places,
Merzouga

Insight on ...

Berbers 64
Interior Design 90
Arts and Crafts................... 204
Shrines 224

Information panels

Sport 51
Ramadan 63
Weddings 69
Barbara Hutton's Parties 75
Matisse in Tangier 116
Spanish Enclaves 130
The Future of the Medina 192
Gardens............................. 259
Film-making 301
Blue Men........................... 319

Travel Tips

Getting Acquainted .. 322
Planning the Trip 324
Practical Tips 328
Getting Around 331
Where to Stay 334
Where to Eat 341
Attractions 344
Nightlife 345
Shopping 345
Sport 347
Language 349
Further Reading 352
◆ **Full Travel Tips index
is on page 321**

Places

Introduction 107
Tangier 111
The Rif 127
Northwest Coast 145
Rabat 153
Casablanca 169
South of Casablanca 177
Fez 185
Meknes Region 209

The Middle Atlas 229
Marrakesh 243
Southwest Coast 263
The High Atlas 271
The South 289
Agadir and the Deep South .. 305

GATEWAY TO AFRICA

Crossing the Straits of Gibraltar to Morocco is one of the most dramatic short journeys a traveller can make

Before the Arabs spread west in the 7th century, settlement in Morocco was characterised by small but numerous Berber settlements and a few trading posts. Not since the Roman era had anything much resembling towns existed. But the Arabs – an urban people whose religion emphasised the communal benefits of the city, exemplified by the holy city of Medina – were quick to build centralised communities, where trade could develop, Islam flourish, and from which the rest of the country could be governed.

But it wasn't until the 20th century that the whole country was subdued by a central city-based authority. Until then much of rural Morocco was known as the *bled es siba* (land of lawlessness), where Berber tribes, led by local sheikhs, fought tooth and nail, while the more easily controlled city and coastal areas were known as the *bled el makhzan* (land of government). As Walter Harris, a late-19th century correspondent for the London *Times*, said, "The whole life in those great Atlas fortified kasbahs was one of warfare and of gloom. Every tribe had its enemies, every family its blood-feuds and every man his would-be murderer."

Unsurprisingly, five of Morocco's seven ruling dynasties have been Berber. Each of these sprang up like a desert storm from the depths of the Atlas Mountains or the harsh Sahara. The decline of a once-powerful dynasty was often blamed on its exposure to the plea-sure-loving decadence of the Andalusian influenced towns.

These days even the remotest town will welcome visitors. But something of the old *bled es siba* anarchy still exists, albeit in the more subtle forms of subterfuge and evasion. For this reason Morocco is not always an easy country for visitors to negotiate and can prove daunting for first-time visitors. The best advice? Be patient and go with the erratic flow rather than fight it. That way you will be rewarded by astonishing beauty, culture and encounters.   ❑

PRECEDING PAGES: skins drying on a hillside near the Merinid Tombs in Fez; winter in the Dades Valley; crossing the courtyard of the Kairouyine Mosque, Fez; date-sellers in the Ziz Valley.
LEFT: Berber woman and daughters from the Dades Valley.

Decisive Dates

8000 BC Neolithic cultures spread through the region. They leave rock drawings of animals such as panthers, lions and elephants.

12th century BC Phoenician sailors establish trading posts along Morocco's coast.

146 BC Carthage falls to Rome. Roman influence spreads west through North Africa. Volubilis, near modern-day Meknes, becomes the capital of the Roman province of Mauritania Tingitana, ruled by Berber kings, the most significant of whom is Juba II (25 BC–AD 23).

AD24 Direct Roman rule under Emperor Caligula.

253 Rome withdraws from northwest Africa. Vandals invade the north coast, followed by the Byzantines in 535, who introduce Christianity.

682 First Arab raids under the command of Oqba Ibn Nafi.

714 Further Arab incursions into Morocco and Spain. Berbers embrace Islam and invade Spain under Arab leadership.

IDRISSID DYNASTY

788 Idriss I, exiled from Baghdad, is welcomed by Berber tribes in Volubilis and establishes Morocco's first Islamic and Arab dynasty.

807 Idriss II founds Fez. Shortly after, Muslim refugees arrive from Córdoba in Andalusia and Kairouan, Tunisia, establishing the Kairouyine University, one of the most important places of learning in the world.

10th–11th centuries The Banu Hilal tribe sweep westwards from the Middle East, destroying infrastructure and devastating agriculture.

ALMORAVIDE DYNASTY

1060–1147 The Berber Almoravide dynasty sweeps up from the south. Youssef ibn Tashfin makes Marrakesh his capital. Among their few remaining monuments is the Koubba in Marrakesh, of seminal importance in the development of Moorish architecture.

1090 Almoravide invasion of Spain.

ALMOHAD DYNASTY

1120 The crusading Berber Ibn Toumert sows the seeds of the Almohad dynasty by establishing a *ribat* (fortified monastery) at Tinmal in the Atlas.

1147–1248 The Almohad dynasty rises from Tinmal. At its peak, the Almohad empire stretches from Spain to Tripoli. Among its notable buildings are the Giralda in Seville, the Koutoubia in Marrakesh and the Tour Hassan in Rabat.

MERINID DYNASTY

1248–1465 The Berber Beni Merin tribe oust the Almohads, establishing the Merinid dynasty. It establishes a chain of Islamic colleges *(madrassas)*, such as the Bou Inania in Fez, and the Chella necropolis in Rabat. Muslim and Jewish refugees arrive, fleeing the Inquisition in Spain. Portuguese and Spanish forces encroach on coastal cities.

THE WATTASIDS

1465–1549 The Wattasids, hereditary viziers of the Merinids, usurp the Merinids. Rule eventually breaks down and Morocco falls under the control of local *marabout* (religious brotherhoods).

1492 Fall of Muslim Spain. Influx of refugees from Spain.

SAADIAN DYNASTY

1554–1669 The Saadians, the first Arab dynasty since the Idrissids, drive out the Christians. Among the dynasty's main monuments are the Saadian tombs and El Badi Palace in Marrakesh. Ahmed el Mansour leads a gold rush to Timbuktu.

17th century Barbary Coast piracy. The piratical Bou Regreg republic is formed at Salé, set up by Moriscos expelled from Spain.

ALAOUITE DYNASTY

1669 The present Alaouite dynasty is founded by Moulay Rashid.

1672–1727 Brutal but effective rule under Moulay Ismail in Meknes.

1873–94 Moulay el Hassan is the last of the notable pre-colonial sultans.

1894–1908 Sultan Abd el Aziz incurs foreign loans, leaving Morocco open to European encroachment.

1906 The Act of Algeciras recognises France's "privileged position" in Morocco.

1912 The Treaty of Fez. Morocco is carved up between France (which gets the lion's share) and Spain. Tangier becomes an international zone.

1975 The Green March. 350,000 unarmed Moroccans claim the Western Sahara for Morocco.

1976 The Polisario, aided by Algeria, disputes Morocco's claims on the Western Sahara. Relations with Algeria deteriorate.

1988 A referendum is promised to determine the fate of the Western Sahara. However, this is repeatedly postponed through the 1990s.

1993 The Hassan II Mosque opens in Casablanca.

1995–6 Five years of drought end in torrential floods, resulting in death and destruction.

1997 Increased democratisation leads to parliamentary elections and a narrow majority for the Socialist Union of Popular Forces (USAP). Abder-

1920s Thami el Glaoui, Pasha of Marrakesh, connives with the French, pacifying rebellious tribes in exchange for power and privileges.

1930s–1940s An independence movement centring on the Istiqlal Party emerges in Fez. Growing unrest is met with repression. Tangier's international set continues to swing.

1956 France grants Independence. Mohammed V changes the title sultan to King.

1961 Accession of Hassan II.

1963–77 King Hassan survives five plots against him, the most serious of which are led by the army.

LEFT: Morocco under the French Protectorate.

ABOVE: mourning the death of Mohammed V, 1961.

rahmane Youssoufi is nominated as prime minister after more than 40 years in opposition.

1999 King Hassan II dies. His son, Mohammed ben Al Hassan, is sworn in as King Mohammed VI. The new king introduces a new era of openness and increased democratisation. He sacks the hated interior minister Driss Basri. Many exiled dissidents are allowed back into Morocco.

2000 In Rabat some 40,000 women march in support of increased rights for women. However a counter-march organised by Islamists in Casablanca attracts some 500,000 women.

2001–2002 Oil is found in the waters off the Western Sahara and in Eastern Morocco. However, its exploitation may not be economically viable. ❑

BEFORE ISLAM

Little is known of the early Berbers, until their land became part of the Roman Empire, and was – temporarily – Christianised and Latinised

Over 50,000 years ago Neanderthal man lived in Morocco. A specimen of his remains was found in caves at Tamara beach near Rabat in 1933. The so-called "Rabat man" seems to have been a boy of about 16 years old. He lived when the region was physically very different from the way it is today. Engravings on flat slabs of rock – some can be seen near Tafraoute southeast of Agadir – show that the area was densely forested and populated by lions, panthers, giraffes, ostriches, elephants and antelopes besides prehistoric man.

There may have been some sort of civilisation about 5,000 years ago, as indicated by the discovery of rock carvings representing a ram with a solar disc between its horns similar to the god Ammon Ra of Thebes in Egypt.

The Greeks have left legends. Fabulous Atlantis is said to have sunk into the sea somewhere west of Spain and Morocco. Then there is the myth of Hercules forcing apart Europe and Africa to create the Straits of Gibraltar, a feat remembered in the Caves of Hercules near Tangier, and in the "Pillars of Hercules" – the rocks of Gibraltar and Ceuta. Some say the Garden of the Hesperides was also in Morocco and that the golden apples Hercules found were in fact oranges – an unlikely tale because oranges originated in Asia and were introduced into Morocco long after this time.

Phoenician traders

We know slightly more about Morocco from the 12th century BC onwards, thanks to the Phoenicians who set up trading posts along the coast. Punic remains have been found at Russadir (Melilla), Tamuda (Tetouan), Ceuta, Tingis (Tangier), Lixus (Larache), Thymiaterion (Mehdia near Kenitra), Sala (Rabat) and Karikon Telichos (Essaouira). These were probably not permanent settlements, although a

number of Punic tombs have been found near Tangier and Rabat.

We know practically nothing of the people who lived in Morocco in Phoenician times up to the fall of Carthage in 146 BC. There is no evidence that the sailors or traders of Carthage ever penetrated inland. Perhaps they were not

interested in colonisation, or perhaps they were unable to conquer the Berbers.

The Romans, who dominated the area for over four centuries until AD 429, found the Berbers, or the Barbarians as they called them, an intractable race who gave the Legions constant trouble when they were founding permanent Roman settlements. Among these outposts of the Roman Empire were Tingis, Zilis (Asilah), Lixus, Valentia Banasa on the Sebou River near Kenitra, Sala Colonia and Volubilis.

The Roman capital

Ruins can be seen today in Rabat at Chella, the Roman *Sala Colonia*. The name survives in

PRECEDING PAGES: *Fantasia in Front of Meknes* by Eugène Delacroix.
LEFT: the Roman outpost of Volubilis.
RIGHT: bronze head of Juba II.

Salé, Rabat's sister town on the other side of the river, still called Sala in Arabic. The most impressive remains are at Volubilis, 30 km (19 miles) north of Meknes, which was probably the capital of the Roman province of Mauritania Tingitana encompassing northern Morocco.

The most remarkable local figure of the Roman period was King Juba II, who ruled Mauritania Tingitana for perhaps half a century until his death, in his seventies, in AD 23. He had three claims to fame: he married Cleopatra Selene (the Moon), daughter of Anthony and Cleopatra; he was one of the most prolific writers of his time in Latin, Greek and Punic; and

he founded a purple dye works at Essaouira.

The Romans also exploited fish factories in Morocco to make *garum*, a salty paste used in cooking. The remains of two garum factories can be seen at Lixus near Larache and at Tangier close to the Caves of Hercules, where the Romans, and probably the Phoenicians before them, used to quarry mill stones.

In the 3rd century, Christian evangelisation of Rome's African provinces began. It seems that many Berbers embraced the new religion as there were numerous bishoprics, including four in Morocco. In some cities the Latin and Christian ways of life survived the fall of the Western Empire of Byzantium. Latin inscriptions in Volubilis date from as late as the 7th century.

During this period Jewish communities also evolved in Morocco, founded after the Exodus from Egypt. Judaism is the oldest religious denomination to have survived without interruption in the country down to the present day, though many Jews left Morocco following the founding of Israel in 1948.

The Dark Age

The Vandal invasion of AD 429 wiped out what was left of Roman Christian civilisation. King Genseric of "Vandalusia" in southern Spain set out from Tarifa with 80,000 people, including 15,000 troops, who swept through Morocco and along the North African coast, destroying everything in their path in an orgy of looting and burning that culminated in the sack of Rome in 455.

It is thought that Vandal depredations were such that the North African Berbers were forced to become nomads – helped by the camel, which had been introduced to Morocco in about the 3rd century. Emperor Justinian restored Christianity to North Africa after the Vandals, considered Christian heretics, were defeated by Belisarius in 533, but the history of the next century in Morocco, and indeed most of North Africa, is obscure.

That is until, 5,000km (3,000 miles) away in the east, a new fire of religious fervour burst into flame, and swept along the Mediterranean coast to bring Islam to Morocco.   ❑

PURPLE DYE FOR CAESAR

On the windswept islets near the coast of Essaouira, deep deposits of murex shells are thought to be evidence of the dye-making industry that supplied the imperial purple robes of the Caesars. The highly prized purple dye was extracted from the shellfish, each of which, it was said, had a drop "no bigger than a single tear".

King Ptolomy, who succeeded Juba II as ruler of the province in the 1st century AD, came to grief because of the dye. He was apparently a vain man, and on a visit to Rome he wore a magnificent robe of imperial purple that aroused the jealousy of Emperor Caligula. The emperor had the provincial upstart assassinated.

LEFT: mosaic in Lixus, now in the archaeological museum in Tetouan.
RIGHT: invasion of the Vandals.

Euq. Delacroix. 1845.

ISLAM AND THE DYNASTIES

In the 7th and 8th centuries Arabian crusaders introduced Islam to Morocco,

where it was fervently adopted by the Berber tribes

El Maghreb El Aksa (the "Farthest West") as Morocco is known in Arabic, was seen in Arabia, the birthplace of Islam, as a reservoir of misguided infidels who needed to be converted to the new faith *besiff* (by the sword). The first of these military missionaries was one of the greatest of North African heroes, Sidi Okba ibn Nafi.

Inspired by fervent dedication to the teachings of the Koran, Okba left Arabia in AD 666, 34 years after the death of the Prophet Mohammed, at the head of an Arab cavalry force. By all accounts, admittedly written by Arab historians centuries after the event, the expedition was a splendid sight as it drove westwards, the curvetting steeds and their scimitar-wielding warriors sweeping through deserts and mountains to spread the divine revelation.

Converting pagans

In fact, Okba made three expeditions, apparently covering over 8,000km (5,000 miles) on horseback to convert pagans, Christians and Jews. He paused for a time to found the city of Kairouan in Tunisia and finally arrived in Morocco on his third thrust westwards in the year 684. Arab chroniclers say that in the Sous valley near Taroudannt Okba defeated a Berber army so big that "Allah alone could count them" – an oriental hyperbole frequently used to describe the exploits of the Arab invaders. Later, perhaps on the curving sands of Agadir Bay, he rode his charger into the waves and cried: "Allah! If this sea did not stop me, I would go into distant lands to Doul Karnein (where the sun sets), forever fighting for your religion and slaying all who did not believe in you or adored other gods than you!"

Okba made no attempt to rule Morocco, but quickly withdrew, only to be slain in a battle with Berbers in Algeria, where his tomb is still revered. Thirty years later another Arab

LEFT: a painting of Sultan Abderrahmen (1822–59) outside Meknes, by Eugène Delacroix.
RIGHT: *Religious Fanatics in Tangier*, by Delacroix.

conqueror, Musa ibn Noseir, arrived to subjugate Moroccan tribes between Tangier and the Tafilalt oases in the name of the Umayyad Caliph of Damascus.

The commander of Musa's forces was a Berber chieftain, Tarik ibn Ziad, a glorious hero enshrined in history and literature as the man

who led the Muslim invasion of Spain. With an army of Berber warriors, he routed the Visigoths in 711 to begin seven centuries of brilliant civilisation at a time when the rest of Europe lived in the Dark Ages.

Zealous Berbers

Tarik's army landed on the bay of Algeciras, near the limestone pinnacle which was named after him, Jebel Tarik or Tarik's mountain, today known as Gibraltar. From this foothold the Muslim armies were to spread with spectacular speed across Spain and into France, where they were finally halted by Charles Martel at the battle of Poitiers in 732. It seems certain that these armies were composed almost entirely of Berbers rather than Arabs. They had voluntarily embraced Islam and, like many recent converts, were the most fervent if not fanatical supporters of the faith, whose simplicity and conquering spirit suited their temperament. In Morocco they revolted against attempts at Arab domination and the exactions of the eastern caliph's tax collectors.

The Berbers founded several independent Muslim kingdoms of the Kharijite sect, which emerged following one of numerous schisms caused by bloody quarrels in the east over succession to the caliphate after the Prophet's

Abbasid caliphs, of whom Harun er Rashid was the fifth. The revolt was one of many, for the Prophet did not designate a successor and had no surviving son. Consequently Islam was plagued for centuries by discord over the legitimacy of its rulers. As we shall see, the lack of a clear-cut tradition, such as primogeniture, to establish succession, and the fact that polygamous rulers often had numerous sons, were a cause of anarchy many times in Morocco, as rival pretenders fought for the throne.

Harun er Rashid sent his army to crush the rebels, and they were massacred near Mecca in 786, but Idriss escaped. After a two-year

death. The heretical kingdoms had already established themselves by the time another Arab hero arrived in 788, accompanied only by an ex-slave, to establish what became the first orthodox Muslim dynasty in Morocco.

The Idrissids

Harun er Rashid, the magnificent Caliph of Baghdad and hero of *The Thousand and One Nights*, was unwittingly responsible for the creation of Morocco's first Muslim dynasty, the Idrissids. Idriss ibn Abdullah, a descendant of the Prophet Mohammed through his daughter Fatima and son-in-law Ali, was among a group of rebels who disputed the legitimacy of the

journey in which he was accompanied by only a faithful ex-slave, Rashid, he arrived in Morocco to take refuge in Walili, the former Roman town of Volubilis. Impressed by his erudition and piety, the superficially Islamicised Berbers made him their leader.

Hearing that the rebel had set up a kingdom, Harun er Rashid sent a Judas-like envoy, who killed Idriss with a poisonous potion in 791. But two months later Idriss's Berber concubine Kenza gave birth to a son. Nurtured by Kenza and the faithful Rashid, the boy became Sultan Idriss II and the dynasty was established.

The Idrissids founded the city of Fez, where they were joined by hundreds of rebel families from Córdoba and Kairouan. They brought with them a sophisticated Arab civilisation which led to the creation of the Kairouyine University, which today is the oldest university in the world.

On the death of Idriss II in 828 (probably also assassinated on orders from Baghdad) his wife divided the small state between their 10 sons. This led inevitably to the decline of the dynasty, and it expired in 974.

Moulay Idriss near Volubilis, the holiest city in Morocco, shelters the tomb of Idriss I, who

> ### ALMORAVIDE LEGACY
>
> Among the Almoravides' few remaining monuments are the mosque at Tlemcen in Algeria, the ramparts around Fez and the Koubba el Baroudiyn in Marrakesh.

or hermitage, in the desert from which to propagate the true faith. His movement was known as El Murabetun (People of the *Ribat*), deformed by Europeans into Almoravides, the first of three Berber dynasties.

In an incredibly short time, the veiled Almoravide sultans created a Berber empire that covered northwest Africa as far east as Algiers and incorporated southern Spain. While the murderous Macbeth was king of Scotland, the Normans were invading England and the First Crusade took the city

is considered a saintly man. His son's shrine in Fez is also the object of pious devotion. Each year a *moussem* (pilgrimage) is made to their tombs to honour the founders of Muslim Morocco and of the only dynasty which did not have to impose itself by force of arms.

The Almoravides

Youssef ibn Tashfin, a Berber from Adrar (in what is now Mauritania) where the men wore veils, was a religious zealot. He set up a *ribat*,

LEFT: the court of Harun er Rashid, the Caliph of Baghdad who sent an emissary to murder Idriss I.
ABOVE: Arabs migrating from the east.

of Jerusalem, the Almoravides, led by Tashfin, swept up from the desert to found Marrakesh in 1060. They captured Fez in 1069, and then pushed on across the Mediterranean into Spain.

Muslim Spain, in the time of the romantic *Cid Campeador* Rodrigo Diaz de Vivar, was divided into 23 *taifas*, or petty principalities. The Almoravides had little difficulty in dominating them on the pretext of helping to defeat Christian armies, as they did at Zallaqa near Badajoz in 1086. They took Granada, Córdoba and Seville in the south, and Badajoz, Valencia and Saragossa in the north, although they were unable to hold them for long.

Tashfin's son Ali ruled the empire from 1120

to 1143, and in his time the fierce and austere Almoravides abandoned the veil to become luxury-loving potentates in Andalusia. The Almoravide dynasty disappeared almost as quickly as it had arisen out of the desert void, but not before spreading Andalusian culture throughout the Maghreb.

The Almohads

Ibn Toumert, popularly known as "the Torch", was another radical religious reformer who emerged at the beginning of the 12th century to preach a unitarian *(tawhid)* doctrine. His followers became known as El Mowahhadidoun, or the Almohads. By the time the fiery Toumert died in 1130, he had gathered numerous Berber tribes around his banner.

DRIVEN TO EXTREMES

The bloody excesses of the Inquisition were matched by Moroccan xenophobia provoked by the presence of infidels on the soil of *Dar el Islam* – "the sacred House of Islam".

The torch was passed to Abd el Moumin, an able warrior chieftain who proclaimed himself Caliph and Amir el Mumineen ("Commander of the Faithful"). Oriental historians called him the greatest of all the Berbers. Moumin seized Marrakesh and Fez, controlled all Morocco by 1148, moved into Spain when called in by anti-Almoravide rebels, and raced across North Africa, defeating the Hilali Arab hordes at Sétif.

By the time he died, Moumin had forged an empire even larger than that of the Almoravides, extending eastwards as far as Tripoli. Most of Muslim Spain was reduced to vassaldom under his son Yacoub Youssef. His grandson, Youssef Yacoub, consolidated Almohad power and won the title El Mansour (the Victorious) when he crushed the Christians under King Alfonso VIII of Castile at the battle of Alarcos, on 18 July 1195.

In their most glorious period between 1160 and 1210, the Almohads built a number of famous landmarks, such as the Camp of Conquest, the Bab er Rouah gateway and the unfinished Tour Hassan in Rabat, the Giralda in Seville, and the Koutoubia Mosque in Marrakesh. But, like their predecessors the Almoravides, they sank, perhaps inevitably, into silken decadence. In their time Alicante boasted 800 looms for weaving silk cloth and minted fine gold coinage. Paper was manufactured in Ceuta and Fez.

Towards the end of the dynasty, in 1230, Sultan el Mamoun was reduced to accepting 12,000 Christian cavalrymen from King Ferdinand of Castile and Leon in order to retake Marrakesh from local dissidents. As part of the bargain he allowed the construction of a Catholic church in the city. A Marrakesh bishopric subsisted until the 14th century to serve foreign mercenaries.

YACOUB'S GOLDEN AGE

Yacoub el Mansour's reign was the zenith of the Almohad dynasty, a golden age of Andalusian brilliance. He surrounded himself with distinguished poets and philosophers, such as the Jewish thinker Maimonides, the court physician Ibn Tofail, and Ibn Rashid Averroes (after whom the main Casablanca hospital is named), who commented on the works of Aristotle and introduced the sultan to Christian monks. Yacoub's enlightened building projects included Rabat el Fath (the Camp of Conquest), a vast, ramparted enclosure used to assemble troops for military expeditions into Spain, and Rabat's monumental Bab er Rouah (Gateway of Souls).

Merinids and the Black Sultan

The Beni Merin was a nomadic Berber tribe from the Sahara, pushed westwards by the Hilali invaders. It settled northeast Morocco in the period when King John was forced by the English barons to sign the Magna Carta (in 1215) and the infamous Spanish Inquisition began to persecute Muslims and Jews.

The Beni Merin tribesmen took part in the battle of Alarcos of 1195, so they were well aware of the potential rewards of the *jihad* (holy war) which they began waging – with the help of Christian mercenaries – against the Almohads. By taking Fez on 20 August 1248, their leader Abou Yahya established the Merinid dynasty.

His son Abou Youssef crossed the Straits of Gibraltar four times to help the Muslims recon-

iron hand. He was less successful in Spain, where his army was beaten at the battle of Rio Salado near Tarifa in October 1340.

Hassan died an embittered man and was buried in Chellah near Rabat. His own son Abou Inan had rebelled against him to rule until 1358, when he was strangled by a vizier in favour of a five-year-old pretender. Inan had lost control of what is now Algeria and Tunisia, the Maaqil Arab invaders started to move in, the Spanish connection was finished, and the Christians began their encroachments. The gangrene of anarchy set in under various infant sultans.

Although their political achievements could

quer lost territory, notably after one memorable battle on 8 September 1275, in which the army led by the Christian hero, Don Nuno Gonzales de Lara, was routed – a black day for the Cross.

Abou el Hassan, the son of an Abyssinian mother and known as the Black Sultan, who ruled the Merinid Empire from 1331 to 1351 (during the Hundred Years War in Europe), was a prodigiously powerful and active man. He reorganised the empire between the Atlantic and the Gulf of Gabes in Tunisia, and held it with an

LEFT: a Moroccan emir.
ABOVE: *Jewish Wedding in Morocco* by Eugène Delacroix.

not be compared with those of the Almohads, the Merinids left a substantial cultural legacy in the shape of *madrassas* , or colleges, in delicate Hispano-Moorish style, which can be seen in Fez, Meknes and Salé. Madrassa Bou Inania in Fez, finished in 1357, is one of the most remarkable, with a clepysdra water clock in the narrow street outside that at one time told the time with 13 brass gongs.

Christian encroachments

At the beginning of the 15th century, piracy became a way of attacking Christians and it thus provided an excuse for the latter to intervene in Morocco. The Spanish kings were undoubtedly motivated also by a spirit of revenge after seven centuries of Muslim domination which was to end with the fall of Granada in 1492.

While Muslim and Jewish refugees began flooding into Morocco to escape the Inquisition, Spanish and Portuguese kings sent armies and navies after them. Henry III of Castile took Tetouan and massacred the population in 1399, Portugal grabbed Ceuta in 1415 and, after three attempts, finally took Asilah and Tangier with a fleet of 477 ships and 30,000 men in 1471.

After *Los Reyes Catolicos* Ferdinand and Isabella ousted the Muslims from Granada,

Spain occupied Melilla in 1497 with a fleet originally intended to take Columbus on his second voyage of discovery. Meanwhile the Portuguese established fortresses on the Atlantic coast at Agadir, Azemmour and Safi, and the Ottoman Turks arrived on Morocco's doorstep at Tlemcen. These were dark days for Morocco, enfeebled for a century by anarchy under the Wattasid dynasty (1465–1549), but they were a prelude to another glorious era.

The renaissance came as a reaction to Christian intolerance: the spirit of the *jihad* (holy war) coalesced around the Saadians, who overthrew the last of the Wattasids in 1557. They astounded Europe when they annihilated a Portuguese army of 20,000 at the Battle of the Three Kings on 4 August 1578.

The Saadians

Members of the Arab tribe of Beni Saad had arrived in the 12th century to settle in the Draa Valley near Zagora and later in the Sous near Taroudant. Claiming descent from the Prophet Mohammed, they founded the Saadian dynasty by taking Marrakesh in 1525. After being driven out of Agadir in 1541, the Portuguese also abandoned the ports of Safi and Azemmour.

These reverses inspired the 24-year-old King Sebastian of Portugal to seek revenge by embarking upon a crusade against the "barbarians", albeit against the advice of his Jesuit mentors. Historians tell us Sebastian was a mystical fanatic who sought personal glory in the name of God. He was joined by one of the Saadians, Mohammed el Mutawakkil, who had ruled as sultan for a brief period but had fled to Spain after being overthrown by his brother

THE BATTLE OF THE THREE KINGS

In 1578, the cream of Portuguese nobility was assembled to fight the Moroccan Muslims, and they embarked with a large fleet to land at Tangier and Asilah. The men marched southwards slowly and ponderously, lugging 36 bronze cannon. Their progress was so slow that Sultan Abd el Malik was able to muster a force of 50,000 cavalry to counter the invading force.

Eventually, on 4 August, the two opposing armies met near Ksar el Kebir, where the Portuguese suddenly found themselves trapped in a fork between the Loukos River and its tributary, the Oued el Makhazin. The tide rose, making it impossible for the men to ford the streams, while

wave after wave of charging Moroccan cavalry cut their enemies to pieces.

The Portuguese king, Sebastian, and his ally, the deposed sultan Mohammed el Mutawakkil, were drowned, and Sultan Abd el Malik died of sickness during the battle. The disaster was complete for Portugal, who later lost both its crown and its African possession, Ceuta, to Spain. Morocco, however, immediately had a heroic new ruler, Abd el Malik's brother Ahmed, who was proclaimed sultan on the battlefield. He became known as Ahmed el Mansour el Dehbi (the Victorious and Golden) after extracting huge ransoms for the Portuguese nobles captured in the battle.

Abd el Malik. Mohammed's purpose in siding with the Christians was to recover his throne.

However, the Saadians achieved a decisive victory on the battlefield, which had a tremendous impact in Morocco after the deaths of the "three kings" (the monarchs of Portugal and Morocco, and the traitorous former sultan: *see panel opposite*). Great prestige was awarded to Abd el Malik's successor Ahmed, who benefited from the glorious outcome as well as the punitive measures he imposed on the vanquished nation.

COMMON ENEMY

Ahmed wrote to England's Queen Elizabeth I, proposing an Anglo-Moroccan alliance against Spain, after the defeat of the Spanish Armada by Sir Francis Drake.

on the way. The rest arrived at Timbuktu after marching for 135 days in probably one of the most gruelling gold rushes of all time. An offer, made by the local emperor Ishaq Askia, to buy them off with 100,000 pieces of gold and 1,000 slaves was spurned by Ahmed as "insulting".

The Songai Empire was destroyed and Ahmed appointed pashas to rule it. Goaded by greed, the pashas were unscrupulous (there were 149 of them between 1612 and 1750). Their unruly troops massacred the population or sent

Ahmed seeks riches

Since Spain was too powerful for him to attempt any exploits on the Iberian peninsula, Ahmed instead set out to conquer the salt and gold mines of the Songai Empire on the banks of the Niger River. A ragtag army of 3,000 Christians, Kabyles, Ottomans and negroes, led by the Spanish renegade Jouder and trained by Turks, trekked across the Sahara Desert. To paraphrase the Duke of Wellington, it was the scum of the earth enlisted for lucre.

Half the troops died of thirst and exhaustion

LEFT: piracy off the Atlantic coast.
ABOVE: bombarding Tripoli, the centre for piracy.

them into slavery in caravans carrying gold back to Marrakesh.

Laurence Maddock, an English trader in Marrakesh, counted 30 mule loads of gold dust arriving in the city in a single day. The historian El Ifrani said court officials were paid in gold and there were 1,400 hammers at the palace to strike gold ducats. Ahmed and his court's notoriety spread throughout Europe.

To match his great wealth, Ahmed built himself a sumptuous palace, El Badi, with Italian marble bought kilo for kilo in exchange for sugar produced by Christian and Jewish renegades in the Sous valley. Foreign visitors marvelled at the magnificence of court ceremonial à la Turk, for Ahmed had spent his youth in Constantinople and had acquired a taste for Ottoman refinements.

Ahmed also organised the Makhzen government, which survived with little change into the 20th century. Of the rest little remains. His palace was razed by the next dynasty. Among the few notable relics are the Saadian tombs built by Ahmed's son Moulay Zidan, which were walled up by his successors and not revealed again until the French came to Morocco.

One consequence of the Saadian era was that the influx of thousands of black slaves from central Africa, white renegades and mercenar-

The Alaouites

The next remarkable sultan was Moulay Ismail, whose 55-year reign (1672–1727) was one of the longest and most brutal in Moroccan history. He was a cruel and profligate megalomaniac reputed to have had a harem of 500 women, over 700 sons and uncounted daughters.

Ismail was the brother of Moulay Rashid, the founder of the Alaouite dynasty and the scion of an Arab family which had emigrated from Arabia to the Tafilalt oasis in the 13th century. The family was descended from El Hassan, son of Ali and the Prophet's daughter Fatima.

Ismail's reign is well-documented by Arab

ies changed the racial composition of the country. The result can be seen in the faces of Moroccans today, ranging from ivory white to brown and ebony black.

Ahmed el Mansour died in August 1603. He was undoubtedly the greatest of the 11 Saadian sultans, eight of whom were assassinated. Three of his sons fought over the succession for seven years, and for a time Morocco was divided into two Saadian states ruled from Fez and Marrakesh. A third state, proclaimed in Rabat-Salé, was an independent corsair republic led by *Moriscos* expelled from Spain. They were the "Sallee Rovers" mentioned in Daniel Defoe's *Robinson Crusoe*.

historians and also by European diplomats, monks and the slaves they came to redeem from captivity at the hands of the corsairs. Some 2,000 Christian slaves and 30,000 other prisoners were employed for half a century in an orgy of building in Meknes, which Ismail made his capital.

A hotchpotch of gigantic structures was built, mostly of adobe, but also with some marble looted from Volubilis and Ahmed el Mansour's palace in Marrakesh, which Ismail had razed to the ground. The city was ringed by ramparts 25 km (15 miles) long. It included palaces with vast colonnaded courtyards, huge gardens, a zoo, stables for hundreds of horses, granaries, barracks for large numbers of troops and, of course, a harem where his legitimate wife the Sultana Zidana, a giant negress, cracked the whip over hundreds of concubines. Each time Ismail granted his favours to one of the oiled and perfumed women she was paraded through the palace on a litter accompanied by singers and dancers.

ALLY TO THE USA

Mohammed ibn Abdullah was the first world leader to recognise the infant United States of America. Washington called him a "great and magnanimous friend".

When Ismail inspected the building sites, he would personally run his lance through slave labourers if he thought they were shirking, or crush their skulls with bricks if he considered their work to be sub-standard. The French diplomat Pidou de Saint Olon saw him dripping with blood after slitting a slave's throat.

The French remember the despot for his plan to marry the Princess Conti, the illegitimate daughter of the Sun King Louis XIV, a proposal that caused hilarity in the Palace of Versailles and not a little bemusement in Meknes when Ismail was turned down.

Ismail's power rested on an army of black soldiers, the Abids, formed from the remnants of slaves brought to Morocco by the Saadians. They were placed in a "stud farm" at Meshra Er Remel on the Sebou river; all their male offspring would then be pressed into military service at the age of 15. Considered more reliable than Arab or Berber warriors, the Abids were garrisoned in kasbahs built at strategic points around the country. They were also used to retake Larache and Asilah, to lay siege for years to Ceuta and Melilla, and to evict the Turks from Tlemcen in modern Algeria. The English left Tangier of their own accord after occupying it from 1662 to 1684.

Ismail's death at the age of 81 in 1727 was followed by a period of chaos such as Morocco has never seen before or since. His numerous sons and the Abids fought over the succession for 30 years. One was proclaimed and dethroned six times and in a generation there were 12 sultans. A contemporary wrote that in this period "the hair of babes in arms turned white" with terror.

In contrast, Sultan Mohammed ibn Abdullah (1757–90) left memories of a pious and peaceful man. He built Mogador (Essaouira),

designed by the French architect Cornut of Avignon and finished by an English renegade named Ahmed el Inglesi. The Portuguese were forced out of their last stronghold at Mazagan, which was then renamed El Jadida, but Mohammed failed to evict Spain from Melilla, which is held by Spain to this day.

There was a bloody two-year interlude under Mohammed's son Moulay Yazid, a sanguinary demon who, among other excesses, had Jews crucified in Fez by nailing them to the doors of their houses. He was followed by his brother Moulay Slimane (1792–1822) and Moulay Abderrahman (1822–59), who were pious and benign.

Decline of the realm

In the second half of the 19th century, Morocco isolated itself, became poor and weak, and was plagued by dissidence in the *bled es-siba* ("land of dissidence"), the parts of the country outside the *bled el-makhzen* ("land of government"). The notable Alaouite sultan Moulay el Hassan (1873–94), spent most of his reign in the saddle trying to subdue rebellious tribes, while European imperialists began gnawing at the country's fragile fabric. ❑

FAR LEFT AND LEFT: Mouly Ismail and his heart's desire, Princess Conti, a daughter of Louis XIV.
RIGHT: a Christian slave at the mercy of his master.

EUROPEAN ENCROACHMENT

After France and Spain waded into Morocco, resentment of foreign rule
simmered for 40 years until independence was regained

In the "last scramble for Africa" at the beginning of the 20th century, Britain, France, Germany and Spain vied with one another to dominate Morocco, one of few remaining parts of the continent outside the colonial grasp.

It had escaped colonialism not because it was considered worthless – on the contrary, it was and remains strategically very important – but because it was an old independent nation with an organised society capable of resisting invasion. That made it different from the rest of the "Dark Continent" with its archaic tribal systems and maps featuring "elephants for want of towns". Also, Morocco had existed as a Muslim nation for more than 1,000 years. It had a long history of dynastic rule, its own culture and civilisation, ancient cities such as Fez, Marrakesh and Tangier, and a record of fierce resistance to invasion.

Until the turn of the century, Morocco had survived by playing one European power off against another. But gradually the rivals were eliminated. In return for a free hand in Morocco, France agreed to allow Italy to colonise Libya and then, as part of the Entente Cordiale, struck a similar deal with Britain, which in return was given carte blanche in Egypt.

This left France with just two other claimants to contend with: Germany, whose Kaiser Wilhelm landed in Tangier and later sent a gunboat to Agadir to demonstrate its "interests"; and Spain, which, because of its centuries-long occupation of the Ceuta and Melilla enclaves on the north coast, maintained "historic rights" in Morocco.

When European plenipotentiaries met at the Reina Cristina hotel in the Spanish port of Algeciras, in January 1906, to decide upon Morocco's future, Britain and Italy supported France. The Treaty of Algeciras proposed a plan of reforms and recognised France's "privileged position" in Morocco.

LEFT: conference members at the Reina Cristina hotel in 1906.

RIGHT: European visitors in the 1920s.

Germany withdrew as World War I loomed, after receiving from France the "gift" of part of Cameroon in West Africa. Spain signed a secret accord with France delimiting their respective "spheres of influence" in Morocco. The European claimants to the Moroccan cake were now reduced to two.

The prodigal son

This coincided with a crisis in Morocco. Sultan Moulay el Hassan, a strong monarch who spent most of his reign in the saddle fighting rebellious tribes, had died suddenly in 1894. He was succeeded by his son Abd el Aziz, a weak spendthrift who emptied the treasury with extravagant spending on frivolous pursuits. Unscrupulous Europeans sold him solid gold cameras, pianos no one at court knew how to play, a German motorboat with its own engineer, and a gilded state coach even though there were then no roads in Morocco.

To solve the resulting financial crisis, large loans were contracted with a French bank consortium. To repay them, Morocco had to forfeit its customs dues, leading to revolts against the growing influence of the "infidels" and encroachments by French troops into areas bordering Algeria. One revolt, backed by powerful tribal chiefs of the south, resulted in 1908 in the overthrow of Abd el Aziz by his brother Hafid. But the new ruler was unable to assert his authority over a debt-ridden country assailed by external pressures and internal dissent. He was forced to sign the Protectorate

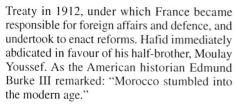

EVADING CENSORSHIP

For independence workers in the French and Spanish zones, post offices in the international zone of Tangier proved useful sources of uncensored news of what was going on in the rest of Morocco.

Because of its strategic location, Tangier and its immediate vicinity became an "international zone". For some time foreign diplomats had been extending their influence in the town. They had been responsible for the building of the Cap Spartel lighthouse and had established a sanitation programme. Good works, they believed, would foster good relations, and no one wanted Spain to control both sides of the Straits of Gibraltar – particularly not Britain. Each nation represented in the interna-

Treaty in 1912, under which France became responsible for foreign affairs and defence, and undertook to enact reforms. Hafid immediately abdicated in favour of his half-brother, Moulay Youssef. As the American historian Edmund Burke III remarked: "Morocco stumbled into the modern age."

Carving up the country

France took over "useful Morocco", the main cities on the central plains and territory bordering Algeria. Spain received the crumbs – the rugged Rif mountain area next to its enclaves, and in the south the enclave of Ifni, the Tarfaya strip and the western Sahara, Rio de Oro.

EMIR DEFEATS SPANISH ARMY

Spain's occupation of the northern zone was marked by the 1920 revolt of the "Emir" Abd el Krim, whose Berber warriors routed a Spanish army of 60,000 at the battle of Anual. It was a remarkable achievement.

Abd el Krim set up an independent republic in the Rif, with an education programme, a state bank and much of the administrative infrastructure of a modern country. He was finally defeated by a combined Spanish and French army commanded by the "saviour of Verdun" Marshal Philippe Pétain, and he surrendered to the French rather than face Spanish execution. He was exiled to the French Indian Ocean island of Réunion and later died in Cairo.

tional zone had its own currency and ran it own post offices and banks.

Penetration of Morocco by France and Spain met with bloody resistance. As soon as the protectorate treaty was signed in Fez, the walled city was besieged by warrior tribes and it was not until 1934 that France was able to pacify the whole of its zone.

Lyautey's way

Marshal Lyautey, the first French Resident-General, was an experienced soldier but also an auda-

THE WISE FRENCHMAN

Lyautey's maxims are still current in independent Morocco: for instance, "Not a drop of water should reach the ocean"; and "Morocco is a cold country with a hot sun."

an active part in all stages of the country's modernisation, otherwise they would become frustrated and rebellious. This proved prophetic.

After Lyautey departed in 1925, succeeding Resident-Generals (14 in 44 years) turned the protectorate into a virtual colony, with direct administration that sidelined the traditional ruling classes and left few outlets for the talents of ambitious young Moroccans. As one commentator remarked, the sultan was reduced to reading the French newspapers to

cious idealist. He believed the protectorate concept should be scrupulously respected: in other words, that all actions must be taken in the name, and with the consent of, the sultan in cooperation with the *makhzen* government, or traditional Moroccan élite.

From the start, he realised the importance of preserving Moroccan culture, and made sure the new French-built towns were located some distance from the medinas. He also insisted that the younger Moroccan generation should take

FAR LEFT: the profligate Abd el Aziz. **LEFT:** Marshal Lyautey, the first French Resident-General.
ABOVE: the Rif presented the most resistance.

find out what was going on in his own country.

Exactly as Lyautey had predicted, intellectuals formed a nationalist movement in Fez to spearhead resistance just as the "pacification" ended in 1934. Some of them were French-educated and inspired by "*Liberté, Egalité et Fraternité*"; others, trained in Fez's old Kairouyine University, were strongly influenced by Middle Eastern politicians.

The movement was amply fuelled by resentment over two grievances. First, the influx of French settlers (which Lyautey had opposed), who took over the best farmland and monopolised the economy. Second, a heavy-handed bureaucracy – which had a mania for regulating everything, right down to the profession of snake charmer – made sure that Moroccans were given only subordinate jobs.

Desirable property

While development of the Spanish zones was minimal because of Spain's civil war and the poor shape of the Spanish economy under Generalissimo Francisco Franco, France poured resources into Morocco: building roads, railways and ports; laying out modern, efficient farms; opening up mines, and setting up education, public health and justice systems on the French pattern. In short, the country was trans-

formed. Ironically, in nationalist eyes, the French protectorate made Morocco even more worth fighting for than before.

When Sultan Moulay Youssef died in 1927, he was replaced by his third son Mohammed, who was 18 and had led a cloistered life. The French thought he would be more amenable to their interests. This was to prove a grave miscalculation. The publication by the French of the Berber *Dahir* (decree) in 1930, to which the young and inexperienced monarch set his seal, was later seen as a serious political mistake. The decree was intended to apply tribal custom law to the Berbers instead of traditional Islamic law. It incensed the Berber tribes, who charged

that its underlying purpose was to convert the Berbers to Christianity.

Disorders broke out and the main nationalist leaders, including Allal al Fassi, Mohammed ben Hassan Wazzani, Ahmed Balafrej and Mohammed Mekki Naciri, were arrested. Along with many others, they were in and out of jail or in exile for the next 25 years.

In the Spanish zone, meanwhile, nationalists were tolerated – more to exasperate the French than out of idealism, since Madrid was still angry at being given the poorest parts of the country. The Franco regime also encouraged rivalry and in-fighting between four nationalist groups to divert attention from the fact that Moroccan troops had been recruited for the "anti-communist crusade" in the Spanish Civil War.

The Glaoui

To counter nationalist agitation, the French enlisted the support of the *grand caids*, the Berber tribal chiefs of the south, led by Thami el Glaoui, the pasha or governor of Marrakesh, whose name meant "Lion of the Atlas". Other personages with grudges against the sultanate were also enlisted. The religious leader Abdelhay el Kettani, whose brother Mohammed was flogged to death on orders from Sultan Moulay Hafid in 1909, was one.

Sultan Mohammed ben Youssef began espousing the nationalist cause shortly before the newly formed Istiqlal (independence) Party issued a "manifesto" in January 1944; it demanded, for the first time, not just reforms but outright independence. The Sultan's support for the cause was said to have been inspired in part by President Franklin D. Roosevelt's advice to him when they met at the Anfa conference near Casablanca during World War II.

As agitation grew, the French reacted by arresting the ringleaders. Riots and demonstrations followed, and finally the Sultan went "on strike" by refusing to seal protectorate decrees.

When General Augustin Guillaume, the 10th French Resident-General, took over in Rabat in July 1951, he found an uncooperative sultan and seething unrest among nationalists. He also inherited a protectorate apparatus that was ready to defy the government in Paris and give in to the demands of the diehard leaders of settlers, who by then had grown to nearly half a million.

By March 1953, the tribal chief El Glaoui, Kettani and other Moroccan "collaborators" in the French zone had decided that Sultan Mohammed ben Youssef, who supported the independence movement, must be replaced. The idea received active support from settlers and their lobby in Paris, where ephemeral French governments of the Fourth Republic were coming and going at dizzying frequency.

The plot thickens

In May 1953 Guillaume, accompanied by Marshal Alphonse Juin, a former Resident-General

But the French Foreign Minister Georges Bidault in April had informed Guillaume in no uncertain terms: "The French government will not accept being placed by anyone before a *fait accompli*... I ask you to oppose without hesitation any new progress towards a situation in which we shall have no choice but to depose the Sultan and use force against our friends."

But El Glaoui and 300 of his fellow plotters, convened in Marrakesh on 13 August – while the Resident-General, Marshal

born in Algeria, inspected tens of thousands of Berber tribesmen assembled near Azrou in the Middle Atlas mountains. Many were French army veterans who had served valiantly under Guillaume and Juin in the final stages of World War II. They were generally seen by settlers as "good Moroccans", in contrast to the "bad" ones represented by the urban nationalists. The latter considered the Azrou parade as a dress rehearsal for a march by massed Berber tribesmen on Fez and Rabat to force the Sultan off his throne.

LEFT: Thami el Glaoui, Lord of the Atlas.
ABOVE: money exchanges in Tangier during its international era.

Guillaume, was in Vichy taking the waters for his liver – and drew up a proposal to depose the reigning monarch and proclaim Sidi Mohammed ben Arafa as sultan in his stead, an obscure 70-year-old who was a distant relative of the reigning sultan.

Despite another Bidault message warning of the "incalculable consequences of such a *pronunciamento*", contingents of tribes began to march on Fez and Rabat, some of them doubtless under the impression they were on their way, as usual, to attend the Muslim feast day ceremonies of Aid El-Kebir, due to start on 21 August that year (when the sultan would perform in public the traditional sacrifice of a ram). Nevertheless, the French government capitulated: Sultan Mohammed ben Youssef was duly deposed and the elderly Ben Arafa was set up in his place.

Crisis at the palace

In an atmosphere of hysteria whipped up by the conspirators and echoed in the colonial press, French Prime Minister Joseph Laniel gave the green light for the Sultan's deposition, apparently believing that the only alternative would be civil war in Morocco. His interior minister,

> **REMEMBERED IN EXILE**
>
> People swore they could see their Sultan's face in the moon, or they would say he was "chez Madame Gascar" on that faraway island in the Indian Ocean.

plotters and their settler friends of the Presence Française association, but their victory celebrations were short-lived. Only three weeks later, on 11 September, the puppet-sultan Ben Arafa narrowly escaped death when Allal ben Abdallah (after whom numerous Moroccan streets are now named) crashed an open car into a royal procession on its way to the mosque in Rabat, then tried to knife him. This signalled the start of violent popular protests against the exiling of the legitimate sultan. They quickly snowballed

Francois Mitterand, did not agree and resigned in protest.

A grim-faced Guillaume went to the palace in Rabat on Thursday morning, 20 August 1953, to demand that the Sultan abdicate in favour of his younger son, Prince Moulay Abdallah, thought to be a more "flexible" prospect than the elder son, Prince Moulay Hassan, the settlers' particular *bête noire*. When the Sultan refused to comply, he and all his sons and daughters were whisked away in a fleet of black cars to the old Rabat airport and flown into exile, first in Corsica and later in Madagascar.

His departure was cheered by the Moroccan

into an urban terrorism campaign coupled with the emergence of a liberation army in the Rif and Middle Atlas mountains.

A bloody end

Resistance fighters – who were not necessarily controlled by the nationalists, but were often small independent groups of patriots – shot French leaders and Moroccan "collaborators", and set off bombs in crowded cafés and markets. On Christmas Eve 1953, in Casablanca's central market, Mohammed Zerktouni (after whom one of the city's boulevards is named) planted a bomb in a shopping-basket that killed 20 people and wounded 28. The choice of the

Christian holiday was symbolic: the Sultan had been exiled on a Muslim feast day.

The terrorists enjoyed the tacit support of the population at large, but extremist French settlers reacted by organising terrorist campaigns of their own, at times shooting indiscriminately from cruising cars and murdering French personages they suspected of pro-nationalist sympathies. There was evidence that they were being helped by the French police.

The campaign reached a climax on the second anniversary of the Sultan's departure into exile, on 20 August 1955, when tribesmen descended on the small farming town of Oued

while being physically attacked and insulted by outraged French settlers.

In Paris, Prime Minister Edgar Faure called a conference of nationalist leaders in Aix-les-Bains, amid fears that a *jihad* (holy war) was about to be launched against France in Morocco and Algeria. The feared uprising broke out in the Rif mountains on 1 October, when the Moroccan Liberation Army attacked three French outposts on the border of the Spanish zone.

The surprise U-turn

The Aix-les-Bains conference was designed to form an interim Moroccan government and

Zem, southeast of Casablanca, and savagely butchered 49 French people, including eight women and 15 children.

The French Foreign Legion was sent in on a punitive expedition. According to Moroccan sources, some 1,500 tribespeople were slain by the Legion, raising tension in the country to boiling point at a time when the latest Resident-General, the liberal civilian Gilbert Grandval, had been trying to solve the crisis

FAR LEFT AND LEFT: Ben Arafa is installed as sultan by the French, and three weeks later he narrowly escapes assassination.
ABOVE: the return of Mohammed V.

hammer out a compromise solution to the dynastic problem in the shape of a "Throne Council". But the Council formula was contested by none other than Thami el Glaoui himself, who astounded everyone by announcing on 25 October that the solution was to restore Mohammed ben Youssef to his throne.

In the circumstances, France could hardly do otherwise. The legitimate sultan was flown back to Rabat on 16 November 1955 to receive a hero's welcome, whose scale and fervour has not been seen in Morocco since. He announced to massed crowds assembled in front of the palace that the protectorate had come to an end. ❑

SINCE INDEPENDENCE

The elation felt at independence soon gave way to rivalries and insurrection.

But strong leadership and wily strategies kept the status quo intact

Sultan Sidi Mohammed ben Youssef changed his title to King Mohammed V in 1956 when Morocco regained its independence. The change symbolised the additional prestige he had acquired as "The Liberator" of the country. His great popularity, together with his religious prestige as Amir el Mumineen ("Commander of the Faithful"), enabled him to rule with uncontested authority during a crucial period when an élite had to be assembled to run a modern nation.

Although he had been humiliated by the French, he proved a moderate and magnanimous monarch. Foreigners were kept on to advise inexperienced Moroccan officials to smooth the transition. Many French settlers fled of their own accord, but others ran farms and industries until as late as 1973 when "Moroccanisation" measures were taken.

Morocco joined the Arab League, was a founder-member of the Organisation of African Unity (OAU), and cultivated cordial relations with France and Spain, who helped create the Royal Armed Forces and supplied aid for economic development. New industries sprang up based on agriculture and phosphates.

The number of schoolchildren grew from a few thousand to over 3 million in 25 years; at the same time improved health conditions stimulated rapid population growth coupled with the emergence of a restive urban proletariat. Providing work, housing and social services became (and remains) an arduous task.

Crisis management

A crisis erupted in October 1956 when the French in Algeria forced down the aircraft carrying Algerian nationalist leader Ahmed ben Bella and his associates from Rabat to Tunis. Rioters attacked French settlers in a violent protest organised by nationalists in support of the Algerian Front de Libération Nationale.

LEFT: Mohammed V.
RIGHT: Mohammed V with the Egyptian leader Gamal Abdel Nasser

Relations with France were strained further because Morocco was channelling arms to the Algerian revolution.

The former Spanish and French protectorate zones and the Tangier international zone were quickly abolished, but it took several years to convince Spain to evacuate the Tarfaya strip

and the enclave of Ifni in the south, in the latter case only after local tribes staged a revolt.

King Mohammed V's main domestic problem was dealing with the old-guard Istiqlal Party, whose leaders considered themselves the real architects of Moroccan independence, deserving to monopolise power in what they called "homogenous governments" (meaning excluding other political parties).

Istiqlal pretensions sparked revolts by other nationalist groups who felt deprived of the fruits of victory. One of the most serious insurrections broke out in 1958 in the Rif mountains after the Istiqlal ordered the arrest of Dr Abd el Krim Khatib and Mahjoubi Aherdan, two

Moroccan Liberation Army (MLA) leaders who had led guerrillas against the French but also contested the Istiqlal party's ascendance.

Although the King ordered the release of Aherdan and Khatib, the rebels defied Rabat until February 1959. There were heavy casualties when 20,000 troops commanded by Crown Prince Moulay Hassan were sent in to wipe out resistance. Nevertheless the King espoused the Istiqlal's claims to large tracts of Algeria, the Spanish Sahara and Mauritania.

DEFYING PREDICTIONS

Hassan II told King Juan Carlos of Spain, 25 years after becoming king, "When I ascended the throne people said I would not last more than six months."

away faction, which came to be known as the *Union Socialiste des Forces Populaires* (USFP), agitated for radical political and economic reforms, attacking the king's "personal power" and accusing the monarchy of being feudal – views shared by the socialist regime in Algeria.

In 1963 newly-independent Algeria rejected Moroccan claims to parts of its territory and a brief war broke out. Moroccan and Algerian troops fought over oases in a disputed area where the frontier had never been formally

At the same time he tried to thwart Istiqlal attempts to dominate the government. Aherdan and Khatib were allowed to create a rival party, the People's Movement, representing the rural majority, which held office in all later governments, while by the end of 1962 the Istiqlal was eased out of power and went into opposition.

Hassan's accession

King Hassan II ascended the throne in February 1961 on the death of his father. By this time the Istiqlal Party had split. A radical left-wing, led by Mehdi ben Barka, emerged with distinctly republican leanings regarded by the palace as a serious threat to the throne. Ben Barka's break-

drawn. The conflict was halted by the Organisation of African Unity, but Mehdi ben Barka was sentenced to death *in absentia* for treason for taking Algeria's side in the dispute.

Just before the border war, Morocco's first constitution was promulgated. It outlawed the one-party regime, guaranteed basic democratic freedoms and provided for an elected parliament, but the king retained substantial powers. The first parliament elected in May 1963 comprised five parties who spent their time in petty bickering.

The King dissolved the parliament in June 1965 because of the "contradictory and irreconcilable demands of the parties" and he declared a "state of emergency". For five years he ruled by decree with a government of independence. He was the Prime Minister.

Plots and coups

Faced by what they saw as the King's autocratic rule, left-wing militants resorted to violence. Many were arrested in connection with five plots against the monarchy between 1963 and 1977; on two occasions, in 1965 and 1973, armed infiltrators entered the country from Algeria; in 1965, 1981 and 1984 there were serious street riots fomented by leftists.

The agitation was severely repressed and

France recalled its ambassador in Rabat and for three years relations were frozen as the King refused to admit Oufkir's guilt, and rejected suggestions that the General be dismissed. Relations with France were resumed after De Gaulle's death and French financial aid to Morocco began to flow again.

At about the same time cordial relations were established with Algeria and Mauritania after the King abandoned the Istiqlal's claims to their territory. He also convened Muslim leaders to a meeting in Casablanca where the Islamic Conference Organisation was created. This enhanced his own prestige and helped to forestall

there were mass trials resulting in death sentences. Mehdi ben Barka, who had been living in exile and was suspected of inciting the agitation, disappeared in Paris in mysterious circumstances on 29 October 1965. He was certainly assassinated. General Mohammed Oufkir, Moroccan Minister of the Interior at the time who had been in Paris at the time of the incident, was convicted by a French court of master-minding Ben Barka's abduction, and sentenced to life imprisonment in his absence.

LEFT: newly enfranchised, Moroccan women queue to cast their votes.
ABOVE: a young Hassan II, ruler 1961–99.

criticism from Islamic fundamentalists. The King now had his hands free to return to more democratic rule.

He decided to rescind the state of emergency, and a second constitution was adopted by referendum; but it was boycotted by the parties, who complained it had been drafted without their consent and was therefore an imposition.

The parties also boycotted the general election so that the second parliament was a colourless assembly with over 90 percent of its members so-called independents. The opposition claimed the vote was rigged. Elected for six years, parliament was a rubber-stamp affair plagued by absenteeism.

In an unsettled atmosphere, senior officers of the Royal Armed Forces staged an abortive *coup d'état* by storming the royal palace at Skhirate on the beach near Rabat on 10 July 1971 while the King was celebrating his 42nd birthday. Nearly 100 guests were gunned down by 1,400 non-commissioned cadets but the King escaped by hiding in a bathroom in a corner of the sprawling palace.

The army's motivations were mixed. Some coup leaders like General Mohammed Medbouh, Minister of the Royal Military Household, who was killed during the raid, were outraged by corruption and extravagance.

and so it seemed politic to avoid alienating loyalist officers and troops. If this was in fact the royal thinking, it proved misguided because, on the following 16 August, the pilots of three Air Force jets tried to liquidate the King and his entourage by pumping cannon shells into his airliner as it was flying home from France.

Once again the King escaped unscathed. As he related later, he spoke to the fighter pilots on the airliner's radio in a disguised voice to tell them "the tyrant is dead", whereupon they called off the attacks.

General Oufkir's alleged suicide during the night after the attacks was at first thought to be

They believed corrupt ministers should be brought to trial and made an example of and not just dismissed. Others were doubtless less idealistic and simply out to seize power in what would probably have been a right-wing military dictatorship.

The Defence Minister, General Oufkir, had the rebels rounded up with the help of loyalist troops. Ten officers including four generals were summarily executed. Just over 1,000 of the troops stood trial in the following February, but only 74 were convicted.

The verdict appeared surprisingly lenient, but the King's contention was that the coup was the work of only a fraction of the armed forces

the act of a dedicated officer who felt he had failed in his duty to protect his sovereign. The official version revealed days later was that he was a despicable traitor who had master-minded the attack and had planned to rule Morocco using as a puppet the King's elder son, Crown Prince Sidi Mohammed, then aged nine. His original plan was to shoot down the royal airliner over the sea and camouflage it as an accident.

At their trial Air Force officers said Oufkir had persuaded them that the King had to be liquidated to save the country from chaos. The truth is difficult to ascertain. The 11 ringleaders were all executed, so their real motives and the loyalty of other officers remain the subject of speculation. In an apparent effort to defuse discontent, six former cabinet ministers and four accomplices were brought to trial for corruption. Eight were sentenced to prison terms ranging from four to 12 years for taking bribes totalling over $2 million, but three years later they were all released.

Divine protection

The two abortive military coups convinced many that the Moroccan monarchy's days were numbered. This may help explain why, in the following year, on 3 March 1973, several hundred armed men infiltrated the country from Algeria with the intention of touching off a "popular uprising" on the 12th anniversary of the King's accession.

The "uprising" also failed, reinforcing the popular belief that the King enjoyed *baraka*, or divine protection. Perhaps misled by their own propaganda which claimed that only a spark was needed to set off a revolution, left-wing USFP activists who led the infiltrators found that, instead of welcoming them as "liberators", peasants in border areas telephoned local security forces. During the trials, at which 22 were sentenced to death, it was revealed that the plotters had also planted bombs at US offices in Casablanca and Rabat, and in the capital's theatre. None exploded, apparently because the myopic activist who had made them got his wires crossed.

In 1974 the non-party government led by Prime Minister Ahmed Osman, the King's brother-in-law, decided to more than double phosphate rock prices to $64 a ton and borrow money on the strength of this to finance capital-intensive development projects. But the higher price held for only a short time because of a world-wide recession.

Taking possession

A sudden surge in the price of crude oil when Morocco had to import at least 75 percent of its energy, combined with substantial increases in dollar and interest rates, and later a series of droughts which made it necessary to import

millions of tons of grain, placed Morocco in an uncomfortable position. But these problems were overshadowed, albeit aggravated from 1975 onwards, by the Western Sahara problem. When Spain announced plans to give its desert colony internal autonomy and hold a referendum there, the King revived Moroccan historic claims to the territory and launched a campaign to recover it for the "motherland".

Asked to decide whether the area was a *terra nullius* before Spain colonised it, the World

Court found that West Saharan tribes had paid allegiance to Moroccan monarchs but that this did not constitute sovereignty, which should be decided by self-determination. The King interpreted this as vindication of Moroccan claims, arguing that in a Muslim society, and particularly in Morocco, allegiance to the monarch constituted sovereignty. With extraordinary speed and great efficiency he organised the Green March, when some 350,000 Moroccans marched into the region, camped for three days under the guns of the Spanish Foreign Legion, which held its fire, and then withdrew when the King announced that they had "accomplished their mission".

LEFT: the Green March into the Sahara Desert.
RIGHT: Moroccan soldiers defend the country's new border against Polisario guerrillas.

The Green March succeeded mainly because Generalissimo Francisco Franco was gravely ill. In their disarray at the prospect of the dictator's imminent death, Spanish leaders were desperately anxious to avoid a colonial war. Thus on 14 November they transferred the administration of the disputed territory to Morocco and Mauritania.

The Algerian President, Colonel Houari Boumedienne, who until then had supported Moroccan and Mauritanian claims to the Western Sahara, suddenly came out in open support of the Polisario Front – a group of left-wing guerrillas led by a former member of the

Moroccan communist party, Mustapha el Ouali, who began campaigning for independence of the Spanish colony.

Algeria trained, armed, financed and gave sanctuary to the guerrillas, who proclaimed the Saharan Arab Democratic Republic (SADR) just as the last Spanish troops withdrew at the end of February 1976.

The war dragged on for more than a decade and imposed a heavy burden on the Moroccan treasury while Boumedienne was able to finance it out of his petroleum resources. Aggressive Algerian diplomacy enabled the SADR to get official recognition from over 70 non-aligned or so-called "progressive" states, among them Libya and the communist regimes of North Korea, Vietnam and Cuba, prompting the King's supporters to say there was a "worldwide communist conspiracy against Morocco".

In the event, the war took on some of the aspects of an East-West conflict, the Polisario were armed with Soviet weapons while pro-Western Morocco received military aid from France and the United States.

The Moroccan view was that Algeria was bent on creating a satellite state in the Western Sahara which would give it access to the Atlantic coast, that Polisario believed its guerrilla war would bring Morocco to its knees, and perhaps that the monarchy would collapse. Algeria on the other hand maintained that it acted on the "sacred principle" of self-determination and equated the Polisario's struggle with its own bloody independence war against France.

However, a major difference was that while the Algerian war became increasingly unpopular in France, and ultimately forced political

THE REIGN OF KING HASSAN II

When Hassan II died of pneumonia in July 1999 after a 38-year reign the nation was struck down by grief. Two million Moroccans lined the streets of Rabat to pay their final respects as the military vehicle carrying the coffin passed by. Royalty and heads of state from around the world attended the funeral, including the US president, Bill Clinton, and the president and prime minister of Israel.

Hassan was one of the moderate leaders of the Arab world. Though autocratic, he was highly intelligent and never out of touch with his subjects. One of his greatest achievements was to keep fundamentalism in check. Though this was partly achieved through exiles and imprisonments, his

most powerful weapon was his lineage to the Prophet Mohammed via the line of Ali (the Alaouite Dynasty), which allowed him to dismiss opponents as heretics.

In the last years of his reign, Hassan realised that to avert a social crisis he needed to embark on a programme of gradual democratisation, which would eventually lead to a constitutional monarchy. Following constitutional changes allowing opposition parties to form a government, the parliamentary election of 1998 resulted in a narrow victory for the four-party opposition, the "Koutla". Islamicists were also allowed to participate for the first time. Nonetheless, King Hassan still had the right to appoint and dismiss ministers.

settlement, the Sahara war produced unprecedented cohesion in Morocco. Far from weakening the King, it created unity as all political parties from left to right rallied around him. In this atmosphere, the King held new elections in 1984 which resulted in a credible parliament.

The small but vocal Party of Progress and Socialism based in Casablanca became the only communist party in the world to oppose the Polisario; leaders of the socialist USPF were even jailed briefly for criticising the King's decision to accept a self-determination referendum at a summit of the OAU in 1981. The irredentist Istiqlal Party not only approved the

withdrew, but he never carried out the threat because of the risk of a devastating war.

The turning point came in 1981 when Morocco began building defence lines composed of ridges of sand and rock studded with electronic sensors to give forewarning of guerrilla attacks. Gradually the lines were extended eastwards until they ran for 1,610 km (1,000 miles) along the frontiers. The army gained control of four-fifths of the territory and forced a military stalemate. By this time Algeria had decided that the war could not be won and it was time for a settlement.

After mediation by King Fahd of Saudi Arabia, Algeria and Morocco restored their rela-

takeover of the Western Sahara, but contained to press Moroccan claims to various parts of Algeria and the whole of Mauritania.

Finally, the King had to restrain his armed forces, many of whose field officers believed that the quickest way to end the war would be to launch a major strike into Algeria and attack the Polisario's rear bases. The King warned several times that he would exercise the "right of hot pursuit" into Algeria as the guerrillas

LEFT: Hassan II, wearing the white *jellabah* traditionally worn in parliament.
ABOVE: King Mohammed VI (right) carries his father's coffin, July 1999.

tions in May 1988. Morocco and the Polisario accepted a peace plan drafted by the United Nations. The plan proposed a ceasefire, to be followed by a self-determination referendum, under international control, to give the people of the thinly-populated area a choice between independence or remaining part of Morocco.

Into the 1990s

Toward the end of the 1980s reconciliation with Algeria paved the way for realisation of an old North African dream of economic union, "The Grand Arab Maghreb", composing Algeria, Libya, Mauritania, Morocco and Tunisia. But many of the promises of the late 1980s failed to come to fruition. The *Union du Grand Maghreb* was abandoned in the face of Algeria's civil war, which made Morocco and Tunisia keen to keep their distance. In the Western Sahara, the promised referendum has yet to take place, though the ceasefire still holds. Attempts at a vote were repeatedly postponed through the 1990s, initially due to US disquiet and Polisario objections when the Moroccan government moved 37,000 Moroccans into the region on the grounds that their families had originated in the area. While

> **PEACEKEEPING PRICE**
>
> UN mediation in the Western Sahara is estimated to cost £2.4 million a month, a sum that many UN members are reluctant to sustain.

Morocco continues to frustrate the referendum, UN peace-keeping forces sweat it out in the desert and *Saharwi* refugees, who fled the Western Sahara when the Moroccans moved in in 1975, face another year in camps.

On the home front, Morocco pressed ahead with an extensive privatisation programme involving over 100 enterprises (including two breweries, a wine-making company and 11 luxury hotels), risking the wrath of fundamentalists in the process. It is vigorously seeking foreign investment and upping its international profile, with Marrakesh in particular becoming a popular international conference centre. Liberalisation was not confined to the economic sphere. In 1997 Morocco held its fairest election to date, resulting in a narrow majority for the Socialist Union of Popular Forces (USAP) and the leader of the opposition Abderrahmane Youssoufi, a former dissident exiled to France, becoming prime minister in February 1998.

Death of a king

In July 1999 King Hassan II died at the age of 70. It was a moment the Moroccan people had dreaded. Life without their King seemed unimaginable. His son and successor, 36-year-old Mohammed Ben Al-Hassan, who received the allegiance of the government within hours of his father's death, was widely perceived as diffident and lacking his father's famous strength of character. Yet within a few months, it was clear that Mohammed VI had a new vision for Morocco's future, and was keen to develop the small seeds of reform that Hassan had planted in the last years of his reign. Mohammed was reported as saying he wanted to reign over a state of law not of fear.

One of his first and most significant acts was to sack the country's much-hated but powerful interior minister Driss Basri, who, as Hassan's right-hand man, had run the country's security forces for some 20 years and was known for his brutal suppression of human rights. At the same time, several leading dissidents were permitted to return from exile in France, including the communist leader Abraham Serfaty and the exiled family of Mehdi Ben Barka, the government opponent who had disappeared in 1965 *(see page 45)*. The King also freed many political prisoners, including Abdessalem Yassine, leader of the Islamic Justice and Spirituality Movement. In the social sphere, the most important development has been a proposal to make sweeping reforms to women's rights, many of which are still derived from Sharia law.

Whether Mohammed can steer the country safely through reform while keeping control of the many opposing forces unleashed by Hassan's death has yet to be seen, but the world is hopeful. As an important sign of Morocco's new dawn, in April 2000 the United Nations launched the Arab World's first centre for human rights training and information in Rabat. ❏

LEFT: Mohammed VI.

Sporting Passions

Morocco may not leap to mind when one thinks of the world's great sporting nations, but in recent years Moroccan sportsmen (and a few women) have been making headlines around the world. Middle distance running has for many years been a forte, but strides have also been made in football and tennis.

In football, Morocco's national team, the Atlas Lions, consistently makes the grade to compete in the World Cup, and under French coach Henri Michel in the 1998 World Cup managed to secure a draw against Norway and beat Scotland 3:0, results that would have put them through to the quarter-finals but for a disputed penalty awarded to group rivals Norway in the last minute of their match against Brazil.

At the start of the 2000 Africa Cup, Morocco was Fifa's highest ranked team in Africa, though in the end it was knocked out early in the tournament, a poor performance considering it hadn't lost a match against African opposition since 1998.

Members of Morocco's national squad play for teams all over world, lured overseas by lucrative contracts. Among the star names are mid-fielders Moustafa Hadji (Aston Villa, UK) ,Youssef Chipo (Coventry City, UK), Salaheddine Bassir (Lille, France) and Noureddine Naybet (Deportivo Coruna, Spain).

The country's passion for football rivals that of neigbouring Spain. Morocco has repeatedly bid to stage the World Cup, and may prove the first country in Africa to do so. Though poor by European standards, it has invested heavily in the sport, with a showcase stadium at Casablanca.

But it is in track events that Morocco really excels. The country has had several middle distance runners of note, most famously the Olympic gold medalist Said Aouta, who inspired a generation of young runners, including Salah HIssou and Khalid Skah, who give the Ethiopians and Kenyans a run for their money in 5,000-metre and 10,000-metre events, and 1500-metre world record-breaker Hicham El Guerroudj.

Morocco is the setting for major meetings of the IAAF (International Amateur Athletics Federation) and also stages a gruelling cross-country event, the Marathon des Sables. Considered the toughest

foot race in the world, it starts from Marrakesh and then crosses the Atlas Mountains to the Sahara, covering mountainous terrain, dried up river beds and trackless sands. Competitors, who travel some 20–80km (12–50 miles) a day depending on terrain, are equipped with backpacks containing flares, signalling mirrors and anti-venom kits in case they get lost or injured. Daytime temperatures can reach 49°C (120°F).

The latest sport to give the whole Moroccan nation something to shout about is tennis. In January 2000 Morocco managed to have two players reach the quarter-finals of the Australian Open, Younes El Aynaoui and Hicham Arazi. Though they

were then knocked out by Yevgeny Kafelnikov and Andre Agassi respectively, this was a terrific achievement for a poor country. Though King Hassan was a tennis enthusiast, and regularly invited top players to his palaces, Morocco has no centres of excellence for junior players.

The late king was also instrumental in promoting golf in Morocco, and was himself a keen golfer, as is Mohammed VI. First-class golf courses are found across the country, and the Royal Dar-es-Salam Golf Club, Rabat, with two 18-hole courses and a 9-hole course, has an international reputation. Designed by Robert Trent Jones, it is the setting for the Hassan II Trophy in November and the Moroccan Open, part of the Volvo PGA, in January. ❑

RIGHT: Morocco's outstanding athlete, the middle distance runner Said Aouta.

THE MOROCCANS

In Morocco, probably more than in any other Arab nation,
traditionalists and modernists comfortably coexist

For centuries Europeans enjoyed explaining the character of the Moor. Early visitors to Morocco would warn of the dark, lazy, deceitful and polygamous infidels on Europe's doorstep. Sir John Drummond Hay, Britain's consul in Tangier for the last half of the 19th century, wrote: "They combine all possible vices."

A popular image

Even these days, some of these Western prejudices and clichés remain, albeit tempered by praise of Moroccan hospitality or family values. In the popular imagination, Moroccans are described as "chauvinists", "fatalists" and "hedonists" – simple stereotypes when one considers Morocco's eclectic racial origins.

Broadly, Moroccans may be divided into the urban and rural populations. The Berbers, the indigenous race, are still more likely to live in the mountainous *bled,* or countryside, where they migrated in the face of the first Arab invaders; and the Arabs, in the towns and cities of the plains. The Berbers are of three main types (sub-divided into countless tribes): the Riffians of the north; the Chleuhs from the Middle and High Atlas; and the Soussi, found in the southwest. Their origins are uncertain, and the many theories include the possibility of European derivations, probably based on the not unusual occurrence of fair colouring and blue or green eyes.

The so-called Arab/Berber divide is now considered to be a myth propagated during the French and Spanish protectorates to help justify colonial policies and undermine resistance. Today most Moroccans are of mixed ancestry – Berber, Arab and black African (the latter originating from black slaves imported from Mali during the Saadi dynasty) – as can be seen from the rich variety of faces, even within the same family. In the countryside, pockets of pure Arabs in mainly Berber regions – for example, Erfoud in the Tafilalt and Tamgroute in the Draa – are unusual. Here the women are shrouded in heavy black *haik* and reveal only one eye to the world, in contrast to their brightly-attired and unveiled Berber sisters.

But the two races have developed much in common. When the Berbers embraced Islam, they adapted it to include pagan customs which were then absorbed into Moroccan culture as a whole. So although Islam isn't supposed to recognise intermediaries between God and man, Morocco is littered with *koubbas,* the white-domed tombs of holy men *(marabouts),* to which the troubled and the sick make pilgrimages.

In fact, women are more likely to visit the tomb of a holy man, or even a sacred stream or tree, than go to pray at the male-dominated mosque. She may camp for weeks at a *koubba,* where she will pray, perhaps grieve and just pass time *(see page 224).*

PRECEDING PAGES: entertainment in Imilchil in the High Atlas; a butcher poses.
LEFT: Berber girl from the Dades Valley.
RIGHT: in the Hassan II Mosque, Casablanca.

Spellbound

Magic, too, is a fecund and potent force. As the late author and composer Paul Bowles *(see page 71)* wrote in his autobiography *Without Stopping*: "Sorcery is burrowing invisible tunnels in every direction, from thousands of senders to thousands of unsuspecting recipients." Every medina contains a *shouaf* to which not only the gullible and uneducated go to purchase weird concoctions or to seek advice; the apothecaries in the markets trade in dried bits of animal skin and pickled reptiles; benevolent and evil *jinn* (spirits) are thought populous; and the power of the so-called "evil eye", meaning the spells cast over one by a jealous ill-wisher, isn't taken lightly. The newspapers are full of lurid tales of revenge through witchcraft, and mothers give their children protective charms – a "hand" or a leather pouch containing fragments of Koranic verses, or perhaps a blue bead – and line their newborn's eyes with kohl, another safeguard. Too much beauty or good fortune are often thought to provoke

LANGUAGE BARRIERS

The Berber languages – Riffian, Tishilhate and Tamsiaght – are completely different from Arabic and totally incomprehensible to most Arabs.

TAKING A SOCIAL BATH

The public bath *(hammam)* is still very much a part of Moroccan daily life, particularly in the medinas. Even families that have well-equipped private bathrooms will, from time to time, visit their local *hammam*. Its function is as much social as practical. Cleanliness is also close to godliness, and ritual cleansing is important before prayer.

Non-Muslims are usually made welcome, though sometimes not in *hammams* next to mosques. Inside you will find a changing area leading into a series of dim, misty chambers of varying temperatures, and be given a bucket for sluicing down. Women, for whom a visit to the *hammam* is a gossipy, social occasion, take all sorts of paraphernalia,

including scrapers for exfoliation, powdered henna and tar-like black soap. These items are often happily shared with ill-equipped foreigners.

The mood in the female *hammam* is animated (women often have small children in tow) and sober in the men's, where the only sound may be the clicking of bones (a rigorous physiotherapy administered by the masseur); but in both a mixture of abandonment and modesty prevails. You may lie in the arms of a semi-naked attendant, who will scrub you mercilessly and examine every pore, but at no point in the *hammam* are underpants removed. That would be considered most impolite.

jealousy and the evil eye. For this reason the most splendid carpet design should never be entirely symmetrical or too perfect.

Again, Islam doesn't endorse the use of magic, but tolerates it – another indication of its flexibility as a religion. In theory, Islam recognises its fellow "written" religions, Judaism and Christianity, and in spite of the colourful accounts of Christian slavery in the 17th century and the departure of most Jews at Independence, Morocco claims historical respect for both. Many Jews

AN ACT OF TREASON

Conversion to another religion is unthinkable for a Muslim and deemed an act of treason by the State. It is illegal to take Arabic editions of the Bible into Morocco.

(giving alms to the poor); and *Haj* (the pilgrimage to Mecca, which should be undertaken at least once in a lifetime). But the Koran (the direct word of God given to the Prophet) and the Hadith (the sayings of the Prophet on Islamic conduct in everyday life) make generous allowances for the frailty of the flesh. Sexual intercourse, providing it is within marriage, is considered beneficial to the holiest of men.

Sufism has adapted Islam to include elements of mysticism, such as asceticism and medita-

emigrated to Morocco from Spain to escape the Inquisition. King Hassan II, in his autobiography *The Challenge*, was proud of Morocco's history of religious tolerance. The Jewish quarter in a city, the *mellah*, was always built close to the palace so that it should benefit from royal protection.

Islam is forgiving towards Muslims themselves. There are five "pillars" of the faith: *Shahada* (the testament that there is no god but God); *Salat* (the observance of prayer five times a day); *Saum* (fasting at Ramadan); *Zakat*

LEFT: sex and kung-fu go down well on the big screen.
ABOVE: women's talk.

tion, which have more in common with monasticism than they do with orthodox Islam. At one time, those claiming *baraka*, a blessing supposedly bestowed by Allah on any direct descendants of the Prophet (quite a marketable asset), acquired the status of saints, deemed capable of miracles. Some of the cults that evolved around these saints inspired trance and self-mutilations in their followers.

Now outlawed, such extreme practices have died out or gone underground, but some remnant of their spirit is still alive in the trance music of the *gnaoua*, black African musician-healers. A group of *gnaoua* are often present on the Jemma el Fna in Marrakesh, dressed in their distinctive hats and waistcoats trimmed with lucky cowrie shells.

Traditionally, *baraka* also endowed its possessor with more civil authority than anyone else – which, in a country of constant tribal feuding, provided at least some kind of independent jurisdiction. Thus it has also helped determine and preserve the succession to the sultancy. Mohammed V's claim to the throne in 1956 was helped by the fact that his lineage could be traced back to the Prophet via Ali (the Alaouite

CURES BY PRAYER

Baraka (religious power) is claimed by *faikirs*, who travel through remote country areas offering herbs and prayers to the sick in return for payment.

dynasty), even though the Koran is against a religious hierarchy and the King's authority is ultimately rooted in a feudal system, not Divine Right. The people offer allegiance in return for the sultan's protection, symbolised by the giant umbrella carried by the King on ceremonial occasions.

French legacy

International consensus is that Morocco has done well since independence – all things considered, including problems caused by earthquakes and droughts. Certainly, arriving in Rabat for the first time or driving into Casablanca along the residential Anfa road, one gets an impression of established prosperity.

France has left its legacy in the country's administration: in common with Europe rather than many other parts of the Muslim world, Friday is a normal working day and Saturday and Sunday a weekend holiday; administratively the country is divided into provinces (or *préfectures* in the cases of Rabat and Casablanca) and sub-divided into communes; when conducting business the educated frequently talk to one another in French rather than Arabic; and until recently bright students were assisted by the Moroccan government to attend foreign, usually French, universities. Inevitably, such students sometimes returned to Morocco with an outlook that had altered.

Superficially, therefore, Morocco can seem European rather than African. In fact, though – unlike other Arab countries, whose cultures bear the heavy-handed stamp of their colonisers – the Ottomans – it retains much of its pre-

---

INSHALLAH, BISMILLAH AND EL-HAMDU LILLAH

A constant refrain in Morocco, and in most Arab countries, is the phrase *Inshallah*. It accompanies most statements of intent. It can mean many things: literally "If God wills", but also many nuances between yes and no, including possibly, perhaps, maybe, of course, absolutely, or why not?...if God wills it. Strictly speaking, the phrase is part of Islamic culture, in which the name of God is constantly invoked. Before starting a meal or a journey, a Muslim will say *Bismillah er-rahman er-rahim* (In the name of God, the clement and merciful), which is a way of giving thanks for the meal, or praying for a safe journey. The King always pronounces it before starting a speech.

El-Hamdu Lillah (Praise be to God) is also heard frequently to express satisfaction, pleasure or simply to give thanks to the Almighty for benefits such as good health, rainfall or prosperity. In times of trouble, the phrase used may be *Allah Akbar* (God is great), the implication being that the deity is above human tribulations.

When in the early 1970s the state television network began broadcasting weather forecasts, they drew a protest from the Ulema (doctors of Islamic law), who said it was sacrilegious to say it was going to rain without adding the phrase *Inshallah*. As a result, all weather predictions are now peppered with the phrase.

colonial character. Its Europeanisation is only a façade, even in the cities. The *bidonvilles* of Casablanca, shanty-towns built by those who migrated to the towns following World War II and the rapid industrialisation of Morocco, exist in conditions that have never improved.

National pride

In the 1970s a delayed reaction to the colonialism of the first half of the century heralded a climate of Moroccan nationalism. Groups of musicians, notably Nass el Ghiwane and Jilala, revived a popular ancient folk music known as El Malhoune, incorporating anti-establishment,

dience. The Moroccan Government was one of the first to demonstrate support for Kuwait and the West (major donors of aid to Morocco) and dispatched 1,500 troops to join the build-up of allied forces in Saudi Arabia. However, when war broke out in January 1991 and Moroccan public opinion rallied round Iraq's Saddam Hussein, King Hassan was forced to moderate his stance. Pro-Iraqi demonstrations in Rabat and Fez were of a size not seen since the Green March into the Western Sahara. In the very speech banning such demonstrations, the King began referring to Saddam as "brother".

By Arab and African standards Hassan pro-

leftist lyrics. It degenerated into popular commercial music before having much political impact, but it didn't go unnoticed in high places. King Hassan II, conscious of skating on thin ice at times (and ever mindful of the demise of monarchs in other parts of the Arab world), was careful to promote national pride, foster useful relations with Europe and America, encourage a popular reaffirmation of faith (while guarding against fundamentalism), and watch his own back, all at the same time.

The 1990–91 Gulf Crisis illustrated his expe-

duced a liberal kingdom, which his son Mohammed VI is carefully taking one step further. It is a country, though, where royal contacts are essential to success in high office– and it is a monarchy in its full sense; constitutionally, the monarch can overrule any decision. The King's authority is underlined at all levels. In every public building, even a humble sandwich shop, a framed portrait of the King is given pride of place.

Modern poblems

One of the biggest problems confronting Morocco is unemployment, particularly among the educated proletariat. A high percentage of

LEFT: prayer time at the Kairouyine Mosque.
ABOVE: a gathering of water-sellers in Marrakesh.

people are engaged in casual, seasonal or itinerant work. There are no state benefits for the unemployed, only weekly handouts of staples such as flour, rice and oil for the extreme needy. Meanwhile the country has seen the sudden growth of a middle class, and inevitably huge disparities between rich and poor cause social unrest. A population of 29 million and an accelerating birthrate exacerbate difficulties and have at last prompted timid attempts at birth control. In recent years royal speeches have made frequent references to the advisability of contraception – something that would have been condemned as anti-religious in the past.

Chronic unemployment also accounts for the surprising number of male and female brothels, particularly in Marrakesh and Casablanca. Although prostitution's claim to be the oldest profession in the world is as true here as anywhere, it proliferated in Morocco under the French and Spanish protectorates, when military brothels were set up. Western homosexuals find a ready supply of catamites in Tangier and Marrakesh, even though homosexuality is illegal, while rich Gulf Arabs, escaping their strict regimes at home, take advantage of Morocco's more liberal climate to establish private female brothels. These are not apparent to the average tourist, whose impression is of veiled women and sexual seclusion.

On the home front

On a more domestic note, social and family traditions, and national and regional festivals, are fervently followed. As well as the big religious festivals (the birthday of the Prophet; Aid es Seghir, marking the end of Ramadan; and Aid el Kebir, commemorating Abraham's sacrifice of a sheep in place of his son, held 70 days after Ramadan), family events such as births, circumcisions, marriages, the return of the *Haj* (pilgrimage to Mecca) and burial are conducted according to cherished rituals. After the birth of a baby a lamb (two lambs if the child is given two names) is slaughtered for a feast on the seventh day; if the family is poor, a chicken or even a rabbit will be substituted for a lamb. For the circumcision of boys at the age of three or four – these days usually aided by a local anaesthetic – another feast is held and the boy is dressed in traditional clothes and plied with money. Arranged marriages are still fairly common, especially in the low and high class families, and lavish weddings are still the norm. But an increasing number of brides and grooms are opting for a simple ceremony, and many couples are living together after the "engagement", an official ceremony equivalent to the wedding itself in the West – which happens a year or so before the wedding (if they do, however, there is no turning back short of divorce or death). Probably more than in any other Arab nation, in Morocco traditionalists and modernists comfortably coexist. ❏

LEFT: a small boy dressed in a circumcision costume. Circumcision normally takes place at the age of three.

Ramadan

The most important time of the year in any Islamic country is Ramadan, the month of fasting when, the Koran stipulates, not even a drop of water should pass a Muslim's lips during daylight. Some people are exempt: pregnant or menstruating women, travellers on a long journey, the very old or sick and children. But almost everyone else, whether they practise their religion or not, upholds this "pillar of the faith".

To Christians, a month of contemplation might seem a poor way to celebrate the revelation of the Koran. More like Lent than Christmas. Not just food and drink, but sex and tobacco too are off the agenda until the hour when a "black thread cannot be distinguished from a white one". If the moveable fast (controlled by the Hegira calendar) falls in the summer when the sun rises early and sets late the mood is particularly subdued. Irrational behaviour, bad driving and short tempers are all blamed on lack of sustenance.

Banking and office hours have to be reduced, and cafés are closed, though their patrons, governed by habit rather than wishful thinking, still tend to congregate on their cheerless terraces. But as each afternoon lengthens and dusk approaches restlessness in the towns and listlessness in the villages metamorphose into a swelling sense of expectation. Just before sundown the streets empty, as everyone heads home.

When the mosque lamps signal nightfall and the *muezzin* calls "*Allah Akbar*" for the sunset prayer, Moroccans everywhere fall upon a bowl of *harira*, a thick broth of lamb, chickpeas, lentils and tomatoes, the traditional break to the fast, as though synchronised by the unseen hand of Allah. In private homes the soup is served with dates, figs and *shebbakia*, deep-fried pastries dipped in honey, either home-made or bought from the special *shebbakia* stalls that spring up during this special time of year.

With everyone replete, the atmosphere turns festive. Cafés catch up on the business they have missed during the day, families parade the main boulevards, and clothes shops do a roaring trade – the purchase of new clothes in preparation for the end of Ramadan, Aid es Seghir, being an essential part of the ritual. Eventually everyone drifts home to bed, where the suburban bourgeoisie, mindful of

their work commitments, sleep soundly until dawn; but in the medinas and villages, the bastions of tradition, the night's rituals are not yet over. Before daybreak drummers patrol the streets and alleyways rousing households for the *assohour*, traditionally thick pancakes spread with honey and served with mint tea or coffee, a sleepy feast which children particularly love.

Each evening is a little celebration, but the 26th day of Ramadan, commemorating the first revelation to the Prophet, is marked by a more elaborate feast and, for the devout, a night spent reciting the Koran in the mosque. A few days later, on the 29th or 30th evening, depending on the appear-

ance of the new moon, the fast ends. The following day is Aid es Seghir, "little feast", a public holiday when new clothes are worn and the country's poor knock on doors to claim alms.

Ramadan has some disadvantages for travellers – the widespread closure of cafés and restaurants during the day and the custom of many bars or restaurants to stop serving alcohol for the month of Ramadan – but the festive atmosphere of the evenings can make up for these. The solidarity that the fast engenders is also impressive: to abstain from the fast is unthinkable for a Moroccan and anyone seen eating, drinking or smoking in public in the daytime would be angrily condemned by his countrymen ❑

RIGHT: honey-laden *shebbakia*, a Ramadan treat.

THE LIVES AND TIMES OF THE BERBERS

The Berbers comprise up to half of Morocco's population, but increasing urbanisation is steadily Arabising their cultural identity

When the Arabs arrived in Morocco in the 8th century, they found a country inhabited by the fiercely tribal Amaziah, who have lived in northwest Africa since before the Phoenicians built their first trading posts along the coast in the the 12th century BC. The Romans called these wild tribes the "Barbarus", a name that has descended to us today as the "Berbers".

Today the Amaziah, as they prefer to be called, represent a widespread group of tribes scattered from Libya westwards to the Canary Islands, and southwards to the Taureg of Algeria.

KEEPING LANGUAGE ALIVE

The Berbers are most strongly identifiable by their language, which is split into three distinct dialects: Riffian in the north, Tishilhate in the western Atlas and Tamsiaght in the east. It was once a written language with its own alphabet, still remembered by the Taureg, but today transliterated into Arabic. Thanks to the efforts of the late King Hassan II and a growing militancy among Berber cultural associations, the Amaziah language is starting to have a small renaissance. It is now regularly broadcast on radio and television, and its literature is being studied in the country's universities.

△ **TO MARKET, TO MARKET**
Souks are vital to the Berbers, especially to the nomads. Here they can buy what they cannot grow or make themselves, and exchange news too.

▽ **FRUIT OF THE LOOM**
Goat hair and sheep's wool are turned into textiles. Designs are inspired by geometrical representations of the natural world.

△ **MOUNTAIN LIVING**
In the mountains the Berbers' stone houses cling to the sides of rocky slopes, perched above intensely cultivated terraced fields.

▷ **UNDER COVER**
Low tents made of goat and camel hair, belonging to the nomadic Ait Atta Berbers of the Jebel Sahro and the semi-arid plains of the Draa.

▽ **THE ART OF IMPROVISATION**
Baking bread on a makeshift stove. To seal the bread, hot stones are placed on top of the dough, with a twig fire on top of that.

THE BRIDES OF IMILCHIL

The most famous of the Berber festivals is the wedding *moussem* of the Ait Haddidou near Imilchil. Each September this enormous tribe meets to celebrate the feast day of the local Muslim saint, and to participate in the last really big market of the year before winter arrives. It is the spectacle of dozens of brides, dressed in blue, white and red shawls, their cheeks rouged and their eyes lined with kohl, coming to sign the government marriage register that has attracted the attention of tourists and journalists from around the world. The Ait Haddidou tribe allows free association between the sexes. During the festival groups of traditionally dressed girls cruise the market, catching the eyes of giggling young lads. The air of the festival is electric with romance.

△ **SONG AND DANCE**
Berber music is communal. Drums, flutes and clapping accompany the lyrics.

▷ **SHY? NOT I**
Berber women are not bashful about accosting strangers. Life is harsh, and communities cannot afford the wasted labour of cloistering their women at home.

A WOMAN'S PLACE

Despite being governed by strict rules of propriety, Moroccan women have a lot more freedom than some of their Muslim sisters – and a voice that is getting louder

The wave of fundamentalism spreading through the Muslim world is not much more than a ripple by the time it reaches Morocco. The late King Hassan, who in the past liked to portray himself as a bit of a swinger, wasn't keen to encourage the zeal of the Eastern *mullahs*. From the start of his reign, he wanted to promote Morocco as a progressive state and it has always been one of the more socially liberal Muslim countries. Alcohol is available, Western women's magazines are sold intact (without the rude bits cut out) and those who choose European lifestyles are, within reason, accepted.

Behind the veil

The majority of Moroccan women still wearing the *l'tam*, or face veil (the Moroccan version covers the nose, mouth and chin), do so out of tradition rather than because they have been influenced by the political Islamicism that spread through the Arab World in the 1980s. More common, and more likely to be inspired by religious or political principles, is the wearing of a simple headscarf.

In the north of Morocco, use of the *l'tam* is confined to older matrons and rarely do they wear the all-enveloping black *haik* worn in the south. Women attired in traditional manner – in a *jellabah*, or kaftan, sometimes slit at the sides – will often be seen with their jeans-clad or short-skirted daughters. Men keen to marry a committed Muslim often have difficulty finding a young woman prepared to express her devoutness by covering her face.

In the countryside, Berber women shoulder a large share of the agricultural work, as life in the mountains and desert is harsh and communities cannot afford to waste precious labour by cloistering their women at home. As a result, Berber women don't wear restrictive veils or *haik,* and are known for their colourful dresses and headscarves.

LEFT: preparing pomegranates.
RIGHT: veiled looks, a woman wearing the *l'tam.*

Nonetheless, laws relating to marriage laid down by the Prophet in 7th-century Arabia are still applied. Polygamy continues to be legal – indeed, outside the Royal Circle it was never known how many wives the late King Hassan had – and a Moroccan man is still within the law if he beats his wife. A male Muslim may

also marry a Jew or Christian, a right not extended to women. If a man wants to divorce his wife, he can simply repudiate her by saying "I divorce thee" three times in front of an Islamic judge. And if a woman wishes to travel abroad without her husband she must be able to show his written permission to the authorities.

Codes of conduct

Women are still governed by strict codes of propriety, especially before marriage. While it is acceptable for an older woman to take snuff, for example, it is unusual for a young woman to be seen smoking in public. And the late-night presence of a group of unchaperoned girls in even an upmarket *salon de thé* will still raise eyebrows. A woman's place, at least after the evening promenade, is in the home.

Speaking out

The succession of Mohammed VI in 1999 introduced a new climate of change for women's issues *(see panel)*, but Islamic fundamentalists are vigorously opposing any divergence from Sharia family law. In March 2000 a demonstration in support of reform attracted some 40,000 women on to the streets of Rabat. But over in Casablanca, around 500,000 female fundamentalists, organised by the Justice and Spirituality Movement, staged their own, much larger demonstration against reform.

Economics help the case for change. Most men can afford only one wife these days, and she will probably goes out to work. Many women have to hold down a job and run a home, in a country where a minimum of four children is still the norm, washing machines are still considered luxuries and the

INHERENT INJUSTICE

According to Islamic inheritance law, daughters receive only half the legacy received by sons, unless the will stipulates other arrangements.

CHANGES SOUGHT

Women's rights were one of the first issues that Mohammed VI sought to address when he succeeded to the throne. However, proposals have met with resistance from Islamicists. Among the issues under discussion are:
● A ban on polygamy
● Raising the legal age of marriage from 14 to 18
● A woman's entitlement to half her husband's wealth in case of divorce
● To place the right of divorce in the hands of a judge rather than a husband
● The abolition of child labour. At the moment, children as young as six can be forced into work by their parents.

midday meal is a full-blown affair that working women rush home to prepare. Many poorer women work long hours as maids in the homes of the middle classes as well as running their own households.

Men do little to help with childcare or housework, although they do sometimes do the shopping, traditionally a male chore because of the desire to protect women from the cut and thrust of the market (and possibly to enable men to keep hold of the purse strings). However, these days, even shopping is being packed into the busy schedule of Morocco's women. ❑

ABOVE: women of Marrakesh.

Wild Weddings

I n spite of the current strides being made in female emancipation, married is what most girls want to be when they grow up. Arranged marriages are still common, but not the rule, and rarely happen against the wishes of the couple involved. In most cases, once a man is ready for marriage he will ask his close female relatives to help him choose a bride or ask them to approach the family of a girl he has already met. A meeting of the two families will then ensue to ascertain the man's prospects and respectability. If the families do not know one another, behind-the-scenes investigations will ensue. It is imperative for the prospective bride to make a good match. Divorce, though not uncommon, still carries a stigma and can be disastrous for a young woman.

Once a couple decide to marry, preparations are made for the "engagement", the legal part of the wedding (after the engagement there is no going back short of divorce or death). Like the wedding itself, it is an elaborate affair, traditionally beginning with the groom proceeding to the bride's home, with donkeys laden with offerings – bolts of fabrics, cones of sugar, baskets of candles and spices – and a fattened calf bringing up the rear. These days, such gifts have symbolic importance rather than material value and, sadly, the tradition is disappearing. However, the groom is still responsible for providing the food for the engagement feast and he will deliver this to the bride's home early in the day; in reality, the bride's family waits by nervously, estimating whether quantities will match demand, and ensuring that items such as salt and oil and charcoal for cooking have not been left out. Invariably the bride's family will need to make a last-minute dash to the market for more supplies.

The wedding itself is usually a two or three-day event (though it can go on far longer) of gender-segregated feasts, regulated by strict protocol. For several days before the occasion, the bride is attended by a *negaffa*, who acts as her personal beautician – supervising depilation, coiffure and the application of henna to hands and feet in lace-like patterns – as well as instructing the bride in conjugal duties. During the celebrations, the *negaffa* flanks the bride at all times, announcing her when she enters a room and attending to her every need (traditionally, the bride would sit motion-less) and supervising her changes of clothes (usu-ally two traditional costumes, plus a white, Western-style dress). Until fairly recently, the *negaffa's* most important job was to witness the consummation of the marriage and confirm the bride's virginity, some-times by brandishing the bloodied sheets.

Most wedding feasts are sexually segregated and held at home or in a hired villa, though mixed gender festivities in hotels are becoming fashionable. On the first night the emphasis is on the groom, whose guests gather from around 5pm for tea and pastries and are entertained by a small orchestra; later on, a meal of two or three substantial courses will be served. The women will also attend, but will occupy

a separate area or floor. At various points in the evening the bridal couple is "presented".

The second evening focuses on the bride's female guests, who will be entertained by an all-female orchestra and possibly by drummers and *gnaou* musicians. More relaxed and more fun than the men's night, it is an occasion for women to put on their finery and let their hair down, dancing with one another and joining in renditions of popular love-songs. To capture the occasion for posterity, professional video-makers are often hired. Though female, these generally cause older and more conservative guests to dive under veils and headscarves, hiding themselves from male eyes that may subsequently view the video. ❏

RIGHT: a Berber bride.

MOROCCO BOUND

Over the years, a multitude of Western writers, artists and musicians have been drawn to Moorish places, in particular to the port of Tangier

The exotic image of Tangier which endures today was largely created by Eugène Delacroix, the leading exponent of Romantic painting in France. In 1832, he accompanied the Comte de Mornay, sent by Louis-Philippe as French ambassador to the sultan of Morocco. He filled sketchbooks with pen and ink drawings, and watercolours of everyday life in Tangier – the bustle of the marketplace and the mysterious streets of the casbah – later using these details in the great series of paintings on Oriental subjects for which he is best known *(see pages 16–17, 24 and 29)*. "I am like a man dreaming and who sees things he is afraid will escape him," he wrote. "The picturesque is plentiful here. At every step, one meets ready-made paintings that would bring 20 generations of painters wealth and glory."

Anything goes

This romantic vision of Tangier persisted, and the town's "anything goes" atmosphere attracted several generations of writers and artists, wanderers and bohemians. Truman Capote summed up the attractions of the city when he first visited at the age of 26 in 1949: "Virtually every Tangerine is ensconced there for at least one, if not all, of four reasons: the easy availability of drugs, lustful adolescent prostitutes, tax loopholes, or because he is so undesirable no place north of Port Said would let him out of the airport or off the ship." Certainly, the first two reasons appealed to William Burroughs, who moved to the city after reading *The Sheltering Sky*, by the American writer Paul Bowles, and the easy availability of drugs was the main attraction for hippies in the 1960s and '70s when Tangier was a key stop on the so-called "hash trail".

Two figures dominated the expatriate scene in Tangier in the post-war years: the Hon. David Herbert controlled the social scene, the

tea parties and high-society gossip of the extensive British colony, but the hub around which all artistic and intellectual activity revolved was the writer Paul Bowles, who lived in Tangier until his death from a heart attack in 1999.

Bowles first arrived in Tangier in August 1931 from France where he had been discour-

aged from writing poetry when critic Gertrude Stein told him, "The only trouble with all this is that it isn't poetry." He subsequently published many volumes of poetry.

He was travelling with the American composer, Aaron Copland, and together they took a house on the Old Mountain. It was not until 1947, that he took up permanent residence in Tangier, and this was as the result of a dream he had in May of that year: "In the late afternoon sunlight I walked slowly through complex and tunnelled streets. As I reviewed it, lying there, sorry to have left the place behind, I realised with a jolt that the magic city really existed. It was Tangier. My heart accelerated… the town

---

LEFT: the late Paul Bowles as a young man.
RIGHT: Some of Bowles's book jackets. His books were usually set in exotic places.

was still present the following morning, fresh and invigorating to recall, and vivid memory of it persisted day after day... it did not take me long to come to the conclusion that Tangier must be the place I wanted to be more than anywhere else."

By this time, Bowles had married Jane Auer, in what the most of their friends regarded as a marriage of convenience between two good friends. It was Jane's success with *Two Serious Ladies* in 1943 that inspired Paul to write short stories. With an

PAUL BOWLES

Although now known as a writer, in the 1930s and 1940s Bowles was busy composing music, including scores for Tennessee Williams's early plays, and for ballet and film.

Friends and lovers

Jane arrived in January 1948, in the company of her latest lover, a hard-drinking, middle-aged tea-shop proprietor from Massachusetts called Cory, and installed herself in the Hotel Rembrandt. She was limping from a knee operation and jokingly referred to herself as "Crippie the Kike Dyke", which also satirised her Jewishness and lesbianism. Paul and Jane, though best friends, kept separate households, often occupying two apartments in the same building.

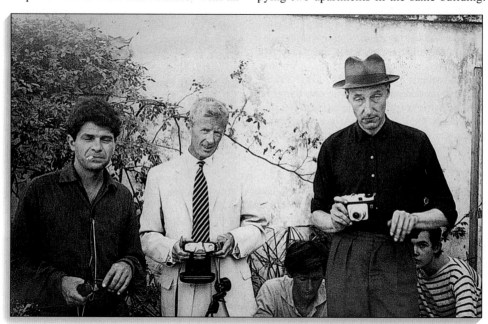

advance for a novel and his dream still fresh in his head, he made plans to go to Tangier: "I got on a Fifth Avenue bus one day to go uptown. By the time we had arrived at Madison Square I knew what would be in the novel and what I would call it... the book would take place in the Sahara, where there was only the sky, and so it would be *The Sheltering Sky*." By the time the bus had reached midtown he had made all the important decisions about this, his most celebrated novel.

Bernardo Bertolucci's film of *The Sheltering Sky* was released in 1989, featuring Paul Bowles himself as the narrator, and starring Debra Winger and John Malkovich.

Paul spent much of his time with the young Moroccan painter, Ahmed Yacoubi. Together they travelled to Ceylon, Italy, Spain and New York, though their friendship was interrupted in 1957 when Yacoubi found himself in court in Tangier for seducing a 15-year-old German boy and began naming names to the authorities interested in the gay ex-pat community. Paul and Jane discreetly left the country for a while, their chauffeur sold the car and used the money to go to Germany, and Jane's Moroccan lover, Cherifa, disappeared into the hills. Yacoubi was eventually acquitted and life returned to normal, but from then on Bowles saw more of Mohammed Mrabet, whom Yacoubi detested.

Paul Bowles was engaged in a stream of projects, from recording traditional Moroccan folk music under the sponsorship of the Rockefeller Foundation and the Library of Congress, to a series of translations from the Maghrebi dialect. He had translated ever since the 1930s; he was the first to translate Jean Paul Sartre's *No Exit* into English, taking the title from a sign on the New York subway. Now he tape-recorded stories told to him by illiterate Moroccan boys, and translated them into English. A dozen books by Mohammed Mrabet have appeared, as well as stories and autobiographies by Driss ben Hamed Charhadi, Mohamed Choukri, Abdeslam Boulaich and others.

Jane's lover Cherifa was a woman from the market, famous for her magic and spells, and even after their sexual relations ended she continued to live with Jane and exercise tremendous power over her, to the concern of Jane's new lover, the Princess Marthe Ruspoli, whom she was with from the early 1960s onwards. When Jane collapsed from a stroke, the Arabs all said Cherifa had poisoned her.

Tennessee Williams visited Tangier in 1956. He and Jane spent every afternoon on the beach. He asked her what she would like as a leaving present and she chose a leg of lamb. After Tennessee left, she would visit the butcher every day and say, "I would like to see my leg of lamb, please," until she was ready to cook it.

In 1962, Paul Bowles wrote the music for Tennessee's *The Milk Train Doesn't Stop Here Any More* and Tennessee came to Tangier to get over his break-up with Frankie Merlo, but Jane was the only one able to make him laugh. Sadly, her eccentricities gave way to depression. She sat in silence day after day, waiting for night to come, and in 1967 Paul felt compelled to place her in a mental hospital in Malaga. Jane died on 4 May, 1973 after a second stroke.

Francis Bacon

Though Matisse delighted in Tangier, the painter Francis Bacon found the light "too bright" for painting, but enjoyed the city's other attractions, as Cecil Beaton tactfully commented in his *Diaries*: "Then a talk about

Tangier – Francis's Tangier, a close intimacy with the Arab world, with the brothel life, and the freedom that can be found only in certain Mediterranean countries where access to women is difficult."

Bacon first arrived in Tangier in 1955, driven there by his friend, Peter Pollock, in his white Rolls-Royce. He liked it so much that he returned the next year, this time with Peter Lacey. They stayed first at the Hotel Cecil, then the Rembrandt, before settling in a flat next door to the Villa Muniria *(see page 121)*. Bacon spent most of the next three years there, returning to London periodically to paint, leaving

Peter Lacey to play piano at Dean's Bar. His life with Lacey was so chaotic, so filled with drunken brawls, homosexual orgies, getting thrown out of the window and being whipped by the demented Lacey that very little painting got done, in fact only three canvases survive from that period.

Robin Cooke, better known as the thriller writer Derek Raymond, gave a thumbnail sketch of Bacon in Dean's Bar one afternoon in 1956: "He had a bottle of champagne beside him and was covered in splashes of paint; he leaned carelessly on the counter with his back to the bottles, his crossed legs adorned with a pair of green Wellington boots."

LEFT: Paul Bowles (centre) with Beat poet Gregory Corso (left) and William Burroughs (right).
RIGHT: Tennessee Williams.

Forbidden fruits

Bacon was a good friend of William Burroughs who moved to Tangier in 1954. Burroughs said of his early days there: "I lived in Tony Dutch's male brothel on the rue d'Arcos for quite a while. Tony Dutch was a big fat strong Dutchman. He still had a heavy accent. He spoke of the Arabs as the Arabics. He had a string of Spanish boys. There wasn't much noise. I liked it in Tangier obviously, I stayed on. I wouldn't say I was in heaven, but I had every drug I wanted. The boys were plentiful, but I was using drugs so heavily that I wasn't interested. Very soon I found a connection for junk, an opiate called Eukodol, and they could sell it across the counter."

After Dutch Tony's, Burroughs moved to the Villa Muniria, where he worked on *The Naked Lunch*, a picaresque novel which contains many scenes set in Tangier. It has since become a Beat classic.

Tangier has always attracted writers. The English novelist Allan Sillitoe wrote one of his most acclaimed books in Tangier: *The Loneliness of the Long Distance Runner* was published in 1958 and made into a successful film by Tony Richardson in 1962. Sillitoe wrote it in the Villa Gazebo, at 282 Monte Viejo (the Old Mountain), a red-tiled, blue-shuttered white-washed house, later occupied by American novelist John Hopkins, author of *Tangier Buzzless Flies*, who described it as having "a wide terrace and large garden, more of a wood than a garden, with a 180° view of the Strait and the coast of Spain. A tower to write in. Paraíso!"

This same villa was the location of an experimental film by Antony Balch called *William Buys A Parrot*, in which we see Burroughs enter the house and admire the view from the garden while standing next to a bamboo cage containing Coco, Hopkins' white parrot.

Less celebrated writers, such as Rupert Croft-Cook and Peter Mayne lived in Tangier in the 1950s. As William Burroughs remembered, "Peter Mayne was very much an old Tangier hand. He wrote *The Alleys of Marrakech*. I remember a line in *The Narrow Smile*, 'There's a boy across the river with an ass like a peach, alas I cannot swim.' I suppose a lot of inland Arabs can't swim."

Another friend of Burroughs, Brion Gysin, arrived in Tangier in the 1930s, and lived there, on and off, until his death in 1986. Though best known as a painter, his quasi-autobiographical novel, *The Process*, is a retelling of his solitary journey across the Sahara. The writer and poet, Edouard Roditi, who had known Paul since the 1930s, arrived from Paris to see them and Jean Genet visited in 1969 and 1970, but he was more interested in the Arab boys and in meeting Moroccan writers than mixing with anyone other than Paul and Brion Gysin. Mohammed Choukri published a journal of his visit, *Jean Genet in Tangier*, translated into English, of course, by Paul Bowles. ❑

THE SUMMER OF '61

The beautiful Muniria villa was the setting for the so-called "psychedelic summer" of 1961, when Allen Ginsberg, his boyfriend Peter Orlovsky, Beat poet Gregory Corso and psychedelic voyager Timothy Leary descended upon writer William Burroughs. Ginsberg had been there before, in 1957, when he managed to offend the painter Francis Bacon by offering him alcohol in an empty tin can taken from the garbage. Later Bacon forgave him and offered to do a "big pornographic painting" of Allen and Peter together, although the distractions of the heady city meant that he did very little actual work during his stay.

LEFT: the painter Brion Gysin.

A Wild Time

*The late Hon. David Herbert was a major protag-
onist in what many have called Tangier's golden
age – the time when the famous and infamous
descended upon the town to make hay while the
sun shone and publicity blazed. Before his death
in 1995, Herbert wrote this account of the
famous parties thrown by Barbara Hutton, the
Woolworth heiress.*

Barbara's house was in an overcrowded part
of the medina surrounded by small Moroccan houses. It was more of a palace than a
house, with a warren of staircases, rooms, mez-
zanines and terraces. As the parties took place on
the terraces, we would be in full view to the outside
world. The Moroccans of the neighbourhood
enjoyed themselves just as much as the guests.
They loved the lights, the music, the ladies' lovely
dresses. They always stayed until the party ended.

The usual form was for Barbara to receive guests
seated on a gilded throne surrounded by Thai silk
cushions. People were brought up to her as though
she were a lady of royal birth. They would practically sit at her feet on the lovely cushions and worship at her shrine. Pretentious, perhaps, but for
Barbara it was pure theatre, the staging of a tale
from the *Arabian Nights*.

As soon as she had a large enough entourage,
she would spring to her feet and dance the night
away with all and sundry, and, this being the international era, that included cabaret artists, hair-
dressers, and pianists from the current nightclubs,
as well as the Tangier élite.

Her most notorious parties, attracting exagger-
ated headlines back in the American and British
press, were those where guests came dressed and
behaving as members of the opposite sex. Straight-
laced diplomats, bankers and respectable Moroccan businessmen would come in full make-up and
decolleté, in spite of moustaches and hairy chests.
Their wives, the elderly and the young, wore din-
ner-jackets or business suits and flattened their
hair with brilliantine plastered over nets. In contrast to such spectacles, Barbara would come
dressed exquisitely as a girlish Robin Hood.

There would be entertainment, including Fla-
menco singers and Moroccan acrobats. Belly-
dancers would be hired from the Koutoubia Palace;

RIGHT: Barbara Hutton.

and on special occasions, such as the annual ball
when guests were invited from all over the world,
the Blue People from the Anti-Atlas Mountains
would come on camels and carrying loaded rifles to
perform their ceremonial dances.

But although Barbara's parties were beautifully
staged, to say they were always a success would
be an exaggeration. If she was in a good and happy
mood, Barbara was the perfect hostess. If she was
tired or sad or had had too much to drink, they
could be a disaster. On these occasions she would
not appear the whole evening. If she had sent a
message saying, "I am not well, but do enjoy your-
selves and have a lovely time," all would have been

fine; but she didn't. The orchestra would play on in
a dreary fashion, and there might even be a little
desultory dancing, but when we eventually realised
that Barbara would not emerge that night, the party
died and little by little the guests drifted home.

In Tangier Barbara remains a legend to this day.
The poor Moroccans had no feeling of resentment
against her or her wealth, or the fact that she had
certain streets in the kasbah widened in order to
accommodate her Rolls-Royce; they remember her
kindness. Guides proudly point out, to tourists of
every nationality, who have probably never heard of
her and so do not know the difference, "You see
over there, that was the Palace of the Woolworth
heiress Barbara Button." ❏

A FEAST OF FLAVOURS

Endorsed by culinary guru and Morocco devotee Robert Carrier as one of the world's great cuisines, Moroccan food is a feast for the senses

Essentially, Moroccan cooking combines the desert nomads' diet of mutton, vegetables and dairy produce with more refined and exotically spiced specialities – the latter of Syrian origin and introduced by Moulay Idriss along with the Muslim religion. But over the centuries it has also incorporated other influences: southern European (olives, olive oil, fruit, tomatoes), black African, and French (particularly apparent in the country's restaurants). The cooking is neither over-oily nor heavy and the seasonings are a blend of sweet and savoury. Almonds, honey and fruit combine with spicy meats; *pastilla (bisteeya)*, the famous Moroccan pigeon pie, is dusted with a generous layer of icing sugar.

Home cooking

Allegedly, the best Moroccan food is found in the home. Certainly, many restaurants are humble affairs, serving charcoal-grilled chicken or *brochettes* (kebabs of marinated liver or lamb), spicy sausages known as *merguez*, and *kefta* (minced lamb shaped into patties and served with a pepper sauce).

There is, however, a growing number of restaurants that reflect the rich range of Moroccan cooking, and in the best places it is usually possible to order specialities not on the menu if the chef is given prior warning. Something such as *pastilla*, for example – wafer-thin layers of *warkha* pastry filled, lasagna-style, with a mixture of pigeon or chicken and almonds – is a complicated dish requiring a full day to prepare. In the home it is a festive dish, popular at weddings. Seafood *pastilla* is a recent addition to the range.

Couscous is regularly cooked at home, often on a Friday, the Muslim holy day. A mound of steamed grain topped with a stew of chicken, lamb or beef and vegetables, it is traditionally served at the end of a meal to ensure that all

guests have eaten sufficient, although these days it is more likely to be a meal in itself. A sauce made from fried onions, crushed into the residue in which the chicken or mutton have been cooked, often goes with it, and almonds and raisins may be either scattered over the couscous or added to the sauce. A salty milk,

lban, is traditionally drunk with couscous.

The ubiquitous *tajine* is a basic beef or lamb stew (sometimes just vegetables) slowly simmered in an earthenware dish with a conical lid. There are very refined variations: *barrogog bis basela*, a lamb stew with prunes; *safardjaliyya*, beef stew with quinces; *sikbadj*, lamb with dates and apricots; and *tajine bel hout*, a fish stew with tomatoes, ginger, saffron, and sweet and hot red peppers. Black olives are invariably added to the honey-flavoured sauce; apples and pears may also be thrown in.

One of the rewards of walking in the Atlas Mountains is to order a *tajine* from a Berber café before setting off and find it ready and

PRECEDING PAGES: displaying the day's catch.
LEFT: *tajines*, a great way to end a day's hike.
RIGHT: couscous, a favourite choice on Fridays.

waiting on your return several hours later. Foreign visitors often buy one of the glazed earthenware *tajine* dishes with the intention of reproducing *tajine* stews at home, but it is worth bearing a couple of points in mind. In Morocco, *tajines* are usually cooked over the low, even heat of charcoal, so when using a more direct heat, such as gas or electric, a heat-diffusing mat should be used. Also, just as you would "season" a new frying pan before using it, it is necessary to eliminate the flavour of earthenware from the pot by doing the same.

The other popular everyday meat is chicken, or *djej*. *Matisha Mesla* is an old Moroccan dish of chicken cooked in tomatoes, honey, ginger and cinnamon; *djej bil loz* is chicken with spices and almonds; and *djej mqualli* is a popular dish of chicken with preserved lemons and green olives, often on a bed of potatoes.

Festive specialities

Special occasions in Morocco are celebrated with special foods. During Ramadan, Moroccans break their daily fast with fresh dates and a bowl of *harira*, a thick soup of beans, lentils and lamb. Every café will have this soup available for those unable to get home by the appointed hour. Outside Ramadan, you

SENSATIONAL SNACKS

The Moroccan pleasure in food is reflected in the amazing range of snacks sold by the country's army of street vendors. These range from cactus fruit peeled to order (said to settle upset stomachs) to freshly roasted chickpeas, and snails in a cumin-flavoured liquor ladled out of giant vats to homeward-bound office workers. You will also find fluffy sugared *sfenj* (doughnuts), still warm from the stove, slices of *tortilla* (a speciality of the north) and freshly fried potato crisps sprinkled with sea salt.

One of the pleasures of motoring in Morocco is the variety of produce to be bought along the way (be sure to keep a knife handy when travelling). In the Rif women hold out plates of tangy white cheese (delicious with flat Moroccan bread) artfully displayed on a bed of leaves; in autumn in the south, boys proffer baskets of freshly harvested dates. In the Atlas, depending on season, you will find almonds, walnuts, pine nuts, strawberries and lychees; on the Atlantic coast honeydew melons costing just three or four dirhams each are readily available, as is freshly caught fish. For more substantial fare when motoring, a multitude of grill restaurants, often doubling as butchers, serve succulent lamb cutlets, kebabs or liver, accompanied by bread and salad and washed down with Oulmes or Sidi Harazam mineral water.

may find *harira* at humble restaurants or sold by itinerant food vendors.

M'choui is the ceremonial dish marking Aid el Kebir, the feast commemorating Abraham's sacrifice of a lamb instead of his son, held 70 days after Ramadan. A whole sheep is roasted on a spit and brought to the table for everyone to carve off pieces and dip into little dishes of cumin. No part of the lamb is wasted: after the feast you will see sheepskins pegged out on rooftop terraces, along with the intestines, which are sun dried for flavouring winter stews.

in the teapot, along with the sugar. When poured, the pot is held high above the glass in order to "aerate" the liquid as it falls. Tea is served throughout the day and after meals. Sometimes, instead of mint, it is laced with pine nuts or orange blossom.

Other drinks include coffee (usually *café au lait* or Turkish), occasionally flavoured with cardamon; milkshakes made with seasonal fruits; and fresh fruit juices – grape, orange, black cherry or pomegranate, depending on the season. ❑

Favourite fish

Established during the French and Spanish occupation, fish restaurants are found along the Mediterranean coast to Ceuta and the length of the Atlantic coast. The most outstanding (with Michelin commendations) is A ma Bretagne, at Ain Diab, the corniche west of Casablanca *(see page 173)* – although, for simpler fare, Sam's in Essaouira or Garcia's in Asilah are hard to beat. Giant prawns caught off Agadir, octopus, squid, boned and stuffed sardines, skate and sole are available at the most modest quayside restaurant: in particular, check out the makeshift stalls set up each morning on the harbours of Agadir and Essaouira. Worth trying anywhere more upmarket is *samak mahshi be roz*, which is any large white fish stuffed with rice, pine nuts and almonds and served with a tamarind sauce.

Liquid refreshment

Islam's prohibition on alcohol means it is not used in cooking other than in French restaurants. Morocco does, however, brew beer and produce wine *(see page 216)*, industries introduced under the French. The beer, light and Continental-tasting, comes in several varieties, but the most popular are Stork (the lightest) and Flag Speciale (in squat green bottles).

The most common refreshment, however, is mint tea, which is prepared in bulbous, silver-coloured teapots and served in glasses. It is an infusion of mint leaves and either green or *nègre* (black) tea – a solicitous host will offer a choice of both. The mint may be placed in the glass or

LEFT: a platter of home-made sweets.
RIGHT: mint tea, a great aid to digestion.

THE ESSENCE OF ARCHITECTURE

The Islamic state, a challenging climate, tribal warfare and foreign

visitors have all left their mark on Morocco's buildings

Moroccan architecture is heavily influenced by Islam. But factors specific to the country – such as natural resources, climate, a tribal history and European imperialism – have modified the Eastern stamp. Early Islamic influences had weakened by the time they reached the extreme west of North Africa, which meant many indigenous practices were left intact. And, as a staging post on the African, Saharan and Mediterranean trade routes, Morocco experienced a long and steady influx of various foreign styles.

High mountains separate the damper, cooler, coastal plains from desert landscapes, where unfired bricks and poor-quality materials dictated a more rudimentary architecture. Mountains also support oak, pine and cedar forests, used lavishly in the internal ornamentation of the larger houses and palaces. In the south, tribal warfare and the struggle of emerging dynasties determined defensive architecture: tall, crenellated *ksour* and kasbahs.

Islamic influence

Nonetheless, the building of towns and villages presented an opportunity to express the ideals of the Islamic state. Islam touches every aspect of a Muslim's life, and Moroccan architecture reflects more than just a series of rules and customs laid down for religious buildings. Its emphasis on the community is reflected in the interlocked nature of domestic architecture.

At the same time, Islam's asceticism finds expression in simplicity of form and respect for space. The Arabs of the 7th century, who had little architectural heritage, were never far from the desert and its incredible vastness. Spaciousness and lack of distraction are well suited to the observation of rituals and prayer.

Because Islam forbids animate representation, all ornamentation was abstract. While this rule was never completely observed and plant and flower forms may often be identified, fine cal-

ligraphy is more usual. Kufic script is highly stylised – to the extent that, practically in cipher, it can be very difficult to read, even for a classical Arabist.

Gold and silver were similarly frowned upon, so less lavish materials were used. Stucco, worked into delicate lace-like patterns, arrived

LEFT: Madrassa Bou Inania, Fez.
RIGHT: detail on a typical pisé building in the south.

in the 13th century, while mosaic *(zellige)* of green, blue, black and red tiling became popular in the 14th century. Both were Eastern techniques perfected in Andalusia and imported to Morocco by the Muslims of Spain. Similarly in the Andalusian fashion, intricate ironwork, which lends itself to abstract design, was employed for window and door grilles and for lanterns.

Mosques and *madrassas*

The mosque, the most important religious building and the principal – although not the only meeting place – for prayer formed a loose prototype for all Islamic architecture. Modelled on the Great Mosques of Córdoba and Kairouan of 8th-century Spain and Tunisia (at that time, the most important cities of Western Islam), which, in turn, were based on Damascene models, most Moroccan mosques are rather plain on the outside. A highly decorated entrance door and a minaret are the most notable external features, and the roof is usually of simple, often green (the colour of Islam), glazed tilework.

FOUNDATIONS OF FAITH

"Believer is to believer," said the Prophet, "as the mutually upholding sections of a building."

MEDINA LIVING

All Arab cities with some history have their medina. The Prophet Mohammed founded the first Islamic community in a city named Medina, second only to Mecca in importance, and it quickly became the prototype for other towns in the Arab world. To a follower of the Islamic faith the pursuit of the ideal of a just and ordered city was obligatory. It is believed that on the Day of Judgement men and women will be assessed not only on their own merits but also on their performance in society. The design of the medinas, therefore, reflected communal values. Each quarter contributed to the benefit of the whole.

Even during the French and Spanish protectorates, the integrity of the medinas was respected. Marshal Lyautey, the first French Resident-General, decreed that new developments serving the European administrators should be set apart from the medinas in order to preserve the old towns' way of life.

In the long run, such good intentions have created their own problems. Though many of the medinas are intact, they have generally lost their administrative and political importance to the new towns. After independence the richer and most influential families often moved to the more modern quarters vacated by the Europeans, leaving the medinas to the powerless and populous poor.

Early mosques did not include minarets; in fact, the earliest mosques were not even formally enclosed. Originally, the faithful would be called to prayer from nearby rooftops. The square-shaped minaret of the Maghreb, unlike the circular minarets of the Middle East, corresponds to the bell-tower of a church (generally, they are four times higher than they are wide) and were copied from early Christian towers in Damascus.

The interior of the mosque comprises a courtyard, known as a *sahn*, with a fountain or basin for preliminary ritual washing, and a hall for prayer, divided into aisles segregating the sexes situated alongside. The *mihrab* (a niche in the wall, often decorated) indicates the direction of Mecca. To the right of the *mihrab* is a pulpit called the *minbar*, often of carved cedarwood with intricate inlay: it is from here that the *imam* (prayer leader) reads the Koran.

Religious buildings open to non-Muslims are the *madrassa*, early universities established in the 12th century for the teaching of theology and Muslim law. While the *madrassa* were often attached to mosques, they developed from domestic buildings – sometimes the homes of the principal teachers. Once again, a central courtyard with a fountain, often cloistered on the ground floor, was flanked by a hall for prayer, as well as classrooms and a library. The pupils' living quarters were situated above, on the first floor.

Many of the *madrassas* were founded by the learned Merinids in the 14th century. The buildings are elaborately decorated with detailed carving, mosaic tiles and glasswork, Kufic script and stucco. The most outstanding are the Madrassa Bou Inania, commissioned by Sultan Abou Inan in 1350, in Fez, and Madrassa Ben Youssef, rebuilt in 1565 by the Saadian Sultan Abdullah el Ghallib in Marrakesh.

Solid defence

As recently as the late 1930s, it could be quite dangerous to travel in Morocco, a fact well illustrated by town defences, which are so evocative of a warlord past. Within the walls are all the

LEFT: reflections on Casablanca.
RIGHT: interior tile detail at the old Glaoui Kasbah at Taouirirt: interlocking polygons are a recurring theme.

necessary buildings for defence: vast stables, barracks, food stores, granaries, arsenals and water cisterns. They are notable for their size rather than their level of architecture, although the design of the *bab*, or gateway, is often the exception to this rule. Generally built of stone blocks and crenellated, two towers flank a central bay in which the gate is set. Above, the arch might be deeply carved in coloured stones, as are the Oudaya Gate in the kasbah of Rabat, Bab Agnaou in Marrakesh and the imposing Bab Mansour in Meknes.

Every dynasty left its own stamp on the defences of the cities, often demolishing much of the work of its predecessors. The Almohads in Rabat (12th century) and the Merinids in Fez and Chellah (13th and 14th centuries) were particularly industrious in this respect.

But it was not only the towns and cities that were in need of fortification. Even the poor, flat-roofed, stone-built farms built on terraces in the Middle Atlas, homes of the Berber Chleuhs, were – and still are – well defended. In the south, these farms give way to the *ksour*, Morocco's most imposing architecture.

In effect, *ksour* are fortified villages, comprising a central square, a granary, a well, a mosque and warren-like streets and housing, contained by high walls punctuated by watchtowers. Made of crude mud brick and rubble or split palm-trunk (a material known as *pisé*), they are permeable to water and can withstand only a very dry climate. Rain constantly undermines this form of architecture, and the south is littered with abandoned and ruined *ksour*, often only a few decades old.

Strictly speaking, the difference between the kasbahs and *ksour* is that the former house individual families, while the latter enclose a whole community. That said, throughout most of Morocco the word "kasbah" refers to the defensive stronghold of a town. The majority of towns possess one, although it is in the south that they are most evident. Square and built of crude brick, they show few openings on the outside. Yet their simplicity is often offset by geometric decorations carved into the mud bricks. Close to the desert, the influence of Saharan Africa is clear.

Fit for a king

Unlikely though it may seem, such blank exteriors have contained some of Morocco's richest palaces. The sheer luxury, colour and decoration, as well as the quality of life within, sur-

FABULOUS PALACES

Known as "the incomparable", El Badi, in Marrakesh, was built for fabulous receptions by Ahmed el Mansour in the 16th century. Its courtyard had five elaborate pools, lined with coloured tiling, the waters of which irrigated a series of gardens. Its marble came from Italy and its furnishings from as far away as China. Its magnificent kiosks, pavilions, towers and galleries made it a legend in Europe. Sadly, today it is little more than an elegant ruin.

The Dar el Makhzen Palace, built in Fez in the 13th century, is probably the finest palace in Morocco – but is now closed to the general public. Several acres in size, its courtyard even contains a *madrassa* and a mosque.

passed even the comforts of Europe for many centuries. Once again, the central feature was the courtyard, around which were grouped suites of rooms in a symmetrical pattern. Service areas would often be built off the sides, and these might have their own central courtyard, as wealth and necessity dictated.

While the original structure of a palace was usually symmetrical, radiating from the central courtyard, later additions were often haphazardly planned. Nonetheless, certain essential features had to be incorporated. There was always a judgment hall and a *mechouar*, an open space to hold large audiences, dominated by a balcony, or *iwan*, where the sultan could receive homage from his tribesmen. The *harem* (the women's quarter), a restricted area, was entirely separate.

The decoration within these palaces required the skills of top Moroccan artists and craftsmen, and while it is true that development and quality of style had degenerated into showy exuberance by the 18th century, there are plenty of examples of good work still preserved.

Nowadays, many former small palaces have been turned into museums and hotels (the

> **MARKETABLE SKILLS**
>
> Moroccan building skills are esteemed throughout the Arab world. When Oman wanted to restore its *ksours* and forts in the 1990s, it had to enlist the expertise of Moroccan craftsmen.

Dynastic contributions

Compared with other forms of building, Islamic architecture has remained relatively static. Following the fall of Rome, urban development in Morocco did not begin again until after the Arab conquest. The Idrissid dynasty of the 8th to 10th centuries resumed building, establishing Fez as its capital.

During the Almoravide dynasty of the 11th and 12th centuries, when many Muslims were expelled from Spain, the brilliant civilisation of Andalusia took

Palais Jamai in Fez; the museum in the Oudayas Kasbah in Rabat; the Dar el Makhzen museum in Tangier, and the Dar Si Said Museum in Marrakesh), providing a chance for visitors to view them at close hand. Royal palaces (there is at least one in every major town) are generally recent but traditional in style, enclosed by extensive gardens and strictly out of bounds. Some sense of their scale may be glimpsed from their perimeters or when approaching a city by air.

LEFT: architecture of the south.
ABOVE: Medina d'Agadir, a new but traditional kasbah designed by Italian architect Coco Polizzi.

root in Morocco. It is thought that Abou Bakr founded Marrakesh and his son, Ali ben Youssef, built enormous fortifications at Taza, a city which, situated on the eastern approach to Fez (the Taza Gap), was an important line of defence. Mosques were rebuilt, and domes, pillars and semi-circular arches, together with plaster sculpture, were introduced.

The Almohads of the 12th and 13th centuries were prolific builders. Additions were made to Marrakesh, most notably the walls. The power of masonry was the symbol of the period, and the Koutoubia Mosque in Marrakesh and the Hassan Mosque in Rabat were both commissioned at this time.

The Merinid dynasty of the 13th to 15th centuries ushered in increasingly sophisticated work rather than particularly imposing buildings. The Merinids were responsible for most of the country's *madrassas*.

Under the Saadians of the 16th and 17th centuries, Morocco became susceptible to foreign influences. The Portuguese took control of coastal towns and built fortifications at Asilah, Safi and El Jadida. Art and architecture tended to repeat the styles of the past rather than innovate, but sheer scale was celebrated by

> ### LOW PROFILE
> In Morocco, the tradition is for low buildings, so that the minaret of the mosque may easily dominate the skyline.

Ahmed el Mansour, who embellished Marrakesh to a degree that impressed a decadent Europe. It is the unflagging industry of the Alaouite Sultan Moulay Ismail of the 17th century that is often so evident today, however. He built and rebuilt constantly. Some 25 km (16 miles) of wall were constructed around the city of Meknes, and he achieved popular public works through the forced labours of slaves and Christian captives. In keeping with his personality, scale and grandeur took precedence over aesthetic considerations.

Modern architecture

There was little further development in architecture until the French and Spanish protectorates, when European styles dominated the northern and coastal cities. Marshal Lyautey, the first French Resident-General, decreed that the European development of towns, to house the influx of European administrators, should be separate from the medinas so as to preserve the traditional civilisation. The new architecture, combining French civic pomposity and Moorish motifs, was called "Mauresque". The 1920s even brought a smattering of Art Deco to Casablanca and Marrakesh.

Nowadays, the newest civic architecture is once again looking towards traditional Moroccan design for inspiration, but it is the Hassan II Mosque in Casablanca (open to non-Muslims, *see page 172*), that shows exactly what modern Moroccan craftsmen can achieve given enough funding. Inaugurated in 1993 and costing more than $750 million, the mosque is the biggest place of worship in the Muslim world apart from Mecca. Though designed by a French architect, Michel Pinseau, the mosque was almost entirely the product of Moroccan craftsmen and, with the exception of Murano glass, Moroccan raw materials – granite from Tafraoute, marble from Agadir and cedar from the Middle Atlas. With some 10,000 craftsmen and apprentices labouring on the building, this single project boosted a huge revival of traditional Moroccan crafts. ❏

LEFT: Inside the Hassan II Mosque, Casablanca.
RIGHT: the enormous doorway of the Hassan II Mosque. Many thousands of master craftsmen and apprentices were employed to work on the mosque.

THROUGH THE KEYHOLE ARCH

Saturated colour, gorgeously patterned tilework, rich rugs and textiles – Moroccan design has taken the world of interiors by storm

Moroccan interior design is now firmly established across the globe, thanks to a number of talented designers and architects and the insatiable thirst for new ideas led by the world's magazines and book publishers. Today it is a synthesis of traditional crafts filtered and adapted by often foreign designers who started off decorating their own homes and quickly found there was an export market for their invented orientalist lamps, cushions or fireplaces.

The concept of Moroccan design is relatively recent and is not so much Moroccan as a fusion of influences, ranging from the paintings of artists such as Matisse to Indian, Spanish and New Mexican traditions. Morocco is as much the crossroads as it is the foundation for this now internationally chic design style.

△ **COME INTO THE KASBAH**
The clear, cool lines of the interior of the Kasbah de Dades in southern Morocco reflect the traditional bare austerity of Moroccan design.

◁ **SAND CASTLES**
The geometric designs of the southern *ksour* have inspired this turret on a house in Marrakesh's palmerie, where the city's most exclusive modern properties are built.

COPYRIGHT? WHAT'S THAT?

An important element of the success of Moroccan style is the adaptability and accessibility of the country's craftsmen. Sketch an idea and you can easily afford to pay someone to make you a prototype. If it works, you can bet that an entrepreneurial Moroccan will be flooding the market with copies within weeks. There is no such thing as copyright in Morocco, and with literally thousands of expatriates and creative individuals ordering up items to their own design, the Moroccan craft industry has one of the best and cheapest research and development facilities in the world. This is by no means a bad thing. The rich exchange of ideas has ensured that thousands of craftsmen are still actively employed and their craft is constantly adapting and developing to new markets. Design is a living activity; once it stagnates and ceases to take on new materials and ideas, it will die.

COURTYARD LIVING

Traditionally, house design consists of rooms built around a square or rectangular courtyard open to the sky. Walls are enormously thick, as insulation against the heat of the sun, and ceilings are high and cool. Arranged around the courtyard are simple whitewashed rectangular salons and bed chambers, one on each side. Additional floors follow much the same pattern, with or without a surrounding veranda supported on arches. Few *riads* extend beyond two floors; kitchens and bathrooms are usually tucked into corners. Small windows look into the courtyard, locking out the bustle of the medina and ensuring privacy. In order to provide additional light, large mirrors often cover the back walls of salons, reflecting light into the darker corners of the rooms. The furnishings are simple: carpets, wall-to-wall padded benches (banquettes) and low tables.

▷ **EAST MEETS WEST**
Western influences have also been absorbed, as in this restaurant in La Mamounia Hotel, Marrakesh.

▽ **CREATING WARMTH**
These days bright folkloric colours, lamps and hand-made textiles are added to create a warm atmosphere.

▷ **BERBER POTS**
Clay pots add interest to the intense, matt colour. While the urban tradition specialises in glazed ceramics, Berber pottery is more utilitarian and the decoration is bold.

MAKING MUSIC

It is difficult to get away from rhythm and song in Morocco, whether it's the
call of the muezzin *or the electric guitars and synthesizers of modern* rai

The 1960s author and painter Brion Gysin thought hearing the music of Morocco was enough to make anyone become a Muslim. The Rolling Stones, friends of Gysin, didn't go quite that far, but they did dress in *jellabahs* and team up with the Master Musicians of Jajouka: following guitarist Brian

Jones's album *Brian Jones Presents the Pipes of Pan at Jajouka*, which was put together in 1968, the Stones recorded the track "Continental Drift" with the Moroccan group for their 1989 album *Steel Wheels*.

Keith Richards summed up the extraordinary sounds of the Jajouka pipes and drums as follows: "It sounds a bit like modern jazz, like John Coltrane or Ornette Coleman, although it's really pagan trance music."

Feel the beat

Wherever you go in Morocco, you are likely to be assailed by wonderful rhythms, whether it's the most common musical phenomenon, the amplified voice of the *muezzin* calling the faithful to prayer, or the tinny sound of Egyptian taped music emanating from the doorway of a shop. Possibly it will be beating drums and the whoops of joyous women celebrating a wedding. But what you should actively seek out – early evening is the best time – are impromptu sessions at music cafés (often identified by the musical instruments hanging on their walls). It is to these that local musicians will come to drink tea and then sing songs.

Chabbi, which means "popular", is the most common music played at these venues. Akin to the folk-music tradition of Europe and North America, it started out as music performed by travelling entertainers, who would collect and compose songs along the way. These days, having received media attention, *chabbi* has moved off the public squares and onto the radio and the television. Abdelwahhab Doukali and Hamid Zahir, two of the most popular singers of this type of music, began their careers, respectively, in Bab el Makina in Fez and in the Jemma el Fna in Marrakesh.

Inevitably, groups have started to electrify traditional instruments (for example, the *buzouk*, a long-necked lute) and to use guitars and keyboards, but at a local level *chabbi* is still confined to the *l'oud* (an 11-string fretless lute), *kamanche* (violin), banjo and assorted percussion instruments. At the end of a *chabbi* song, an instrumental section called *leseb*, which is twice the speed of the rest of the piece, induces shouting, dancing and syncopated clapping from the audience.

Classical roots

Interestingly, some of the more complex traditional forms of Moroccan music – Andalus, now exemplified by the orchestras of Fez, Meknes and Tangier (towns that were most influenced by Moorish Spain), and *milhun*, an ancient form of sung poetry – have been combined with *chabbi* to produce a mixture of sophisticated instrumentals and popular lyrics.

In contemporary *rai* music, too, which originated in the border towns of the Rif and western Algeria (although, in the Maghreb, one must remember that borders are political rather than ethnographical), style and lyrics have come a long way from their Bedouin roots.

Rai's preoccupations these days tend to be sex, drugs and cars; while the instruments used are brass, accordions, electric guitars and synthesizers. Modern *rai* music is becoming increasingly popular in Europe and Morocco's own stars include Chaba Zahouania and Cheb Kader.

RISKY *RAI*

With lyrics such as, "Hey, Mama, your daughter she wants me," and, "Beer is Arab, whisky is European," *rai* has not endeared itself to the establishment.

from the Atlas region: itinerant bands of four members, known as *imdyazn*. Playing drums, the double clarinet and the *rebab* (a single-string flute), the role of the musicians was to bring news of world affairs, and they would improvise as they went along. This still happens, but nowadays, outstripped by television and radio, the function of the *imdyazn* is merely to entertain rather than inform the public.

Outside of wedding celebrations, it is in the entertainment squares of towns and villages

Rural rituals

Berber music, generally found in the country areas, is quite distinct from Arabic-influenced *chabbi* or rock-style *rai*. It includes ritual music, which is closely linked to the agricultural calendar or performed during exorcism or purification ceremonies, and sung poetry called *tamdyazi*, which is performed with just drums and flutes for accompaniment.

At one time, it was common for towns and villages to be visited by professional musicians

---

LEFT: street music.
ABOVE: no city wedding would be complete without its traditional ensemble.

that one is also likely to witness the music of the *gnaoua*, dancing musician-healers in distinctive hats and waistcoats trimmed with cowrie shells, whose wild drum rhythms induce states of trance. The *gnaoua* brotherhood has devotees all over Morocco but particularly in Marrakesh. It claims spiritual descent from Bilal, an Ethiopian who was the Prophet's first *muezzin*. Most of their ceremonies are held with the intention of placating spirits (*jinn*), whether good or evil, which have inhabited a person or place. Undoubtedly, the origins of these rites are in sub-Saharan Africa, and a black African influence is evident in the music's rhythms and the appearance of the musicians. ❏

SKIING

Skiing in Morocco is exotic and exhilarating, even though facilities and opportunities for après-ski are still rudimentary

It may be thought that skiing, an invention of the late 19th century imported from Scandinavia and developed as a pastime in the Alps, could have bypassed the hothouse of the Atlas. In fact, experiments in Moroccan *piste* skiing originated in the 1930s – before the winter sports fanfares of Courchevel and Val d'Isère could be heard.

During World War II expatriate Frenchmen installed primitive ski-tows in clearings of the Anti-Atlas cedar forest and so set up the first equipped nursery slopes in the country. In 1942–3 they mounted several ski sorties into the Great Atlas, the spearhead led by the now legendary André Fougerolles. By 1952 an 80-page guide to *piste* skiing and cross-country ski expeditions in Morocco had been issued, covering many ambitious projects – then achieved perhaps only once.

High hopes

Climatically, snow precipitations may occur in Morocco down to 1,000 metres (3,330ft). Snow that is likely to lie for more than two months raises the minimum level to 1,700–2,000 metres (5,600–6,500ft). From an early date, *ski de haute montagne* was considered more rewarding than oscillating up and down short, sometimes artificially maintained, nursery slopes.

Multinational parties confirmed during the 1950s that the High Atlas was essentially a mountain skiing domain, and the purpose-built resort of Oukaimeden was conceived and completed in a few years. The modest weekend practice grounds at Mischliffen-Jebel Hebri on the west rim of the Anti-Atlas remained fairly basic.

Nothing much has changed at Mischliffen in 40 years. Skiers generally commute to the three lifts from agreeable amenities in Azrou and Ifrane, 5–20 km (8–12 miles) away. Equipment hire is a hit-or-miss affair. In a poor year the season is short – maybe only five weeks, though usually extending to eight with runs

falling through a modest vertical interval of 100–200 metres (330–660ft). Mischliffen is not a package-tour destination. Skiers are invariably locals from Fez, Meknes and Rabat. Youngsters and school groups, with amateur instructors, are much in evidence.

To widen the horizon, bolder skiers persuaded the authorities to open up Bou Iblane in the Anti-Atlas as a high altitude resort. A road was pushed beyond the Taffert forestry hut to a site at the foot of the mountain, where an initial ski-lift was built. However, the car-park here, about 140km (85 miles) from Fez, often cannot be reached in late winter because the road is not kept open by snow-ploughs – a case, as so often in Morocco, of economic viability versus the small number of participants. Those attending sleep rough at the hut, for there is no accommodation or restaurant – or indeed any other services – at the "resort". *Dortoirs* (self-catering flats) are on the drawing-board.

Across the quite suitable north-facing slopes

LEFT: cross-country skiing in the High Atlas.
RIGHT: roads to the ski resorts are not always open.

and hollows of the several Bou Iblane summits, from 3,100 metres (10,200ft) downhill sweeps of 700 metres (2,300ft) are possible. The main problem is that good snowfalls may not last long. With a deteriorating surface, the skiing soon becomes of poor quality and, in the absence of waymarks, eventually a hazardous slalom among boulders. So here, too, one must count the season as short.

Oukaimeden

Oukaimedan, 75km (47 miles) from Marrakesh, ranks as the premier ski-station in the country. The road is normally swept clear of

An excellent French Alpine Club hostelry, with low charges, vies with the best commercial chalets for standards of comfort, but the *après-ski* lacks the sophistication of Alpine resorts.

Youth clubs and schools are encouraged to assemble parties to train at Oukameidan for competitive downhill and cross-country skiing. Special firms now aspire to arrange ski journeys supported, below the snowline, by mules and porters. In the Toubkal Massif, British parties have excelled in formulating tactics for unique long-distance experiences on skis. *Ski-mulet* is a description that figured prominently in holiday brochures of the 1980s.

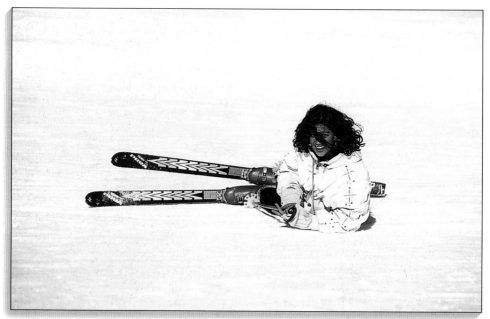

snow and the season lasts from mid-December until early April. Now 40 years old, this resort has had Alpine-type trappings grafted on to it.

The chair-lift to the top of Jebel Oukaimeden (3,273 metres/10,740ft), the highest cableway in Africa, may be closed by mid-March. Following irreperable breakdown of the ski lifts in 1999, new lifts are to be installed for 2001. The graded runs are limited unless one is prepared to use skins and make out of bounds circuits.

Accommodation is available in two hotels, four skier-chalets, various apartment blocks (including some for renting), and hired private chalets. There are general food shops for self-caterers; equipment hire; but no garage repair.

Spurious, misleading claims abound about ski climbs in the Toubkal Massif. Most of the desirable peaks cannot be reached on skis; these must be shed some way below the summits and parties proceed on foot using climbing techniques as conditions dictate. Mount Toubkal itself is an exception, though even here skis are removed by most parties 30 minutes from the top.

One for the professionals

The outstanding expedition ski ascent in the area is Tazaghärt – coincidentally offering the best winter gully climbs as well – but it is very serious stuff, helped along by the strong Berber backup available at Imlil.

The high level routes of summer become popular ski tours in winter, threading the high valleys and crossing passes to reach their ultimate destination. The rigours of these excursions demand a brand of enthusiasm usually confined to mountain skiing fanatics.

Central High Atlas

Ambitious plans are on the drawing-board for turning the Bou Guemez valley in the Central High Atlas into a skiing paradise. Specifically, a consultative document has been produced detailing certain options. A fundamental disagreement between the promoters pivots on downhill infrastructure – lifts and tows, chalets and shops, or a chain of huts, to link up with other valleys, for touring.

Another scheme, favoured by ecologists and environmentalists, would have the district preserved altogether from pylons and cables, and allow only wealthy heli-skiers to be flown in from Beni-Mellal hotels and collected the same way. Clearly, the Berbers are totally opposed to this idea. Finding the funds to realise any of the grand designs published so far will hinder advancement, but Azurki and Izourar huts should soon be open for business.

A lot of skiers make the rough journey to Azurki mountain 3,677 metres (12,000ft). As long ago as 1950, this huge smooth-sided mass was pronounced potentially the finest skiing location in Morocco – coupled with its equally bulky neighbour Ouaoulzat. Skis have glided over every facet, spur and depression where trails of 1,000 metres (3,300ft) can be plotted. Snow retention on mountains round the Bou Guemez is good and skiing in favourable years continues until around mid-May.

Skiing further east enters the realms of wilderness exploits. The amount of pre-planning, organisation and local knowledge that is required will defeat many hopefuls.

Jebel Masker, near Tounfite, has been singled out as a solitary noble ski ascent objective. This has been accomplished many times, but it is strictly the province of the well-trained alpinist and is avalanche-prone in some prevailing conditions.

Close to Midelt, the gigantic Ayyachi will tax

HELICOPTER SKIING

Air charter is a growing business in Marrakesh and Beni-Mellal and the demands of skiers have made a considerable contribution.

the fittest exponent. Doubtless a gratifying feat, it has half a dozen ascent-descent routes described in specialist publications, with a preciseness suggesting scores of ascents have been made. In fact, some of these are believed to have been helicopter-assisted. .

In the skiing season, daily forecasts of weather and ground conditions for Mischliffen and Oukaimedan are available in towns and cities all over Morocco. If based in Marrakesh or Meknes, one can go at short notice to either in a couple of hours. ❑

A FINAL WORD OF ADVICE

Although it may be an attractive idea to decide on the spur of the moment to go skiing while in Morocco, with the intention of hiring equipment *in situ*, remember it is crucial to be properly equipped. In particular, personal, portable rescue beacons are absolutely essential. Small battery-operated radio transmitter/receiver devices of the type worn by cross-country and touring skiers in Europe cannot function in the Atlas where rescue services are distant and in any case have no compatible electronic receiving equipment. You must also be certain you have adequate rescue and air repatriation insurance for skiing in the Atlas.

LEFT: falling down is part of the fun.
RIGHT: preparing for ski school in Oukaimedan.

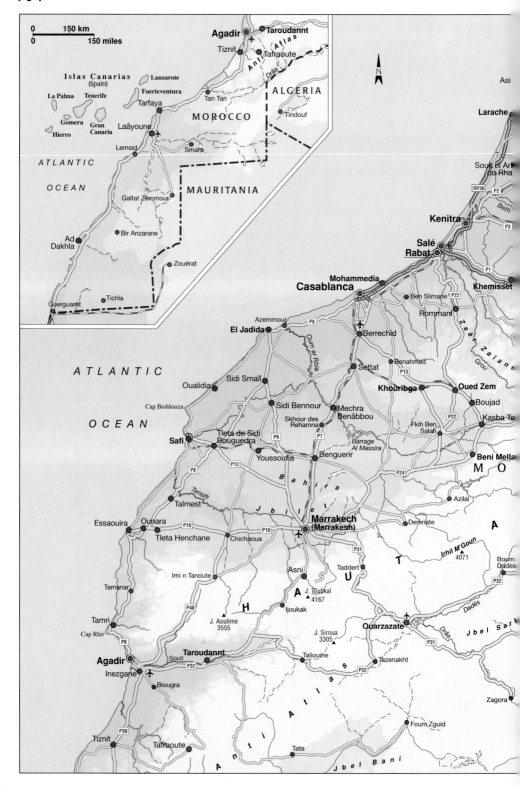

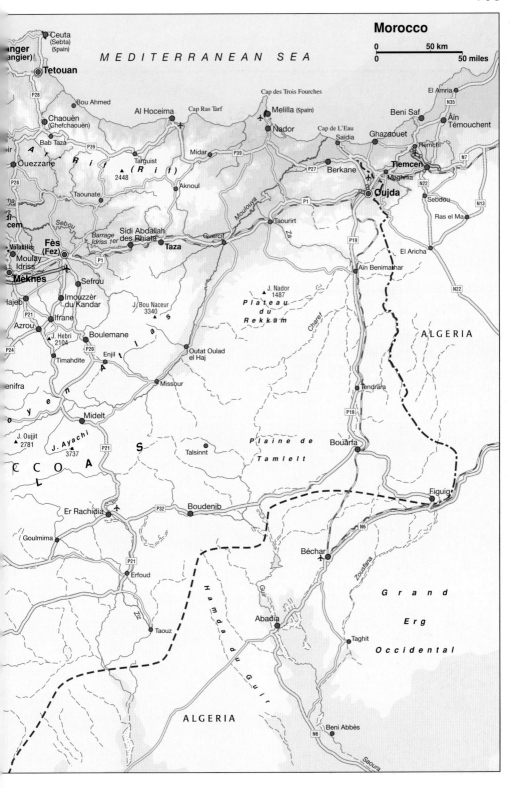

PLACES

*A detailed guide to the entire country, with principal sites
clearly cross-referenced by number to the maps*

Travel in Morocco has come a long way since the days when Europeans needed to disguise themselves in *jellabahs* and veils in order to penetrate anywhere beyond Tangier. Dusty old tomes on Morocco all contain photographs of their authors in native dress – though the writer Wyndham Lewis seemed to think this had more to do with a desire to dress up as Arabs than any real fear of attack.

In fact Berbers, being naturally resourceful, have proved the very opposite of their famously fierce image; they have welcomed tourism and at a local level, particularly in the Atlas, have been quick to profit from it, often undermining the government's broader attempts to capitalise on big spending by foreign visitors.

Some hotel development has spawned on the north coast, especially south of the Spanish enclave of Ceuta, and in Agadir in the south, but, amazingly for a country with sandy beaches and reliable sunshine so close to Europe, Morocco has escaped the type of intensive development that mushroomed elsewhere on the Mediterranean. The Moroccan government, reputedly seeking a better class of holidaymaker, has focused on the southern valleys for upmarket tourist development, with well-hidden, traditionally designed luxury hotels proliferating yearly.

But, despite long blonde, blue-skied beaches, fortified Portuguese fishing ports, lush oases in pink desert plains, mountains offering walking, climbing and winter skiing, the extraordinary attractions of Morocco are the imperial cities of Fez, Meknes and Marrakesh. Founded in the Middle Ages and expanded by succeeding dynasties, they contain superb examples of early Islamic architecture and ways of living that have barely changed since medieval times.

Morocco's capital, Rabat, though with similar historic claims, seems European by comparison, with French-style cafés, "Mauresque" architecture and a conservative image. Here, more than anywhere, is a reminder that a large part of Morocco was governed by the French. If Rabat seems bourgeois, Azrou and Ifrane, south of Fez in the Middle Atlas, with their steep roofs and carved gables, would not be out of place in the Alps. Incredible, then, that just 320 km (200 miles) away, radiating from the foothills of the Atlas, lie the rolling dunes and palm oases of the south – landscapes that helped win acclaim for David Lean's classic film *Lawrence of Arabia*. ❏

PRECEDING PAGES: the Ziz Valley; overview of Fez from Bab Guissa; taking a ferry from Rabat to Salé.
LEFT: village in the High Atlas.

TANGIER

Notorious for its libertine ways when it was an international zone, Tangier has only recently shaken off its louche image. Today it is expanding rapidly and facing a bright future

I n its heyday, **Tangier** was up there with Cannes on the international set's calendar. It was frequented by Tennessee Williams, Cecil Beaton, William Burroughs and Tallulah Bankhead. Brion Gysin, Paul Bowles and the British aristocrat David Herbert, the younger son of the 16th Earl of Pembroke, made the town their home, and Barbara Hutton, the Woolworth heiress, bought a house in the medina. Tangier's tax-free status attracted world bankers and unscrupulous profiteers. In its squares, the Grand and Petit Soccos, whose very names reflect the town's hybrid character, anything could be found and purchased. It was truly an international zone.

Until, that is, six months after Morocco's independence in 1956, when Tangier's international status was revoked and the administrative infrastructure dismantled. It was typical that Tangier, a city of indulgence, should be granted these few months' grace. Nonetheless transition was a shock to a city whose prosperity was based purely on its free-port status. It underwent a sharp decline from which it only steadily recovered.

Vestiges of its former character survive. There are still a few retainers from the international era, though, sadly, stalwart Paul Bowles, died in 1999. The famous bars it used to boast have nearly all closed, but there are others and Tangier remains a late-night city, much more so than Fez, Marrakesh or Rabat.

The homosexual mecca that it became in the 1950s still pertains to some extent. Around mid-afternoon Café de Paris in the Place de France continues to attract a sprinkling of genteel old men in white linen trousers and shaded spectacles.

Covetable asset

Tangier has a long history of foreign interest – hardly surprising, considering its strategic importance at the mouth of the Mediterranean. The Carthaginians established a trading port and gave it the name Tingis. Next came the Romans, followed by the Vandals, Byzantines and Visigoths (when Christianity gained a foothold). By 705 the Arabs had arrived.

Tangier prospered under the Berber dynasties until the 14th century, when internal order broke down and Morocco's north and northwest coast became infested with pirates. This prompted the Portuguese to intervene. Having already captured Ceuta, they went on to seize Tangier. Mosques were destroyed and churches were built in their stead. But Berber resistance was persistent, and in 1661, after two centuries, the Portuguese finally handed Tangier over to Britain as part of Catherine of Braganza's dowry on her marriage to Charles II.

PRECEDING PAGES: a view of Sidi Hosni, the one-time home of Barbara Hutton. **LEFT:** a fisherman in the Port du Pèche. **BELOW:** summer on the beach.

Britain deemed Tangier a covetable asset. Even Samuel Pepys, who loathed Tangier and described it as an "excrescence of the earth", reckoned it would be "the King's most important outpost in the world". But the British were unable to repel the constant Berber attacks and they withdrew in 1684, after deliberately destroying the principal improvements they had introduced. From then on, Britain's prime objective in Tangier was to uphold the authority of the sultan and keep any single European power from colonising it. Britain had held Gibraltar since 1713 and it was vital for it to have a close, cooperative source of food and supplies for its tiny territory. Other powers were equally keen to control Tangier, and by the 19th century the town was overrun by diplomats.

Foreign control

Europe tightened its hold on the town by making social improvements: a lighthouse was built at Cap Spartel (by then the treacherous rocks, not pirates, were the main hazard along the Strait), and in 1872 a Sanitary Council was formed to manage outbreaks of plague. But there was nothing altruistic in European involvement; special privileges granted to natives working in the legations and consulates included exemption from sultanic taxes and justice, and before long the consulates were selling "protection" for exorbitant sums of money.

By the signing of the Treaty of Fez in 1912 establishing the French and Spanish protectorates Tangier was already virtually an international zone. The Treaty of Algeciras put this on an official footing, and in 1923 another statute handed Tangier to the victors of World War I – France, Spain, Britain, Portugal, Sweden, Holland, Belgium and Italy. For the next 33 years Tangier was a centre for unregulated financial services, prostitution, smuggling and espionage.

The indigenous Tangier aroma, compounded of flowers, spices, hashish and Arab drains, is infiltrated by the pungent smell of typewriter ribbons from the overheated portables of best-selling London and New York novelists.

– KENNETH ALLSOP
London' *Daily Mail,* 1959

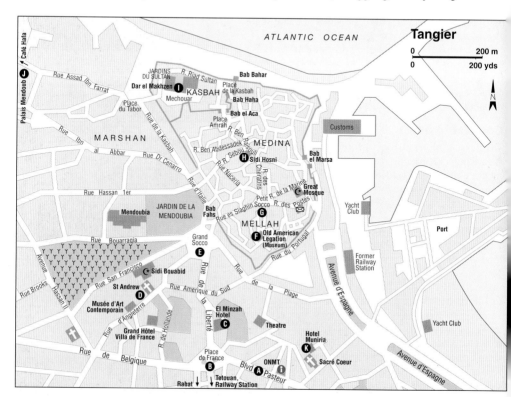

Tangier today

Following independence, and the collapse of Tangier's spurious economy, the town was left to recover, somewhat neglected by the Moroccan government. Then closely huddled around its corniche, medina, Boulevard Pasteur, Marshan and The Mountain (the latter leafy suburbs populated by the villa-owning classes), it slowly expanded into a large town with suburbs and an industrial region to the south. Food and textile manufacturing and the port apart, tourism is now its biggest industry.

Even in the 19th century, Europeans visited Tangier for its weather, and climate is supposed to be one of the town's enduring attractions. In the summer, it rarely becomes unbearably hot. It is warm well into October, and even when it is cold and wet there are always some hours of sunshine during the day (be warned though, mid-winter nights can be very cold, especially as central heating is rare). However, the *chergui*, an eastern wind, bearable in the town, seems always to be at its most violent on the beach. It guarantees a steady business for the long line of beach clubs, sometimes the only convenient respite.

Tangier's low cost of living and proximity to Europe have made it a popular package-tour destination – witness the rash of medium-priced hotels, nearby holiday complexes, and Club Méditerranée towards Malabata on the eastern side of the bay. The town attracts many Brits (pleased to discover it is one of the few places in Morocco where English is widely spoken), some of whom are on day trips from the Costa del Sol and Gibraltar. However, Tangier is primarily a summer resort for Moroccans. Any summer evening the streets between Boulevard Pasteur and the Grand Socco are solid with freshly-dressed families "*faisant le boulevard*". Many are visiting Fassis escaping the intense heat of summer in Fez.

Map on page 112

Tangier's port is Europe's gateway to Africa.

BELOW:
an overview.

TIP

Most of Tangier's car
hire companies are
located at the
southern end of
Boulevard Pasteur and
in the side streets off
neighbouring
Mohammed V. If you
want to hire a car, visit
as many of these as
you can to compare
prices – and be
prepared to haggle.

RIGHT: on the
Boulevard Pasteur.

Orientation

Boulevard Pasteur Ⓐ (also known as Avenue Pasteur) running up from Boulevard Mohammed V and the central post office, is Tangier's high street. To its right, on the ocean side, streets containing small hotels wind steeply down to the sea and the port; behind it, away from the coast, are shops, restaurants, nightclubs and bars. The railway station, which used to be situated next to the port and just a short walk from the centre, has been relocated to the outskirts of town, near the coach station on the road to Tetouan.

The large banks and the **tourist office** (No. 29) are on the Boulevard, along with the well-stocked European bookshop **Librairie des Colonnes** (southern end), a lifeline to expatriates living in Tangier, and the perfumier **Madani**, a local institution, where as well as finding local favourites such as musk and amber you can have your favourite "designer" perfume replicated.

The Boulevard, lined with the pavement terraces of the town's more upmarket cafés and *salons de thé*, runs down to a paved platform, complete with cannons and a good view over the harbour. It joins Rue du Mexique, the main shopping street, in the **Place de France** Ⓑ, an animated circus containing the 1920s-style Café de Paris, which was something of an institution during the international era. From here Rue de la Liberté curls past El Minzah Hotel and the Galerie Delacroix, while the Rue de Belgique leads to Rue d'Angleterre and the English church. Following either route you can find your way to the Grand Socco, a large sloping square overlooked by the coloured, tiled minaret of the **Sidi Bouabid mosque**, the first mosque (1917) to be built outside Tangier's old walls. Directly opposite the top of the square is the main, horseshoe-shaped gate into the medina.

Rue de la Liberté

The **El Minzah Hotel**  is the top hotel in Tangier. It was originally the home of a wealthy American and later the Palmarium Casino, but its design reflects traditional Moorish architecture: a discreet entrance off the street precedes an elegant lobby leading to a tiled open courtyard overlooked by the hotel's upper storeys. An exit on the opposite side of the quadrangle leads to a terrace, small pool and gardens – a cool spot for afternoon tea.

The **Galerie Delacroix**, part of the **French Cultural Centre** directly opposite El Minzah, is a small gallery containing works by Eugène Delacroix, the French painter who toured North Africa in 1832, as well as paintings by aspiring Moroccan artists and images of Morocco by foreign painters. The French Cultural Centre is extremely active (check noticeboard for forthcoming events), and the French Lycée, off Boulevard Pasteur, contains the **Salle Bastianelli**, a venue for good French theatre and international films. Spanish culture is offered at Ramon Y Cajal, Lycée Polytecnico Español.

The old British Consulate building, at 52 Rue d'Angleterre (from Rue de la Liberté, cut up Rue Amérique du Sud), has been turned into the **Musée d'Art Contemporain de Tanger**, an attractive modern art gallery. Close by, the Anglican church of **St Andrew**  was built to serve British expatriates. It contains an exotic mix of styles. Islamic features – delicate stucco tracery, thin pencil pillars, Kufic script and keyhole arches – combine with English village-church trappings: pews and hassocks, organ and pulpit, copies of the Book of Common Prayer and, on the wall, an order of hymns and a flower-arranging rota.

In the graveyard, the venerable Moustafa, the church's enthusiastic and Muslim caretaker, will point out Walter Harris's grave. Harris, famous correspondent

Map on page 112

Walter Harris's tombstone in St Andrew's cemetery.

BELOW: inside St Andrew's, where Anglican features are given a Moorish twist.

Matisse in Tangier

In 1941 Matisse told Pierre Courthion: "The chief goal of my work is the clarity of light." And it was the special quality of light that Matisse was seeking when he arrived in Tangier with his wife Amélie on 29 January 1912 on the packet *S.S. Ridjani* from Marseilles, in those days a 60-hour trip. Unfortunately when they got there it had been raining continuously for 15 days, and to Matisse's consternation continued to do so for most of February. They were installed in the Grand Hôtel Villa de France. Their room looked over the Grand Socco, St Andrew's church, the medina and the beaches along the bay, all of which Matisse drew and painted. Because of the rain, his first painting in Tangier was of a vase of irises.

Shortly after his arrival, Matisse's old friend, the Canadian painter James Wilson Morrice landed from Montreal and checked into the same hotel. They had not known of each other's travel plans but they renewed

their friendship and, once the rain stopped, explored the city together, setting up their easels in the medina.

Amélie returned to Paris on 31 March, leaving Matisse to follow two weeks later after he had completed a painting. The rains produced luxuriant foliage and Matisse gained access to a private garden attached to the Villa Brooks where he worked for over a month on *Park In Tangier*. He loved the intensity of colour in the lush vegetation and when his friends back in Paris exclaimed delightedly over his painting he demurred, "That's not how it is, it's better than that!"

He did three paintings of a Jewish girl called Zorah whom he found in the medina; He had to obtain special permission from the hotel, who let him use a studio where the guests would not see her entering; it was easy to find male models and he did a number of studies of Sudanese mercenary sodiers as well as Riff tribesmen.

Inspired by the work he achieved in Tangier, Matisse returned on 8 October and stayed once again at the Hôtel Villa de France. He only intended to stay a short while but his work went so well that he changed his mind. Amélie joined him in November, travelling there with their mutual friend, the painter Charles Camoin; together the artists painted and sketched in the streets and cafés.

Morocco was a turning point for Matisse. Coming at the end of his Fauvist period, it ushered in the glorious decorative canvases that are his best known work. He wrote: "The trips to Morocco helped me to accomplish the necessary transition and enabled me to renew closer contact with nature than the application of a living but somewhat limited theory such as Fauvism had turned into made possible."

Though he never returned, the influence of Tangier stayed with him. The wooden screens and bright embroidered wall hangings he collected became key motifs in many of his subsequent paintings. Elements of the work he did in Morocco are present even in his last great work, the 1951 chapel at Vence where the robes of his figures echo those of Zorah, all those years before. ❑

LEFT: Matisse at work. Sadly, the Grand Hôtel Villa de France where he stayed, is now derelict.

for the London *Times* and devoted Arabist, wrote many revered tomes on the country, including the classic *Morocco That Was*. His tombstone reads: "He loved the Moorish people and was their friend". Other notable tombs include those of Caid Sir Harry McClean, an Englishman who was appointed to train the sultan's army in 1877, and Emily, Shereefa of Ouezzane, a 19th-century English governess who married the Shereef of Ouezzane. One of the latest of the colourful expatriates to be buried here is David Herbert *(see page 71)*, who presided over the expatriate life of Tangier right up until his death in 1995.

Not far from the church, in Rue de Hollande, is the **Grand Hôtel Villa de France**, where Henri Matisse stayed and painted on two fruitful visits to Tangier in 1912 and 1913 *(see opposite)*. Sadly, the dilapidated but still elegant hotel was closed in 1992 and its fate has yet to be decided. It is now in the hands of an Iraqi businessman, who also established **Dawliz**, an entertainment complex just opposite the hotel which has a good cinema, various upmarket restaurants and an attractive *salon de thé*.

Downhill from the church is one of Tangier's main market areas. Small shops, not much larger than cupboards and selling everyday items such as *babouches*, the open-backed leather footwear (traditionally in yellow, white – for the mosque – or red), earthenware cooking pots and clothing, extend to the edge of the Grand Socco. Halfway along, through a gap lined by *Jiballi* women crouched over bunches of mint and coriander and fattened hens, is one of Tangier's three food markets – spices, vegetables, cheeses, olives, meat and eggs – fulfilling every touristic expectation of a Moroccan souk.

The **Grand Socco ⑤**, where Rue d'Angleterre and Rue de la Liberté converge, is a large irregular-shaped area, ringed by cafés, that used to be the main

Map on page 112

TIP

For one of the most enchanting views of Tangier, visit the *salon de thé* on the first floor of Dawliz. Its terrace overlooks the medina, port and bay – a scene that would have been enjoyed by Matisse from his room in the nearby Grand Hôtel Villa de France.

BELOW:
the high walls and stepped streets of the Kasbah.

TIP

Tangier is a late-night city. As a rule, *Tanjawis* rise early and dine and sleep late. Many bars do not open until 9pm, and close around 2am or later. Nightclubs are usually open until almost dawn.

BELOW: a child takes his mother's home-made bread to the oven of the local baker. Such ovens often heat the water for the neighbourhood *hamman* too.

market square. It is still a gathering point, where women come to sell bread and men sell second-hand clothes and other bits and pieces. On the far side of the *socco* is a keyhole gate, the main entrance to the medina.

The medina

Rue es Siaghin, to the right as you pass through, leads to the Petit Socco; **Rue d'Italie**, steep with broad steps on either side, leads directly up to the **Kasbah**, passing on the way the old **British telegraph office**. During the international era all the European powers had their own communications systems, and it was through the telegraph and post offices that Moroccan nationalists gleaned news of events in the French and Spanish zones. A turning into the medina off Rue d'Italie (opposite Café Excelsior) leads to the **Tomb of Ibn Battouta** (turn right at first junction and look for the green doors), the 14th-century Arab geographer and traveller, who was born in Tangier. Pilgrims visit the tomb, which is only about 1.5 metres (5 ft) long, dimly-lit and draped in a green cloth.

The other route, **Rue es Siaghin**, meaning silversmiths' street, cuts deep into the medina. It was to the right of here, in the *mellah*, that the Jews lived, the traditional dealers in silver. Some jewellers still trade, but most Jews have moved on.

The **Old American Legation ❻** (Mon, Wed, Thurs 9.30am–12.30pm and 4–6.30pm or by appointment; tel: 935317) also off the beginning of Rue es Siaghin, in the Rue d'Amerique, is less easy to find (strike right just past No. 77 on Rue es Siaghin), and consequently rarely visited by the droves of tourists heading for the Petit Socco (an easier approach is from Rue du Portugal, outside the medina's walls). Although the building has served Britain's New World colonies since 1684, the sultan gave the Legation to the US in 1821. Morocco

IBN BATTOUTA

Tangier's most famous son is probably the 14th-century Arab geographer and traveller Ibn Battouta. He is commemorated, appropriately, in the name of one of the main ferries between Morocco and Spain. The son of a judge, he was born in Tangier in 1304, and at the age of 21 set off on a pilgrimage to Mecca. But his intended trip of around six months became a 29-year journey, in which he vowed never to travel the same route twice. He ventured east to India and China, down the coast of East Africa to Somalia and what is now Tanzania, and through the Sahara Desert to Niger and Mali. On the way, he stayed in colleges or with local rulers and holy men.

Back in Morocco in 1354, he related his adventures to the Sultan of Morocco, who asked him to dictate an account of his journeys to a young scribe called Ibn Juzayy. The account, which weaves observations, chunks of history told to him by scholars and kings, anecdotes and personal opinions, plus lines of poetry added by the scribe, evolved into *El Rihla* (The Travels). It was copied by hand in full and in part for libraries and was used as a guidebook by other travellers. Much later, in the 19th century, it was translated into French, German and English, and became a travel classic.

was the first country to recognise US sovereignty and this legation was the first American government property outside the United States.

Today the elaborately decorated 17th- and 18th-century interior is used for concerts and exhibitions. Its permanent collection contains some of the best paintings, lithographs and photographs in Morocco, including work by Eugène Delacroix and contemporary Moroccan painters such as R'bati and Hamri; one by Yves St Laurent; and various naive and impressionist works. Tours are conducted by a knowledgeable French woman (who also speaks English).

The **Petit Socco** Ⓖ at the end of Rue es Siaghin still retains some of the low-life glamour that drew the likes of William Burroughs and Brion Gysin. It was here, on the terrace of the Café Central, that Burroughs gained inspiration for *The Naked Lunch*. The cafés here are very different from those on Boulevard Pasteur. Most are packed with men seemingly watching television, but, in fact, watching each other. Individuals constantly sidle in and out to whisper in an ear or beckon. Sit inside one of the cafés for long enough and you are bound to be hustled to buy hashish and be told of "upstairs rooms".

From the Petit Socco, **Rue des Cheratins** and **Rue Ben Raisouli**, festooned with souvenirs, meander up to the Kasbah, which used to comprise the sultanic palace (now a museum), administrative quarter and prison. Within its walls are some of the most sought-after properties in Tangier. Barbara Hutton had a house here, **Sidi Hosni** Ⓗ and so did Richard Hughes, author of *A High Wind in Jamaica*. To see where Hutton held her famous parties *(see page 75)* climb the stairs of Café Ali Baba (identified by its psychedelic mural on the outside wall), for it overlooks Sidi Hosni's terraces. Before Hutton, Sidi Hosni, named after a local holy man buried on the site, had belonged to Walter Harris, correspon-

Map on page 112

William Burroughs raises a glass. Burroughs gained inspiration for episodes in The Naked Lunch *in the Petit Socco.*

BELOW: the Carmen Macien Foundation, behind Sidi Hosni.

dent of the London *Times*, and then to the American diplomat Maxwell Blake. Hutton's bid for the property had beaten that of Generalissimo Franco.

The old palace, the **Dar el Makhzen** , was occupied as recently as 1912 by the abdicate Sultan Moulay Hafid, though by all accounts his stay was uncomfortable. Like most Moroccan museums, the **Palace Museum** (summer 9am–noon and 3–6pm; winter 9am–3.30pm, closed Tues), on the west side of the *mechouar* (courtyard), is a feast for the eyes – the original Arabesques and *zellige* providing a stylish context for the artefacts. But typically, too, it is short on relevant literature. Exhibits, arranged in rooms lining the sides of two courtyards, include carpets, ceramics from Fez and Meknes, costumes, musical instruments, household implements and jewellery. The kitchen quarters house an **archaeological museum** containing a mosaic from Volubilis.

North of the *mechouar*, and accessed by the palace's Andalusian Gardens, the **Rue Riad Sultan** curls left around the ocean side of the Kasbah to pass a door leading to an upstairs café called **Le Détroit**. This used to be the most exclusive restaurant in Tangier, where owner and writer Brion Gysin entertained an élite circle of friends. Now custom is mainly reduced to package groups in the afternoons; it affords exciting views, though, with a clear sight of **York House**, the machiolated residence of the English governors in the 17th century and now a private house belonging to the designer Yves Vidal.

From Place Tabor, Rue de la Kasbah leads down to Rue d'Italie *(see page 118)* while a five-minute walk west along **Rue Assad ibn Farrat** and **Rue Mohammed Tazi** (also reached by taking a No. 1 or No. 11 bus) is **Palais Mendoub** ❶. The former Tangier home of the late American billionaire, publisher and Arabist Malcolm Forbes, this large white villa was for many years

The colonial-style Continental Hotel overlooks the port. Its terrace is a pleasant spot to enjoy a pot of mint tea.

BELOW: the courtyard of the Palace Museum.

devoted to a museum of military miniatures, which were a passion of Forbes. It was here that Forbes held his much-publicised 70th birthday bash in 1989, an event that recalled the extravagant parties given by Barbara Hutton in Tangier. The event cost $2 million and the entertainment included 600 drummers, acrobats and belly dancers and 300 Berber horsemen. Guests included Henry Kissinger, a Getty or two, and Elizabeth Taylor, who also honeymooned here with her eighth husband, Larry Fortensky.

Life after dark

Perhaps more than any other Moroccan town or city, Tangier has the most concentrated nightlife and it certainly keeps the latest hours; many restaurants and clubs don't open until 9pm and don't close until 4am. It was once famous for its bars, in particular the Safari, Les Liaisons and The Parade, none of which remain. A bar's success depended upon the personality of its owners and in the late 1940s and early 1950s Tangier attracted its fair share of charismatic hosts and hostesses. Dean's bar, at one time more a fashionable club than a bar, is still here in Rue Amerique du Sud, but the eponymous Dean, who began his career as the lover of a rich and titled English gentleman, has long gone and it is now very much a dive. The quaint Tanger Inn, attached to **Hotel Muniria Ⓚ**, setting for the "Psychedelic Summer" of 1961 *(see page 74)* and where William Burroughs wrote *The Naked Lunch*, is still going. You will find it on Rue Magellen, running towards Boulevard Pasteur from the corniche. Burroughs wrote his novel in Room 9 of the hotel. David Cronenberg's film of the book was not shot in the hotel but in a studio mock-up of it. The room concerned, which has barely changed since Burroughs' time here, was copied in painstaking detail.

TIP

Turn left as you leave Palais Mendoub and left again after the hospital to reach Hafa, a secluded cliff-top café fragrant with the scent of hashish and with far-reaching views over the Straits.

BELOW: a ferry docks. Over 4 million passengers cross the Straits each year.

The beach bars

Tangier's beach is frequently plagued by the *chergui* (east wind), which ensures a steady business in its beach bars. These provide changing facilities, sunbeds and a place to buy refreshments (all for around 50 dirhams a day), and many of them are open until the early hours of the morning. Although rentals are renewed at the start of each season, the bars only occasionally change hands and each one has developed its own character: some are gay (Miami Beach and Macumbu, for instance); the Yacht Club (belonging to the port Yacht Club) is private; BBC Emma's Bar is popular with Europeans; the Chellah Beach Bar and the Golden Beach cater mainly to residents from the Chellah and Solazur hotels. Fans of the British playwright Joe Orton may want to visit the Windmill, frequented by Orton during his stays in Tangier.

East and West of Tangier

To the west of Tangier, the lovely headland of **Cap Spartel** ❷ offers alternative beaches to Tangier's well-populated sands and, if the wind is blowing from the east, more sheltered conditions for sun-bathing. The most interesting route to the cape is via the S701 Mountain Road, passing Tangier's most exclusive properties, including houses belonging to Morocco's royal family and a residence of the King of Saudi Arabia. The Mountain itself is, in the words of the Joe Orton, "a replica of a Surrey backwater… twisty lanes, foxgloves, large pink rambling roses, tennis courts and gardens watered by sprinklers".

The road loops the headland, passing the turn for the Cap Spartel lighthouse, erected by foreign diplomats in the 1870s, and a series of sandy bays, each with a makeshift café. A little further along are the **Caves of Hercules** (9am–sunset;

The Caves of Hercules. As all the guides point out, their entrance to the sea is roughly similar to the shape of Africa.

BELOW: the lighthouse at Cap Spartel.

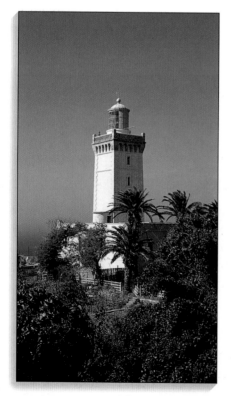

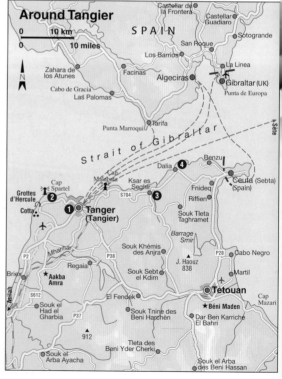

Around Tangier

admission charge plus small tip for the guide), rock chambers inhabited in pre-historic times and in the international era used as a venue for parties, including one hosted by Cecil Beaton, who served sea-cooled champagne and hashish. Robinson's Hotel, opposite the caves, has a terrace overlooking the bay; it is a good spot to enjoy a late afternoon beer.

Further on still, you pass the ancient Roman ruins of **Cotta**, dating from the 2nd and 3rd centuries, which include a small temple and a bath-house. Also here is the surface terminal for a vast new US$3.5 billion pipeline taking natural gas from Algeria to Córdoba (from here the pipe disappears under the Straits) and which will eventually extend into northern Europe. A turning left before the road to Rabat leads back to Tangier via the town's prison (opposite which, the Sompei petrol station has an excellent grill restaurant serving first-rate *harira* and kebabs), where a large contingent of Westerners found guilty of drug smuggling languish. Continuing down the coast, a magnificent beach stretches the length of the 45km (28 miles) to the fortified town of Asilah *(see page 145)*.

Alternatively, east of Tangier, are **Cap Malabata** (also with a lighthouse and a pleasant café), now a residential area, and, further east along the recently improved road to Ceuta, a string of good beaches, beginning with **Plage des Amiraux** (signposted), a few kilometres from Tangier, and then, about 28 km (17 miles) from the city, **Ksar es Seghir** ❸ with its pretty fort overlooking the mouth of a small river. The most idyllic beach along this stretch lies below the village of **Dalia** ❹, 11km (7 miles) on from Ksar es Seghir (turn left before Dalia, along a track after passing a hilly outcrop just to the left of the road); its silky white sands are backed by pines and, apart from at weekends and in August, when it attracts a fair number of campers, it is often deserted. ❏

Map on page 122

TIP

If you are travelling back to Tangier after exploring the coast east of the city, stop for a fish supper at the restaurant Lachari, overlooking the river at Ksar es Seghir. Its superb fish and shellfish platter is excellent value.

BELOW: boys on the beach.

THE RIF

Morocco's Mediterranean coast is backed by the rugged Rif Mountains, a poor but very beautiful region with huge potential for tourism

Map on pages 128–9

Rabat

After decades of neglect, the Rif has been welcomed back into the kingdom of Morocco. In all the years of his reign, King Hassan II never once set foot in the area, and it was left to his son, King Mohammed VI, to overcome years of hostility between the Rif and the palace by making a triumphal tour of the north within months of his succession. Along with this symbolic act has come a new government intention to improve the lot of the region's desperately poor rural population. One major project of great importance is the planned construction of a new coast road between Tetouan and Oujda, a journey that currently takes around four days with stops. This will open up some of Morocco's most beautiful coastline to development and is expected to give a much-needed boost to tourism in the area.

At the moment, despite its surrounding beauty, the existing coast road from Tetouan is rarely used as – unless you're lucky enough to possess a four-wheel drive – it is usually a one-way trip due to the poor state of the road from El-Jebha to the P39. However, it is still worth doing the loop to Oued Laou (campsite and hotel) and then inland on the tarmac road S8304 through an idyllic agricultural plain and gorge, before joining the P28 just before the bridge that crosses the river north of Chaouen (or Chefchaouen).

The Rif has always had an image problem, despite being home to some of the country's most beautiful landscapes. One of the reasons is the Riffians' fierce reputation. Blood revenge used to be a serious cause of population depletion and possibly deforestation, since trees and property as well as life were destroyed in a feud. It was said that a male Riffian who had not taken a life before he was married was not considered a man. (Strictly speaking, the term "Riffian" should be applied only to the tribes of the middle Rif around Ketama; the *Jiballa* – Arabic rather than Berber-speaking tribes – inhabit the extreme western Rif close to Tetouan. But generally the term "Riffian" is used in relation to the inhabitants of the whole of the mountainous area in the north.)

Red mountains

The Rif Mountains rise sharply from the Mediterranean, where a craggy coast is punctuated by sandy coves. East of Tangier their foothills lie close to Tetouan. Here, contrasting strongly with the low hills and gentle colours of the Tangier hinterland, the landscape is impressively rugged.

To the immediate east, trees begin to cloak the limestone peaks as you climb towards the central Mount Tidiguin, dominated by the often snow-capped peak. Squat holm- and cork-oaks give way to high cedar forests and the kif plantations of Ketama. The further

PRECEDING PAGES: a winter day in Chaouen. **LEFT:** *jibatli* woman in typical dress. **BELOW:** mist settles on the Rif.

east you travel, the redder the hue of the mountain range becomes, a change that strikes the traveller on the road to Al Hoceima where the terrain becomes denuded and barren. From Al Hoceima to Oujda on the Algerian border, south of a fertile coastal plain, the land is desolate, crossed by cracked riverbeds.

More inviting, on the Rif coast directly below the range, are some of the finest sandy beaches in Morocco, a fact which has led to an explosion of large hotels and holiday villages, fed by the international airport of Tangier and by the increasing custom of well-off Moroccans from Fez and elsewhere who are escaping from the intense summer heat inland. But many of these resorts are half-empty and it is still possible to find unspoilt, secluded beaches between the pockets of development. Some of the country's best fish restaurants are along this shore. The resorts include Restinga Mdiq, Cabo Negro (which also has an impressive new golf course), Martil and Amsa.

The people

The Rif has for centuries been influenced by Spain, as an Andalusian style of architecture in the towns, a common fluency in Spanish and foods such as paella, tortilla and tapas all testify. Many of the Andalusian Muslims who fled Spain in the 15th and 16th centuries settled here; and from 1912 until 1956 the Rif, plus the short stretch of Atlantic coast south to Larache but excluding the international zone of Tangier, formed the bulk of the zone governed by the Spanish. Until this time, the Riffians had existed outside the authority of the sultan – the inhabitants refused to pay taxes or accept his garrisons.

The Spanish found the Rif tribes difficult to govern. The Rif Rebellion of 1926, led by Abd el Krim and finally quashed by the Spanish with French rein-

BELOW:
a shepherdess
and her charges.

forcements *(see page 36)*, was the precedent for nationalist demands in the rest of Morocco. And since independence, the Riffians, disappointed by their lot, and still retaining some of their famous *bled es siba* ("land of lawlessness") mentality, have continued to prove irksome to the government. In December 1958, a rebellion broke out near Al Hoceima, which the then Crown Prince Moulay Hassan was sent to quell.

Despite the illegal smuggling of goods from the tax-free ports in the Spanish enclaves of Melilla and Ceuta, the creation of a new steel plant at Nador, and a developing tourist industry, the area remains poor, and its inhabitants still complain of economic deprivation and neglect by central government, which is why the illegal cultivation of kif is proving so hard for the government to combat *(see page 136)*. When processed the spear-shaped leaves of the plant are turned into the resin hashish, a much more concentrated product that is easier to transport. A suitable climate, remoteness from Rabat and proximity to Spain and Gibraltar (the latter a key base in the trans-Mediterranean drugs trade) made the region a perfect base for kif cultivation.

Heading east

By Moroccan standards, the P38 from Tangier to Tetouan is a busy stretch of road. As part of the main thoroughfare from the densely populated northwest of Morocco to the Spanish enclave of Ceuta, it is used by people heading to buy the cheap electrical goods and garments smuggled out of Ceuta to Tetouan. Consequently, it is lined by Riffians intent on selling the motorists their produce, too. *Jiballi* women dressed in typical pom-pom sombreros, red and white striped *ftouh* and what can only be described as bathtowels (often rigged into a papoose

TIP

In the Rif, you should expect to be stopped by customs officers and police looking for hashish, especially east of Tetouan and Chaouen, towards the kif-growing areas of Ketama. Road-blocks can be tiresome, as are the juvenile antics of the roadside drug vendors, who try to force cars to stop by leaping into their path.

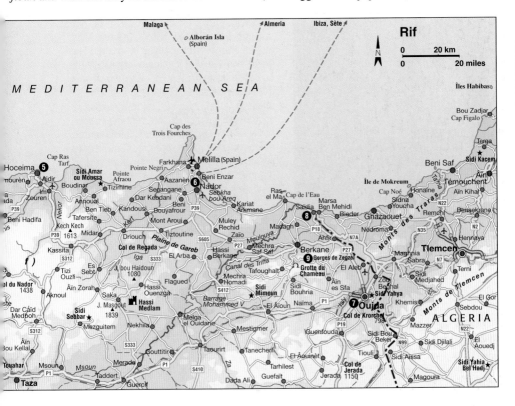

The Spanish Enclaves

A Spanish possession long before Morocco ever became a nation, Ceuta continues to embarrass both Morocco, which wants it back, and Spain, which doesn't want to give it but which also realises that its own continued presence there – and in Melilla, its second enclave further along the coast – rather erodes the argument for wresting Gibraltar from the British.

Such friction has meant that crossing into Ceuta can be an exercise in frustration, with long queues of traffic and pedestrians. When, after the war, it belonged to the International Zone, it was not uncommon for passengers to be stripped and their cars taken apart. Things are not much better these days. As a tiny piece of Spain in Africa and, of the two Spanish enclaves on this coast, the closest to the Spanish mainland, Ceuta is a beacon of hope for many economic migrants keen to

make a new life in Europe. Many of these travel here from deep inside Africa, sometimes trekking most of the way on foot. Once inside Ceuta, they can apply for asylum (a special camp has been set up for asylum seekers) or, if they have the money, they may risk their lives on dangerous journeys across the Straits in vessels supplied by local mafias (people-smuggling attracts a less severe punishment than drug-smuggling). But currents in the Straits are unpredictable and the boats usually of poor quality, so the bodies of drowned Africans frequently wash up on Spanish and Moroccan beaches.

An anti-immigrant fence has been built between Ceuta and Morocco. Equipped with security cameras and fibre optic sensors, it is the latest attempt to deter people from getting into "Fortress Europe". Its cost, £22 million, was paid for by the European Union.

In recognition of the extensive and profitable trade between Morocco and Ceuta, inhabitants of the province of Tetouan in Morocco are allowed to make day trips to Ceuta without a visa. Their chief aim on these day-trips is to stock up on duty-free goods.

As a rule, most visitors to Ceuta do not stay more than a few hours. The buildings resemble grey wedding cakes, hotels are few and expensive, and it is more interesting for its past than its present, not least that it was the Moors' point of embarkation for their conquest of Spain. In the Plaza de Africa is the church containing the 15th-century wooden effigy of Our Lady of Africa, Ceuta's patron saint and also, oddly, Mayoress – an office granted in perpetuity by a unanimous vote of the municipality.

A stroll around Ceuta relieves one of the desire to visit Spain's other enclave, Melilla, half a day's drive to the east. Again, the character of a modern duty-free garrison town (Franco served here as a colonel in 1925) drowns out a proudly bugled past. Melilla was Spanish 192 years before Le Roussillon became French and 279 years before the birth of the United States. These years have condemned, not enhanced, the place. Apart from a few wide streets, a bull-ring and some gardens, it has little to offer. ❑

LEFT: Ceuta's church of Our Lady of Africa in the Plaza de Africa.

…o contain a baby) hold covered dishes of crumbling white cheese (either salted or unsalted) or honey. Men tout amethysts and pottery, and small boys straw-berries, pinenuts, walnuts or whatever else can be harvested for sale.

Map on pages 128–9

Spanish flavour

Tetouan ❶, flanked on all sides by forest-clad limestone mountains, is a sur-prising sight worthy of its name (meaning in Berber "open your eyes"). In autumn it is prone to rain and low cloud, and in the winter to snow. It isn't until you arrive that you appreciate the town's location and realise how high the road has climbed. The town's past importance as the capital of the Spanish zone, where the Spanish High Commissioner lived, is apparent in its civic architec-ture. Imposing balconies beneath tall windows and curlicued grille-work are reminiscent of those in Seville. Place Hassan II, where a royal palace has been built on the site of the old Caliphate palace, has a sweep of old market buildings that look distinctly Andalusian, but more interesting is some of the older domes-tic architecture. The large old mansions at the lower end of the *mellah* (Jewish quarter) at the foot of Rue Luneta are in a state of dilapidation, but even so, the intricate enamelled tiling and fancy wrought-iron work decorating their exteri-ors demonstrate the difference between Spanish and Moroccan domestic archi-tecture; on Moroccan houses adornment is all internal.

A tiled facade, characteristic of Tetouan.

Tetouan was a busy trading centre even before the Spanish protectorate added to its importance. At the beginning of the 16th century, the Jews and Muslims who arrived here from Spain practised piracy. They made slaves of passengers and crews, then extracted fabulous ransoms. Ships of all nationalities were attacked, but Spanish vessels suffered particularly badly, Philip II closed down

BELOW:
on Place Hassan II.

Tetouan's port on the River Martil, leading to a decline in the city's fortunes. Later, under Moulay Ismail the town's economy prospered again.

Nowadays, Tetouan strikes the visitor as a busy, bustling town, its energetic character stemming perhaps from its history as the focus of political resistance in the Rif. It was here, in 1954, that a rally of 30,000 tribesmen protested against the deposition of Sultan Mohammed V. In more recent years, it has seen bread riots – demonstrations against the high prices of basic foodstuffs. Even café life is not as idle as elsewhere. During the afternoon and early evening the numerous cafés are packed with men playing board games.

Shopping is another important activity. Visiting Moroccans interested in buying cheap smuggled electrical goods and inexpensive clothing head for the Souk Nador in the west of the town, its entrance marked by a stall selling huge television sets. (Like many other activities in the Rif, this trade is illegal but tolerated by the state.) The souks within the medina running off an attractive, trellis-covered street, entered through the Bab el Rouah on Place Hassan II, are more geared towards the numerous tourists, but the Souk el Houts ("fish market") behind the Spanish Consulate remains local in character. Turning right at this souk leads to the Bab Oqla and an excellent **Museum of Moroccan Arts** containing examples of Riffian and Jiballi traditional crafts. In the Place el Jala there is an **archaeological museum** (9am–noon and 2.30–5.30pm, closed Tues) displaying Moroccan artefacts from the Roman and Phoenician periods.

Picturesque Chaouen

Chaouen ❷ (usually signposted Chefchaouen), tacked into the hills south of Tetouan, ranks among Morocco's prettiest places. The town is startlingly clean,

and its buildings, their corners rounded by repeated layers of whitewash. Women wear the white, rather than black, *haik* (unless they are in mourning when the reverse is true). In winter the town is visited by snow. Colour comes from the trellises of violet clematis, the red-tiled roofs and the tiled lintels around the doors. Curving window grilles and studded doors also add variety.

The town was founded in 1471 by Moulay el ben Rashid as a base against the Christians, although the kasbah was built in the 17th century by Moulay Ismail. The town was virtually closed to Christians until 1920, when the Spanish finally managed to conquer it. They discovered a community of Jews descended from the first refugee settlers speaking 10th-century Castilian, a language extinct in Spain for over 400 years, and leather craftsmen working in tanned and decorated leather, just as their ancestors had done in 12th-century Córdoba.

The P28 road leading to the town arrives just below the old walls. By climbing up through the marketplace you reach a brown gate called Bab el Ain, overhung by one of the town's typical wrought-iron lanterns. This leads to the main square. The cobbled **Plaza Uta el Hamman**, shaded by trees, strung with lights and lined by bowed cafés, is an excellent place to sit, appreciate the light and inhale the mountain air (not to be confused with the scent of kif drifting from the cafés' upper storeys). It was here, until 1937 – when the practice was outlawed by the Spanish – that boy homosexuals were auctioned. The Riffian tribes were staunchly anti-homosexual – Abd el Krim, leader of the Rif Rebellion, made homosexuality illegal – but the Jiballi, Gomara and Sehhadja tribes, who populated this area in the western Rif, didn't share their aversion and homosexual relations between young men was common.

In glowing sandstone on the opposite side of the square, in vivid contrast to

Map on pages 128–9

مدينة شفشـاون
VILLE CHEFCHAOUEN
سـاحة محمـد الخـامس
PLACE MOHAMMED V

BELOW:
Chaouen, set in the foothills of the Rif.

Chaouen is well-watered by springs in the surrounding hills, and fountains abound in the town.

the tiled-roofed, sugar-cube housing, is the unpainted walled **Kasbah** (daily 8.30–noon, 2.30–6pm) with its quiet gardens. To the right of this are the cells where Abd el Krim was eventually imprisoned in 1926. Next door is the 15th-century **Grand Mosque**, with its distinctive octagonal minaret.

By following the main thoroughfare to the back of the town, through the Place du Makhzen and its cluster of pottery and gemstone stalls, past the succession of tiny shops opening directly on to the steep, cobbled street, you reach the point under the mountains where a waterfall hits the river. Here women wash clothes and also sheep's wool, which they will then card and spin into yarn for home weaving. The medina is jammed full of often charming little pensions and hostels, each with their own character. One to be recommended is the tiny Hostal Gernika (tel: 98 74 34), run by an artistically inclined Spanish woman. It is very reasonably priced, spotlessly clean and with a lovely little terrace. Nearby, the brothers Boujida have a small handicrafts shop where they produce some original woven tapestries. A superb view of the town can be had from the swimming pool/bar terrace of the 1970s-style Hotel Asmaa (tel: 98 60 02), above the town, next to the municipal campsite.

Holy places

BELOW:
a whitewashed courtyard.
RIGHT: Chaouen's steep and cobbled streets.

The Berbers of this region are renowned for their reverence of *marabouts* and it is an area with many religious associations. Chaouen is considered a holy city, as is **Ouezzane ❸**, reached along the P28 travelling southwest of Chaouen. It was chosen by Moulay Abdullah, a descendant of Idriss II, to found the Taibia brotherhood in 1727. The *zaouia*, or centre, prospered. Its shereef, who lived in a sanctuary separated from the town, is considered one of the holiest men in the

land. Historically the shereef of Ouezzane held more sway over the region's tribes than the sultan. Pilgrims from all over Morocco would come for his blessing and criminals sought immunity here.

Map on pages 128–9

The sanctuary, surrounded by gardens, was supposed to represent the Islamic paradise. In reality, it had at least one foot in hell. Wine, spirits and kif were sold along its approach and the shereefian family had its share of mortal troubles, caused by congenital insanity. Sidi Mohammed, shereef in the middle of the 19th century, had a psychopath and a kif-addict among his sons. And he, at the least, was eccentric. Admiring all things European, he decided to marry an English governess called Emily Keene. The marriage was not a success, foundering on Sidi Mohammed's drinking and womanising.

The shereef of Ouezzane is still a person of moral influence consulted on matters of religious philosophy. Pilgrims are particularly noticeable in the spring when they arrive for the annual *moussem*. Today the town is an important market for the surrounding olive-growing region and is famous for its woven wool textiles used for making *jellabahs*. In character, Ouezzane is rather like Chaouen, though more sprawling, its white houses climbing up Bou Hellol mountain. Again, there is a strong Andalusian flavour, partly due to Ouezzane's once important Jewish population, whose large houses, faced with decorative tiling and fronted by wrought-iron balconies, are still much in evidence.

Switchback ride

Ouezzane, some might argue, does not really fall in the Rif at all. Below it stretches a fertile plain and the heavily populated triangle of Souk el Arba, Rabat and Meknes. It formed part of the French zone during the protectorates

BELOW: a *moussem* in Ouezzane.

and it was one of the places where French troops rallied to help Spain defeat the Rif Rebellion. The Rif proper continues along the P39 to Ketama.

This journey along the spine of the range passes through the most spectacular scenery in the region. Each switchback reveals a new panorama or unexpected scene, such as a whole village celebrating a wedding on an otherwise deserted mountainside, bride and bridegroom carried shoulder high. Driving is slow, but the road is wide and, apart from in winter, the route is safe enough.

Vegetation is a mix of holm-oak, cork-oak pine, gorse and cacti. **Ketama** ❹ is heralded by cedar and kif plantations and a large number of Berbers, in heavy brown *jellabahs* – designed to exclude the cold in winter, and the sun in summer – attempting to persuade drivers to stop and buy chunks of hashish. The town has little to recommend it apart from its location, although the Tourist Office plugs its virtues as a boar-hunting and (doubtful) skiing centre.

Cork-oaks grow abundantly in the Rif and are often seen stripped of their bark. The cork is harvested every 10 years or so for use in domestic and industrial products.

BELOW:
a kif plantation.

To Al Hoceima

East beyond Ketama, trees become fewer, and the red sandstone of the mountain a more violent colour. **Targuist**, the last stronghold of Abd el Krim and from where the Riffians' ammunition was distributed on muleback, is a gritty, workaday place situated on a small plain. Its streets are laid out in grid fashion.

Al Hoceima ❺ to the north, on the other hand, reached by taking the P39A from Ait Yussef ou Ali (birthplace of the Abd el Krim brothers), is a seaside resort popular with Moroccan tourists, although it has seen more exciting visitors in its time. It was at Al Hoceima that Hassan II, then the crown prince, emulating Spanish tactics in the capture of Abd el Krim, landed with 15,000 troops in a rented British-owned ferry, managing to surprise and defeat the small-scale

THE HASHISH INDUSTRY

The Rif mountains are internationally associated with the cultivation of hashish. It is a huge business that was initially licensed in the 1940s, along with cigarettes. Cultivation was eradicated from the south of Morocco in 1954, while the country was still a French Protectorate, but the Spanish refused to criminalise kif in their northern enclaves. Hashish production was eventually made illegal throughout Morocco in 1961, although little progress has been made in curbing the industry in the north.

As in most drug-growing areas around the world, the major obstacle is the grinding poverty of the cultivators and the lack of any viable alternative economic activity. Despite cooperation with the United Nations in 1988 and the European Community in 1993, after which the Moroccan Government promoted alternative agricultural schemes, the area devoted to kif is expanding, with the latest Spanish estimates counting 85,000 hectares (210,000 acres) under cultivation, producing 1,750 tonnes of cannabis a year. It is a hidden export industry with an estimated value of more than US$500 million a year and a European street value 10 times higher.

The Moroccan authorities jump at the chance to imprison naive foreign tourists as proof of their hardline attitude towards the narcotics trade.

Map on pages 128–9

Rif rebellion of 1958–59. His repression of the uprising was characteristically ruthless, using napalm and flame throwers to literally raze Al Hoceima and many surrounding villages to the ground. It was the last time Hassan ever ventured into the north of Morocco and marked the beginning of an estrangement between the monarch "and his beloved people" of the region that lasted until his death in 1999.

The town, on the west side of a large crescent-shaped bay, has a large number of small hotels. A much larger hotel complex, with the full-range of amenities, appears to take up most of the beach and gives the impression of owning it; in fact, it is perfectly possible for people not staying at the hotel to bathe here. The beach and bay are overlooked by a pleasant public garden. Further to the west of the town is the attractive port, with an active fishing fleet, and the panoramic Restaurante du Port. It is possible to visit the fishing harbour, but be careful where you point your camera as the port is also used by the Moroccan Navy and the police are particularly sensitive.

For a real bargain, and some local character, try the unusual Hotel Florido in Place du Rif. It is a round, tiered, 1930s building whose rooms have elegant French windows. The ground floor is a popular café, though the haze of tobacco smoke and general animation makes it feel more like a saloon.

Sun and fun on the beach at Al Hoceima.

Summer retreat

If you are in search of a more peaceful spot on the Mediterranean, head for **Cala Iris**, west of Al Hoceima, at the end of the tarmac S610 road. It is a tiny fishing port, with a few cafés, at least one of which can produce a tasty meal of grilled sardines. The cobblestoned port was rebuilt in 1998 with Japanese help

BELOW:
Al Hoceima.

as a sign of friendship between the two countries. Nearby is a tiny beach and pleasant campsite open all year, with a seasonal restaurant-café.

To the border

Immediately east of Al Hoceima, off the P39A, take a narrow tarmac road, signposted Asfiha Plage, down a very steep descent to a grey sand beach with showers and a good view of the Penon de Alhucemas, a tiny inhabited rock in the bay. The best beach with a view of the rock is monopolised by the Club Med at **Ajdir**. Towards Nador, the landscape changes from the fertile Nekor River plain to virtual desert just south of the Spanish enclave of Melilla. **Nador ⑥**, below Melilla, is known for its steel plant, an industrial scheme, that was implemented in the wake of independence. It has developed into a sprawling industrial town of no great interest except as the entry point to the Spanish zone.

It is, however, also a university town which, along with Oujda, draws all students from the eastern Rif (in the west they go to Tetouan), but it can't be the most stimulating environment for the young. Along with Tetouan and Marrakesh (also a university town), Nador has experienced bread riots in the past.

Beyond this is a cultivated plain, watered by the River Moulouya. This river, whose Barrage Mohammed V has greatly aided irrigation, marked the boundary between the French and Spanish protectorates. Historically, it has helped form a barrier against Algeria. However, the Beni Merin tribe, from which sprang the Merinid dynasty, entered Morocco at this point by taking control of the river valley, then cutting a route through the Taza Gap. The leader of the tribe, Abou Yahya, captured Fez in 1248.

Borders in the Maghreb are determined by politics rather than cultural dif-

Drawing water from a well near Al Hoceima.

BELOW: Cala Iris.

ferences, and an Algerian influence is felt instantly in **Oujda** ⑦, Morocco's easternmost city. The language is similar to Algerian Arabic and many women have adopted an Algerian style of dress (the veils of Algerian women are relatively short, covering only the nose and mouth, not extending to the chin and neck as they do in Morocco. The music of Oujda, too, is more in tune with Algeria. The type known as Andalusian, which forms the classical music of Northern Morocco (Tangier, Tetouan, Fez) evolved from that of Seville and Cordoba. The Andalusian music of Oujda and Algeria, on the other hand, has its origins in Granada and is more structured. Modern *rai* music, now fashionable in Europe as well as the Maghreb, developed in the brothels of the border towns of Oujda and Algeria's Oran.

Owing to its strategic importance, Oujda has always been prized. Since its founding in 994, it has passed through many hands: the Almoravides, the Almohads, the Merinids, the Saadians, the Alaouites, and the Turks, whose vast empire did not penetrate much further west than this. It was also the first town to be threatened by the French, who were hovering on the Algerian border long before their protectorate was agreed in 1912.

Today Oujda is a modern city, with a large university. Comparatively few Western tourists venture as far as this, for despite its turbulent history there is little to see, and since the closing of the border with Algeria the economy of the town has all but died. At one time its appeal derived from an upbeat and prosperous feel, the combined effect of its large contingent of students and busy traffic to and from Algeria. If you stay here in summer, when it is stiflingly hot, you are advised to choose a hotel with a pool.

Saidia ⑧, some 50km (30 miles) to the north, was once a busy beach resort

Map on pages 128–9

Oleander, with its deep root system, flourishes in the driest terrain, including the eastern Rif.

BELOW: the eastern Rif.

Taking the plunge in the Zegzel Gorge.

for Algerian tourists. Literally on the border, it has a very long yellow sand beach lined with a double row of holiday villas (some de luxe), with a few hotels, plenty of cafés, restaurants and some nightclubs. It must be a happening place during the summer holidays, but out of season it is a bit forlorn, like beach resorts the world over. Camping Mansour, the modest Restaurant de la Paix and a little unlicensed restaurant known as Chez Said's (next to the Sûreté National), which can rustle up a surprisingly good fish lunch or supper, are all open out of season.

Suburban rituals

Sidi Yahya, 6km (4 miles) off a built-up suburban road leading southeast of Oujda, is a popular excursion for Moroccans and Algerians. The body of Sidi Yahya, reputed to have been John the Baptist, is said to be buried here, and Jewish, Muslim and Christian pilgrims all gather. It is a strange place, associated with hermits and steeped in religious rites, rather at odds with its suburban setting. At weekends, and particularly at the August and September *moussems*, it is packed with visitors. Water or oil is placed in the domed tombs to receive the saint's blessing, after which it is administered to the sick, and female petitioners wash in the streams and knot strips of fabric to the trees in order to bind their contract with the saint. There is also a grotto called the Ghar el Houriyat, or Cave of Houris, the handmaidens of Paradise.

Since 1988, tensions between Algeria and Morocco have fluctuated. After easing in the late 1980s, tensions resumed in the 1990s when fundamentalist violence gripped Algeria. The stalemate in the Western Sahara *(see page 47)* continues to exacerbate the difficult relations between the two countries, and travel across the border to Tlemcen to see the Almoravide mosque, or to Mansoura for the Merinid ruins is out of the question while the Moroccan/Algerian border remains closed and Algeria continues to be riven by violence. The road south to Figuig – a long and dusty drive of over 360km (224 miles) – is inadvisable.

The Beni Snassen

The P27 road from Nador to Oujda skirts the forest-clad Beni Snassen mountains, where an agreeable detour from Berkane is possible. The road to Zegzel is a bit rough at first but soon improves and launches into the **Gorges de Zegzel ❾** after passing through a few modern villages. The road meanders along the bottom of the gorge, past inviting pools of cool, clean water, until it climbs up to give superb views of craggy, forest-covered, flat-topped hills. Parts of the route are flanked by orchards growing the most amazing array of fruits, including tangerines, apples, quince, pomegranates, almonds and apricots. Beehives fill in the spaces between the trees and viewpoints look down over brown stone villages with cool white courtyards.

The drive through the peaceful farms of the Beni Snassen Berbers continues to the S403 junction, where a left turn leads to **Tafoughalt** (pronounced Taforalt), which is worth a visit on a Wednesday for its weekly market, or right back to the P27. From afoughalt it is possible to visit the **Grotte du Chameau**, a large limestone cave system that derives its name from a camel-shaped stalagmite situated near the entrance. The drive down to the main road from the junction soon opens out into a spectacular view back to the Beni Snassen mountains and northwards over the Moulouya plain towards the sea.

Map on pages 128–9

Routes through the Rif

There are three main passages through the Rif. The P26 from Chaouen via Ouez-zane *(see page 134)* skirts the range, and for those wanting only an impression of the Rif, with less tricky driving, this is the best route to Fez; it offers plenty of impressive scenery along the way. A more spectacular route, however, is the S302 from Ketama. This is known as the Route de l'Unité, which was built along the old caravan passage to Fez by voluntary national effort after independence. Initiated by Mehdi ben Barka, a prominent figure in the nationalist left before his radical views led to his exile and later disappearance in Paris, it was intended to link the French and Spanish zones. Like Operation Ploughing, a scheme to cultivate over 120,000 wasted hectares (300,000 acres), it was as much a public relations exercise as a useful development of the country.

Nevertheless, begun in 1957 when the country was still enjoying the euphoria of independence, this was the first road to be built from north to south in the Rif, the Spanish never having been very active in the development of their zone. The other main thoroughfare through the mountains is the equally beautiful S312 off the P39 at **Kassita**, which eventually arrives at Taza on the edge of the Middle Atlas *(see page 236)* after a drive though naked white hills. Both of these routes are punctuated by fuel stations. ❑

BELOW: *marabout* near Taza.

Map on page 146

THE NORTHWEST COAST

From Cap Spartel 40km (26 miles) of golden sand runs all the way to the fortified town of Asilah, famous for its vibrant summer arts festival. A little further along the coast is laid-back Larache

Rabat

The triangle of land delineated by the main roads connecting Souk el Arba du Rharb, Fez and Rabat/Casablanca is the most densely populated in Morocco. The P2 from Tangier, therefore, is one of the busiest stretches of highway. It links the rest of Morocco, and indeed Africa, to the point closest to Europe. In July it is packed with migrant workers returning home from Europe for their annual holiday. Eventually Rabat and Tangier will be linked by a toll (very cheap) motorway; this has so far extended as far north as Larache.

Moroccans are frequent stoppers and constant eaters on any journey, and so roadside stalls, selling anything from melons to pottery, are many, and "meat-sandwich" cafés abound, their smoking braziers casting a veritable cloud over the road. Don't be nervous about eating at these cafés; the meat is usually of good quality and very fresh.

The coast along this Atlantic stretch has been heavily influenced by Spain and Portugal. In the 15th and 16th centuries the Moroccan ports were regularly besieged, and one by one they fell to either Spanish or Portuguese forces. In the 17th century, the area, along with Tangier, Ceuta, Tetouan and Rabat, formed part of the Barbary Coast and was plagued by pirates. The Iberian influence is strongest in Asilah and Larache, towns colonised intermittently by Spain and Portugal until 1691 and 1689 respectively. These early influences were compounded by the Treaty of Fez in 1912, when both towns fell under the Spanish protectorate. They contain large populations of Spanish origin and Spanish rather than French is the second language. Architecture and food also reflect a Spanish heritage.

Arty atmosphere

From the outskirts of Tangier, the road and railway south cross a breezy agricultural plain, keeping the sea within sight for most of the way, sometimes across small lagoons. After **Gzanaia** it passes the so-called Diplomatic Forest, a favourite spot for picnics on weekends and holidays, and, on the inland side, an American base, with its forest of transmitters and aeriels. **Asilah ❶**, 46 km (30 miles) south of Tangier and a favourite excursion from the city, is a model town. Citrus trees and good, informal fish restaurants, with outdoor tables, line its streets, and its walled medina is scrupulously clean. There is a short string of low-key hotels and holiday complexes north of the town. Also here is the railway station – a 2-km (1-mile) hike from the town.

Like Essaouira, in the south, the town is a magnet for artists, and many of the white houses of its medina are enlivened by brightly-painted murals. At the end of July an annual music festival attracts popular, classical, jazz and folk performers from all over the

PRECEDING PAGES: mural in Asilah. **LEFT:** in Asilah's medina. **BELOW:** melon seller on the coastal road.

world (well worth attending), and at any time of the year its cafés are good places to experience live Moroccan music – usually in the late afternoons.

The main entrance to the medina, **Bab el Kasaba**, is easily found off Place Zellaca, just around the corner from the seafront. Asilah's walls, punctuated by vantage points with views of the beach and the harbour (where they are now building a marina), were originally built by the Portuguese. The **Palace**, one of the main venues for events in the summer music festival, is more recent. It was built in 1909 by Shereef Ahmed el Raisuli, a self-styled leader credited with considerable *baraka* by the *Jiballi* tribesmen in the hills around Tangier. He achieved fame through a series of kidnappings, most notably of the London *Times* journalist Walter Harris, who, though imprisoned with a headless corpse, was forgiving enough to befriend his captor and later invite him to his villa in Tangier. Reflecting on Raisuli in his book *Morocco that Was*, Harris said, "In Morocco, one mustn't be too critical... it was seldom one dined with any great native authority in the country who had not a record behind him that would have outdone Newgate's historic annals."

El Raisuli's relationship with the Spanish protectors was more wary, and out of fear rather than admiration they made him governor of the region, a role he fulfilled for four years. Revelling in his new-found grandeur, he established his palace in Asilah. The peasants who were forced to build it called the palace "the House of Tears", alluding to the hardship of their labours. Being a restless spirit, however, Raisuli was not content to languish in splendour and was soon in revolt again. He fought the Spanish sporadically for a further eight years. An Englishwoman called Rosita Forbes visited Raisuli in 1924 and recorded his biography, a classic work on Morocco.

A door knocker in Asilah. Studded, carved or painted in geometric designs, doors in Morocco are often works of art in themselves.

BELOW: sorting the day's catch.

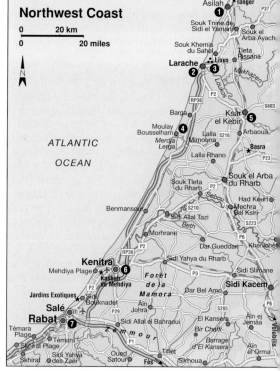

To Larache and Lixus

Larache ❷, 87km (54 miles) south of Tangier, on the mouth of the Oued Loukos, is more Spanish than Portuguese in character. **Stork's Castle**, the fortification overlooking the bay, was built by its 17th-century Spanish masters. The **Place de la Libération** (previously Plaza de España), the main circus, was built during the time of the protectorate, when Larache served as the chief port for the Spanish zone. Hotels, bars and restaurants – many serving excellent fish – all reflect the Spanish influence, though the blue and white paintwork is badly peeling and the stucco embellishments are a little knocked about. Larache's decayed elegance combines with a laid-back charm, and the town is becoming a popular summer resort for European families.

The beach is on the far side of the **Oued Loukos**, approached by a circuitous route following the turn off to Lixus, a kilometre or so to the north of the town (buses ply the route), or by crossing the estuary by ferry (5–10 DH per person). From here, there is a pretty view of the town: a foreground of moored fishing vessels is backed by the walls of Stork's Castle and the medina rising in a higgledy-piggledy crown. The estuary is a good site for spotting birds, including crested coot, red-crested pochard, moustached warbler and Spanish sparrow, though the lagoon at Moulay Bousselham *(see page 148)* is the most important bird-watching area along this stretch of coast.

The ruins of ancient Lixus, above Oued Loukos near Larache.

The Roman town of **Lixus ❸** (open site; no admission charge), its remains scattered over a hill on the right-hand side of the road leading to the beach, was founded by Phoenicians in about 1100BC, possibly as their first trading post in North Africa. As a Carthaginian and later Roman town, like Cotta *(see page 123)* it was employed in the production of *garum,* an anchovy paste pop-

BELOW: the moon rises over the ramparts of Asilah.

TIP

A motorway runs
south to Rabat and
Casablanca from just
north of Larache. Tolls
are inexpensive (by
European standards)
and the route is well
punctuated by rest
areas, equipped with
petrol stations,
lavatories and cafés.

ular in Roman cooking. It is one of several claimants to the site of the mythical
Garden of Hesperides containing the golden apples sought by Hercules in his
penultimate labour. Apart from some megalithic stones, built into the acropolis
and oriented towards the sun, few remains pre-date the Roman period. At the top
of the hill there are foundations of temples, a theatre and amphitheatre, ramparts
and houses and, near the bottom, the remains of the salt and *garum* factories.
Most of the floor mosaics have been removed to the museum in Tetouan *(see
page 132)*, though there is one of Oceanus in situ in the baths by the theatre.

South of Larache

From Larache there is a choice of three routes south: the coast road, the motorway and the P2 striking inland. On the coastal route is the resort and holy village of **Moulay Bousselham** ❹ across a large lagoon. A *moussem* is held in the
village every summer, when pilgrims visit a cave containing a sacred stalactite.
The lagoon is popular with birds, most noticeably ducks and waders, including
the Greater Flamingo. Winter is the best time to bird-watch, though the chances
of seeing the rare slender-billed curlew, seen in the area in the 1980s, have
proved slim in recent years.

If you are planning to travel on to Fez from Larache, take the P2 inland to
Ksar el Kebir ❺, once an important power base coveted by the Spanish and
Portuguese in Larache and Asilah. It was near here that the Portuguese fought
the Battle of the Three Kings in 1578 *(see box on page 30)*, resulting in the
death of the Portuguese King Sebastian and the eventual rise of Ahmed El Mansour, the star of Morocco's Saadian Dynasty.

Beyond Ksar el Kebir, outside **Arbaoua**, is the old protectorate border –

BELOW: outside the
old walls of Asilah.

where the former checkpoint is gathering weeds. During the French and Spanish protectorates, passports had to be shown in order to pass this point. After independence, Mohammed V made an ceremonial visit to the spot to declare the checkpoint formally closed.

Beyond is the turning to Ouezzane (a rewarding detour: see the chapter on the Rif, *page 134*). On the P2, the surrounding hills level out onto a rich, well populated plain whose focus is **Souk el Arba du Rharb** (*arba* meaning Wednesday, the day of its souk, and *rharb* meaning west). Thanks to the rich alluvial soil and the use of up-to-the-minute technology, this one of the richest agricultural regions of Morocco, specialising in cereals, sugar cane, early vegetables and fruit for export, as well as livestock. Southeast of here is **Sidi Kacem**, an industrial centre and rail junction, through which most people pass on their way to Meknes or Fez. As a major transport hub, it is well served by good grill-restaurants.

Back on the coastal route, on the other side of the Mamora Forest (Forêt de Mamora) of cork-oaks, acacias and eucalyptus, lies **Kenitra ❻**, the administrative centre of the region. Founded by the French in 1913 on a bend in the Oued Sebou, one of the most important rivers in Morocco, it is industrial in character and not particularly interesting for visitors, but the **Kasbah de Mehdiya**, 11km (7 miles) to its south on the mouth of the Oued Sebou, is impressive. The Spanish who captured the point in 1614 built the fortress upon a prototype conceived by Louis XIV's military engineer. Moulay Ismail, however, drove the Spanish out and established his own man there, the Caid Ali er Rif, the governor responsible for the Moroccan gateway and palace.

South of Kenitra, routes cross the edge of the Mamora Forest before hitting the suburbs of **Rabat ❼** *(see page 153)*. ❑

Map
on page
146

The vast Mamora Forest is fast diminishing. Constantly plundered for firewood and cleared for agricultural use, it has almost halved in size over the past 50 years.

BELOW: a donkey and trap, a common form of transport along the Atlantic coast.

RABAT AND SALÉ

Morocco's capital is conservative in character, with gracious architecture, verdant boulevards and pleasant cafés. Just across the river lies its twin – the former pirate base of Salé

Map on page 154

Rabat

The most recent of the imperial capitals, Rabat has less in the way of historic *madrassas* and mosques than Fez, Meknes or Marrakesh, but it is nonetheless an appealing city, with an attractive medina and kasbah, a good choice of restaurants, and a lovely setting on the Oued Bou Regreg. It also has one of the great monuments of Islam in North Africa, the Tour Hassan, one of a trio of minarets built by the Almohads (the other two are the Giralda in Seville and the Koutoubia in Marrakesh), as well as a merinid necropolis outside the city walls.

If you are arriving in Rabat by train, be sure to get off at Rabat Ville and not Rabat Agdal, a leafy suburb west of the centre. Rabat Ville railway station is conveniently situated next to the Parliament building at the top of Avenue Mohammed V, the city's main commercial spine. From here it is an easy walk to a number of small hotels or a short taxi ride to the more upmarket options *(see Travel Tips)*. The medina lies at the other end of Mohammed V, in the shadow of the Kasbah of the Oudayas overlooking the sea and the mouth of the river.

Rabat's history

Rabat was founded in the 10th century near the ruins of the Phoenician and later Roman port of Sala Colonia at the mouth of the Oued Bou Regreg. This first *ribat* (Islamic military community), later became the capital of the great 12th-century Almohad conqueror Yacoub el Mansour, who ruled an area that extended from Tunisia to northern Spain. Ribat el Fath, the Fortress of Victory, was the assembly point for his armies, which bivouacked in the shelter of its 5-km (3-mile) long massive walls.

With the death of Yacoub el Mansour, Rabat lost much of its importance and was not to recover its status as capital until the French occupation in 1912. By then the town of Rabat – the present medina – was one of five separate entities: the medina itself; the adjoining Kasbah of the Oudayas; the *mechouar,* or palace complex, situated some distance away; beyond this the ruins of Chellah; and finally, across the Bou Regreg from the Oudayas, the old town of Salé.

The centre of the modern town was then grazing land between the medina and the *mechouar*, still partly enclosed by the ruins of the Almohad walls. Horsemen galloped across this plain in the traditional *fantasia* to pay homage to the sultan on his infrequent visits to his Rabat palace.

Modern centre

Now all is engulfed in the Rabat-Salé conurbation of over 1½ million inhabitants. Modern **Rabat** is staid, heavily policed and respectable, with its poor areas conveniently well out of sight or camouflaged by

PRECEDING PAGES: ceremony at the Tour Hassan. **LEFT:** Hassan II's funeral in Rabat, 1999. **BELOW:** a city waiter at work.

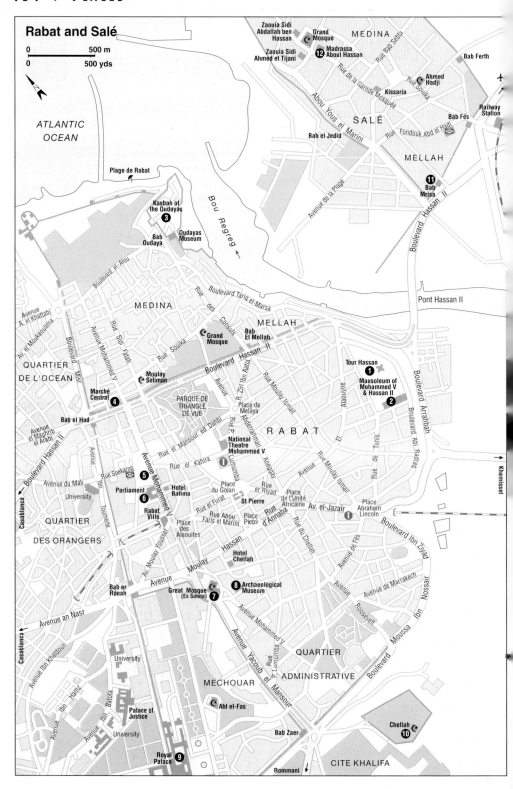

Rabat and Salé

0 — 500 m

0 — 500 yds

N

ATLANTIC OCEAN

MEDINA

Zaouia Sidi Abdallah ben Hassan
Grand Mosque
Zaouia Sidi Ahmed et Tijani
12 Madrassa Aboul Hassan
Rue Bab Sebta
Bab Ferth
Rue de la Garnde Mosquee
Rue Souika
Ahmed Hadji
Kissaria
Abou Yous el Marini
SALÉ
Bab Fès
Railway Station
Bab el Jedid
Rue Fondouk Abd el Hadj
MELLAH

Plage de Rabat

Avenue de la Plage

11 Bab Mrisa

Boulevard Hassan II

Kasbah of the Oudayas **3**

Bab Oudaya
Oudayas Museum

Bou Regreg

Pont Hassan II

Boulevard Tariq el-Marsa

MEDINA

Rue des Consuls

Boulevard el-Alou

Rue Soulka

MELLAH
Bab El Mellah

Grand Mosque

Tour Hassan **1**

Boulevard Hassan II

Mausoleum of Mohammed V & Hassan II **2**

Boulevard Arrahah

Boulevard Abi Badraz

Khemisset

Avenue A. el Khattabj
Av. el Moukaouama

Av. el Moukaouama

Boulevard Misr

Avenue Mohammed V

Rue Sidi Fatah

Moulay Soliman

QUARTIER DE L'OCEAN

Marché Central **4**

Bab el Had

Avenue

Avenue el Maghrib el Arabi

Boulevard Hassan II

Avenue du Mali

University

Casablanca

Rue Soekarno

Rue el Mansour ed Dahbi

PARQUE DE TRIANGLE DE VUE

Place de Meliiya

Rue Ziri ton Aatia

Rue Moulay Ismail

R. Abderrahman Anagay

RABAT

Rue Moulay Ismail

Rue de Tunis

National Theatre Mohammed V

Rue el Kahira

P. Lumumba

5

Parliament **6**

Hotel Balima

Place du Golan

Rue et Forat

St Pierre

Rue er Riyad

Rue d'Annaba

Place de l'Unité Africaine

Av. el-Jazair

Place Abraham Lincoln

Rabat Ville

Place des Alaouites

Rue Abou Faris el Marini

Place Pietri

Avenue

Boulevard Ibn Ziyad

QUARTIER DES ORANGERS

Av. Moulay Youssef

Avenue Tourneta

Ibn Toumert

Hotel Chellah

Hassan

Avenue de Fas

Bab er Rouah

Great Mosque (Es Sunna) **7**

Archaeological Museum **8**

Avenue Mohammed V

Avenue de Marrakech

Moulay

QUARTIER ADMINISTRATIVE

Ibn Nossair

Boulevard

Moussa Ibn

Casablanca

Avenue an Nasr

Avenue Ibn Khaldoun

University

MECHOUAR

Ahl el-Fas

Avenue Yacoub el Mansour

Avenue Roosevelt

Avenue Ibn Hanz

Avenue Ibn Batota

Palace of Justice

University

Bab Zaer

Chellah **10**

Royal Palace **9**

Rommani

CITE KHALIFA

"walls of shame". Casablancais may call it provincial, but by Moroccan standards Rabat is a tolerant and (unlike Salé) a Westernised city. The *ville nouvelle,* or New Town, built during the French Protectorate has filled the space between the medina and the Almohad walls and spilt over into other *quartiers.*

Despite the overflow, seen from the outside, these ochre walls still seem to encircle the town. From the great gate of Bab Rouah, the finest of the five city gates, they run down past lawns and orange-trees to Bab el Had at the corner of the medina, where the Marché Central stands. It was at Bab el Hed that the last pre-protectorate sultan exhibited the heads of defeated rebels. Now for most of the year, swifts and martins flock to the spot at dusk, nesting in the regular holes in the masonry (designed to support the crossbeams of small mobile platforms for repair work to the walls). On the other side of town another well-preserved section of Almohad wall encloses the palace area and, beyond the palace, Chellah overlooks the valley.

Map on page 154

Detail on the Tour Hassan.

Principal sights

Following the road round above the valley, one comes to the principal Almohad site in Rabat, and the city's invariable symbol, the **Tour Hassan (Hassan Tower)** ❶, magnificently situated on the crest of a hill commanding both Salé and Rabat. This is the unfinished minaret of the great Hassan Mosque, constructed by Yacoub el Mansour in the last five years of his reign after his victory over the kings of Castile and Leon at Alarcos.

At his death in 1199 work seems to have ceased, but the main structure of the mosque was well advanced. The design was monumental. Twenty-one east-to-west aisles in the prayer-hall, with space for 40,000 worshippers (double the capacity of the Kairouyine in Fez) made it the largest mosque in the west and the second in all Islam. El Mansour, it is said, wanted his whole army to pray together here.

BELOW: a guard on duty at the tomb of Mohammed V.

The shell of the mosque was destroyed at the same time as the city of Lisbon in the earthquake of 1755. Many of the 400 columns have now been re-erected upon a foundation of modern flagstones. Parts of the mosque's outer wall survive, and a large sunken water-tank near the tower, which was to have fed the fountains in the ablutions court, has been converted into a monument to the victims of the independence struggle. But the site of the mosque is now no more than a great white open space between the modern mausoleum of Mohammed V and Hassan II on one side and the Tour Hassan on the other.

The tower, designed by the same architect as the Giralda in Seville and the Koutoubia in Marrakesh, rises to only 50 metres1 (65ft) – the height of the Koutoubia – out of its projected 81 metres (265ft). Within the tower's 2.4-metre- (8ft-)thick walls is an internal ramp up which mules carried building materials and which (intermittent restoration permitting, of course) is usually open to visitors. The climb itself and the splendid view from the top are convincing proof of the real height of the truncated structure despite its stocky look.

With its 16-sq.-metre (172-sq.-ft) cross-section, as

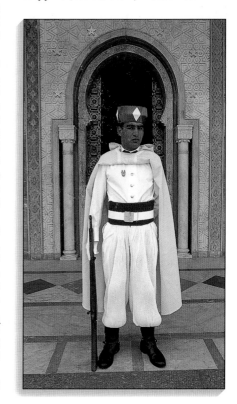

TIP

From the riverside
below the Tour
Hassan, rowing boats
ferry passengers over
to Salé *(see page 163)*
for a few dirhams.
Without a car, this is
the easiest way to
visit Salé.

against the Koutoubia's 12 sq. metres (39 sq. ft), the Tour Hassan would, if completed with its upper ranges of tilework and its lantern, have appeared more slender than either of its sister towers. But the harmony of its decorative carving (different on each face at the lower level, the same on three faces at the upper), the magnificence of the site and the rich ochre of its stone make it one of the most memorable pieces of architecture in Morocco.

It is, however, towards the white marble **Mausoleum of Mohammed V** and **Hassan II ❷**, on the other side of the rows of columns, that most visitors direct their attention. It is the costly but uninspired product of architectural and decorative styles that haven't changed in 400 years, but is redeemed by the genuine popular piety of the many Moroccan visitors. At the funeral of Hassan II in July 1999 an estimated 2 million Moroccans, many distraught with grief, flooded Rabat's streets to say farewell to their king as the military vehicle in which the body was carried made its way from the palace. Contrary to expectations, King Hassan has a modest tomb, which is dwarfed by that of his father.

The Kasbah of the Oudayas

From the Tour Hassan, roads lead down to the rather seedy **riverside** where fishing boats dock. It is from here, looking towards the sea, that the **Kasbah of the Oudayas ❸** can be best seen. Built by Yacoub el Mansour on the site of the original *ribat*, in former times the fortress of the Oudayas, itself a small town, it also contained the sultan's residence in Rabat. In the 17th century, the period of the corsair state known as the Republic of Bou Regreg, the Kasbah's inhabitants lived by piracy. Their captives used to be sold in the **Old Wool Market**, a triangular space still used by the wool trade, across the road from the Oudayas entrance.

BELOW:
into the Kasbah
of the Oudayas.

Moulay Ismail, whose reign spanned and paralleled that of Louis XIV *(see page 33)*, put an end to the vicious little republic, took over the corsair business himself and constructed a new palace within the Kasbah, which is now the Oudayas Museum *(see below)*. He also installed in the Kasbah the warlike Oudayas tribe whom he charged with the tasks of subjugating the equally fractious Zaer tribe south of Rabat and keeping the corsairs in line.

Approaching the main entrance, the **Bab Oudayas**, you may want to purchase half an hour's peace and quiet by engaging one of the many freelance guides (although the kasbah is not as bewildering as in other towns). Thus protected, you can begin to take in the façade of this superb Almohad gate, with its extraordinary superposition of arch around arch, working outwards from the basic keyhole profile of the entrance to the massive square block of the whole gate. Contemplated at length, the façade begins to shimmer and dance with the tension between inward and outward pressures around the arch and the interplay of the different geometrical motifs.

Pass through the angled entrance in the side tower and you find yourself next to the interior face of the gate and in the main street of the Kasbah. Halfway along this street on the left is the **Oudayas Mosque**, rebuilt in the 18th century by the renegade English architect Ahmed el Ingles.

Any turning to the right off the main street followed downhill will bring you to the Café Maure on the ramparts overlooking the river, which connects with the Andalusian gardens and the **Oudayas Museum** (10am–5pm, closed Tues). The latter not only contains a fine display of jewellery, costumes and carpets, but is of interest in itself as a handsomely decorated royal residence, with elegant reception rooms opening on to a central courtyard.

Map on page 154

Hibiscus bloom in the Andalusian gardens in the Kasbah of the Oudayas.

BELOW: through the kasbah, toward the Café Maure.

The medina

The Oudayas Kasbah stands at the northeast corner of Rabat **medina**, the four sides of which run first along the river, then past the cemetery on the coast, down the Almohad walls running from the lighthouse in to Bab el Hed, and finally along the Andalusian walls on Boulevard Hassan II. When in the 17th century the last wave of Muslim refugees were expelled from Spain, many of them settled in Salé and Rabat. They found the latter in ruins and almost deserted, and the area within the old Almohad defences far too large for their needs. So they put up the Andalusian walls to contain the part they settled, and this – the present medina – they rebuilt in the architectural style of their Spanish homeland.

When, in 1912, the French made Rabat the protectorate capital, Marshal Lyautey, in a pattern later followed in all the old towns of Morocco, forbade the development of the medina by European builders and ordered the creation of a new town outside its walls. The initial consequence of this policy was urban segregation, which was much criticised by Moroccans, but in the long run it has preserved the traditional Moroccan towns better than any others in North Africa.

The entrance to the medina is a little downhill from the Oudayas Gate by the **Rue des Consuls**, the only street in which foreign consuls could formerly set up shop, and today largely but not exclusively a tourist shopping street. The first section is occupied by carpet, rug and wool merchants. Popular types of carpet include the urban-style Ribati, characterised by strong reds and blues in geometrical patterns, and the generally smaller Taznacht with their softer-hued vegetable dyes and cruder patterns often including animal and plant motifs (never as strictly taboo in the Maghreb as elsewhere in the Muslim world). Most of the big carpets are now produced by sweated labour in carpet factories, but private carpet-makers sell in the souk held in this street every Thursday morning.

Halfway up the Rue des Consuls, side by side on the left, are two old *fondouks* (inns for travelling merchants and their pack animals) which now house leather workers. A few yards further up on the left, a more modern *fondouk* has become a cloth-sellers' *kissaria* (shopping arcade), arranged round a small garden. The street continues with leather and clothes shops until you come to a small crossroads. Ahead and on the left is the former Jewish quarter, or *mellah*, while to the right the road leads through a covered market (mainly jewellers – closed on Fridays – and shoe shops) and past the medina's **Grand Mosque**. On the corner of the side street beside the mosque is a 14th-century Merinid fountain, a survival of pre-Andalusian Rabat which has been incorporated into the facade of a bookshop.

The covered market leads straight on into the **Rue Souika**, the medina's main shopping street, which emerges at the **Marché Central ❹**. While the Rabat medina is too Westernised to have preserved the strict street-by-street trade groupings, there is still a tendency for sellers of roast sheep's heads and cows' feet to cluster in one stretch and those of lingerie, spices, ironmongery or audio cassettes in others.

The area behind the Marché Central is veined with *derbs* – narrow cul-de-sacs between windowless walls

BELOW: *babouches* and bags for sale.

leading off the main thoroughfares. Within the *derb,* massive iron-studded doors open, through the traditional blind entrance-way with a right-angle bend, into the courtyards of private houses. These old-style, inward-turned houses were described by Leonara Peets in 1932 as "lidless clay boxes in which the Moroccan man hides his women and his home life… a rectangular well of two storeys, with all the windows directed onto the internal patio." It was on the roof terraces of such houses that the womenfolk, who otherwise never went out except to visit the baths, were allowed to emerge in the late afternoon, when men were banished from the rooftops.

Behind the Marché Central, to the left as one faces the medina, there is a small **flea-market** in which interesting oddments are sometimes found.

To the Archaeological Museum

The Marché Central faces **Avenue Mohammed V** ❺, which runs through the centre of the New Town shopping area before broadening out into a rather elegant palm-lined promenade, the scene of the evening walkabout, past the modern **Parliament building** ❻ and straight on up to the 18th-century **Great Mosque** ❼ of Rabat at the top of the hill. Those disappointed by the ruins of *Sala Colonia (see page 162)* should visit the **Archaeological Museum** ❽ (9–11.30am and 2.30–5.30pm, closed Tues) – by no means the least of Rabat's splendours. A five-minute walk from the Great Mosque, in a side street next to Radio Télévision Marocaine, this collection is notable for the superb bronzes recovered from the excavations at Volubilis, the Romano-Berber capital of Mauritania Tingitana *(see page 211).*

When Rome ordered the evacuation of Volubilis in the 3rd century, the citi-

TIP

Early evening activity in the capital centres on Avenue Mohammed V. Hotel Balima has a nice terrace from which to watch the promenade. Behind the hotel are several good places to eat, including La Mama's, a bustling Italian restaurant.

BELOW: inspecting a possible purchase, the Central Market.

zens, expecting to return shortly, quickly buried their works of art outside the city, where they were to remain undisturbed for 17 centuries. These pieces are kept apart in the **Salle des Bronzes**, a separate building which you will probably have to ask the attendant to open for you (for reasons of security).

In addition to many charming small Graeco-Roman statuettes, there are three or four pieces of such grandeur that one wonders at most visitors' neglect of this excellent museum: the Guard-Dog (centrepiece of a fountain); the ivy-crowned Youth (the Ephebus, copied from Praxiteles); the Rider; and above all the busts presumed to be those of Cato the Younger and the young King Juba II of Mauritania Tingitana *(see picture on page 21)*. The Head of Cato, austere and fastidious, is entirely convincing as the enemy of Octavius Caesar who killed himself for a principle.

The Head of Juba, however, is the *pièce de résistance* of the collection – the product of *"pays berbère, occupant romain, esthétique grecque"*. Undoubtedly a Berber youth, it could easily have been a sculpture of their king. The short *retroussé* upper-lip is characteristic and seen all over Morocco to this day. It is the Chaplinesque appearance (all moustache and front teeth) seen hunched over the wheel in all Rabat taxis as they edge their way through the traffic, cautious and scrupulous, and unlike any other taxis in the country. The historical Juba, a famous scholar of his time, was a protégé of the Emperor Augustus, and married Cleopatra Silene, the daughter of Anthony and Cleopatra. He reigned for 45 years. Their son Ptolemy, summoned to Caligula's games at Lyon, was murdered by the mad emperor, allegedly for wearing a more brilliant purple toga than Caligula himself. (Apart from animals for the amphitheatres, wheat and indigo dye derived from a shellfish was ancient Morocco's main export.)

BELOW: the Chellah.

The Royal Palace

A short distance west of the museum, on the busy intersection joining Avenue an Nasr and Avenue Moulay Hassan, stands **Bab er Rouah**, the "Gate of the Winds", the most impressive of the surviving Almohad gates, which now doubles as an art gallery with changing exhibitions.

Do not, like many tourists, take the school entrance next to the Great Mosque for that of the **Royal Palace ⑨**, which is actually 200 metres/yards further to the right, halfway between the mosque and Bab er Rouah. Visitors are allowed to walk or drive through the archway into the *mechouar* (palace area, containing **Dar El Makhzen** – the House of Government). Here one enters a town within a town, containing the modern palace, the Prime Minister's office and the Ministry of Religious Affairs. The resident population of 2,000 includes extended branches of the Alaouite ruling family (others are distributed among the palaces in other towns) as well as retainers (serving and retired), a guards regiment and cavalry. The complex also contains a mosque, at which the King, when in Rabat, leads the midday Friday prayer on feast days.

Burial of the dead

The central road through the *mechouar* brings you out through the Almohad walls on the far side, just 10 minutes' walk from the **Chellah Necropolis ⑩** (9am–7pm) towards the left. The walled area of Chellah, stretching down the hillside almost to the level of the valley, was for 1,500 years the site of the port – Phoenician, Roman, Berber and Arab – of Sala, until, in the 13th century, its inhabitants took themselves and the name of their town across the estuary.

But Rabat remained the assembly point for armies bound for the Spanish

Map on page 154

The Moorish gateways of the Royal Palace.

BELOW: inside the Chellah Necropolis.

wars, and the first three Merinid sultans in the 13th and 14th centuries used Chellah as a burial place for their dynasty. (The other Merinid necropolis is outside the walls of Fez, their main capital.)

You pass through an unusual gate, more ornamental than defensive, since Muslim graves contain no treasure) with stalactite corbels surmounting the gate towers like hands upraised in Muslim-style prayer. This gateway, whose style is positively sprightly after the massiveness of the Almohad gates, must once have blazed with colour from its now lost tilework.

Inside, paths lead down through half-wild gardens and scented trees (notably the huge white trumpets of the hallucinogenic *dattura* or belladonna tree, also known as the "jealous tree" for its power to send people mad) to the cluster of domed saints' tombs to one side of the ruined Merinid mosque and *zaouia*, and over on the left, the excavations of the Romano-Berber town. These remains of *Sala Colonia* – or what was left of it after the Merinids had quarried it for their own buildings – can be viewed from the outside only, but visitors can walk all over the ruins of the mosque and the royal tombs behind the mosque.

This is, incidentally, the only mosque in Morocco apart from Moulay Ismail's tomb in Meknes and the Hassan II Mosque in Casablanca that non-Muslims are allowed to enter (following the ban imposed by Marshal Lyautey). One feels here, even more so than elsewhere in Morocco, the haunted charm of ruins which are not sterilised and minutely patched but are intertwined with fig-trees, overgrown with flowers and grazed by sheep – much as travellers discovered Italy in the 17th century.

The doorway into the mosque leads first into what was the ablutions court, and then into the prayer-hall, behind the rear wall of which were the burial chambers.

BELOW:
a view of Rabat from across the river in Salé.

Ahead and to the right is the **tomb of Abou el Hassan**, known as the Black Sultan, with part of a richly decorated wall still standing behind it. His wife, the former Christian slave Shems Ed Duna (Morning Sun), whose saintliness is commemorated in local legend, is buried to the far left (the sexes being segregated in death as in life). This mosque was built by Abou el Hassan's grandfather, Abou Youssef Yacoub, the "King of the *jinns*", who is believed to have buried his gold nearby and set the jinns to guard it.

To the left of the mosque stand the ruins of the Black Sultan's *zaouia*, a place of religious retreat and study. Small cubicles surround a courtyard with a central pool, beyond which a small prayer-hall culminates in a *mihrab* (niche pointing towards Mecca) encircled untypically by a narrow passageway, now blocked with thorn branches and rubble. Legend has it that walking seven times around this *mihrab* is as good as a pilgrimage to Mecca – perhaps the reason why it is now blocked up. At the other end of the central court, down some steps beside the minaret, are the old latrines with accommodation for eight (remarkably generous provision for the occupants of only 16 study cells). The inmates would have slept in dormitories above the cubicles. The minarets of both *zaouia* and mosque, as well as some of the plane-trees and saints' shrines, are hosts to that bringer of good luck, the stork's nest. Emerging again from the mosque on the side opposite the Roman remains, you find the ground slopes down to the ruins of a *hammam* (steam bath), in which a sunken pool houses a colony of eels.

Twin city

The main Hassan II bridge over the **Oued Bou Regreg** (Father of Reflection) leads directly to the centre of Rabat's twin city. It is hard to believe that **Salé** and Rabat are nowadays part of a single conurbation. Crossing the river is a journey in time and certainly in moral space. For Salé, despite its prodigious current growth, remains strictly Muslim (a dry town), culturally resistant and (theoretically) maintains an anti-European tradition going back to the last wave of Andalusian refugees from the Spanish Inquisition and the tradition of the corsairs, who were active well into the 19th century. But the *Slawis'* courtesy today compares well with many other towns, and foreigners have no hassles here.

The town of Salé has been so called since 1260 when, following the sack of the former town on this site by Alfonso X of Castile and the enslavement of most of its inhabitants, the population of Chella (Sala) crossed the river to settle here and rebuild the town. For the next six centuries Salé's economic importance was greater than that of Rabat.

From the 13th to the 16th centuries it was Morocco's principal trading port and when, after the last wave of Andalusian resettlement in the early 17th century, Rabat and Salé formed the short-lived corsair state of Bou Regreg, Salé was predominant. The hero of Daniel Defoe's story *Robinson Crusoe* was captured and sold into slavery by the Sallee Rovers.

From the Salé end of the Hassan II Bridge, the first town gate you see is the unusually tall **Bab Mrisa** ⓫ (Port Gate), built by the Merinid sultans to admit sea-

Map on page 154

The eels in the pool of the Chellah's hammam are thought to confer fertility. They are supposedly ruled over by a giant eel with long hair and golden rings, and draw their magic from the saintly Shems, as does the small spring rising in the gardens below the ruins.

BELOW: making bricks.

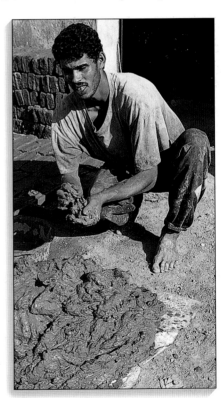

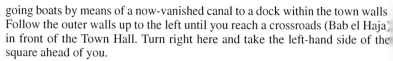

going boats by means of a now-vanished canal to a dock within the town walls. Follow the outer walls up to the left until you reach a crossroads (Bab el Haja) in front of the Town Hall. Turn right here and take the left-hand side of the square ahead of you.

Straight ahead and bearing left, you enter the main trading streets of the **medina**. Here craftsmen and shopkeepers flock together by trades, grouped guild-like in their own narrow streets. This is very much a traditional Moroccan town, visited by few tourists and entirely free of hustlers. The long straight road up to the left (Rue de la Grande Mosquée) takes you to the area of merchants' mansions and religious centres *(zaouias)* around the Grand Mosque. Behind the mosque to the right is the **Madrassa el Hassan**  – a lovely little Merinid religious college, just as finely wrought and well preserved as the great Bou Inania *madrassas* in Fez and Meknes, but much smaller. There is the same ubiquity of decoration – first *zellige* (faïence mosaic), then incised stucco, and finally carved cedar-wood. Visitors are admitted to the dormitories in the upper storey and even to the roof, with its view across the river to Rabat. Beyond the Grand Mosque on the seaward side lies the **Shrine of Sidi Abdallah ben Hassan**, a 16th-century saint revered by the corsairs. His cult survives in an annual procession on the eve of Mouloud (the Prophet's birthday); men in period costume carry large lanterns, intricately made of coloured wax, from Bab Mrisa up to the saint's shrine, where they dance and sing.

Birdlife in the zoo, Temara Ville. Among the other inhabitants are Barbary lions. Though the last wild Barbary lion was shot in the 1920s, a project was launched in 1999 to return the species to the wild.

BELOW: Madrassa el Hassan.

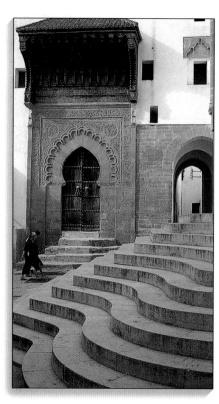

Pots and botany

Away from the town, there is a thriving cooperative of **potteries**, on the Salé side of the river, beside the airport road out of Rabat. Salé pottery is marked by delicate economical designs in white and pastel shades, often including the Roman *fibula*, or brooch fastener – a traditional motif in Berber decoration. Unfortunately this faïence work chips easily, unlike the hotter-fired Fez stoneware with its characteristic scrollwork and resonant blues and whites.

About 10km (6 miles) north of Salé on the Kenitra road, recognisable by the coloured sun-hats for sale on racks outside an arched metal gate, are the **Jardins Exotiques** (10am–5.30pm), a botanical adventureland with liana bridges and winding jungle paths. Designed by a French conservationist to illustrate a variety of ecosystems, the gardens are rather run down, but the obstacle course is still fun.

A further 6km (4 miles) north there is a turning off to the five-star Hôtel Firdaous and the attractive sandy beaches of the Plage des Nations (but beware: the sea here is dangerous).

From Rabat to Casablanca

Anyone travelling without their own transport can get to Casablanca easily by train (get off at Casa-Port station). Drivers have a choice of three clearly indicated roads, the motorway (toll payable), the P1 or the coast road, which can be busy at weekends when it becomes ensnarled with beach-bound city dwellers.

Many of the Atlantic beaches are subject to currents which make swimming dangerous, but a number of small sandy bays between Rabat and Casablanca are both attractive and safe. About 10km (6 miles) south of Rabat on the coast road brings you to **Temara Plage**, with a series of beaches – Contrebandiers, Sables d'Or (Sidi el Abed) and Sehb ed Dahab. Around Sables d'Or there are several restaurants, discos and sports facilities, and Sehb ed Dahab has a marina. In summer, however, these beaches are appallingly crowded.

Temara Ville, a couple of kilometres inland, has Morocco's main zoo (there is another one in Agadir), a well-maintained collection (originally the King's own) in extensive grounds. A little further south, where the coast road crosses the small Oued Ykem river by the Ain Atiq motorway exit, two campsites and two restaurants cater for visitors to the attractive **Plage Rose-Marie**. The Hôtel Le Kasbah hires out horses which you can ride along the beach, has a good swimming pool and, in summer, a nightclub. If you are considering camping in summer, be warned: in the holiday season Moroccan campsites are often chock-a-block with semi-permanent tent cities, and camp life is far from restful.

At **Skhirat**, 30km (19 miles) south of Rabat, the King's seaside palace – scene of a bloody attempted coup against Hassan II in 1971 – is flanked by excellent beaches and smart villas. Some 70km (40 miles) from Rabat and 30 km (19 miles) before Casablanca lies the long thin coastal strip of **Moham-media** – a town with a split personality: on the Casa side, there are an oil port, factories and poor districts; on the Rabat side (described as East Moham-media), a playground for rich Casablancais, with hotels, good beaches and sports facilities that include an 18-hole golf-course, a marina, water sports, rid-ing (Hôtel Samir), a casino and a racecourse. It's a relaxing sort of place and has two excellent Spanish-style fish restaurants. ❑

Map on page 154

TIP

The Robert Trent Jones-designed Royal Dar-es-Salam Golf Club, on the outskirts of Rabat off the Rommani Road, comprises two 18-hole and one 9-hole courses. Visitors can have access to the club as temporary members.

BELOW: the coast south of Rabat.

CASABLANCA

Though nothing like its Sin City image in the classic Hollywood movie that appropriated its name, Casablanca is an exciting and fast-changing metropolis

Map on page 170

Morocco's economic capital is developing at an astonishing rate. Its streets are choked with traffic and noise. Modern high-rise buildings have transformed its skyline, and up-market shops and huge advertising hoardings have changed the atmosphere downtown. Casablanca is no longer a poor version of a modern city. A burgeoning middle class and a rapidly expanding professional service sector has launched the city into the 21st century.

It is also a city with extensive poor areas and sealed off bidonvilles (shanty towns) which were the scene of murderous bread riots twice during the last two decades of the 20th century. The first bidonvilles sprang up back in the 19th century; they mushroomed during the postwar years and the country is still struggling to address their problems. Combating poverty is King Mohammed VI's stated priority.

The original Berber town of Anfa was destroyed by an earthquake in 1755. Rebuilt as Dar el Beida (the White House, or Casa Blanca), its population had barely reached 20,000 by the turn of the century, not a tenth of that of Fez at the same time. Since then, however, it has risen to be the main port and industrial capital of Morocco, with a population variously estimated from the official figure of nearly 3 million to an unofficial 5 million. This makes Casablanca Africa's second city after Cairo.

Casablanca has never had any real link with the film of the same name that made the city famous. Not one scene was shot within a thousand miles of Casablanca and it bears even less resemblance to today's city. The nearest hint of the film that a visitor will find nowadays is in the decor of the Hyatt Regency bar or the frequent reruns of the classic at the Cinema Lynx.

PRECEDING PAGES: view over Casa. **LEFT:** the Hassan II Mosque. **BELOW:** on Place Mohammed V.

Orientation

At the centre of Colonial Casablanca are two large squares, the **Place Mohammed V ❶** and the **Place des Nations Unies ❷**. From the latter, a road runs down to the port entrance and Casa-Port railway station. This road marks the eastern edge of Casablanca's small and rather dull old medina, at the lower end of which, facing the sea, stands the 18th-century fort, the **Borj Sidi Mohammed ben Abdullah**, built to resist Portuguese raids. The only reason for visiting the medina is to go shopping in **Derb Omar**, where the Casablancais' boast that you can buy anything is its only resemblance to London's Harrods.

Over the other side of the Place des Nations Unies you will find a more modern pedestrians-only shopping precinct, between the Place d' Aknoul and the Boulevard de Paris. The real centre of town, however, has moved from the tired area of the Protectorate era

A touch of Art Deco at the city's Hyatt Regency Hotel.

to the crossroads of **Boulevards Zerktouni** and **d'Anfa**. Designer decorated cafés and European name shops line the wide avenues and streets, while the neighbouring offices house banks, advertising agencies, computer companies and architectural practices. Casablanca has money, and nowhere is this more evident than in the recently completed **Deux Tours**, a huge office and commercial development that is now the downtown landmark.

However Casablanca does not abound with the usual attractions that the rest of Morocco offers the visitor. There are no other museums or historic attractions of note. Simply wandering the streets, visitors would soon tire of the constant traffic and pollution. The city is the country's economic powerhouse and the culture is that of the young urbanite. Casablanca's real attraction is its complete contrast to the rest of Morocco. There is as yet no listings magazine, but Casablanca has a number of websites that list current and special events. Other sources of information are the women's press (*Citadine and Femmes Du Maroc*) and Teleplus, the weekly television magazine. They are worth checking out as

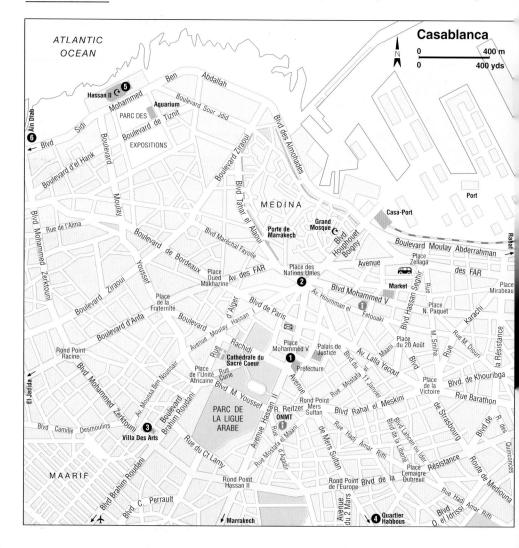

it is through visiting the exhibition openings, fashion shows and night-spots that the real life of the city can be seen. Highlights of the annual calendar are the Caftan Show (winter), which attracts international designers, and the national film festival (spring).

The gourmet is well served in Casablanca *(see Travel Tips)*, but shopping is the other big attraction. One of Morocco's largest industries is textiles and clothing manufacture, which means it is possible to pick up factory surplus bargains especially in women's fashion. The most expensive and higher quality shops are found along the Boulevards Zerktouni and d'Anfa, while the Maarif area is crammed with hundreds of small boutiques that will easily provide a day's bargain hunting for the fashion conscious. Interior decoration shops are also numerous, with the best of their offerings a synthesis of traditional Moroccan style and European design.

Architecture and art

The city is famous for its Art Deco and neo-Mauresque architecture. The latter was a product of the French Protectorate administration and is well represented in the public buildings around the Place Mohammed V, on the other side of the Place des Nations Unies from the medina. Four monumental public buildings from this period dominate the square: the Grande Poste; the Wilaya (Prefecture), with its clock tower, the Palais de Justice, with elaborately tiled courtyards; and the Banque d'Etat. The first three are in the neo-Mauresque style cooked up by French architects in the 1920s and 1930s. Other examples of the exuberant exploitation of exotic themes by European architects, combined with local craftsmanship, are seen in particular along the Boulevard Mohammed V and in the surrounding streets, where carved facades abound, often with decorative tiles or zellige mosaics, ornate entrance-ways and some striking Art Deco grille work on staircases and balconies.

Many of the Art Deco villas that once lined the city's boulevards have now been demolished or converted into private offices – the Shems Advertising agency, 162 Boulevard d'Anfa, for example – though ideas of establishing an Art Deco historic district are occasionally proposed. The **Villa Des Arts** ❸ (30 Boulevard Brahim Roudani; open Tue–Sat 11am–7pm; tel: 022-29 50 87), a privately funded museum, is a beautifully restored example of the style. The museum is dedicated to collecting contemporary Moroccan art and is financed by the ONA Foundation, which also funded the restoration of the Tin Mal Mosque in the High Atlas *(see page 276)*.

Highly contemporary is the **Home d'Enfants Murdoch-Bengio** (51 Rue Abu Dhabi, Oasis, tel: 022-99 49 40/41; visits by appointment) a small museum of Jewish Moroccan culture in a super modern building designed by architect Aime Kakon, built on the site of a postwar Jewish orphanage. Other noteworthy exhibition spaces are the **Institut Français** (121 Boulevard Zerktouni, tel: 022-25 90 78) and the **Theatre Sidi Bellyout**. The **Cybergallery**, 14 Rue Ain Harrouda, holds contemporary art exhibitions as well as having a modern café.

Map on page 170

Casablanca has some of the country's best pâtisseries.

BELOW: a pastry and a *café au lait.*

The Minaret of the Hassan II Mosque.

BELOW: the mosque's massive marble courtyard.

Quartier Habbous

A 10-minute drive from the centre (take a *petit taxi*) takes you to the new medina, called **Quartier Habbous** ❹ built in the 1930s in the neo-Mauresque style by the French. This attractive complex, is now a shopping district (not primarily for tourists) specialising in Arabic bookshops and traditional utilitarian objects. It is also the site of the Adul offices where men go to repudiate their wives under Islamic law. It is easy to walk around and agreeably hassle-free. Worth visiting here is the famous **Pâtisserie Bennis** in the Rue Fkih El Gabbas. Nearby is the Royal Palace in Casablanca, with its high walls and hidden gardens (it is rumoured that the new king, Mohammed VI, is planning to open it to the public as a museum).

The Hassan II Mosque

West along the corniche (it is best to catch a *petit taxi*) is the **Hassan II Mosque** ❺ (open to non-Muslims Sat–Thurs for guided tours only at 9am, 10am, 11am and 2pm; admission charge), the gift of a grateful nation to its previous sovereign on the occasion of his 60th birthday in 1989 (it was inaugurated in 1993). This magnificent and costly building, complete with library, museum, steam baths, Koranic school and conference facilities was built on the sea-bed, with water on three sides. It was designed by French architect Michel Pinseau and financed by voluntary subscriptions. Its position complies nicely with a Koranic saying: "Allah has His throne on the water." As far as possible it incorporates Moroccan materials – cedar wood from the Middle Atlas and marble from Agadir and Tafraoute.

The cost, in all more than US$750 million, was met by various means. Special

officials collected contributions from every home in the land, and some employers deducted a percentage from their workers' wages. The late king's highest officials are said to have fallen over themselves to be generous.

The prayer hall, with an electrically-operated sun-roof over the central court, has space for 20,000 worshippers while another 80,000 can pray on the surrounding esplanade. The marble minaret is 25 metres (82ft) square and 175 metres (575ft) high, which makes it the tallest religious building in the world, beating the Great Pyramid of Cheops by 30 metres (98ft) and St Peter's by 40 metres (131ft). It took 35,000 workers 50 million man-hours to complete. Visible for hundreds of kilometres out to sea, this is the largest mosque outside Medina and Mecca. A 32-km (20-mile) Star Wars-style visible laser beam, points, like a giant finger, from the top of the minaret towards Mecca.

Along the Corniche

Casablanca's playground is the corniche of **Ain Diab ❻**, a rich residential area, westward from the port, past the mosque. Here the local population comes to jog and lie on the beach during the day, while at night it is lit up with restaurants and nightclubs. One of the best French restaurants in Africa, the award-winning **a ma Bretagne** (closed Aug) lies at the western limit of the corniche, not far from the **Marabout of Sidi Abderahmen**, a picturesque cluster of white tombs rising on a rocky outcrop just offshore. At low tide pilgrims wade through the waves to reach it. A couple of nightclubs worth checking out are Villa Fandango (Rue Mer Egee, Boulevard de la Corniche, tel: 022-39 85 08) and the Revolver Café (corner of Rue Mer d'Oman and Rue de la Mer Adriatique, tel: 022-39 71 85). The clubs come to life around midnight. ❑

Map on page 170

On the rocks at Ain Diab.

BELOW: under cover on the corniche.

SOUTH OF CASABLANCA

Map on page 178

This stretch of coast is little visited by foreigners, but it is worth exploring for the old Portuguese port of El Jadida, the oyster beds of Oualidia and the pottery of Safi

Rabat

The Atlantic coastal strip south of **Casablanca** ❶ is served by two roads: the busier and not necessarily faster P8, and the S121, the more scenic coast route (without the attendant poor surface that the description usually implies). The scenery, though, is not as obviously dramatic as elsewhere in the country. To the west vast stretches of Atlantic breakers are intermittently hidden by sand dunes, still lagoons or long lines of wind-breaking canes sheltering tomato plantations. To the east is a still and tussocky plain grazed by sheep and punctuated by scattered farm buildings.

Occasionally the melancholy character of the region is relieved when the road sweeps within feet of an unexpected and inviting sandy cove. Mules and carts (complete with number plates) suggest a more affluent peasantry than that of the south. Even the occasional horse is spotted.

Portuguese legacies

About 80km (50 miles) south of Casablanca at the mouth of the Oued Ouem Er Rbia (Mother of Spring) the main road passes the little town of **Azemmour** ❷ The view of the town from across the river is one of the most memorable in this country of set-piece, almost painterly views. The white cube buildings stacked up behind the walls are set off in this case by the astonishing colours of the river, either reds or greens depending on whether it has rained in the hills or not.

The town was called Azama by the Portuguese who occupied the place for only 30 years from 1510 until 1540. It is the first of a string of one-time Portuguese ports along this stretch of coast. From within, the town is unspectacular but pleasant. One can walk round the Portuguese ramparts and reflect on the extraordinary energy of that small country in the 14th and 15th centuries, when at one time or another it held most of Morocco's Atlantic ports.

The town's annual *moussem* commemorates a Jewish holy man, but the Jewish population, like the majority of Moroccan Jews, fled to Israel in 1967 fearing reprisals for the Six-Day War. The *mellah* is now in ruins, but the rather plain little synagogue is opened for determined sightseers.

About 16km (10 miles) further south, 100km (63 miles) from Casablanca, is the seaside resort of **El Jadida** ❸ a refuge in summer for *Marrakshis* fleeing the suffocating heat of the *chergui*, the east wind. Its miles of sandy beaches (often obscured by warm mists), its carefree atmosphere and the interesting old Portuguese Town make it a pleasant stopping place, though it is usually crowded in summer. Many of the town's main routes are beautiful avenues planted with mature long-trunked palm trees.

PRECEDING PAGES: fortified El Jadida. **LEFT:** El Jadida's characteristic long-trunked palm trees. **BELOW:** poised for take off.

El Jadida's coat of arms.

The Portuguese held the town, which they called Mazagan, for 250 years and built the fortified and moated medina adjoining the harbour. The cobbled streets and Portuguese architecture of the citadel still have a rare atmosphere not found elsewhere in Morocco. The most remarkable Portuguese relic is the underground cistern (daily 8.30am–noon, 2–4pm; admission charge), pillared and vaulted like a church crypt, and astonishingly lovely with oblique shafts of sunlight reflected in the shallow water. Orson Welles filmed part of his *Othello* here in 1952. The cistern was once the armoury and fencing school for the Portuguese garrison. Round the corner the old Church of the Assumption, now restored, stands in a quiet square in the centre of the Portuguese Town. The minaret of the nearby mosque was once, as you will see, the Portuguese lighthouse. There is now a Portuguese restaurant almost opposite the cistern and a new exhibition space nearby called L'Espace Culture.

The fortifications of the citadel are in an excellent state of preservation and a walk around its ramparts provide a series of superb views, with the Bastion d'Ange giving a good view over the port area. However, to get the best view of the walls, and really appreciate the setting of the citadel, hike out at high tide to the end of one of the city's two breakwaters, which reach out on either side of the port. They give a beautiful view back towards the citadel, its monumental walls lifting out of the sea to protect the seaward postern into the old city, the foreground framed by colourful fishing boats.

The city once had a large Jewish population, increased in the 19th century by the Sultan Abder Rahmam, who resettled Jews from Azemmour here. There is a large Jewish cemetery south of the citadel and a synagogue within its walls.

BELOW: local lady.

The Muslim medina is a busy commercial network of shops and souks. Par-

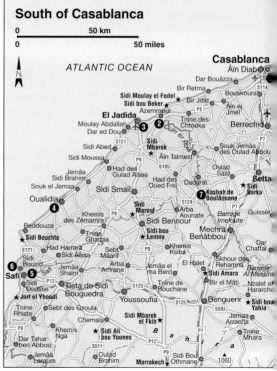

icularly worth visiting is a small square to the south of the main thoroughfare, immediately opposite the arched entrances to the citadel. This is the woven wool market and auction place. El Jadida is justly famous for its woven *jellabahs* and *haiks*, and the shops in the square are full of tailors, slipper shops and haberdasheries full of colourful silk. During the afternoons auctioneers tour the square selling individual lengths of textiles to the highest bidder.

To the north of the citadel along the coast there is a covered fish market that is well worth a visit. It is also an excellent place to eat, as is the licensed Restaurant du Port (right in the port, past the police barrier). Open for lunch and dinner it has a privileged view of the citadel walls.

Pilgrims and oysters

A few kilometres south of El Jadida, on the picturesque coast road, is the site of the annual Moussem of Moulay Abdallah, usually held in the third week of September. The festival is based around the whitewashed and green-tiled *zaouia* of the same name, situated within the ancient 12th-century walls of Tit. The *moussem* has one of Morocco's most famous displays of *fantasia* (Moroccan horsemanship). Not much further along the S121 coast road is the huge chemical and phosphate development **Port de Jorf** that provides El Jadida's economic impetus.

About 90km (55 miles) further south, past a series of coastal salt-marshes, you come to the pretty little bay of **Oualidia** ❹ famous for its oyster-beds. There are two hotels with good seafood restaurants and two campsites built around the ruined 17th-century kasbah of the Saadian Sultan El Oulid and a royal villa. Oualidia is now the preferred beach resort south of Casablanca and is often

Map
on page
178

TIP

El Jadida's corniche on the northern side of town is the place for cafés. A whole string of them line the pavement, each with its own subtle character. The most respectable, and recommended for women on their own, is the most northerly.

BELOW:
boys will be boys.

Prickly pears are sold all over Morocco, but are especially common on the Atlantic coast. They are a tried and tested local remedy for upset stomachs.

BELOW: in Safi.

crowded in summer, especially at weekends, but the atmosphere is pleasant and the swimming excellent. The final 66km (40 miles) of the S121 to Safi is an enjoyable drive along dramatic cliffs, including **Cap Beddouza**, with enticing views down onto difficult-to-access sandy beaches.

Ceramic capital

About 150km (94 miles) south of El Jadida, **Safi ❺** is an important phosphate and fishing port with a thriving and very smelly chemical industry to the south of the town. Its two main monuments were left behind by the Portuguese, who occupied Safi briefly in the early 16th century. The Dar el Bahr (Chateau de la Mer), on the shore below the medina, is well preserved. The different origins of the cannon on its ramparts reflect the European competition for commercial influence after the Portuguese were driven out. In the 17th century Safi was Morocco's chief port of trade with the Christian world, until overshadowed by Essaouira. However, its origins are much more ancient and it may even have been the Phoenician city of Mysokoras.

Up on the hill behind the medina, another Portuguese stronghold, the Kechla, was enlarged and beautified by a spendthrift son of Moulay Ismail, who, inheriting the extravagant tastes but not the industry of his father, squandered on high living the money the sultan had earmarked for military purposes. Today the restored building is the **National Ceramic Museum** (Sat–Thurs 8.30–noon, 2.30–5pm; admission charge) containing pottery from all over the country and worth a visit both for the ceramics and the delightful green tiled courtyard.

In the middle of the medina, the Portuguese St Catherine's Chapel, once part of a now-vanished cathedral, bears the arms of King Manuel I and is an attractive blend of Gothic and Renaissance elements. On the hillside to the north of the medina are the Safi potteries, which turn out brightly coloured earthenware plates and vases with distinctively bold geometrical patterns, as well as an explosion of more contemporary designs which originated as commissions by European importers, and have since spread. Safi pottery is found all over the country, but rarely as cheaply as at the numerous roadside stalls and ateliers that pack the roads along this stretch of coast. They make great buys if you can get them home.

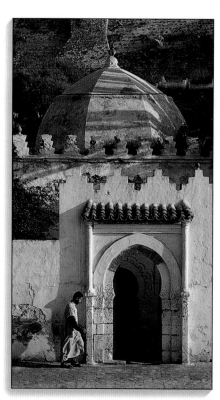

The road up to the cliff top north of the town brings you to the village of **Sidi Bouzid ❻** with its *zaouia*, a good restaurant and magnificent view of town and port. One can watch the long procession of sardine boats returning to port while sampling the deliciously spiced sardines that are the local speciality.

The hinterland

Inland from the coast the Rehamna Plain is a vast rolling agricultural area settled by the descendants of Arabian Bedouin, who migrated west as early as the 11th century, laying waste to the land as they went. Their arrival in Morocco marked an agricultural catastrophe as they destroyed the ancient irrigation systems and denuded the landscape with their insatiable herds of livestock. Today the coastal plains are known for huge phosphate mines.

Of most interest in the area is the rarely visited **Kasbah de Boulaouane** ❼ a picture of which use to adorn the label of Boulaouane wine bottles. The site is best visited en route to or from El Jadida. It makes a perfect picnic spot between the interminable P7 Casablanca–Marrakesh road or the El Jadida–Marrakesh P9, where the only remarkable features are the huge cement works at Sidi Smail (producing thousands of irrigation canal sections) and the phosphate mine of Youssoufia.

The kasbah was a huge fortress set within a tight meander of the Oum er Rbia River that rises among the cedars of the Middle Atlas and drains into the sea at Azemmour. It was built by the great Alaouite Sultan Moulay Ismail in 1710, as one of a series of kasbahs in southwestern Morocco to contain the march of Portuguese conquest. The walls are still in very good condition and it is possible to tour the fortress along their tops, appreciating its superb defensive location, protected on three sides by steep slopes and the river far below. Much of the interior is now rubble, except for the elegant arched inland gatehouse, a few interior walls, some underground chambers, the mosque (still partially used by local villagers) and a small adjacent *marabout*. The short stubby minaret can be climbed via a narrow staircase, but the view is disappointing for all except the very tall, as its parapet is just too high for most people to see over.

Elsewhere in the kasbah, the friendly old guardian will point out, among the ruins, remains of *zellige* tiles, carved plasterwork and columns of pure white Carrara marble, which Moulay Ismail acquired from Italy in exchange for an equal weight of sugar. Outside the walls, on the northern side, a walled corridor leads down the slope to a tower, which was presumably designed to give the kasbah access to water from the river. ❑

Map on page 178

BELOW:
potters' kiln, Safi.

FEZ

The old city of Fez is one of the world's last pockets of medieval civilisation. It is peppered with mosques, madrassas and palaces, and its trades and crafts have barely changed in 1,000 years

Map on page 186

High up by the fort that dominates the two cities of Old Fez, students in their *jellabahs* sit in the evening sun surrounded by Coca-Cola cans and test each other for their university exams. Below them in the valley lies their past: the old medina, with its domes and minarets, embraced by high walls behind which hooded figures move down narrow streets, trains of heavily-laden donkeys with baskets full of rubble pass through the crowds, and beggars crouch by the gates of the mosques.

Three kilometres (2 miles) to the west, up on a plain that is bitterly cold in winter but full of summer breezes, stretch the boulevards and squares of the new town. For the students, this land of bougainvillea and comparative Western plenty holds the promise of the future. The medina – the hotly debated, anachronistic, wholly impractical, decaying yet treasured, lauded and always loved medina – represents everything that made Morocco. For the casual visitor, Fez is mysterious, exotic and, for all the warmth of the people, a hidden place. Once the poets praised it for the beauty of its mosques, the quality of its water and the palms that lined the banks of the sweet river flowing through its centre.

But where rulers once fought for it and craftsmen gave their lives to adorn it, today politicians and historians fight to preserve this chipped and battered jewel of North Africa. In places the river now runs fetid and the palaces are falling down, but the world watches to see if it, along with Venice, can survive the ravages of an industrial world.

PRECEDING PAGES: night falls over Fez. **LEFT:** Fez el Bali, with the Kairouyine Mosque in the foreground. **BELOW:** visiting the tomb of the city's founder, Moulay Idriss II.

Motorbike escort

There's no need to look for Fez. If you arrive by car, you'll be flanked at the first traffic-lights by motor-biked guides offering to lead you into the city for a few dirhams. The route to the New Town, where the majority of hotels are, or to Old Fez (Fez el Bali and Fez el Jdid) is clearly marked, but it's a question of keeping your nerve. The boys will drop back quickly if you look as though you know what you want and where you're going. They watch carefully the movements of newcomers; after a few days the hustle-patter will die down.

If you are staying in the New Town (most hotels are here), it is easy to find your way around. Built by the French after World War I on a simple grid system, it doesn't have the charm of Rabat (or even Casablanca), where the French incorporated their design into the Moroccan structure. The streets here are plain and wide, with lots of cafés, restaurants, banks and shops, but not much atmosphere and not even a very exciting nightlife.

Marshall Lyautey declared Fez el Bali and Fez el Jdid, which make up the medina, a historic monument

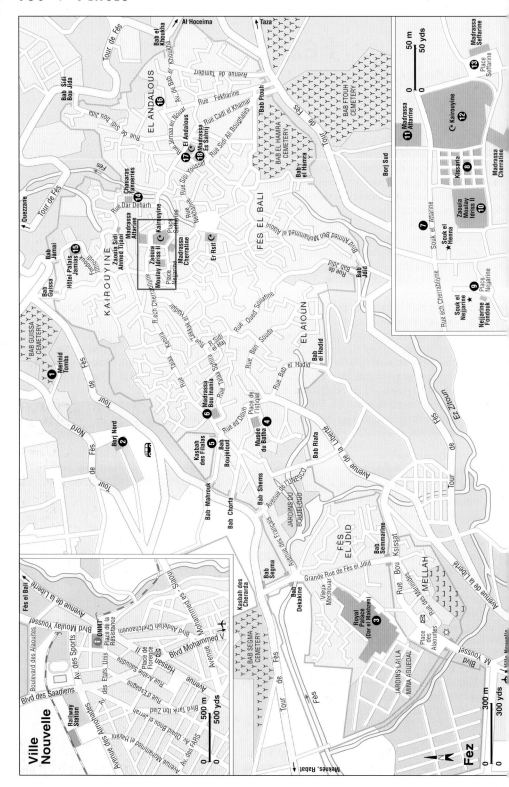

Fez

Ville Nouvelle

and slapped a preservation order on it. New Fez was built as the industrial and colonial centre. The administrative buildings are here and so are most of the hotels. Transport between the new and old town is frequent and easily available (buses and taxis leave from the main squares).

For an overview

The best way to get your bearings and a feeling of the size and complexity of the Old City is to take the route **Tour de Fes**. It circumvents the city walls, taking you first to the west of the palace and up to the **Merinid Tombs ❶** on the hillside. There is some mystery attached to the tombs, mausoleums of the last Merinid sultans; it is not known exactly who is there. Described in the chronicles as beautiful white marble with vividly coloured epitaphs, they are now a crumbling ruin, more a landmark than of any particular architectural interest. If the King is in residence, the tombs are guarded and you cannot clamber among them, but you are still allowed on the hillside.

The view is sensational. Once you are in the Old City, there is seldom an opportunity to see the overall structure and dimensions of the mosques and *madrassas* to such advantage. From here you can appreciate the layout of the town and the scale of its finer buildings. The view is best at dawn and dusk; then the light is magical.

At the foot of the hillside Fez el Bali stretches out on both sides of the river. The Kairouyine quarter on the west bank of the Oued Fes dates from about 825 when over 2,000 Arab families from Kairouan in Tunisia came here as refugees. The Andalous quarter on the east bank had been established a few years earlier, when 8,000 Arab families settled here, expelled from Andalusia by the Christians. With them came skills and learning which were to make Fez an outstanding centre of culture and craftsmanship.

As Arab rule in Spain drew to its end, further influxes of refugees from Cordoba, Seville and Granada arrived. They introduced the mosques, stucco, mosaics and other decorative arts and a variety of trades that are still central to the medina's economic survival. The strategic division between the two quarters was used by warring factions through the centuries until Youssef ben Tashfine of the Almoravide dynasty took control in the 11th century. Although Marrakesh was his capital, he did great things for Fez. He began by demolishing the wall dividing the two quarters and building a bridge across the river; this helped, but even today you are aware of the distinction between the two.

Mosques were built in each quarter and, seen from above, the quarters appear to form a kind of amphitheatre around the Kairouyine Mosque (Fez's most important building), the green tiles marking out its total area. To the right of the Kairouyine as you look down on the city, a thin minaret marks the other great religious monument of Fez, the Zaouia of Moulay Idriss II. The Andalous Mosque, a similar focal point, is on the east bank.

To the right of the two minarets you can see the vast area of royal palace and grounds, with Fez el Jdid

If you like your romance dark, Fez is probably the most romantic city on earth. It might have been dreamed up by Edgar Allan Poe – almost sinister in its secretiveness, a twisted city, warped and closed

— JOHN GUNTHER
Inside Africa, 1955

BELOW: the streets are too narrow for delivery vans.

Map on page 186

TIP

For one of the best
dusk- or night-time
views of Fez, take a
taxi to Hotel les
Merenides, near Borj
Nord, for a drink on its
pleasant terrace.

(Fez the New) beside it. Built by the Merinids in the 13th century, Fez el Jdid primarily provided a superior royal residence for the sultan and those connected with the palace, the administration and the army. The *mellah* is at the east end. With the emphasis on grandeur and open space, Fez el Jdid's layout is very different from Fez el Bali.

The two parts of the Old City are linked by the Avenue des Français, which borders the peaceful and attractive Jardins du Boujeloud (Boujeloud Gardens) on one side. The walls between the two were joined at the end of the 19th century and some of the buildings around this area date from that time.

This is probably the clearest view you will get of the layout of the city. Once down in the medina there are no vistas and it's only by design that you can get a glimpse of a minaret or a roof top. Most of the *madrassas* have good views from their roofs, if you are able to reach them. The carpet emporiums frequently use their roof-top views as bait to entice tourists.

Behind the Merinid tombs is the five-star Hotel les Merenides, an ugly but brilliantly positioned hotel, not surprisingly a matter of contention when planned. The hotel suffered extensive fire damage when it was attacked during riots in 1991, but has since been restored. The **Borj Nord** ❷, a fortress dating from Saadian times is just below the hotel and houses a collection of arms. Its opening times are erratic, so unless you are particularly interested in weaponry it is probably not worth a visit. However, if you are up here, and it is open, why not? Again there are superb views.

On the opposite hillside the **Borj Sud** stands sentinel amid olive trees and gravestones; there are plans to build additional housing around this area. Many of the hillsides surrounding Fez are dotted with white tombstones – the ceme-

BELOW:
the Merinid tombs.

teries have to be outside the medina as there is no room for graves inside the city. The Tour de Fes takes you on from the tombs and the Borj Nord past the Bab Guissa to the Borj Sud and then sweeps back towards the New Town, leaving Fez el Jdid on its right.

Map on page 186

A look at Fez el Jdid

Despite its name, **Fez el Jdid** (New Fez) was planned by the Merinids during the 13th century to incorporate an impressive royal palace and gardens (entry to both now prohibited) and as the administrative centre of Fez. The role of this part of the city diminished when the governmental function was moved to Rabat by the French. At about this time it became known as the red-light district of Fez and now remains a slightly melancholy area with the almost deserted *mellah* (Jewish quarter) tacked on to the southeastern corner. The **Royal Palace ❸** entrance, however, on Place des Alaouites, is impressive, with huge brass doors surrounded by bands of plasterwork, *zellige* and calligraphy. The grounds, said to cover 40 hectares (100 acres), are enclosed by high walls.

Detail on the mighty bronze door of the Royal Palace.

The *mellah* was originally sited by the Bab Guissa. When Fez el Jdid was built the Jews were ordered to move to their new quarter near the sultan's palace. Many Jews who had interests in the medina preferred to become Muslims and thus stay in Fez el Bali. Those who did move were promised protection in consideration of supplementary taxes.

This ghetto was given the name *mellah*, which means "salt" in Arabic, because it was the Jews' task to drain and salt the heads of decapitated rebels before they were impaled on the gates of the town. The Jews' position has always been ambiguous and, although ostensibly under the sultan's protection,

LEFT: the Place des Alaouites.
BELOW: entrance to the Palace.

their freedom before the protectorates was limited. No Jew was allowed to wear shoes or ride outside the *mellah*, for instance, and further restrictions were placed on their travel elsewhere.

Very few Jewish families remain; most left for France, with a few setting up home in Casablanca. What remains are their tall, very un-Arab buildings retaining a certain dignity even in their fast-decaying form. There is a rather run-down souk mainly of clothes and household item, audio cassettes, T-shirts and other cheap, generally low-quality Western goods. One of the oddities of this area – on the edge of the *mellah*, opposite Place des Alaouites – is the Hebrew cemetery (7am–sunset, closed Sat). Rows of pristine white gravestones very close together cluster on the slope of the hill stretching down towards the river.

From the *mellah*, Bab Semmarine, which separated the Jewish and Muslim quarters, leads to the **Grand Rue de Fez el Jdid**, lined with souks selling vegetables, textiles and household items. Though the street lacks the cohesion and mystery of Fez el Bali it is a lively souk, particularly from around 5pm, when the cool of evening releases a surge of shoppers on to the streets.

At the end of the street is the Petit Mechouar, enclosed by high crenellated walls and bordered by the tradesmen's entrance to the palace. A right turn here leads to Avenue des Français running alongside the Jardins du Boujeloud, a shadowy venue for romantic trysts. This eventually leads to Bab Boujeloud, one of the main gateways to Fez el Bali.

Museum first

The area between Fez el Jdid and Fez el Bali, joined in the late 19th century by Moulay el Hassan, contains the Dar Batha Palace. Formerly part of the link

The sign for the Hebrew Cemetery on the edge of the mellah.

BELOW: image maker.

between the two, with gates at both ends, it now houses the excellent **Musée du Batha** ❹ (8.30am–noon and 2–6pm, closed Tues; admission charge). Inside, rooms open off a central garden, each one dedicated to a particular Moroccan craft and its application in everyday life. The guide (small tip) will shed light on the purpose of the various articles on display, from the measure for determining the optimum level of alms to the bristle necklace placed around the necks of male calves so that their mothers, painfully pricked when their young came to suckle, would kick them away, forcing them to graze on the herbs which made their meat so sweet. The museum offers many interesting examples of stucco work and carving – useful to see before embarking on the tour of the *madrassas* and mosques because they give a useful insight into developing techniques.

A guide to guides

Finding your way around **Fez el Bali** is a challenge. It is a good idea to hire a guide; he can take you to all the main sights, which can serve as landmarks on your own excursions later. Fix a price before you start. This is important, although at the end he will disarmingly suggest you pay what you think he's worth. Don't get drawn into that – your evaluation and his may radically differ and things can then get complicated and even unpleasant. There are fixed rates for official guides, so work on that basis, adding extra for things like qualifications and language skills. You can arrange an official guide through your hotel, an unofficial guide will find you. Students are many, and in some cases are much more interesting company than a bored official guide.

The close relationship between the people and their city means that everybody knows somebody with something to sell – and a sale helps the community. Part

Map on page 186

According to a survey by the World Bank, 48 percent of households in Fez el Jdid live below the locally defined poverty line. This compares to 34 percent in Fez el Bali.

BELOW: houses in Fez el Jdid.

The Future of the Medina

Fez embodies all the problems facing medinas in the modern world. For centuries it was the political and cultural capital of Morocco. and is still seen as the centre of intellectual endeavour. But its 1,000-year-old medina relies upon the interdependence of industries and social structures for its survival and this is gravely threatened. Contrary to some visitors' impressions, it doesn't exist as a museum, and its souks do not stock merely tourist trinkets; the *Fassis* rely on their industries, and their leather goods, silverware and cedarwork are sold throughout the country – to Moroccans. Over 200,000 people live and work in the medina and it's clear to anyone wandering through the packed souks that tourists are irrelevant to most of the inhabitants.

Old methods are still used by the dyers, tanners and the brass and silver craftsmen.

There isn't room in the city to introduce new technology, open new factories and streamline production, even if they were wanted. So far only some of the potteries have been moved out of the centre to hillsides close by, where new technology could be introduced. But such progress is beset by problems: break a part of the vast structure of the medina and it all might crumble.

Overcrowding is the main cause of Fez's ills. Over the past 50 years people have been moving into the town from the countryside to find work and fulfil dreams of prosperity, putting Fez under severe strain. Certain public infrastructures, such as water supplies and 13th-century sewage systems, are at breaking point. There is no new housing available and shanty towns have spawned on the hillsides near Fez. The different quarters of the city, once so well defined, are gradually losing their individual functions.

Sadly, demographic, social and economic constraints have had detrimental effects on the city's architecture. Fez's ancient mosques, *madrassas*, palaces, *fondouks* and houses – only a fraction of which the tourist sees – are crumbling. Toxic waste is being poured into the rivers and sewers; the small but numerous machines used by the craftsmen produce damaging vibrations. Once-magnificent mansions are being split up into tiny flats to accommodate the ever increasing number of rural migrants.

In 1980 UNESCO launched an appeal and introduced an ambitious programme of restoration. Now working in partnership with the World Bank, it has set up ADER-FES (Agence Pour la Dédensification et la Rehabilitation de la Médina de Fés). Their task is enormous and would seem impossible, but work is underway. The objective is to keep the medina as a working structure – reinforcing its foundations both physically and administratively. The project has extended to include Fez el Jdid as well as Fez el Bali.

To survive, the medina has to take account of progress. The task of "up-dating" may be impossible, but the most urgent objective is to lighten the pressure within the city walls and allow the medina to breathe. ❏

LEFT: a broom salesman goes from door to door, selling his wares.

Map
on page
186

of your tour will inevitably include a visit to a carpet emporium or co-operative. If you have no desire to buy and are short of time, try and make this clear at the outset, although you won't be believed. If you *do* find yourself being sucked into the sales patter, retreat politely as soon as you can; the longer you're there the more difficult it becomes.

If you are guideless and taking your chance alone in the medina, remember that any young lad will guide you out (for a few dirhams) should you get lost. Contrary to some first impressions, Fez is not a frightening city.

A tour of Fez el Bali

One of the main entrances to the medina is through the **Bab Boujeloud ⑤** to the east of the palace area. Cars are not allowed in the medina but parking is easy around the gates, which are also ringed by simple cafés and restaurants. Expect to pay a small sum for a "*gardien* of the car", who will appear as you draw up. Taxis can be taken from Place Baghadi just by the gate, though all long-distance buses, which at one time dropped passengers here, now depart from a well equipped bus station up near Borj Nord. As dusk falls this area is thronging with people. A dusty flea-market stretches out across the waste ground just outside the city walls.

The Bab Boujeloud, a brace of keyhole arches built in 1919, is one of the most recent *babs* but is traditionally tiled and decorated: blue and gold outside, reputedly to represent the city of Fez, and green and gold inside to represent Islam. Just inside the gate the square splits into the two main streets, **Talaa Kebira** (Grand Tala), the upper one on the left (inside the gate make a left turn followed immediately by a right), and the much less interesting **Talaa Sghira**,

BELOW: Bab Boujeloud. The blue *faience* on the exterior of the gate is said to represent Fez, while the green on the inside represents Islam.

Sounds and smells stimulate and soothe in turn in Fez's medina. One of the nicest aromas is of fresh mint, large bundles of which are sold on every street corner.

BELOW: the Attarine Madrassa.

running parallel straight ahead. Much quieter than Talaa Kebira, Talaa Sghira can provide a speedy return route.

Just off the square, on the upper reaches of Talaa Kebira, is one of the most famous sights in Fez, the **Madrassa Bou Inania** ❻ (8am–6pm; closed Fri am; being restored but still open to visitors), an exuberant example of a Merinid monument. *Madrassas* used to play an important role in Morocco. Essentially urban, these buildings were used as lodging houses for students who were strangers to the town; the idea was that the isolation would help them concentrate on their religious studies. *Madrassas* were supported by endowments from the sultans and revenue from local inhabitants. For convenience, they were built close to the mosque where the students went for their lessons. Similar in structure to mosques and private houses, they centre on a courtyard and are highly decorated with *zellige* (mosaic tiling), lacy stucco and cedar carvings. Students often spent more than 10 years at university, so places to live were at a premium.

According to local sources – almost certainly unreliable in view of the Moroccans' love of cautionary tales – the origins of the Madrassa Bou Inania are rooted in a rich sub-soil of sex and scandal. The Sultan Bou Inan was renowned for his high living and extensive harem, but there came a point in his dissolute life when, having falling deeply in love with a concubine, he vowed to atone. He made his lover his wife and as a public display of his new-found piety he commissioned the Madrassa Bou Inania to be built on the site of public latrines inside Bab Boujeloud.

But unfortunately the object of his love was a former prostitute-dancer and his viziers, though impressed by the new *madrassa*, were outraged by the sudden elevation of a whore. The clever sultan took them to the newly completed build-

Map on page 186

ing, "Did you not used to piss where now you pray?" he asked, inviting them to see the parallel. From that moment the sultan's new wife was considered a pillar of respectability.

Abou Inan wanted his *madrassa* to rival the Kairouyine Mosque and it did become one of the most important religious buildings in the city. He failed in his aim to have the call to prayer transferred here from the Kairouyine, but it was granted the status of Grand Mosque, unheard of for a *madrassa* in Morocco, and Friday prayers are still heard here (the only time when the *madrassa* is closed).

The building follows the usual layout, but the quality and intricacy of the decoration are outstanding. The courtyard facade is decorated with carved stucco, above which majestic cedarwood arches support a frieze and corbelled porch. The examples of cedarwood carving, stucco work, Kufic script writing and *zellige* work are outstanding. It is one of Morocco's few buildings in religious use that can be entered by non-Muslims.

Opposite the Bou Inania is a remarkable water-clock. Thirteen wooden blocks balancing 13 brass bowls (only seven original bowls remain) protrude beneath 13 windows. Sultan Abou Inan erected it opposite the *madrassa* to ring out the hour of prayer, hoping its originality would bring further fame to his beloved *madrassa*. Unfortunately, its 14th-century mechanics have defeated modern horologists and the clock has been silent for over five centuries. According to legend, a curse was put on the clock when a passing Jewess was so alarmed by its chime that she miscarried her child. In 1990, following the discovery of documents detailing the working of the clock, a programme of restoration was begun. However, the work is proving more complex than expected and the clock is undergoing yet more investigations.

As Talaa Kebira starts to go downhill a few hundred metres past Madrassa Bou Inania, look out on the right for the one-time home (marked by a plaque) of Ibn Khaldoun, a famous 14th-century historian from Tunis who wrote a seminal history of the Arabs.

BELOW: facade of the Nejjarine Fountain *(see page 198)*, one of the finest in Fez.

WATER, WATER EVERYWHERE

Islam blossomed in dusty, dry lands where trees, flowers and water were (and are) especially treasured. Great minds were therefore engaged in solving problems of irrigation, and in cities water was introduced as much as possible, in splashing fountains and pools.

The fact that Fez has so many fountains is thanks to the vision of the Almoravide sultan Youssef Ben Tashfine, who re-routed the river to achieve his aim. Engineers were instructed to create an elaborate system of channels and by the late 11th century every mosque, *madrassa, fondouk*, street fountain and public bath, as well as most of the richer households, had water. The system included a successful method of flushing the drains.

The sound and sight of Fez's many drinking fountains refresh the senses. They are notable for their elaborate *zellige* settings. Though the Nejjarine fountain is the most magnificent example, many others are splendidly decorated. Wear, tear and pollution have dulled their brilliance, and in some cases destroyed the pipes feeding the fountains, but the Arab Fund of Economic Development is supporting the restoration of some 42 of Fez's historic drinking fountains and they are gradually being restored to their former glory.

Talaa Kebira

The Talaa Kebira leads eventually to the Kairouyine Mosque and the Zaouia of Moulay Idriss *(see page 187)*, but along the way are plenty of interesting souks. Smells and sounds are enthralling; if you walked through blindfold, despite a lack of air and draughts, the pungent aromas of mint, spices, wood and leather would act as guides. The overall impression of the medina is chaotic but in fact its structure is distinct. Each quarter has its own mosque, *madrassa, foundouk,* Koranic school, water fountain, *hammam* and bakery, where everyone in the quarter brings their own dough to be baked in the central ovens (marks of identification help avoid confusion). Daily prayers are taken in the mosque of the quarter, the Grand mosques being used on Fridays, when people flock from all areas for this special prayer day.

Daily life continues. Shouts of *"Balek! Balek!"* ("Get out of the way") precede the long-suffering tread of the mules carrying huge, often precariously balanced burdens, forcing the flowing crowd to pin themselves against the walls. If Westerners weren't so obvious by their dress, they would certainly still be identified by their sudden movements interrupting the otherwise smooth flow of the *Fassi* crowd. The *Fassis* are so familiar with the sounds that they duck and weave past obstructions, keeping on the move, but there is the occasional impossible load that brings even the *Fassi* to a standstill. It perhaps isn't surprising that these tend to be mechanical trucks going about the restoration programme rather than the malleable beasts of burden.

Walking down the street, you come across large buildings now mainly used as warehouses by traders in the souk; these are the *fondouks*, another integral part of the medina, created at about the same time as the *madrassa,* as hotels for

A common sight in the medina is of children making the braid that is used to trim kaftans. They secure the ends of the thread to the corners of buildings and then painstakingly weave the different strands.

BELOW: a *bakal,* a corner grocer.

traders and doubling up as stables. There were over 200 *fondouks* in Fez el Bali; many survive and it is remarkable to see such highly decorated buildings being used as warehouses. They have the familiar structure of a courtyard with galleried sleeping area. In particular, look out, on the left-hand side of the street and through a vine covered arch opposite a white mosque with a stumpy minaret, for an old *fondouk* occupied by the butter and honey market (announced by the strong smell of *smen* – the aged butter used in the best *couscous*). Further down, where the narrowing *talaa* takes cover under a shady roof of rushes watch out for another turning on the left-hand side, this time leading to an old *fondouk* in which workers sit paring the fat from sheepskins.

Nearing the end of Talaa Kebira, you might get a whiff of the strong smell from the leatherworkers' *fondouk*, which stores the drying skins from the slaughterhouse before they're sent to the dyers. Soon the road becomes **Rue ech Cherrabliyne** (slipper-makers' street), and you will see ahead the green and yellow minaret of the late 18th-century Cherabliyine Mosque framed by the bulging upper storeys of the buildings.

Babouches, the soft leather slippers, are sold here. With their backs turned down so that they are easy to slip on and off on entering a home or mosque, they come in several colours, with yellow popular for everyday and white for Fridays and other holy days (when white is often worn from head to foot). Women's *babouches*, in velvet, silk and nylon, as well as leather, come in a huge range of colours, often embroidered with gold thread.

The street bends down towards the Kairouyine Mosque. This area is the commercial and formal centre of the medina. Islam strongly approves of trade. Straight ahead, the **Souk el Attarine** ❼ (the perfume and spice-sellers' souk),

Kaftans in the souk. Underneath their sober jellabahs, Moroccan women love bright colours.

BELOW: a quiet corner.

where modern toiletries are found side by side with traditional Arab perfumes such as musk and amber, as well as baskets of spices. Just off the souk, to the right is **Souk el Henna**, a pretty square shaded by an old fig tree. Here baskets of green henna leaves, camomile, antimony (from which kohl is derived), pumice, red salves for the lips and cheeks and a tar-like black soap are some of the more orthodox items on offer. Also available are aphrodisiacs and charms to ward off the evil eye.

Also off Souk el Attarine is the **Kissaria ❽**, a covered market selling the luxury items traditionally sold in the vicinity of the Great Mosque – embroidery, silks and brocades, as well as imported goods. The fire that wiped out the Kissaria in 1954 leaves it rather characterless in structure with modern roofing, but the dazzling display of goods quickly distracts the eye.

Carpenters and saints

Below Souk el Attarine is the *horm*, a sacred area around the Shrine of Moulay Idriss II, the effective founder of Fez. The easiest way to find it is to return to the start of Souk el Attarine (with its entrance behind you) and turn left. The shrine is a little way along on the left, but before seeing that take the second turning on the right, to reach **Place Nejjarine ❾** (carpenters' souk), heavy with the scent of worked cedar and thuya wood. Here craftsmen crouch over finely carved tables, bed heads, chairs and every kind of wooden creation. Most Moroccan furniture seen in hotels and private houses is wooden and made with meticulous care in the medinas. Place Nejjarine is one of the oldest in Fez, and the *fondouk* at the corner of the square dates from the late 17th century. The **Nejjarine Fountain**, the focal point of the square, is an outstanding example of *zellige* decoration and

As well as adding lustre to hair, henna is used to decorate women's hands and feet, particularly for special occasions such as festivals and weddings. The henna leaves are boiled to produce a green paste that is piped onto the hands in elaborate designs and fixed with lemon juice. When dry the crusty paste is removed, leaving lace-like orange patterns.

BELOW: the green-tiled roofs of the Kairouyine Mosque.

stands almost like a shrine to water. The large, beautifully painted octagonal trays being made here serve a variety of festive occasions – to carry boys undergoing circumcision, or to carry a bridegroom's gifts for his bride; the larger kind may even carry the bride or bridegroom. Well worth visiting is the three-storey **Nejjarine Fondouk**, which has been beautifully restored and now serves as a museum (10am–7pm) devoted to wood-working techniques and tools. A roof-top café offers good views over the roofs of the Kairouyine Mosque.

Map on page 186

The **Zaouia of Moulay Idriss II ⑩** is introduced by bright stalls selling candles, incense, padded baskets for gifts and nougat, dates and nuts, the usual signs in Morocco that one is approaching a shrine. A wooden bar at donkey-neck height denotes the area; until the French protectorate this barred not only mules and donkeys but also Jews and Christians. It also marked a refuge for Muslims, who could not be arrested in this area. Today it is a popular spot for beggars hoping to tap pilgrims on their way to devotions. The tomb was built by the Idrissids in the 9th century but was allowed to fall into decay by ensuing dynasties until it was rebuilt in the 13th century by the Merinids. The Wattasids rediscovered the tomb and from this period it became the revered shrine it is now. A glimpse through the doorway reveals a colourful and mystical scene – the smell of incense and the flickering lights of candles surround prostrate figures. In September the shrine is the focus of a huge *moussem*.

Minaret of the Kairouyine Mosque, trimmed with green tiles, the traditional finish to important mosques and zaouias.

The street follows the wall of the *zaouia* (look out for a brass slot inviting alms in the wall), and through another very richly decorated doorway you can see the room of prayer. This contains innumerable chandeliers and, around the tomb, a rather surprising collection of clocks, considered an upmarket offering in the 19th century. If you continue to follow the walls of the *zaouia* (bearing in mind that shops cleave to its walls, making it difficult to identify) you will come out on the other side of the Kissaria *(see page 198).* Passing through here, you emerge back on the Rue Attarine, between the Madrassa Attarine (on the left) and the principal entrance to the Great Mosque of Kairouyine *(see below).* The **Madrassa Attarine ⑪** (9am–1pm and 3–6.30pm), one of several *madrassas* around the Great Mosque, was built by Sultan Abou Said from 1322 to 1325 and is similar in design to the later Bou Inania *(see page 194)*; no doubt many of the same master craftsmen worked on its interior. As the *madrassa* is no longer in religious use, you can enter the prayer hall. A good view of the courtyard of the Kairouyine Mosque is available from the *madrassa*'s roof (tip to gain access).

BELOW: the Nejjarine Fountain.

The Great Mosque

All roads in the medina lead to the **Kairouyine Mosque ⑫** (closed to non-Muslims) which serves as the Great Mosque of Fez el Bali. Rivalled in size only by the Hassan II Mosque in Casablanca, it covers 16,000 sq. metres (4 acres) and can accommodate more than 20,000 people. It was founded in 859 by Lalla Fatima al-Fihrya, a pious woman from Kairouan, Tunisia, one among the wave of immigrants from Kairouan. The mosque, then merely a small prayer hall, was built in memory of her father.

In Place Seffarine cooking utensils come in all shapes and sizes, but mostly very large to cater for extended families and wedding parties.

BELOW:

the raw materials – usually goat or calf skin or sometimes horse hide.

Each of Morocco's sultans added to the mosque and changed it. The Merinids' alterations in the 13th century cast it in its present mould. Green tiled roofs cover 16 naves and the tiled courtyards have two end pavilions, added by the Saadians, and a beautiful 16th-century fountain reminiscent of the Court of Lions of the Alhambra Palace in Granada. It is jealously guarded from the eyes of non-Muslims but you can probably snatch glimpses of the interior from one of its 14 doorways and views into the courtyard can be obtained from the roof of the Madrassa Attarine *(see page 199)*.

The sanctuary interior is austere, with horseshoe arches over some 270 columns. It was one of the first universities in the Western world and was considered a great seat of learning; its reputation attracted over 8,000 students in the 14th century, and it even boasted a future pope, Sylvester II (pope 999–1003), among its students. A noted mathematician before becoming pope, Sylvester II introduced the West to Arab mathematical concepts, including the zero.

The **Kairouyine Library**, on the far side of the mosque, is also thought to have been built in the 9th century. Closed to the public, it contains one of the largest collections of Islamic literature in the world.

Below the library is **Place Seffarine** ⓭ (devoted to metalworkers), an enchanting square shaded by trees. Huge cauldrons are stacked in every available space, donkeys are loaded up, work is in progress – all accompanied by a cacophany of hammering. The same skills were used on the redecoration of the great doors to the King's palace, visible across Place des Alaouites as you approach Fez el Jdid from the New Town *(see page 185)*. Place Seffarine is one of the prettiest squares in the medina, and if you can gain access to the **Madrassa Seffarine** close by, climb up to its roof for a view of the overall scene.

A dyeing trade

From here it is an easy walk to the tanneries on the Oued Fez. Take the north exit from Place Seffarine (the exit next to the one from which you entered the square), passing a small shop selling items carved out of animal horn, a by-product of the leather industry. After a few minutes walk, and taking the left route when you reach a T-junction, you reach **Chouaras Tanneries** , the largest of the three tanneries in Fez, accessed through a gap on the right-hand side of the street. Your nose will inform you of your arrival; this time the smell is pretty unpleasant – of fresh animal hides steeped in urine to make them supple. Sprigs of mint are proffered as pomanders.

Map on page 186

The area has hardly changed since medieval times. The position of stone vats, one against the other, make shifting the skins in and out of the different dyes an athletic achievement. Scantily-clad men crouch and balance over vats dipping the hides; roofs around are thick with drying skins. The tanneries are run as a co-operative, with each foreman responsible for his own workforce and tools. Jobs, which are strenuous and smelly but well paid, are practically hereditary. Visitors are trooped through the walkways and helped up small uneven steps to vantage points for photographs. Terrible bottlenecks of mint-sniffing visitors move hesitantly along the walls and roof tops.

Finished leather goods. At one time, whole libraries were sent to Morocco to be morocco bound and tooled with gold.

From here you can continue north to Bab Guissa and the Palais Jamai Hotel, for lunch or tea on the terrace by its pool or backtrack to Place Seffarine and cross over to the Andalous Quarter and Bab Ftouh *(see page 202)*, from where buses head back to the New Town. The route to the Palais Jamai is unremarkable, save for passing the elaborate stucco entrance of the **Zaouia of Sidi Ahmed Tijani**, the inspirer of a Sufi sect important in North and West Africa. Ahmed Tijani (1737–81) began his journey to sainthood at the age of seven, by which time he had memorised the Koran.

BELOW: dyeing in the tanneries.

The **Palais Jamai Hotel**  beside **Bab Guissa** was built at the end of the 19th century as a palace by the Ulad Jamai brothers, viziers of Sultan Moulay Hassan. The brothers eventually fell foul of the political machinations of the day and when Moulay Abd el Aziz succeeded to the throne in 1894 they were sent in fetters to Tetouan. Walter Harris, correspondent of the London *Times*, related their fate in his book *Morocco That Was*: "In the course of time – and how long those ten years must have been – Haj Amaati died. The Governor of Tetouan was afraid to bury the body, lest he should be accused of having allowed his prisoner to escape. He wrote to Court for instructions. It was summer, and even the dungeon was hot. The answer did not come for eleven days, and all that time Si Mohammed Soreir remained chained to his brother's corpse."

The Palais Jamai's position on the edge of the medina, enclosed in a walled garden of palm trees and roses lulled by the sound of water and birdsong, is probably the best in Fez. The sound of the 5am call to prayer – "*Allah Akbar*" – echoing across the medina from the Kairouyine Mosque, joined by a chorus of *muezzins* from neighbouring mosques, is in itself a good reason to stay within earshot of the medina – it

Map on page 186

is a voice of Morocco and should be heard at least once during your stay. If you do decide to stay in the Palais Jamai, it is well worth paying the extra cost of a room with a medina view (the back of the hotel overlooks the Merinid Tombs).

The Andalous quarter

Back at Place Seffarine, take the opposite direction from the tanneries and cross the bridge to the east bank of the river to explore the **Andalous Quarter ⑯**. This area, named after the Arab refugees from Spain who settled here in 818, is less intense than the Kairouyine Quarter, both in its structure and number of inhabitants, but its long neglected ancient monuments are at last beginning to receive the restoration they so richly deserve. The most noted of these is the **Andalous Mosque ⑰**, founded shortly after the Kairouyine Mosque in the 9th century and embellished by the Almohads at the beginning of the 13th century. It is the main sanctuary on the east bank, with a great north gate decorated with *zellige* and surmounted by a magnificent cedar porch. Of the two *madrassas* in this quarter, the **Es Sahrij ⑱** (daily 9am–1pm and 3–6.30pm) is early 14th-century and has an ablutions pool in the centre of the courtyard. Its *zellige* decorations are some of the oldest in the country and it has an impressive ancient wood *minbar* (pulpit).

Walking up the hill towards the **Bab Ftouh**, which marks the eastern limits of the medina, you pass the potters quarter. Fez pottery, with its distinctive blue design, is sold all over Morocco and its craftsmen are much admired; you will find affordable examples in the Souk el Henna, off Souk el Attarine *(see page 197)*. From Bab Ftouh, buses and taxis leave for the New Town via the ring road.

Across from Bab Ftouh is the main **cemetery**, which on Fridays becomes as busy as a railway station, as families come to sprinkle water on the graves, leave sprigs of myrtle and picnic beside the tombs of their dead loved ones. Non-Muslims are not welcome.

BELOW: the doors of the Palais Jamai.
RIGHT: the egg-box design of the tanneries.

The New Town and beyond

If you are travelling by rail, you will arrive in the New Town (the station is a short walk west off Boulevard Moulay Youssef). But even if you are driving, you may well want to base yourself here (unless you intend staying in the Hotel Palais Jamai, *see page 201*); it has the best choice of hotels, good cafés and restaurants and is livelier than the medina at night.

Exit routes west of the New Town head through fertile landscapes to Sidi Kacem or Meknes *(see page 215)*. A few kilometres in the other direction are the hot springs and cool sources of **Sidi Harazem**, where the ubiquitous mineral water is bottled. Site of the shrine of Sidi Harazem, a Sufi mystic, this is also another popular pilgrimage site, and can get very crowded at weekends. Unfortunately much of what was once an attractive spot has been concreted over, making it a disappointing escape from the harsh summer heat in Fez.

Much further afield, but more rewarding, is the P24, the main route south of Fez to Marrakesh, a glorious journey through the Middle Atlas Mountains via the cedar forests of Azrou and Ifrane. ❏

MADE IN MOROCCO – ARTS AND CRAFTS

The medinas of Morocco are hives of traditional industry, where you will see exquisite examples of the country's flourishing arts and crafts

Exploring the souks of Fez and Marrakesh is like walking down the corridors of time. More is revealed the more you delve, for it is in the hidden *fondouks* and courtyards off the main drag that traditional crafts and industries thrive in ways that have barely changed since Andalusian refugees introduced them over 1,000 years ago.

Crafts are grouped according to type, with the finer crafts located close to the Great Mosque. Each craft is organised into a guild, with apprentices working under master craftsmen for several years. Only when an apprentice is deemed to have the necessary skills and mental application will the master craftsman declare him fit to work alone.

URBAN INSPIRATION

While the rural tradition is inspired by nature and animistic beliefs, the urban craft tradition takes inspiration from the Koran. Koranic verses in highly stylised script are engraved, sculpted, carved, painted and embroidered on metals, plaster, wood and textiles. Allied to this abstract art is the use of complex patterns, often in the form of *zellige* (mosaics of tiny hand-cut glazed tiles), repeated again and again to produce a meditative effect on the beholder.

▷ **ZELLIGE IN THE MAKING**
Zellige is an ancient art form. The late King Hassan II boosted its revival by establishing several special *zellige* schools.

▽ **COMPELLING EFFECT**
Beautiful *zellige work* can be seen in Morocco's *medersa*, where mesmerising *zellige* patterns reflect the power and infinity of God.

◁ **HEAVY METAL**
In the metalworkers' souk. Copper, brass and silver are turned into trays, lamps, pots and tableware, often incised or damascened.

◁ SOUK NEJJARINE
Fez's Place Nejjarine is the best place to see traditional woodworking techniques such as marquetry. Its nearby *fondouk* has been turned into a museum of woodworking

△ SPINNING A YARN
Rural weavers frequently use wool from their own sheep, which they will wash, card and spin themselves, but sometimes they will buy it from the towns.

MOROCCO'S MAGIC CARPETS

Weaving is one of Morocco's oldest and most esteemed craft traditions. The flat-woven *mergoums* of the Berbers are particularly dazzling for their striking geometric designs.

Rugs have many purposes. In the home they are laid over floors, hung on walls and slipped over couches. But they may also be used to wrap up a Berber bride on the way to her new home or to cover a funeral bier. Their symbols (snakes, crosses, tattoos, lozenges and "eyes") are believed to have magical and prophylactic powers.

One of the best sources of quality weavings is the Middle Atlas region. Midelt's carpet cooperative is a good place to make a purchase. A new initiative supported by the World Bank, called The Virtual Souk, is attempting to help women sell directly to buyers through the internet. Already successful, the experiment, which cuts out the middle men, is changing the lives of women weavers.

△ PAINTED ARABESQUES
Painted wood is popular in Morocco, and the work of top *zawaaga* (the craftsmen specialising in the art form) can be exquisite.

◁ CHIP OFF AN OLD BLOCK
Thuya wood grows in the region of Essaouira, where master carpenters turn the wood into richly coloured furniture and ornaments.

▷ MODERN APPLICATION
Modern Moroccan *zellige* is making its way into Western homes in the form of table tops, often surmounting a wrought-iron base – perfect for summer dining alfresco.

THE MEKNES REGION

Map on page 210

This region is perfect for short explorations by car. As well as the imperial city of Meknes and the Roman outpost of Volubilis, it has rolling vineyards, shrines and natural springs

Meknes, the imperial city of Sultan Moulay Ismail, is considered the third most interesting city in Morocco after Fez and Marrakesh, and so sees its fair share of foreign visitors. However, its proximity to **Fez ❶** means that it is often treated as a day's excursion from there rather than as a base in its own right, even though it has several further places of interest on its own doorstep, including the Roman city of Volubilis, and nestles in attractive countryside peppered with shrines and springs. It also has a good selection of medium-priced hotels, plus a long-established luxury hotel, the Transatlantique.

For chronological reasons it is probably best to visit Fez before Meknes, and then travel to Meknes via Moulay Idriss, the shrine of the founder of the first Islamic kingdom in northwest Africa, and nearby Volubilis, a slightly roundabout but rewarding route which, with stops, will take a full day to complete. A car is recommended, although it is possible to complete the journey in stages by bus and *grand taxi*. To follow this route, take the main P1 Meknes/Rabat road west of Fez and turn off right towards Sidi Kacem/Ouezzane after about 8km (5 miles). At the village of Nzala-des-Beni-Ammar take a sharp left to Moulay Idriss and Volubilis (signposted) along a single-track road through hills covered in olive groves. It arrives at Moulay Idriss after 10 winding kilometres (6 miles). There is a car park on the right as you enter the town.

PRECEDING PAGES: Bab el Khemis, Meknes. **LEFT:** Moulay Idriss. **BELOW:** a candle seller outside the tomb of Moulay Idriss.

Moulay Idriss

Although hundreds of tourist buses visit Volubilis, only 1km (½ mile) away, only a few stop off in **Moulay Idriss ❷**, the small town clustered around the shrine to Moulay Idriss I, whose tomb rests here. It is considered a holy town – at one time Christians were forbidden to enter – and visitors should bear this in mind. Its chief appeal for non-Muslim visitors is its picturesque setting, which can be enjoyed over a mint tea in the square below the town. There is no accommodation in Moulay Idriss itself (the nearest is the Volubilis Inn on a hill outside town).

At the end of the 8th century, Moulay Idriss el Akhbar (the elder) arrived in the village of Zerhoun. The great-grandson of the Prophet Mohammed, he had fled to Morocco to escape persecution and death. He stopped first at Volubilis, later building his town nearby, and set about converting the Berbers to the Islamic faith. He was well received by the mountain people, who recognised him as their leader, and he became the founder of the first Arab dynasty in Morocco. A year later he began founding Fez – a labour completed by Idriss II, the son of his Berber concubine Kenza.

News of his popularity and success reached his eastern caliph and an emissary was sent to poison him

in 791. His dynasty lived on through his son, born two months after his death.

Set in the spur of the hills just east of Volubilis, Moulay Idriss looks a compact, predominantly white whole, but it is really two villages; the Khiber and the Tasga quarters join together around the mosque and shrine. Although Meknes is only 25km (16 miles) away, the town is seemingly oblivious to the 21st or even 20th century. There are few concessions to Western visitors; the souks – insofar as they exist at all – sell basic wares and are in the Khiber quarter, spreading rather thinly back up the hill from the *zaouia*.

The best views of the town are from the terrace **Sidi Abdallah el Hajjam**, above the Khiber quarter. The narrow streets make up a complicated network and it's easy to climb into a dead end. There are, however, plenty of boys happy to lead you to the terrace for a few dirhams. From here the structure of the town is clear: white and grey cubes cascade down to the point where the quarters merge beside the tomb and *zaouia*, the green-tiled roofs and arched courtyards of which are clearly visible. Also look out for the **Madrassa Moulay Idriss**, whose striking cylindrical minaret (very different from the usual square minarets of the Maghreb) was inspired by minarets seen in the Arabian Gulf. It was commissioned by a pilgrim returning from Mecca in the 1930s; its green ceramic tiles are inscribed with verses from the Koran.

The shrine

BELOW: the harvest *moussem* in Moulay Idriss.

The **mausoleum** was rebuilt by Moulay Ismail, who destroyed the first structure at the end of the 18th century in order to create a more beautiful one. This was later embellished by the Sultan Moulay Abderrahmen. The main square – more of a rectangle – opens out from the holy area. It is the busiest part of the

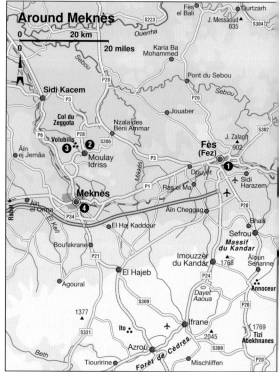

own, especially around the tiled fountain, with several pleasant cafés. Opposite the entrance to the shrine makeshift stalls sell candles and padded baskets to present offerings. Nougat, giant poles of it, like furled umbrellas in every imaginable colour, is a speciality of the town, as it is in many other places of pilgrimage in the Arab world.

Map on page 210

Annual moussem

As the most important shrine in Morocco, Moulay Idriss is the focus for a huge annual *moussem*, attracting pilgrims from all over Morocco as well as several Sufi fraternities, such as the Hamaacha and Dghoughia, once famous for their violent trance-induced rituals. The more extreme activities of these sects have been outlawed by the government, but it is rumoured that they continue in places unobserved.

The *moussem* is held after the harvest, usually beginning on the last Thursday in August. Originally a purely religious festival, it has come to include *fantasias,* singing, dancing and markets. The hillsides are covered with tents, and prayer, feasting and general rejoicing continue throughout the festival. Tourists are tolerated, but it is a purely Muslim festival and it's probably sensible to visit during the daytime rather than in the evening.

Volubilis

A wide road with a smattering of stalls leads down to the city gate, where most public transport departs and people wait for lifts. For **Volubilis** ❸ (8am–6.30pm) take the right fork as you leave town and at the next junction take the Ouezzane road. Entrance to the site is on the left after about 3km (2 miles); the sand-

TIP

If you don't have your own transport and it is too hot to walk, you will probably need to hire a taxi to take you the 3km (2 miles) between Moulay Idriss and Volubilis. Ask the driver to return at a pre-agreed time.

BELOW: ceremonial serving dishes are prepared for the *moussem.*

TIP

Enjoying a perfect rural setting some distance above the site is the modern Volubilis Inn, the only hotel in the area. The inn is comfortable, with superb views and a pool on its terrace. It is worth staying here if you can; otherwise you may like to come for lunch or a drink. Tel: (055) 544405.

BELOW: Volubilis is noted for its fine Roman villas.

coloured buildings around the entrance will be visible. Beside these is a well-positioned shady café looking across to the site, and a small, open-air museum with many pieces of inscribed stone and other fragments lying haphazardly around. Most of the important finds have been removed to the archaeological museum in Rabat.

It is frequently possible to have Volubilis to yourself, but you may be unlucky and your visit coincide with a coach party or two. The best times to visit are early morning or late afternoon.

The history of the site

Traces of a Neolithic settlement have been found in Volubilis, and also those of an important Berber village, thought to have been the capital of the Berber kingdom of Mauritania. Caligula was responsible for taking over this kingdom and from AD 45 Volubilis was subject to direct Roman rule, making it the Empire's most remote base. During this time, olive oil production and copper were the city's main assets. The profusion of oil presses on the site confirms this – one or two to a house. It benefited from local springs as well as the Fertassa stream running through the site. Most of the buildings date from the beginning of the 3rd century, when the number of inhabitants was probably around 20,000. By the end of the 3rd century the Romans had gone.

After this, change was very gradual; Volubilis maintained its Latinised structure and when the Arabs arrived in the 7th century the mixed population of Berbers, Jews and Syrians still spoke Latin. The culture and teachings of Islam took over and by 786, when Moulay Idriss I arrived, most of the inhabitants were already converted. He chose to build a new city (Moulay Idriss) nearby, and Vol-

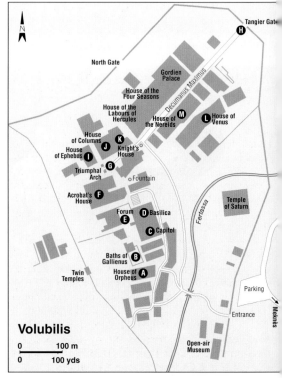

Volubilis

0 ——— 100 m
0 ——— 100 yds

ubilis began to decline. Much later, in the 18th century, Moulay Ismail dese-
crated Volubilis by removing most of its marble to adorn his growing complex
of palaces in Meknes.

The Lisbon earthquake in 1755 damaged the city and it fell into ruin. It didn't
come to the attention of the outside world again until two foreign diplomats
stumbled upon it on a tour of the area at the end of the 19th century, though it
is hard to believe it could have been ignored for so long considering the splendid Triumphal Arch, the only edifice to remain standing after the earthquake.
Excavations were begun during the French protectorate in 1915 and continue
today, funded by the Moroccan government.

A tour of the ruins

Following a well-worn path through olive groves and across the small **Fertassa River**, clamber leftwards up the hill to the start of the site, where an arrow
will direct you around to the left. Volubilis is small and easy to cover; the most
important remains are clearly labelled and the arrows describe a roughly clockwise tour. Some of the main buildings have been half restored or reconstructed.
The most remarkable finds include bronze statues (now in the Salle des Bronzes
in the Archaeological Museum in Rabat, *see page 160*) and the amazingly well-
preserved mosaics, many of which remain *in situ*. For purposes of identification,
the houses are named after the subject of the mosaic they contain.

All the houses follow the same basic structure: each had its public and private
rooms. The mosaics usually decorated the public rooms and internal courtyards;
the baths and kitchens being the private areas of the house. The first house you
come to on the clockwise tour of the site is the **House of Orpheus Ⓐ**, the
largest house in its quarter, identified by a clump of
cypresses to the left of the main paved street. It has
three mosaics: a circular mosaic of Orpheus charming
the animals with his lyre, remarkable for its detail and
colours; another of nine dolphins, believed by the
Romans to bring good luck; and a third portraying
Amphitrite in a chariot drawn by a seahorse.

From here, cut up to the new square building containing a reconstructed olive press, one of several that
have been found on the site. Next to it are the 3rd-
century **Baths of Gallienus Ⓑ**, originally the most
lavish public baths in the city, as their proximity to
Volubilis's main civic buildings – the Capitol, Basilica and Forum – required. The public baths provided
a meeting place to chat, gossip, do business, exercise,
eat and drink, but grand houses also had their own
elaborate heating systems providing hot water and
steam for baths and heat.

From here, the street leads to the Forum (public
square), Capitol and Basilica, an impressive collection of administrative buildings which comprised the
centre of the city. The **Capitol Ⓒ** is distinguished by
a crop of free-standing Corinthian pillars and a flight
of 13 steps on its north side. Originally the central
area would have contained a temple fronted by four
columns and been surrounded by porticoes. An
inscription dates the temple to AD 217 and dedicates
it to the cult of Capitoline, Jove and Minerva.

Maps:
area 210
site 212

*Mosaic detail –
a Medusa head.*

BELOW: the
stones of Volubilis.

The **Basilica** ● is a larger building beside the Capitol. It isn't easy to see its structure now but it would have been divided into five aisles (note the stumpy columns) with an apse at both ends. It doubled as the law courts and commercial exchange. The **Forum** ●, which completes the administrative centre, is an open space which was used for public and political meetings. It is of modest proportions and nothing remains of the statues of dignitaries that would have adorned the surrounding buildings.

Between the Forum and the Triumphal Arch is the **Acrobat's House** ●, containing two well preserved mosaics. The main one depicts an acrobat riding his mount back-to-front and holding up his prize. Another house nearby contained the famous Bronze Dog in the archaeological museum in Rabat.

The **Triumphal Arch** ● is the centrepoint of Volubilis. It was an impressive, if non-functional, ceremonial monument. Contemporary with the Capitol, it was built by Marcus Aurelius Sebastenus in honour of Caracalla and his mother Julia Domna. It is supported on marble columns and decorated only on the east side. Records and the inscription suggest it was surmounted by a huge bronze chariot and horses. It was built to celebrate the power of the Emperor Caracalla and remains a remarkable edifice.

The main paved street, **Decumanus Maximus**, stretches up to the **Tangier Gate** ●, the only gate out of a total of eight which remains standing. Off the street are the ruins of many fine houses, the fronts of which were rented to shopkeepers, who would have sold their wares from shaded porticoes on either side. The layout is not unlike a Moroccan street today.

Exploration of the houses will reveal more splendid mosaics. The **House of Ephebus** ●, for example, boasts a Bacchus mosaic, depicting the god of wine

BELOW: the House of Orpheus.

Map on page 212

in a chariot pulled by panthers. A wonderful bronze statue of of an ephebe (young man) wearing a leafy diadem was found in this house and is now in the Salle de Bronze in the archaeological museum in Rabat *(see page 161)*. The **House of Columns ❶**, recognisable by the remains of columns guarding the entrance to the courtyard, has an ornamental basin surrounded by brilliant red geraniums. The **Knight's House ❷**, next to this, is in a poor state except for the stunning mosaic of Dionysos discovering the sleeping Ariadne, one of the loveliest sights of Volubilis.

Many of the larger houses off Decumanus Maximus contain well-preserved mosaics; but in particular don't miss the **House of Venus ❸** (marked by a single cypress tree) and the **House of Nereids ❹**, a couple of streets in. The former contains stunning mosaics of mythological scenes, including the abduction of Hylas by nymphs and one of the bathing Diana being surprised by Acteon. The House of Nereids yielded the stunning bronze heads of Cato and Juba II – also in the museum in Rabat.

The well-worn path curls round behind the Basilica and Forum, leading back to the entrance, where one can adjourn for a mint tea in the café, and examine some of the statuary in the garden.

To Meknes

To continue to Meknes from Volubilis, turn right as you leave the site, proceed back towards Moulay Idriss, but carry on along the main road instead of turning up to the town. The fast road runs through rolling fertile hills planted with vines and dotted with the white domed tombs of *marabout*. About 27km (17 miles) after leaving Volubilis the road leads into the modern

The position, atmosphere and mosaics of Volubilis combine to make the site a worthwhile stop. Geckos running up and down crumbling walls, darting into invisible holes, occasional whiffs of highly scented flowers, the clear air and the silence on the plateau all enhance the magic.

BELOW: the Triumphal Arch.

quarter of the imperial city of **Meknes** , a prosperous provincial town. Local industry and excellent farm land account for its wealth; vineyards cover nearby hills. As usual, the New Town contains the most comfortable accommodation in town (see Travel Tips) while the main areas of interest for visitors are in the medina. Following signposts for the medina, turn down Avenue Moulay Ismail and cross the river to the old city lying on the west bank. A one-way system follows the wall around to the main gate, Bab Mansour (signposted), where parking is available in the surrounding area.

Meknes has been called the "Versailles of Morocco" and there is evidence that Ismail saw himself as a Moroccan Louis XIV. Ismail recommended the Muslim faith to the French monarch and offered himself as husband to one of the French princesses – suggestions that were politely turned down.

Moulay Ismail

Meknes was the imperial capital of Moulay Ismail, an effective but ruthless sultan who ruled Morocco for 55 years (1672–1727), more or less as a united country. During that period Morocco became a significant country in the world and the sultan considered Louis XIV, his contemporary in France, a close friend.

But Moulay Ismail was renowned for his ruthless tyranny, and his love of blood is legendary. As a celebratory gift to mark the beginning of his long rule in the mid-17th century, he displayed 700 heads on the walls of Fez, thus setting the tone of what turned out to be a reign of terror.

The British diplomat John Windus, who visited Ismail's palace in 1725 and recorded his impressions in *A Journey to Mequinez*, observed how "about eight or nine [in the morning] his trembling court assemble, which consists of his great officers, and alcaydes, blacks, whites, tawnies and his favourite Jews, all barefooted; and there is bowing and whispering to this and the other eunuch, to know if the Emperor has been abroad (for if he keeps within doors there is no seeing him unless sent for), if he is in a good humour, which is well known by

BELOW: local wines.

THE WINE INDUSTRY

The low hills around Meknes are the main centre of Morocco's wine industry, though the vine-growing area stretches from Rabat/Casablanca to Fez. The industry was set up by the French, who did the same in Tunisia and Algeria, both of which also continue to produce wine, in spite of the Koran's admonishments against alcohol. North African wines are now being exported to Europe and are beginning to be found on the shelves of a few mainstream supermarkets.

Reds are generally considered better than the whites. Two of the best reds are the rich and fruity Guerrouane and Vieux Papes, though the more widely available Toulal is also palatable. Among the whites frequently found on wine lists are Oustalet and Spéciale Coquillage, both of which are quite acceptable when well-chilled, though one of the best of the lighter wines is Gris de Boulaouane, a fruity grey-rosé produced near Casablanca.

If you want to buy wine in Morocco, you need to go to an upmarket épicerie (of the kind also selling a wide range of imported goods) in the New Town of a city. Wine is not usually sold in the medinas, although the more exclusive of the medina-based restaurants will have wine-lists. Many restaurants do not serve alcohol during Ramadan.

his very looks and motions and sometimes by the colour of the habit he wears, yellow being observed to be his killing colour; from all of which they calculate whether they may hope to live twenty-four hours longer."

Even before Moulay Ismail took control, Meknes was an important city, well placed between the Middle and High Atlas mountains and the coast and the interior. Founded in the 10th century by a Berber tribe known as Meknassass, it passed through the hands of all the major dynasties, from the 11th-century Almoravides and the 12th-century Almohads to the Merinids, who built a *madrassa* here, and the Saadis. It was customary for the viziers of the Fez-based Merinid sultans to keep second residences in Meknes.

Before becoming sultan and moving the court from Fez to Meknes, Ismail had been the governor of Meknes on behalf of his father, the Alaouite Sultan er Rashid, whom he succeeded in 1672. Both as governor and sultan, Ismail's excesses were notorious. Reports vary wildly but some say he had a harem of 500 wives and concubines, and of the hundreds of children he fathered he had the girls strangled at birth and was not averse to slicing off the limbs of erring sons. To enforce his rule as sultan, he formed an army of 30,000 Sudanese soldiers – a "peace-keeping" force – who roamed the country, keeping the tribes in check.

Maps:
Area 210
City 218

A nougat-seller plies his trade outside Bab Mansour.

Grand designs

Although surrounded by fertile land and a good choice in terms of trade connections, Meknes's location on a high plateau meant it was not easy to defend, and so Moulay Ismail immediately set about building a complex defence system comprising vast fortifications, a granary and reservoir. Stone was plundered from Volubilis and from El Badi, the grand Saadian palace in

BELOW:
Bab Mansour.

Marrakesh. Some 25km (16 miles) of walls were built around Meknes. More than 25,000 unfortunate captives were brought in to execute his vision of grand palaces, walls and fortresses. At night they were herded into dark, subterranean chambers dug for their habitation. Describing Ismail's brutal treatment of his slaves, the British writer Scott O'Connor, in *Vision of Morocco*, adds: "When the slaves died they were used as building material and immured in the rising walls, their blood mixed with the cement that still holds them together in its grip."

Ismail's vision of power has left Meknes a graveyard of huge palaces and buildings, and the medina and imperial city now present rather a tragic sight, "Miles upon miles of cemented walls run their mournful course about the city" is how it was described early in the 20th century. Within these walls lie the remains of a dream of some 30 royal palaces, 20 gates, mosques, barracks, and ornamental gardens. It is magnificent and lunatic in its scale of conception, and Moulay Ismail has to be admired for his single-mindedness. He built Meknes into one of the four great imperial cities and it remained capital until his

Signposts help show the way in this vast walled city.

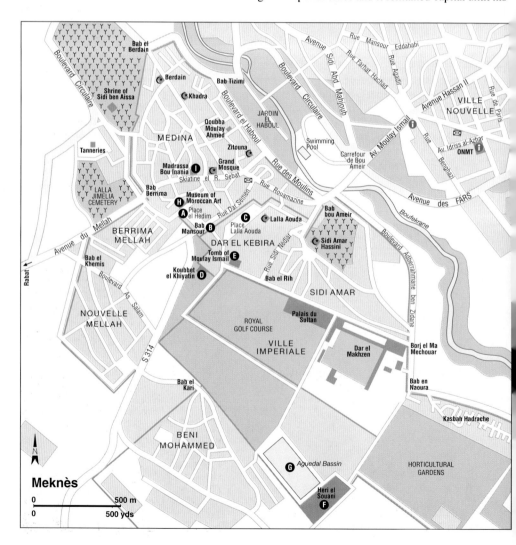

Meknès

death in 1727 when his heir removed the court to Marrakesh. The son destroyed a number of buildings as a parting shot and from then the city declined.

Map on page 218

A tour of the town

Begin a tour of Meknes on **Place el Hedim** (the sinisterly named Place of Destruction), from where the medina spreads northwest and the imperial city southeast. Now a huge square graced by shooting fountains, it used to be part of the medina but was razed to the ground by Moulay Ismail to create an approach to the main entrance of his palace via Bab Mansour. The square is almost too large to be lively. Stalls cling to the east side and benches line the west. A fairly constant stream of people cross from the medina to Bab Mansour and round towards the new town; though it no longer serves as the bus terminus (which is now outside Bab Khemis), buses forever disgorge their bulging loads into the square. Briefly the square fills, then just as quickly it empties.

The area is dominated by the imposing **Bab Mansour** , commissioned by Moulay Ismail himself but finished during his son's reign, in 1732. Brilliantly decorated with green and white tiles, it is flanked by two square bastions supported in part by marble columns plundered from Volubilis. Though remarkable for its size and symmetry, like much of Ismail's grand vision it proves overpowering and heavy.

Preparing to grill merguez, the spicy Moroccan sausages.

A tour of the Imperial city should start from here. Although a guide – picked up in Place el Hedim or around Bab Mansour – can be useful, the layout of the city is easy to grasp and it is possible to manage without one.

Proceeding through Bab Mansour, you come to **Place Lalla Aouda** , a popular gathering place for womenfolk in the late afternoon. Close by (walk to the right as you come from Bab Mansour) is a simple pavilion, the **Koubbet el Khiyatin** (9am–noon and 3–5.30pm; admission charge), thought to have been used for receiving visiting ambassadors and for bargaining over the ransoms demanded for Christian victims of Barbary Coast piracy, in which Moulay Ismail had a controlling interest. Adjacent to the pavilion is a stairway leading into subterranean chambers used to house either grain or slaves – no one is certain. The chambers, which were blocked off by the French, who also added the sky-lights, once extended 7km (4 miles) in each directions.

BELOW: a water-seller.

The gardens stretching out behind the walls have been turned into a **royal golf course**. Following the road round, through another gate, you come upon one of Meknes's chief attractions, the **Tomb of Moulay Ismail** (9am–12.30pm and 3pm–sunset; closed Fri pm; free admission). Restored by fellow Alaouite Mohammed V in the 1950s, it is one of the few shrines in Morocco that can be visited by non-Muslims. The others are the mausoleums of Mohammed V and Hassan II in Rabat and the shrine of Sidi Yahiya *(see page 140)* near Oujda. Only the courtyards are open, but you can peek through the door of the sanctuary to see the tomb. The fine tile panels are in excellent condition; simple geometric patterns contribute to the splendour. The walls and courtyard are highly patterned and the stucco work is striking.

Moulay Ismail's reputation for violence and cruelty does not seem to have diminished the reverence paid to him. It is perhaps odd that such a keen blood-letting ruler should have a shrine of such magnificence, and one that still attracts pilgrims from all over Morocco. People believe that his tomb has *baraka* (magical powers) which will rub off on believers. A doorway off the mausoleum opens on to a private cemetery (no entry) containing the tombs of people who wished to be buried alongside this famous ruler.

Heri el Souani

From the tomb it is possible to walk along a corridor-like road (follow the signs: it is a 25-minute walk): in summer you may want to flag down a *petit taxi*) to the Heri el Souani, the vast granaries and store rooms for the imperial complex. Massive walls, riddled with nesting birds, rise on both sides of the thoroughfare. Most of the palaces behind them are crumbling ruins, but a few have been restored for military or educational purposes; you can catch glimpses of these through breaches in the walls.

The **Dar el Kebira**, Moulay Ismail's main palace complex, was destroyed by his son and remains a sad ruin. The **Dar el Makhzen**, one of the last palaces completed at the end of the 18th century, has been restored and is used by the present royal family as an occasional residence.

One of the most remarkable sights within the Imperial city is the **Heri el Souani** ❻ (9am–noon and 3–6pm; admission charge) – high vaulted chambers divided into 23 aisles which were used as store-rooms and granaries. The chambers are immense. Moulay Ismail was always ready for a siege or drought. For a good overview of the complex, climb the stairs to the café on the

The door to Moulay Ismail's tomb. Non-Muslims are allowed into the courtyards.

BELOW: the mausoleum of Moulay Ismail.

Map
on page
218

remaining part of the roof. Olive trees provide shade. The **Aguedal Basin** ⊙, round the corner from the Heri el Souani and visible from the roof-top café, covers 4 hectares (10 acres) but, as with all the sights within the Imperial city, its abandoned grandeur creates a mournful and gloomy atmosphere. Moulay Ismail's vision was mighty but the spaces he created were never filled – the scale was too huge.

The **Royal stables** (not open to visitors), 3km (2 miles) further along the route in the quarter of Heri el Mansour, are the most extreme example of Moulay Ismail's excess, They were built for more than 12,000 horses, each with its own groom and slave. The grain – sufficient for a siege lasting years – was stored below in the granaries, at a temperature kept constant by the thick walls. Ismail also constructed a canal providing fresh water for the horses without them having to move from their stalls. The crumbling remains still give an indication of the extent of decoration that once existed; tiles and *zelliges* are visible on pieces of partially overgrown wall. By and large, though, the place now belongs to goats.

Not far from here is the modern-day **Haras Regional**, a stud farm and training centre for Arabian horses. Experienced horsemen or women can take out temporary membership and help exercise the horses, but anyone can pay a visit. Some of the horses are pure Arabian, some Berber and others mixed (the exact percentage of Berber to Arab is posted on their stalls). More compact and delicate-looking than the thoroughbred, the Arabian is famed for its power as well as its beauty, but its most valuable asset historically was its endurance, a quality prized by the Bedouin, its human counterpart in weathering the hardships of the desert. A tribe's horses were its chief pride, its partners in raiding and war. Years of working and living together – horses often bedded down in the family tent – forged a bond of affection between the Bedouin and their horses which transcended usual human/animal relationships and inspired legends and poetry.

The medina

Returning to the Bab Mansour, enter the **medina**, at the west end of the Place el Hedim. The **Museum of Moroccan Arts** ⊕ (9am–noon and 3–6pm), housed in the Dar Jamai, is discreetly positioned at the corner of the square beside the entrance to the medina. It is worth a visit to see the fine examples of Berber rugs, especially if you are interested in buying one at some point in your trip. It also has an interesting collection of local artefacts and pottery. The building itself was built for Mohammed Ben Larbi Jamai, grand vizier at the court of Moulay Hassan (sultan 1873–94) by the same architect who built the Palais Jamai in Fez, though it is on a less grand scale. Some of the upper rooms are decorated and furnished to give an idea of domestic life in the 19th century. Like all the other grand palaces, it has an inviting garden filled with flowering shrubs and birdsong.

Follow Rue Sidi Amar to reach the Great Mosque and the heart of the medina. Close by is the **Madrassa Bou Inania** ⊕ (9am–noon and 3–6pm), started by the Merinid sultan Abou Hassan, who built

BELOW:
the granaries.

the Chellah in Rabat and the Madrassa el Hassan in Salé, but finished by Sultan Abou Inan (1350–58), builder of the Madrassa Bou Inania in Fez. It is similar to other Merinid *madrassas* with a central ablutions fountain in a tiled courtyard, quarters on two levels for around 50 students and a prayer hall on one side. As usual, every inch of wall is painstakingly covered in stucco, *zellige* work and wood carvings in abstract patterns and arabesques, creating a mesmerising intensity designed to reflect and reiterate the greatness and oneness of God. Go up to the roof of the *madrassa* for good views of the surrounding area, including the green tiled minarets of the mosques of each quarter and the roof of the Great Mosque.

The souks

The main street, covered by a corrugated iron roof, contains most of the usual stalls and is an animated, bustling thoroughfare. The **carpenters' souk** is permeated by the sweet smell of cedar and thuya wood. If you continue through the souk, you eventually emerge at the west end, site of most of the artisan markets. It is quite a scruffy area but has some interesting co-operative workshops, including basket-makers and saddlers. Fruit and food stalls are found spasmodically, both in this area and in the souk.

Outside the medina, beside the vast **Bab el Berdain** (Gate of the Saddlers) spreads a huge cemetery containing the shrine of **Sidi Ben Aissa** built in the 18th century (closed to non-Muslims),which is the focus of a *moussem* on the eve of Mouloud (the Prophet's birthday). The event is one of the biggest *moussems* in Morocco, attracting members of the Sufi-inspired Aissawa Brotherhood from all over North Africa *(see panel, page 223)*.

BELOW:
the vast enclosing
walls of Meknes.

The new and old *mellahs* (Jewish quarters) to the west of the medina and Place el Hedim have markets and souks of their own. It is a busy but very run-down, with ramshackle buildings incorporated into the crumbling walls. This is one of the poorest parts of town.

Whether because of the bloody actions of Moulay Ismail, reputed to have slaughtered over 36,000 with his own hands, or the combination of grandeur and decay, Meknes has a strange atmosphere. The emptiness of the vast crumbling edifices in contrast to the intensity of the slightly shabby medina reinforce the impression. Meknes lacks the cohesive feel of Fez; its inhabitants have none of the proud confidence in their city that the Fassis show.

The New Town and beyond

The French built the **New Town** on the opposite side of the **Oued Boufekrane**, which runs through the valley between the city's two halves. There is little of interest, but it does have a good selection of hotels, restaurants and cafés. Fairly lively by day, Meknes, new and old, has died by about 10pm.

Just outside Meknes there is a highly recommended diversion, for those who like horses or who would prefer an alternative base to the city centre. The **Tijania Ranch** (tel: 061 20 38 14 or 055 53 35 06), signposted off the tiny tarmac road to El Menzah (in the direction of Boufekrane) off the S316, is in the heart of the wine-growing region of Meknes. It is a stud with Arabian race horses, and as well as offering horse riding excursions into the surrounding hills, it has what must be Morocco's first fully organic restaurant, with an original menu of entirely home-grown food. If you fall in love with the ranch, very satisfactory accommodation is available in the farmhouse. ❑

Maps:
city 218
area 210

BELOW:
Place el Hedim.

THE AISSAWA BROTHERHOOD

One of the best-known Sufi fraternities in Morocco is the Aissawa Brotherhood, founded in the 15th century by Sidi Ben Aissa and quickly spreading throughout North Africa. Like other Sufi sects, it advocates trance induced by music as a means of drawing closer to God.

One of the ways in which Sidi Ben Aissa revealed his mystical powers was through his immunity to scorpion and snake bites, and he was said to confer the same magical powers on his followers. Once in a state of trance, they could eat anything, however grim, without ill-effect. At one time, on the eve of Mouloud (the Prophet's birthday), the date of their annual *moussem*, over 50,000 devotees would gather and, in a state of trance, devour live animals and pierce their tongues and cheeks. Their rituals were similar to those of the Hammaadcha of Moulay Idriss, whose *moussem* is described in Paul Bowles's *The Spider's House*.

The Moroccan government has outlawed the most extreme practices of these cults, but their annual *moussems* still take place, and they are very much involved in the everyday lives and rituals of their followers and of Moroccans in general. They perform healing ceremonies and attend circumcisions and are paid to capture snakes that have invaded houses.

A LAND OF SHRINES AND PILGRIMS

Pilgrimages play an important role in Islam.
Though the Haj is the greatest pilgrimage of all,
many smaller journeys are made to local shrines

Shrines are everywhere in Morocco, from simple white domed *koubbas to* large and elaborate *zaouias* that are centres for religious brotherhoods. They are magnets for pilgrims, who come to pray, grieve and ask for cures. Women will petition their favourite saint for help in childbirth or for a cure for infertility. They may bring small offerings or knot strips of fabric to the grille of the tomb to bind their contract with a saint. Water or oil may be put into tombs to receive a saint's *baraka* (blessing), after which it will be administered to the sick.

IN PLACE OF MECCA

Completing the Haj (pilgrimage to Mecca, the birthplace of the Prophet) is a life goal of most Muslims. It is saved for over many years, and families will club together to finance the trip for ageing parents. The return of a Haj is celebrated by the whole family, who will organise a welcome party at the airport. Presents from Mecca – prayer beads, watches, gilded tissue boxes or verses from the Koran embroidered in gold thread – are treasured, even though many will have been manufactured in the Far East.

Moroccans too poor to travel to Mecca will undertake a series of pilgrimages to local holy sites, such as Moulay Idriss or the tomb of Moulay Idriss II in Fez.

▷ **SWEET CELEBRATION**
All important shrines are flanked by stalls selling nougat, nuts, figs and dates. Moulay Idriss is known for its wonderful nougat.

▷ **MARKING THE DEAD**
In Islam, burials generally take place on the day of death. The washed body is wrapped in a simple shroud, and buried on its side, facing Mecca.

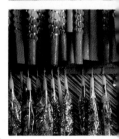

◁ HIGH AND HOLY

All over the world high places are often also holy places, as is frequently the case in Morocco. White *koubbas* stand out against the brown hills.

△ FOCAL POINT

Inside a *marabout* or *koubba*, the tomb is draped in cloth, which is usually green (the colour of Islam) and red.

▽ A PEEK INSIDE

Non-Muslims are not usually allowed into shrines, but they can get a glimpse into the antechambers of the shrine of Moulay Idriss II in Fez.

▷ BESIDE THE SEASIDE

A simple shrine at Tamsgid N'oufdas, south of Essaouira. Many *koubba* occupy coastal headlands.

◁ SHEDDING LIGHT

Coloured votive candles are popular buys among pilgrims to larger shrines, such as the shrine of Moulay Idriss II in Fez.

GOING TO A MOUSSEM

Moussems are annual festivals, usually held to honour a local saint but sometimes also celebrating the harvest. They can be huge affairs, attracting pilgrims and celebrants for miles around, and in the case of the biggest *moussems* from all over Morocco. Equal to their religious significance is the opportunity they present for trade. Huge tented encampments spring up overnight, livestock of all types is haggled over, and every conceivable utensil of rural life is bought and sold. The festivals are accompanied by music, dancing and *fantasias* (displays of horsemanship) and often the ritual slaughter of an animal in a ceremony that mixes pagan and Islamic elements.

Since the days of the French protectorate the government has used the opportunity presented by the *moussems* to keep tabs on the tribes, in particular to register marriages and collect taxes.

THE MIDDLE ATLAS

Map on page 230

Relatively few foreigners explore this vast area. Those who do will discover outstanding mountain scenery filled with lakes and waterfalls, the royal resort of Ifrane and fabulous Berber carpets

The Middle Atlas is a huge under-visited region of mountain ranges filling much of Morocco, between the High Atlas and the Rif, from the Atlantic coast up to Taza. The mountains emerge in the west as the Zaër Zaïane highlands, inland of the Rabat/Casablanca coastline, and dip down towards the High Atlas at Kasbah Talda. They then re-emerge from the High Atlas north of the great artificial lake, Bin el Ouidane, to become the Middle Atlas proper, crowned with stands of lofty cedars and running northeast between Midelt in the south and Azrou in the north. The range continues past the beautiful cities of Fez and Sefrou, becoming the Jebel Tazzeka, then falters at the Taza Gap, guarded by Morocco's least touristic medina city. It is a stunning region of forests, upland pastures, running rivers and lakes. High enough to be blanketed in snow in winter, the mountains are home to the Beni Mguild Berbers, some of Morocco's most gifted nomadic weavers.

PRECEDING PAGES: typical Middle Atlas landscape. **LEFT:** powderplay at a local *moussem*. **BELOW:** transporting charcoal.

The Zaër Zaïane Highlands

The P22 southeast of Rabat winds through the cork-oak trees and steep valleys of the Temara Forest, over rolling hills and through cleared rich agricultural land up to **Rommani** (Wednesday souk), where the S106 turns left to **Maaziz** and the S209 leads up into the heart of these highlands. Crossing the Bou Regreg, Tiddas is set in a large agricultural valley dominated by neat rows of apple orchards. Leaving the town, the road climbs steeply through forests of fir trees towards **Jebel Mouchchene** (1,086 metres/3,563ft), the journey punctuated with scattered hamlets and fields offering views to the south of tree covered hills.

After El-Harcha, a dead-end road leads on to **Tarmilate ❶**, home of the Oulmes and Sidi Ali bottling plant. The town is set on a spur, surrounded by higher forested peaks. Accommodation is available in the once stylish 1930s Hotel des Thermes (tel: 07 52 31 73). Company owned, the hotel is rarely visited by tourists, but has clean rooms, hot baths, a licensed restaurant and a congenial atmosphere at a very reasonable price. From the hotel there is a pleasant walk down the deep valley to **Lalla Haya**, the source of Morocco's most famous mineral water. The spring emerges hot and slightly sulphurous, and gushes through an iron pipe into a large basin streaked with red iron deposits. It is a great place for a bath.

The nearby town of **Oulmes** has very little to offer except its souk each Tuesday. The place has an air of rural poverty and, like Tarmilate, is surrounded by shanty town housing, the homes of peasants who work on the surrounding company-owned farms. From here the S2516 makes its way southwards

through holm-oak forest, past the shrine of Sidi Otmane to Khenifra. Northwards the S316 is an equally enjoyable drive to Meknes.

The real Middle Atlas

The real Middle Atlas emerges out of the northern hills of the High Atlas north of the dam and reservoir of **Bin el Ouidane ②**. This has become a centre for watersports and nowadays there are a few luxury holiday homes, with private jetties for Morocco's inland sailing enthusiasts. From the lake the road leads via impressive hairpins to **Afourer**, where there is more upmarket accommodation, and to the main P24 route between Fez and Marrakesh. However, to really follow the emerging Middle Atlas, take the S1805 towards **El Ksiba ③**. It now has a tarmac surface and, after Taguelft, climbs up from the Abid Valley through red hills with scattered juniper bushes onto a rolling cultivated plateau. The surrounding peaks become increasingly higher and the valley more contorted, with cultivation eventually restricted to a narrow band alongside the river, until

TIP

The Hotel du Lac (tel: 023 44 24 65), beautifully situated on the river below the reservoir of Bin el Ouidane, offers rooms, a summer campsite, a bar and a reasonable little restaurant.

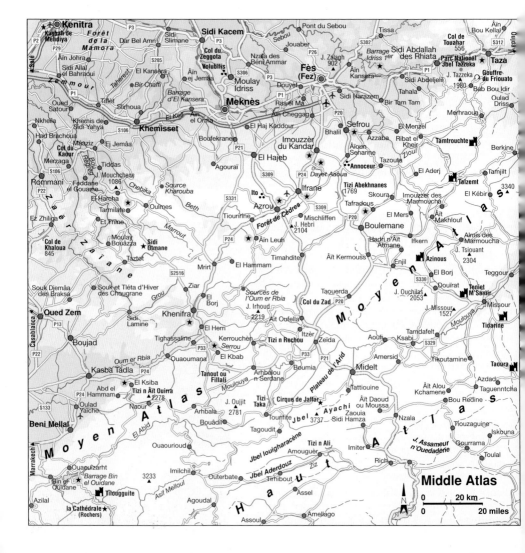

it emerges through a defile at Ait Aghzif, and suddenly opens out into a valley plain covered with orchards, some 25km (15 miles) before El Ksiba.

Shortly afterwards, the S1805 joins the S1901. A left turn leads to El Ksiba over the Tizi N'Ait Ouirra, and back to the P24 for an attractive stretch through to Khenifra. To the right is the southern road to Imilchil. Taking this road allows you to turn off towards Arhbala and eventually the P33, while always staying on tarmac. The road initially climbs over the Tizi N'Ifar and passes through Mediterranean oak woods, where you'll see numerous charcoal makers, to emerge at the main Imilchil/Arhbala junction.

About 13km (8 miles) to the left is **Arhbala**, once a French administration centre, which still retains the red tile and stone houses that are so typical of towns in the Middle Atlas. Beyond the town the increasingly potholed road continues over a pale barren plateau, until eventually improving and descending to give a dramatic view down over the town of **Sidi Yahya Ousaad**, with its striking green tiled administration building and a fertile valley below. About 1 km (½ mile) after the town, at a turning next to the Magnoua café, the P33 leads on to Khenifra or Midelt.

El Kbab ❹ can be reached by turning off the Khenifra road onto the S3409 which, after winding through fuzzy green hills, descends via a series of hair-raising turns to the town and the S3217. The road to the Oum er Rabia from El Kbab, via Kerrouchen, is a mix of piste and tarmac not suitable for normal road vehicles. However the route around **Jebel Irhoud** (2,219 metres/7,280ft) is well worth the effort for those equipped with a four-wheel-drive vehicle. The sealed road into the heart of the cedars leads from Khenifra on the S3485.

Khenifra ❺, on the rubbish-strewn banks of the Oum er Rbia, is built around

Map on page 230

Sun-seeker in the Middle Atlas.

BELOW: a shepherd in winter.

a small, tightly packed medina. Houses are a dark brick red with the wood-work of windows and doors painted turquoise. There are a few hotels in town, some of them fairly expensive. The more reasonable Hotel Restaurant de France (tel: 055 58 61 14), in the military quarter, can offer a good lunch and reasonable rooms, but there is no bar. For those with an unquenchable thirst the Bar de la Poste is just next door, and across the road is an off-licence. The way out of town towards the mountains is via a busy street that offers tantalising glimpses up cobbled side alleys.

The S3435 climbs past holiday homes, alternating with small peasant farms, to meet the S3211. Here it is worth taking the time to visit the small **Azigza lake** at the end of a highland sheep meadow, surrounded by a half moon of cedar forest and limestone cliffs. Beside the lake is a half-built and abandoned café. It's a favourite spot for hunters and sportsmen, judging by the number of spent shotgun cartridges lying around.

Cedar country

The road northwards runs through evergreen oak forest that gives way to lofty dark stands of cedar, some of the trees reputedly measuring over 60 metres (195ft) tall, before descending into the picturesque hollow containing the springs that form the **Oum er Rbia**. The main spring has a car park beside a pool, a pleasant spot for a summer dip and a walk towards the spring itself that gushes from underneath the mountains. But it is not an ideal spot to camp due to the over-enthusiastic attention of locals trying to cadge money. A few kilometres further north some accessible clearings in the forest can be found where you can camp without being pestered.

BELOW:
downtown Azrou.

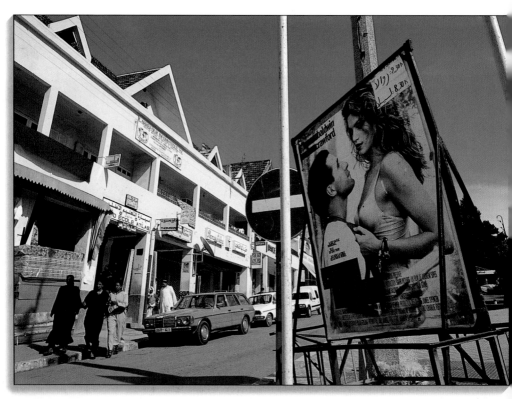

A gentle drive through the forest comes out at the French-built **Ain Leuh**  which has a thriving Wednesday market, frequented by Hamid Kassimi, an itinerant carpet seller who plies the local souk circuit. His stall is usually near the impressive chalet-style post office. From Ain Leuh take the Tagounit road to join the P21 and on to Azrou. It is a rewarding drive along the edge of the forest with frequent views down into the fertile valley below.

Map
on page
230

Hiking centres

The centre of **Azrou** ❼, the impressively clean French-era Place Mohammed V, is bordered one side by the Hotel Restaurant des Cedres (tel: 055 56 23 26) and the Relais Forestier restaurant. The other side of the square gives onto a small souk. While in Azrou look out for Mohammed Kallal (tel: 055 56 19 49), one of the few licensed mountain guides in the region. Absolutely passionate about the Middle Atlas, he is a perfect choice if you want to organise a more exhaustive exploration of the area on foot or by four-wheel-drive. His past experience includes guiding Jean-Yves Collet on a six-month expedition to film a wildlife documentary about Barbary apes, which are often to be seen alongside the road throughout the area.

A cedar tree rises near Azrou.

South from Azrou a rough track off the P21 takes you to the huge and ancient Cedre Gouraud. More practical if you haven't got a four-wheel-drive vehicle is the route further south to the turn-off for the Mischliffen and Jebel Hebri ski resorts. At the moment there is not much to see out of season at either resort, just a couple of static chair lifts, but **Mischliffen** will soon have a small modern hotel with a sun terrace and outdoor swimming pool. It should then be a good base for long walks through the forest.

BELOW: camping in the Middle Atlas.

East of Sefrou is one of the main olive-growing areas of Morocco. There are some 50 varieties of olives altogether and as many ways of preparing them.

Further south again on the P21 is the isolated lake of **Sidi Ali**, surrounded by 2,000-metre (6,560-ft) peaks but no facilities.

Ifrane , a short drive northeast from Azrou on the P24, is something of a shock. Cool and tranquil with manicured lawns and the outward appearance of a Swiss alpine resort , it seems out of place, particularly as it is overlooked by the grey hulk of the royal château. Scratch the surface of the town, however, and you soon realise that few of the hotels or services quite live up to Swiss standards. The population appears to be very young and very chic. The celebrated Al Akhawayn University (where courses are taught in English) is on the edge of town. Ifrane does have a tourist office with a willing staff and they produce a useful leaflet on the area.

More Moroccan and more affordable as a base, **Imouzzer du Kandar** is about 24km (15 miles) further north on the P24. Characterised by tidy avenues lined with deciduous trees (splendid in autumn) and a cheerful square, the town offers a plethora of cafés, a park with a couple of ponds and a choice of places to stay. The Hotel Royal (tel: 055 66 30 80), on the southern edge of town has a busy bar and modern rooms with balconies overlooking the park. On the northern end is the family-run, Hotel Les Truites (tel: 055 66 30 22), a fabulous traditional French-style country hotel with a cosy bar, conservatory terrace restaurant and small garden at the back. The bathroom facilities are a bit lacking, but they are in the process of renovation.

Touring the lakes

A few kilometres before Imouzzer du Kandar, off the P24, is the begining of the lakes tour, initially passing the once-magical **Dayet Aaoua** , which in recent

years has been suffering the sad effects of drought. On the lakeside is the imposing Chalet du Lac (tel: 055 66 31 97), which despite its repressive exterior has a wonderful, if slightly expensive, restaurant and the most enormous pot belly stove to ensure that the place stays warm even on the coldest nights. A little beyond the lake is the Gîte du Lac Dayet Aoua (tel: 055 60 48 80), offering accommodation in an Andalusian-style house with a pool, set in an orchard of young apple trees frequented by resident peacocks.

The lake tour continues around the less visited Dayets Afourgah, Iffer, Ifrah and Hachlaf, via a series of tiny tarmac roads, each reasonably signposted. The area is particularly frequented by fishermen and, apparently, the late king Hassan II liked nothing better than taking off from his palace in Ifrane for the day to fish here. The eastern side of the lakes region is bordered by the P20 that travels northwards to the delightful city of Sefrou.

Cherry country

Sefrou ⓫, rarely disturbed by tourists, was once a major centre for Morocco's Jews and its walled white pedestrian medina is still characterised by their houses with wooden balconies. The whole medina is dissected by the River Aggai, that enters the town via a small waterfall above the separate walled ksar. Beside the Bab Makame, the Cooperative Artisanale offers good quality handicrafts at very reasonable prices.

Immediately east and south of Sefrou there are few roads open to normal road vehicles, but one recommended drive is on the S4614 to Tazouta and then the S4163 and S4653 via Skoura to Boulemane. The latter has no accommodation but you can visit the Café Snack Tijnt, which claims a *"cadre romantique"*

Map on page 230

Sefrou is famous for its cherries. A festival to mark the cherry harvest is held in June.

BELOW: in country areas washing is still done in the river.

Map on page 230

(romantic setting). The S4653 section in particular is a rewarding meandering drive, following the Gigou Valley, with views of the towering cliffs of the Tichehoukt Massif (2,796 metres/9,170ft) to the south. On one particularly tight twist in the river stands **Tafradous** ⑫, accessible only via a footbridge that leads up an enormous ramp to a village built like a crusaders' castle. This one site alone makes the whole drive worthwhile. A few kilometres south of Boulemane the S4656 leads up to Imouzzer des Marmoucha before the tarmac road runs out. It is a one-way trip for normal vehicles but, road conditions permitting, off-road vehicles can continue on the track over the Bou Zabel Pass which becomes the sealed S326, and complete the loop with a vertiginous descent towards the P1.

Due east of Sefrou, the El Menzel road travels through rolling olive groves and crosses the Sebou River, with views into its gorge, before joining the S326 and the P1 above the enormous **Barrage Idriss Ier** ⑬.

The Jebel Tazzeka and Taza

Eastwards on the P1, an easily missed turn-off to the north at Sidi Abdallah des Rhiata quickly twists back on itself to go under the main road and climb immediately up into the spectacular rust-red stained Zireg Gorge. This is the start of the **Jebel Tazzeka National Park**, perhaps the most beautiful upland landscape in northern Morocco. The loop road (which eventually comes out at Taza) climbs through cork, evergreen oak and pine trees with spectacular views over forest wilderness inhabited by reintroduced Barbary deer. Along the way are a couple of picnic sites with kiosks and display maps. To the north of the S311, the 1,980-metre (6,495-ft) summit of Jebel Tazzaka is easily identifiable by its aerial mast and is accessible via a signposted track.

BELOW: going shopping in Sefrou.
RIGHT: the ancient city of Taza.

The road passes **Bab Bou Idir**, a lonely alpine outpost with a picnic lawn beneath two cedar trees, before descending to the highland pasture of Dia Chiker, bordered by limestone crags. From here a signposted turn-off leads to the **Friouato cave**, one of many in the park. The final dramatic descent to Taza begins by cutting through a limestone cliff to where a series of steep bends pass a picnic area in the Valley of Birds. The little village of **Ras el Ma**, halfway down the mountain, has a superb rustic café of the same name, where it is possible to sip mint tea and admire the view of Taza in the gap between the Middle Atlas and the white naked hills of the eastern Rif to the north.

Taza ⑭ grew to importance when the Almohads occupied it in the 12th century, making it their second capital (Tin Mal being the first), after failing to capture Marrakesh from the Almoravides. The medina today is set on a hill above the new town. There is little in the way of historic monuments to visit, although glimpses of the Andalous (a 12th-century minaret which predates the Koutabia in Marrakesh) and grand mosques can be seen from the twisting pedestrian alleys of the pale ochre medina. More impressive is the complete and utter lack of any kind of tourist influence. You can't even buy a postcard, never mind visit a carpet bazaar. This is something of a refreshing change after Marrakesh and Fez. ❑

↑ Safi

Hospital
Ibn Tofaïl

Avenue de la 4ème D.M.M.

Rue du Sergt Levet

Rue du Bani

Rue du Capitaine Arrighi

Rue du Draa

Rue du Draa

Avenue Mohammed Abdelkrim el Khattabi

Rue Mohammed el Begal

Avenue Mohammed

Rue Abdelouahad Derraq

Rue Ibn Sina

Rue Ibn Aïcha

Avenue Yacoub el Mansour

Boulevard Mohammed Zerktouni

Rue de la Liberté

Boulevard de la Youqoslavie

ONMT

Rue de l'el Mansour

Eddahbi

Rue Souriya

Avenue el

Iman Malik

R. Khalid Ibn Oualid

VILLE NOUVELLE

Avenue de France

Avenue el Mouqaouama

GUELIZ

Avenue Moulay Rachid

Avenue Hassan II

Place du 16 Novembre

Avenue des Nations Unies

Avenue Mohammed V

Avenue Yacoub el Marini

Place de l'Empereur Hailé Sélassié

Railway Station

Rue el Qadi Ayad

JARDIN DU HARTSI

Saints Martyrs

Avenue Hassan II

Rue Jabir Ibn Hayane

Rue Ibn el Qadi

Rue el Qadi

Route N° 10

QUARTIER INDUSTRIEL

Rue Abou Bahr Seddia

Rue el Jahed

Rue Mohammed el Hansali

Avenue de France

Avenue Moulay el Hassan

HIVERNAGE

Avenue du Président Kennedy

Rue Ahmed Chaouqi

Rue Hafid Ibrahim

Avenue de Paris

Avenue Echchouhada

Boulevard

Essaouira

Rue el Ikhaa

Avenue el Qadissia

Avenue el Qadissia

FERME EXPERIMENTAL

Casino

JARDIN MÉNARA

Avenue de la Ménara

OLIVERAIE DE BAB JDID

N

Marrakesh

0 — 500 m
0 — 500 yds

✈

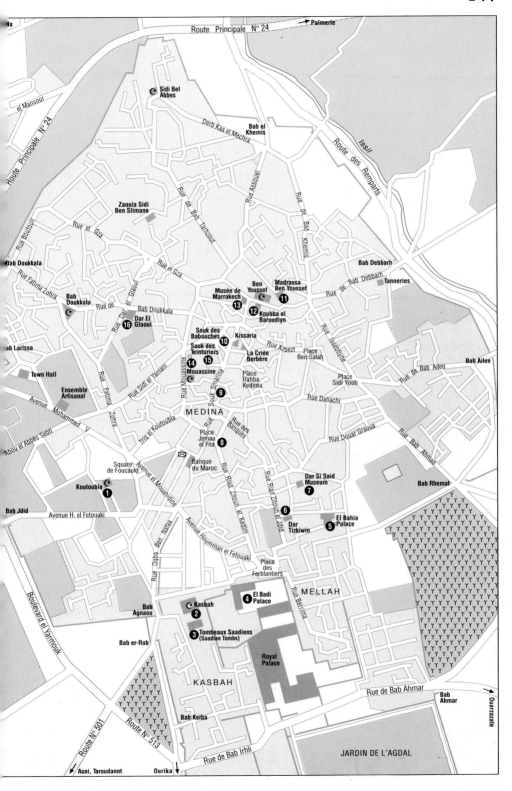

Route Principale N° 24 → Palmerie

el Mansour

Route Principale N° 24

☾ Sidi Bel Abbes

Derb Kaa el Mechra

Bab el Khemis

Route des Remparts

Issil

Rue de Bab Tarhkout

Rue Assouel

Rue de Bab Khemis

Zaouia Sidi Ben Slimane

Rue el Gza

Bab Doukkala

Rue Boukouil

Rue Fatima Zohra

Rue el Gza

Bab Debbarh

Rue de Bab Debbarh

Tanneries

Bab Doukkala ☾

Rue de Dar el Glaoui

Bab Doukkala

Dar El Glaoui 16

Musée de Marrakech
13

Ben Youssef ☾

Madrassa Ben Youssef 11

Koubba el Baroudiyn 12

ab Larissa

Rue Isseahbyne

Rue de Bab Ailen

Bab Ailen

Town Hall

Ensemble Artisanal

Avenue Mohammed V

Abou el Abbes Sebti

Rue Fatima Zohra

Rue Sidi el Yamani

Rue Mouassine

Souk des Babouches

Kissaria 10

Souk des Teinturiers

Mouassine 14 15

Rue Azbezt

La Criée Berbère

Place Ben-Salah

Souk Smarine

Place Rahba Kedima

Place Sidi Youb

9

MEDINA

Rue des Banques

Rue Dabachi

Rue Douar Graoua

Rue Bab Ahmad

Triq el Koutoubia

Place Jemaa el Fna
8

Square de Foucauld

Avenue el Mouahidine

Banque du Maroc

Koutoubia ☾ 1

Bab Jdid

Avenue H. el Fetouaki

Rue Dqba Ben Nafaa

Avenue Houmman el Fetouaki

Rue Riad Zitoun el Kedim

Rue Riad Zitoun el Jdid

Dar Si Said Museum 7

6

Dar Tizkiwin

El Bahia Palace 5

Bab Rhemat

Boulevard el Yarmouk

Place des Ferblantiers

MELLAH

Rue Berima

Bab Agnaou

Kasbah ☾

2

El Badi Palace 4

Bab er-Rob

3 Tombeaux Saadiens (Saadian Tombs)

Royal Palace

KASBAH

Rue de Bab Ahmar

Bab Ahmar

→ Ouarzazate

Route N° 501

Route N° 513

Bab Ksiba

Rue de Bab Irhli

JARDIN DE L'AGDAL

→ Asni, Taroudannt   Ourika ↓

MARRAKESH

Set on a plain below the Atlas Mountains, the city is capital of the south. Its character is as much African as Arab, reflecting its former role as a caravan station on trans-Saharan trade routes

Map on pages 240–241

Marrakesh is probably the most exotic city in Morocco, for it is the meeting place of cultures and continents. It was the first capital of a united Morocco (back in the 11th century) and it is where tribesmen from the so-called Bled El Siba (land of lawlessness) meet those from the Bled El Makhzen (land of government). Situated at the geographical centre of the country, it is the first great city north of the Sahara.

A vibrant centre of trade, with a population of about 1 million, Marrakesh is expanding rapidly, with satellite suburbs under constant construction. Its modern economy, apart from tourism, includes textile and light manufacturing industries. Hermes has a factory here, as do various other knitwear and clothing companies. Designers export metal furniture, and painted wood and jewellery made to order, and Marrakesh craftsmen and foreign investors have discovered a lucrative market for their well-made goods.

In recent years, especially since the building of the Palais de Congres on Avenue de France, the city has become a popular venue for international conferences. Good facilities, plentiful hotels and interesting possibilities for R & R attract everyone from associations of opticians to heads of state. It was in the Palais de Congres that the 1994 GATT (General Agreement on Tariffs and Trade) was signed, and almost every week Marrakesh hosts an international conference of some sort. General Motors, in 1998, held a long series of conferences here to launch its new range of Opel cars, flying in some 20,000 employees and agents from around the world over a period of a month. The city's central location, varied scenery and skilled technicians also make it a favourite location for filming commercials, fashion shoots and feature films, including *The Mummy* and *Hideous Kinky*.

In winter, the city is dominated by the towering Atlas Mountains. The snow-capped peaks loom over the city in the clear winter air, an unbroken wall filling the entire southern horizon. In summer, the city roasts under a desert sun, which can push temperatures up to 50°C (134°F) in the shade. But winter or summer, the city has a perpetual party atmosphere. The *Marrakshi* accent is rough, crude, full of a barely controlled sensuality.

PRECEDING PAGES: late afternoon on the Jemaa el Fna. **LEFT:** the well-kept boulevards and gardens of Gueliz. **BELOW:** speeding round the souks.

History

Marrakesh was founded by the Almoravides, fanatical religious nomads who exploded out of the Western Sahara in 1060. Austere veiled warriors, much like the Tuareg, they built a walled kasbah and mosque that eventually became the capital of an empire that not only united all of modern Morocco, but also most of Spain and much of Algeria. Under the leadership of

A warm welcome at La Mamounia, one of the world's great hotels and beloved of Winston Churchill.

Youssef ben Tashfine, Marrakesh became a cosmopolitan centre of culture and learning with Andalusian-style mosques and palaces. The legacy of the Almoravides remains most tangibly in the city's walls and system of underground irrigation channels that fed the new city and its fabulous gardens.

Orientation

Marrakesh is split into at least two distinct cities, the walled medina and **Gueliz**. Of most interest to visitors is the **medina**, with its winding markets and historical monuments enclosed within pink walls of sun-baked mud. The medina can be further divided into quarters, with the most obvious partition falling between north and south of the central square, the Jemaa el Fna. North of the square are twisting alleys and densely packed souks, each specialising in a particular trade. Behind and on either side of the souks are residential quarters that offer little to the passing tourist, except for the odd eccentrically placed restaurant or mosque, with the exception of the area around the Medrassa ben Youssef which is the old historical centre of the medina.

South of the square is the *mellah*, the kasbah and the royal palace, and the greatest concentration of historical monuments. Three main arteries serve this quarter: Avenue el Mouahidine/Avenue Houmman el Fetouaki running from Avenue Mohammed V (Marrakesh's main street) past the Koutoubia mosque and *mellah* market and ending at the busy junction next to the Place des Ferblantiers (an easily recognisable square that acts as a useful reference point in navigating the area), and the streets Riad Zitoun el Kedim and el Jdid (old and new), direct routes from the Jemaa el Fna to Place des Ferblantiers, filled with workshops where tin lanterns and lampshades are made.

BELOW: *gnaou* musicians on the Jemaa el Fna.

While the medina holds most of the city's sights, its range of western-style accommodation, restaurants and bars is decidedly lacking. For middle- to upper-range hotels (3-star and above), visitors are forced to look in Gueliz, the new part of town outside the walls. The Office National du Tourisme and the local GRIT Marrakesh information office (Mon–Fri 8.30am–6.30pm, Sat 8.30am– noon) are also found here on Avenue Mohammed V. The French built the basis of this modern city. It is dominated by the broad Avenue Mohammed V, the main artery linking the modern city with the old Arab medina. Running north from the medina, beginning at the Koutoubia Mosque (where a busy junction leads off right to the Club Med and the Jemaa el Fna), this cuts through the walls at the Bab Nkob and ends on the far side of Gueliz at a busy traffic circle marking the start of the Casablanca road. Most of the bars, restaurants and hotels lie on this main street or in side streets running off it.

Map on pages 240–241

The historic sights

The tallest feature on the medina skyline is the **Koutoubia Mosque ❶** (Mosque of the Booksellers). Built by Sultan Abel Mouman at the beginning of Almohad rule, it is the city's most important landmark and serves as a useful point against which to relate the other sites in the city.

A mosque was originally built here by the Almoravides; the Dar el Hajar (House of Stone) can still be traced in an excavation alongside the Koutoubia Mosque. The original Koutoubia Mosque was destroyed by the Almoravides' successors, the Almohads, who descended from Tin Mal in the High Atlas and captured the city in 1147. The Almohads soon built their own Koutoubia Mosque, but evidence suggests that this may have been wrongly aligned to

The Koutoubia minaret, built by the Almohads and a useful orientation point in the city.

BELOW: carrying it all back home.

Mecca, for a second mosque was completed in 1158 as an extension of the first, presumably to correct the original alignment of the prayer hall. Excavations undertaken in 1948 revealed the foundations of columns which would have supported the roof of the first Almohad mosque, and it is still possible to see, on the northern wall, the bricked-up arches that connected the two buildings. The same excavations also revealed evidence of a machine to raise and lower a screen (a *maqsurah*) to separate the ruler from the general populace. This would have been a sensible precaution, as many a Muslim leader has been assassinated on his way to or from prayer.

The present-day mosque, like nearly all mosques in Morocco, is closed to non-Muslims but a spectacular *minbar* (a moveable staircase from which a mosque's imam delivers his Friday sermon and leads prayers) from the Koutoubia Mosque can be seen in the Dar Si Said Museum *(see pages 251)*. Inscriptions on the *minbar* show that it was made in Córdoba for the Koutoubia Mosque but was most likely commissioned by the Sultan Ibn Tashfine, around 1120, for the original Almoravide mosque. The workmanship involved in the marquetry decoration of the staircase – no two of the 1,000 panels are exactly the same – shows something of the splendour of Marrakesh during the 12th century.

It is the minaret that is the pride of the mosque today. After many years of being shrouded in scaffolding the Koutoubia minaret has now been beautifully restored. The mosque tower served as the model for the Tour Hassan in Rabat *(see page 156)* and the Giralda in Seville, later buildings of the Almohads. The minaret is nearly 70 metres (230ft) high, and follows the Almohad proportions of 1:5, with the tower five times as high as it is wide. This proportion is found in nearly all Almohad mosques. The exterior of the tower is

BELOW: keeping a watchful eye.

decorated with carved stone tracery, each side displaying different patterns. The rough stone of the tower would once have been covered with plaster and decorated. Remnants of this decoration can be seen in the lines of coloured tiles at the top of the restored tower.

The surrounding excavations of the original mosque have also been completed. The resulting piazza and garden now provide an alternative early evening focus to the Jemaa el Fna for *Marrakshis* and visitors alike. The assembled families and the children playing create an enjoyable atmosphere in which to stroll and admire the mosque. It is a relaxing way to while away an hour or two before heading off in search of dinner.

The Kasbah Mosque and the Saadian Tombs

Due south of the Koutoubia, and most easily approached from Bab Agnaou, is the 12th-century **Kasbah Mosque ❷** (look out for its minaret). This mosque is the second Almohad monument in Marrakesh, although practically nothing of what you see today belongs to the original construction. Rebuilt for the first time about 30 years after the Koutoubia, but before Rabat's Tour Hassan, it is built from brick rather than stone and has been much restored.

Next door to the mosque (and clearly signposted "Tombeaux Saadiens") are the **Saadian Tombs ❸** (daily 8.30–11.45am, 2.30–5.45pm; admission charge), built by Ahmed el Mansour, the second Saadian sultan, on the site of an older cemetery which was reserved for descendants of the Prophet. The Saadians emerged from Tamgroute in the Draa Valley during the 16th century, when Morocco was in turmoil after the collapse of the Merinids. On a wave of religious fervour and nationalist sentiment, they swept through the country,

The lovely Saadian Tombs, built by Ahmed el Mansour.

Map on pages 240–241

BELOW: a close shave below the medina walls.

capturing Marrakesh in 1524. When the religious leaders of Fez rebuffed their claims of Sheriffian descent (from the Prophet), they made Marrakesh their capital instead of Fez.

Abdallah el Ghalib succeeded to the Saadian throne after the murder of his rivals. A strong leader, he made a considerable impact on Marrakesh, rebuilding the original Medrassa Ben Youssef (founded by a Merinid Sultan in the 14th century) and the kasbah; he also built the Mouassine mosque and founded the mellah. His successor and half-brother, Ahmed el Dehbi (also called el Mansour, the Victorious) built El Badi Palace and the Saadian Tombs.

After the collapse of the Saadian dynasty, the tombs were bricked up by Moulay Ismail in the late 17th century, and only rediscovered by a French aerial survey of the medina. At one time the entrance to the tombs was either via El Badi Palace or through the Kasbah Mosque; today, visitors follow a narrow passage alongside the outside wall of the mosque's prayer hall. The mausoleum is built in the late Andalusian tradition and post-dates the Alhambra by two centuries. It is one of the top historical sights of Marrakesh, containing the tombs of Mohammed ech Cheikh and Ahmed el Mansour, as well as those of numerous other members of the Saadian royal families. To appreciate the beauty and peace of the cemetery, it is best to visit in the early morning, before 10am.

El Badi

El Badi Palace ❹ (daily 8.30–11.45am, 2.30–5.45pm; admission charge), near the Place des Ferblantiers, is an elegant ruin between the *mellah* and the imperial city. Built by Ahmed el Mansour in the 16th century, it was once a palace of outstanding beauty, covered in white Italian marble. Little remains

Fez is Europe but closed; Marrakesh is Africa, but open. Fez is black, white, and grey; Marrakesh is red.

– JOHN GUNTHER
Inside Africa, 1955

BELOW: the ruins of El Badi Palace.

except an enormous open courtyard housing a rectangular pool and traces of the underground water system that once irrigated its gardens. The palace took 25 years to complete and, at the hands of Moulay Ismail less than a century later, only 12 years to destroy.

In 1999 the Marrakesh Folklore Festival, held in the palace in June, was revived and expanded to include folk troupes from other Arab countries, which give it an international flavour. Although perhaps not as much fun as when it was a purely local affair, the nightly folk parade along Mohammed V, and related events in the square and outside the Bab Jdid, create a festive atmosphere in the city in general.

Past the Place des Ferblantiers, in the *mellah*, is **El Bahia Palace** ❺ (open daily 8.30–11.45am, 2.30–5.45pm; admission charge) built in the 19th century by grand viziers to the Alaouite sultans. Depending on your own taste, El Bahia (which translates as "the brilliant") is either an impressive display of the period's post-Alhambra decoration or a degeneration of Andalusian art which borders on kitsch. Either way, the series of gardens, courtyards and cool reception halls are impressive if only for their scale and opulence. During the French Protectorate it served as the governor's residence. Today, the palace is officially part of the Royal Palace and parts of it, including most of the upstairs rooms, are used for lodging guests. Jackie and Aristotle Onassis once stayed here.

Hidden riads

Contemporary with the palace are many grand merchants' houses, some of which have been converted into restaurants or small, often exclusive, hotels and *maison d'hôte*, offering a much needed alternative to the usual hotels. Many

A fantasia is staged at 5pm every evening of the El Badi Folklore Festival. A well-loved part of most large Moroccan festivals, fantasias involve charging horsemen performing daring manoeuvres and acrobatics to the accompaniment of gunfire.

BELOW: a restored *riad*.

RESTORED RIADS

For a few years now it has been fashionable to buy up a *riad*, an old Arab house with a courtyard in the medina, and have it renovated into a holiday hideout for yourself, your friends and even paying guests. The result is that the visitor can now find an amazing array of accommodation available in a city which, although full of hotels, has few of any great charm. These houses for rent, called *maisons d'hôte*, come in all sizes, and to suit all pockets, from the palatial (complete with pool) to the simple. For no more than you would spend on an equivalent hotel, it is possible to rent a house with four or five bedrooms and enjoy the real Marrakesh medina experience.

A number of agencies have grown up to facilitate the purchase and renovation of houses for the orientally-inspired foreigner. Some will even find you clients to rent the house once it is finished, to help finance your dream. One of the oldest and most established agencies is Marrakech Medina (102 Rue Dar El Pacha, tel: 044 42 91 33; www.marrakech-medina.com). They also have a rental department for visitors looking for a house to rent during their holiday. Independent *maisons d'hôte* include Riads Dalia (tel: 044 44 21 96), Malika (tel: 044 38 54 51) and Riad Enija (tel: 044 44 09 26).

TIP

On Rue Riad Zitoun el Kedim, off the Jemaa el Fna, is a *riad* signposted in English and advertising itself as "restaurant". It is run by Fakitah, who specialises in arranging weddings and women-only henna parties with sumptuous food and dancers. She will also lay on soirées for parties of foreign visitors if contacted in advance.

BELOW: snacks on the Jemaa el Fna.

of these private enterprises are run by expatriate Europeans who have been seduced by Marrakesh's combination of modernity and oriental tradition (*see page 249*). Marrakesh has always attracted creative people from all over the world, artists and designers, actors and even ex-ambassadors unwilling to retire to their own cultures and looking for an outlet for their often considerable energies. Most famous of these today are Yves St Laurent, who restored the Majorelle Gardens, and Patrick Hermes with his love of polo. However, there is an ever-growing group of the less famous who have nonetheless fallen in love with the city and are launching private schemes that will eventually benefit the city as a whole. Newly opened in the medina is the Riad Tamsna (tel: 044-38 52 71/72; daily 9am–7pm) offering a chic combination of exhibition space, tea house, restaurant and design shop in a beautifully restored white *tadalakt riad*, in Derb Zanka Daika, off Rue Riad Zitoun el Jdid. Another is the Dar el Bellarg (tel: 044-44 45 55) (House of Storks), a public arts centre, set up by a Swiss foundation, housed in one of the medina's most beautiful *fondouks*. Both of these places are open to the public most days and are a new phenomenon in Marrakesh. They are likely to become places that all visitors to the medina will want to see, and their cafés may well become favourite rendezvous points.

Off the Rue Riad Zitoun el Jdid is a narrow alley that passes Bert Flint's beautiful house, **Dar Tizkiwin ❻**, which is both his home and a private museum (visits are limited to half an hour). It contains a superb collection of Berber textiles and pottery (his jewellery collection is housed in his Agadir museum, *see page 307*). Bert Flint is an original and tireless collector who should be given great credit for making good Moroccan craft available to the visiting public.

Beyond Dar Tizkiwin, at a small fountain, a street leads to the excellent **Dar Si Said Museum ❼** (Wed–Mon 8.30–11.45am, 2.30–5.45pm, closed Tues; admission charge), marked by a Moroccan flag. It contains a mixture of artefacts of varying interest in a particularly impressive *riad*, built in the 19th century by the brother of the Grand Vizier Ba Hmad who was responsible for El Bahia Palace *(see page 249)*. There are the usual examples of doors and *mashrabiya* (wooden screens), showcases of weaponry and Berber jewellery and examples of copper, brass and silverware: kettles with a compartment for burning the charcoal, conical-lidded containers intended for bread, long-spouted vessels for pouring water over the hands of dinner guests, and incense holders – the latter two essential preludes and postscripts to any elaborate meal in a traditional household to this day.

Evening assembly

The **Jemaa el Fna ❽** is the heart of street life in Marrakesh, a huge square-cum-open space between the souk and Koutoubia Mosque that is a magnet for foreign and Moroccan tourists alike, who are drawn to its jugglers, snake charmers, orange juice sellers and fakirs. Here teeth are pulled and fortunes told. Though activity is round the clock, it is at night, from around 5pm, that the Jemaa is at its most exciting. Night vendors set up stalls selling a huge variety of food at rock-bottom prices. It is possible to eat anything from goats' heads to snails, *merguez, tajines* and couscous. Best value is the *harira* soup at just 1 dirham a bowl. The atmosphere is intoxicating: lamps glow amid swirling clouds of smoke, pick-pockets and con men dart through the crowds while dazed-looking foreign visitors clutch their bags and gape. A less intimate way of enjoying the

Map on pages 240–241

Snails in cumin-flavoured liquor are a good way to begin a feast on the square.

BELOW: charming the crowds.

spectacle is from a terrace of one of the many ringside cafés, with the Café de France and Café Argana (which offers a backdrop view of the snow-covered Atlas in winter) the favourites.

Men should beware of poor Berber girls bearing gifts of cheap jewellery. They are certainly after your money, and some will suggest that you sample the delights behind their exotic veils. If you do fall into temptation you will certainly come out poorer, if not wiser, than you expected.

The souks

Flowing northwards from the Jemaa el Fna, on the opposite side from the palaces, are the souks of the medina, a warren of shadowy tunnel-like streets punctuated by pools of electric light from tightly packed boutiques. Stout matrons swathed in veils chaperone fashionably dressed daughters. Shouts of *"balek"* clear a path for over-laden handcarts, bicycles and mopeds. Foreigners are urged to "Come in" and are bidden *"Bienvenue"*.

On a first visit, the souk can feel overwhelmingly aggressive, as would-be guides appear and disappear at your side offering their services. However, since the establishment of the Tourist Brigade (a special squad of plain-clothes police dedicated to protecting tourists from the less savoury side of the medina) visiting the souk has become a positively hassle-free experience in comparison to earlier years. Though the souk appears to be a disorganised jumble of shops selling a head-spinning array of goods, the maze of twisting streets is really a network of specialist markets. Each separate souk has its own name, although there is little point in trying to remember all but a few of these, as you will never see any signposts. What the experts call rebound navigation, relating

TIP

As a change from the cafés overlooking the square, try the café of the Hotel Islane on Avenue Mohammed V, which offers a fine view of the Koutoubia Mosque and gardens from its first-floor terrace.

BELOW: elegant dining in the Tobsil Restaurant.

RESTAURANTS

If you want to splash out and dine in style at least once on your trip, Marrakesh is the place to do it. Restaurants abound here. The medina is best known for converted courtyard houses serving traditional Moroccan cuisine. Among those vying for attention are **Dar El Yacout** (tel: 044-44 19 03), designed by the acclaimed American architect Bill Willis and now run by Britain's Honorary Consul in the city, **Stylia** (tel: 044-43 40 66), **Ksar Chahramane** (tel: 044-44 06 32) and **Dar Marjana** (tel: 044-44 57 73). All have reputations for stunning interiors, good food and tasteful oriental entertainment.

However, there are variations on the super-swish restaurant-in-the-medina theme. The **Pavilion** (tel: 044 38 70 40) specialises in the best French cuisine in town, while arguably the most refined Moroccan cooking anywhere is found in **Tobsil** (tel: 044-44 40 52). Set in a beautiful and intimate *riad (see left)*, the Tobsil has a subdued and elegant atmosphere and not a belly dancer in sight (unless you really want one). These last two places are among Marrakesh's most exclusive restaurants, attracting the very beautiful and very famous. An evening in either would be a gastronomic highlight of a visit to the city.

For other possibilities, see the Travel Tips section.

everything to a few easily recognisable landmarks, is the best method of finding your way around. Of most interest are the areas that have kept their medieval character and are still highly specialised.

Access is via two streets that lead off the square. The **Souk Smarine** ❾ is hidden by a few alleys selling olives, dried fruits, cheap shoes and ladies underwear. Its entrance proper is through a prominent arch also identified by a regular hawker of a bird-imitating whistle. Hear its high pitched warbling and you cannot be far away. The entrance is a busy junction. Straight ahead, through the keyhole arch, is the broad paved and covered Smarine, its shops dominated by upmarket fabric vendors and a couple of huge tourist emporiums. A small but fascinating antiques shop a few metres down on the left offers insights into Moroccan culture over the past century.

The Rue Smarine eventually forks, a junction heralding the heart of the souk. On the right is a square dominated by spice shops, strung with animals in various stages of desiccation. An entrance on the square's north side, flanked by Berber carpet stores, leads to the former slave market (Marrakesh was an important centre for the trans-Saharan trade). The left fork, Souk Attarine, leads to **Souk des Babouches**, ❿, the slipper alley lined by small kiosks crammed with *babouches*, the characteristic slippers with a turned down heel. Weak electric bulbs reflect off the brilliant gold thread of wedding slippers. Further on, the sound of hammering will guide you into the blacksmith's souk where metal garden furniture and weathercocks are almost as popular as the more traditional ornate window grilles.

The right-hand fork off Semmarine passes jewellery and leather souks before arriving at the **Madrassa Ben Youssef** ⓫ (daily 8.30–11.45am, 2.30–5.45pm;

Map on pages 240–241

Women's babouches *embroidered with gold thread.*

BELOW: views on the Madrassa Ben Youssef.

BELOW:
the dyers' souk.

admission charge) and mosque. When the original 14th-century, Merinid *madrassa* was rebuilt by Abdallah el Ghallib, the Saadian sultan made it the largest Koranic school in Morocco in a deliberate attempt to snub the imams of Fez, the religious centre of the country. The tortuous entrance is unusual but succeeds in enhancing the visual impact on entering the main courtyard, where a rectangular marble pool reflects the intricately carved cedar wood and plaster of the walls and the sky above. The open sky is an integral part of Andalusian architecture. The spacious courtyard leads to a prayer hall whose proportions, balancing detailed carving and *zellige* decoration, gives an impression of serenity through exquisite but disciplined beauty.

The Ben Youssef Mosque is more interesting for its history than for the building that now exists on the site. Rebuilt several times, the current mosque dates back only to the 19th century and is thought to be only half the size of the original. A mosque was first built by the Almoravides in the 12th century and would have been contemporary with the **Koubba el Baroudiyn ⓬** (a small ablutions chamber opposite the mosque), one of the very few surviving examples of Almoravide architecture in Marrakesh. Embodied in the *koubba*'s small carved dome and keyhole arches is the kernel of all Andalusian art that followed, right up until the present day.

Nearby is the **Musée de Marrakech ⓭** (Place Ben Youssef; daily 9am–6pm; admission charge; tel: 04 39 09 11), opened in 1997 and funded by the Omar Benjelloun Foundation. In the restored 19th-century Dar Mnebhi Palace, the museum displays a wonderful collection of Islamic calligraphy and, in the former *hamman*, a collection of 18th- and 19th-century lithographs and watercolours of Moroccan seaports, but its real purpose is to build up a collection of contempo-

rary Moroccan art and to hold exhibitions and other cultural events. In this it is hugely successful and is providing inspiration for other private foundations to follow. It also has a pleasant café in the courtyard, and a great bookshop.

Map on pages 240–241

The dyers' quarter

To reach the remaining sights on this tour, it may be easier to return to the Jemaa el Fna. From there, the short street leading past the Café Argana connects to a little square. From this, approach a discreet covered alley, the Rue Mouassine, directly ahead on the left. This is an often less crowded and more hassle-free entrance to the souk.

Follow the road northwards with a final right turn by some high-class jewellery shops to reach the Saadian **Mouassine Mosque and Fountain ⓮**. This mosque is probably the most impressive in the medina, and dates from the Saadian dynasty. However, little can be seen from the ground as it is heavily surrounded by shops and houses, so you should enquire in any of the nearby shops for access to a roof. You will be rewarded by the sight of green tiled roofs masking peaceful open courtyards that are hard to imagine in the bustle of the souk below. The fountain, with its plain white arches and discreet carved beam has an elegant beauty in marked contrast to the heaped brass of the souvenir superstore opposite.

Not to be missed is the **Souk des Teinturiers ⓯** (wool and silk dyers), past the square at a small junction of alleys, with a convenient but tiny café nearby. It is a constant miracle that the dyers can produce such vibrant colours from their cramped and blackened workshops. Rich iridescent skeins of green, yellow and red silks blaze against the bright blue sky. The dyers souk has become all the

Marrakesh is a good place to buy hand-woven carpets.

BELOW: an array of silks.

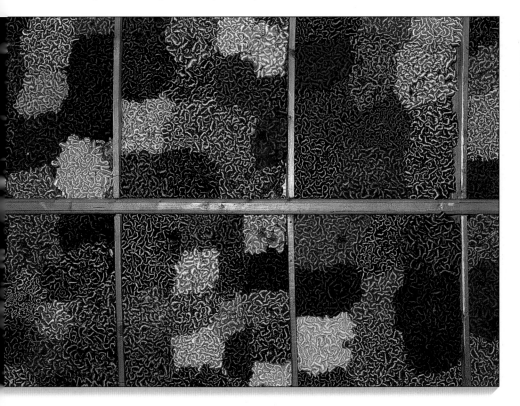

more important as an example of a traditional craft since the one in Fez is now defunct, replaced by industrial dyeing processes elsewhere in the city.

Past the wool dyers is a small covered alley identifiable by an old twisted vine. One side of it is dominated by stalls selling thuya wood carvings from Essaouira, but there are also a couple of junk shops and a small shop crammed with folk pottery, mostly from the Rif Mountains. This short covered souk links the dyers area to the Souk Attarine, and from there a right turn leads back to the easily recognised Souk Smarine.

The Pasha's Palace

Also in the northern part of the medina is the **Dar El Glaoui** , part of which today houses the offices of the Delegation du Culture. This was formerly the palace of the Pasha Glaoui who collaborated with the French to rule Morocco. The Glaoui, a Berber clan from the region of Telouet, were the last of the old-style despotic rulers of Morocco. While they never laid claim to the title of sultan it was their power and alliances that allowed the French to subdue the country *(see page 38)*.

The Glaoui were tribal overlords in the most traditional sense. With their own army they controlled the ancient medina, as they did the whole of the south, with a mixture of terror and generosity. On the one hand, they ran hundreds of brothels catering for French Legionnaires and had a posse of informers and spies who blackmailed and murdered on their behalf. On the other, they showered mistresses with riches, held lavish banquets and gave away fortunes to the poor. While the Pasha entertained Hollywood film stars, and even attended the Coronation of Queen Elizabeth II, his enemies where tortured and executed in dungeons straight from the pages of a tale of medieval horror.

A corner of the Majorelle Gardens. The intense cobalt blue of the buildings is used to enhance the green of the foliage – a trick Matisse learnt in Morocco.

BELOW: in the Jardin Menara.

Great escapes

The 16km (10 miles) of Marrakesh's city walls are best seen from a caléche (fares are posted on a wall, but it is best to agree a price before setting off) or a hired bicycle. Built originally by the Almoravides as a defence against the Almohads, the walls now have eight working gates, although many more are buried under rubbish or bricked up and built into houses. Worth visiting is the Almoravide **Bab Debbarh**, which gives access to the tanneries (just follow your nose). The **Bab Aghmat/Rhemat** is the gate through which the Almohads captured the city after Christian mercenaries betrayed the Almoravides by opening the gate to their attackers.

Outside the southern walls is a fortress called the **Squallet el Mrabit**, which once housed a squadron of cavalry to help defend the city. Close to the **Bab er Rob**, from where taxis and buses travel to the Ourika Valley and Imlil in the High Atlas *(see pages 271–2)*, is the much photographed **Bab Agnaou**, a small arch with a carved facade that was once an entrance from the medina into the imperial city.

After a day in the souk, escaping the medina can be a tempting prospect. Tea in the **Mamounia Gardens** is a favourite among visitors, but most *Marrakshis* head for a stroll in the Agdal or Menara gardens. The **Menara**, created in the 12th century by the Almohads, is the smaller though more famous of the two: if, however, you want to see the snow-covered Atlas rising over the 19th-century pavilion and rectangular pool, a view captured on countless postcards, you must time your visit for sunset during the first few months of the year.

The **Agdal** is much larger and has several pools but is less visited because of its greater distance from the centre. The **Jardin Majorelle**, in Gueliz, are a delight, with more botanical interest. The gardens were built by Jacques Majorelle, a French orientalist painter, in the 1920s, and a few of his pictures can be seen in the small museum in the gardens.

The city's role as an oasis is brought home on a circuit around the **Palmerie** (said to have sprung up from the discarded date stones of the Almohad army besieging the Almoravide city). The palmerie, sandwiched between the Casablanca and Fez roads (signposted "Circuit des Palmeries"), is also home to Marrakesh's rich and famous, who are numerous, and palatial villas set in luxuriant gardens abound. The **Café Palm d'Or** provides the chance of refreshment on the tour. The palmerie also has several large hotel complexes, such as Palmerie Golf Palace and the Palmeriva, offering riding, tennis, mountain biking and golf. Independent operations also cater for non-resident visitors who would like a round of golf or a gallop on a horse.

Arabian Nights

Elsewhere on the edge of town are the "dinner and spectacle" tourist experiences in which you can enjoy Arabian Nights-style entertainment. Of these Chez Ali is the original, and probably still the best. Catering for hundreds of guests each

Map
on pages
240–241

TIP

If you want a real break from the heat and hassle of Marrakesh, take off to the Ourika Valley, an hour's drive into the Atlas Mountains *(see page 271)*. For those without their own transport, buses for the valley depart from Bab er Rob.

BELOW: the El Badi Palace folk festival held in early June.

Map on pages 240–241

lunchtime and evening, it is a logistical phenomenon on the scale of a mini Disneyland. They may not be genuine cultural experiences, aimed as they are at the coach tour crowd, but the entertainments are fun and you can be sure children will love the *fantasia* horsemen and the camels, not to mention the laser projected girl on a flying carpet.

Royal favourite

On the northern edge of Gueliz, the French Institute (open Tues–Sat 8.30am– noon, 2.30–6.30pm) offers a library, exhibition space and occasional events and films. It also has a vibrant little café. Its programme is always posted at the main entrance to the Central Market in Gueliz.

All this merely scratches the surface of a city rich in monuments and with many still-inhabited palaces secreted away in its medina. King Hassan II spent more time in Marrakesh in the last months of his life and consequently inspired efforts to beautify the city. As a result gardens were planted around the medina walls, between the Bab Jdid and Bad Nkob, and much of the pavement along Avenue Mohammed V was repaired, as well as some inevitable tinkering with the city's fountains. It is to be hoped that the process will continue, although there is little sign that the Opera House (Marrakesh's premier example of an increasing number of white elephants) is any nearer completion. There are still no public parks of note and the Avenue Mohammed V remains the firm favourite for an early evening stroll, with the Avenue de France providing a lively alternative on a hot summer's night.

Above all, however, it is the atmosphere of the city that is compelling. Marrakesh is a place where you feel you could fall in love, or be murdered, make a fortune or be lost forever in its winding alleys. It is a city of conspiracy, of magic openly displayed, of pleasure bought, sold and given freely. It is no coincidence that the opening sequence of Carol Reed's *The Third Man* (1949) was filmed in the city's medina. It is the perfect place for a mystery.   ❑

BELOW: the rush hour in Gueliz.

A Garden City

Some 160km (100 miles) from the coast and too far from the cooling Atlas, Marrakesh is a furnace in summer. By two o'clock in the afternoon the sun's rays are so fierce that the air itself trembles from the onslaught. For the *Marrakshis*, relief is found in dark interiors, private courtyards and most pleasingly of all in the city's gardens.

The gardens of Marrakesh have always surprised and delighted visitors. The British writer Osbert Sitwell, in *Escape with Me*, called Marrakesh "the ideal African city of water-lawns, cool, pillared palaces and orange groves." It was the promise of gardens and flowers that drew Matisse to North Africa. He went in the footsteps of the writer Pierre Loti, who found "nothing but carpets of flowers", and the painter Eugène Delacroix, who remarked on "innumerable flowers of a thousand species forming carpets of the most varied colours".

The image of a carpet, though well-worn, is apt. The favourite theme of carpets all over the Islamic world is the flowering garden. Hung on walls and slipped over couches, rugs are winter reminders of summer's bounty.

Gardens are also earthly intimations of Paradise, the Eden of the after-life described in the Koran as "gardens watered by running streams". Entwined foliage, a constant motif of Islamic decorative art, runs riot over stucco carvings and faience tiling in Moroccan mosques and *madrassas*.

Marrakesh's great gardens are 19th or early 20th-century creations, though in most cases they replace earlier gardens which, starved of water during tribal warfare, had withered and died. Originally, they were agricultural estates, where the sultan would reap olives and citrus fruit for profit. On a smaller scale is the city's most recently renovated garden, the Majorelle Gardens, named after its creator, the French painter Jacques Majorelle, who lived in Marrakesh in the 1920s. Lovingly restored by the couturier Yves St Laurent, the garden is a kaleidoscope of tropical colour. Walkways are painted a dusty pink, flowerpots bright yellow, the ornamental carp in the lily-padded pools a vibrant orange.

Smaller gardens are found all over Marrakesh, in particular in the old palaces that have been turned into museums. The garden in El Bahia, for example, is a walled oasis, where the Grand Vizier's wives and concubines came to stroll and play to the accompaniment of birdsong. Pathways are laid out symmetrically, but plants, flowers and trees intertwine and overarch, creating an enclosed world where secret assignations would be veiled by curtains of accanthus and sweet-scented jasmine. This is no prissy arrangement of neat flower beds and clipped box hedge. Instead it is an intense explosion of perfume (roses, jacaranda, jasmine, orange blossom), juicy fruits (pomegranates, figs, carob, peaches, grapes), and the intoxicating pollen from the datura tree, said to drive people mad and known as the "jealous tree". The overriding effect is sensual. It is no accident that the best-loved plants in Morocco are those which release their scent at night, when their heady perfume contributes to the voluptuous courtship of lovers.   ❑

RIGHT: the Jardin Majorelle.

THE SOUTHWEST COAST

*Crashing Atlantic waves, eerie sea mists and darkly brooding
battlements lend drama and romance to the coast
between Essaouira and Agadir*

Map
on page
265

The southwest coast, between Essaouira and Agadir, is starting to see some changes. Once a forgotten strip of land with minimal rainfall, where local people fought to cultivate barren looking fields in a constant struggle against poverty, today there are the first signs of a burgeoning interest in tourism and the economic development of the region.

The area has become a popular trekking destination, with agencies offering camel treks along the coast between the extreme western edge of the High Atlas and Essaouira. It is the only way to visit some of the most magnificent unspoilt beaches in Morocco. Argan oil, a local produce, is also achieving international recognition as a healthy component in everything from salad dressings to cosmetics. There is talk of reviving the once annual Argan festival in Tamanar.

Essaouira ❶ is the region's prime attraction. It first attracted international attention when, Orson Welles chose it as a location for his 1952 film of *Othello*. It lies beneath low Mediterranean-type hills, carved up into small stony fields dotted with olive trees and thorny argans. After the wide lemon and pink coloured plain west of Marrakesh, or the flat Atlantic coastlands to the north, scales suddenly seem small and human. Houses are painted a jaunty white and blue, there are hanging flower-baskets and a thriving fishing harbour.

Yet the Atlantic beats against Essaouira with vigour, and the town's fortified walls, rooted in a ragged outbreak of rocks above a sandy bay, and a crop of rocky islands opposite, endow a sense of romance and drama. It has long been associated with artists, as numerous private galleries testify. In the 1960s the most idealistic of youth cultures congregated here, when Essaouira became a haven for hippies.

PRECEDING PAGES:
donkey riding
near Essaouira.
LEFT:
the battlements
of Essaouira.
BELOW:
climbing a palm
tree is possible.

Pirate enclave

Until quite recently the town was known by its Spanish or Portuguese name, Mogador. It was founded in the 18th century by Sultan Mohammed ben Abdullah as a free port for Europeans and their Jewish agents engaged in trans-Saharan gold, ivory and slave trading. Before this, it was a pirate enclave. In the 19th century it quickly became a thriving town and many of Morocco's Jews migrated here. In 1860 a traveller and writer called James Richards recorded in his *Travels in Morocco* that "the population is between thirteen and fifteen thousand souls, including four thousand Jews, and fifty Christians".

Both Christians and Jews incurred the dislike of the native people. The law of protection, under which men working for European merchants were exempt from Sultanic laws and taxation was blatantly abused. "Protection" was sold for large sums of money or for goods in kind.

One of the European-made cannons poised for action on the ramparts.

BELOW: Essaouira – a location for Orson Welles's *Othello.*

Designed by a European engineer, a captive of the Sultan Mohammed ben Abdullah, Essaouira has wider, more regularly shaped streets than is usual in Moroccan medinas. James Richardson wrote, "The houses are regularly built, with streets in direct lines, extremely convenient though somewhat narrow... There is a large market place, which on days when the market is not held furnishes a splendid parade, or corso for exercising cavalry."

Place Moulay Hassan, set back from the harbour and the tourist office, is the town's social centre; men congregate outside the Café de France or play pool in its once-elegant interior; the young gather at Café Sam's Macdonalds, and women, who are without exception veiled, come to sit in the square during the late afternoon.

Essaouira's main shopping thoroughfares lie behind Place Moulay el Hassan in **Avenue de l'Istiqual** and **Rue Mohammed Zerktouni**. Between Avenue Oqba ibn Nafi and Place Moulay el Hassan you will find an enclave of tourist shops and cafés. The **ramparts**, called the Scala (reached via Rue de Souka, past the sign for Hotel Smara), are Essaouira's main attraction. European cannons, several of British manufacture, gifts from the merchants to the Sultan Mohammed ben Abdullah, face the nearby islands, Isles Purpuraires, where Juba II established a factory for the manufacture of a purple dye derived from a shellfish, much in demand in 1st-century Rome. At the end of the 19th century, the islands were used as a quarantine station for pilgrims returning from Mecca who might be importing plague. It is possible to visit the islands by fishing-boat but permission must be gained from Le Grand Gouverneur in the province, a formality which is easily arranged through the tourist office.

In the potently-scented carpenters' souk beneath the ramparts, craftsmen

carve everything from small items such as boxes, bracelets and picture frames to large chess sets, tables and cabinets out of thuya and cedar wood. One of the finest woodworkers' souks in Morocco, it supplies shops and bazaars all over the country and abroad. To bring out the rich patina of thuya wood, the handicrafts are rubbed with cotton balls soaked in vegetable oil.

The **Museum of Sidi Mohammed ben Abdallah** (Wed–Mon 8.30am–noon, 2.30–6pm; admission charge) in Rue Laalouj, opposite the Hotel Tafoukt is well worth a visit for its collection of jewellery and costumes documenting the long Jewish presence in the city.

Music makers

Essaouira has now been discovered and is developing at an ever-increasing rate, thanks largely to the efforts of André Azoulay, a talented international banker, a native of the town, who was once one of King Hassan II's most trusted advisers. The annual Gnoua Festival, which began in 1998, has been a great success, featuring international musicians and attracting tens of thousands of Moroccan and foreign tourists. Until now the music festival has been free, although there is talk of making it a ticket only event in the future. Essaouira has a heritage as a hippy Mecca, once welcoming personalities such as Jimi Hendrix, and the festival fits easily into the town's easy-going atmosphere. During the week of concerts it feels rather like a Moroccan Woodstock.

The European fashion for buying up and renovating old Arab houses, which started in Marrakesh, has spread to Essaouira, giving the still largely sleepy town an international atmosphere, perhaps reminiscent of the time when it was Morocco's primary international port. The influx of interest and money is ben-

Map on page 265

Thuya trees grow in the flat sandy conditions around Essaouira. Short, like scrub oaks, they seem an unlikely source of the beautifully grained and coloured wood.

BELOW: beneath the battlements.

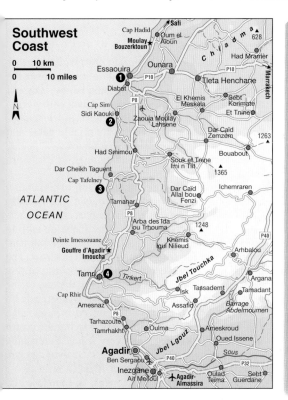

efiting the town as a whole. New hotels, *maisons d'hôtes* and restaurants are opening in the medina *(see Travel Tips)*. One of its most celebrated establishments, attracting reviews in the international glossy magazines and featuring in books on Moroccan architecture and style, is **Villa Maroc**, bordering the old city walls. Blending character and comfort, the aim of its British owners has been to create an authentic experience of Moroccan culture without sacrificing comforts such as freshly pressed linen, modern bathrooms and telephones. It offers individually decorated rooms, furnished with Moroccan handicrafts, open fires and Moroccan home cooking.

Another British expatriate, Jane Loveless, has helped organise the town's music festival and even set up an annual camel race along the beach. A kind of unofficial Essaouira promoter, she is one of several other enthusiasts who are helping to put the town back on the map and reinvigorate an economy that all but died with the large exodus of most of its Jewish population in the 1950s.

Small restaurants are popping up across the medina, some trying to create a bistro-type ambience. Châlet du Plage and Chez Sam, near the harbour, remain the best restaurants in town, although there is now no shortage of small, clean establishments where one can eat a decent meal cheaply. Another sign of Essaouira's new status is the reopening of its airport with – at the moment – limited flights to and from Casablanca and Agadir. Flights between the town and Marrakesh are likely to begin soon.

Essaouira has long attracted European tourists, but so far remains unspoilt. It tends to appeal to independent holidaymakers, looking for peace and quiet, although organised tour groups from Agadir and Marrakesh often visit the town during the day. It is also a good option for children (a sandy beach, interesting rock pools and battlements being the main attraction), and for surfers *(see below)*.

Best beaches

An arc of sand lies to the south of town, but further along the coast, off the P8 rolling its way over the foothills of the High Atlas to Agadir, minor roads and tracks lead to what the Moroccans call *plages sauvages* (wild beaches), long stretches of white sand-duned beaches thickly fringed by prickly gorse and argan trees and disappearing into thin mists in the distance. Surfers, who have been coming to Essaouira for years, frequent **Cap Sim** and **Diabat**.

Sidi Kaouki ➋, a beach just south of Essaouira, and dominated at its northern end by a spectacularly sited *koubba* is an excellent and very accessible alternative. It has become the focus for the wind-surfing brigade, with a kind of beach bum camper van park springing up for several months each summer. The increased trade has encouraged a little string of tiny cafés around the car park that marks the end of the road into the village, and the excellent Auberge de La Plage (tel: 044-47 66 00) with rooms overlooking the sea. Sidi Kaouki's superb sandy beach goes on for miles but it is prone to being very windy. Sunbathing often means trying to relax while a sandstorm rages all around you at a height of about 10cm (4 inches).

Cap Tafelney ➌, a white sandy bay enclosed by

hills and sheltering a small community of picturesque fishing huts (some of which sell a frugal selection of sea-damp provisions), can suffer from an off-putting surfeit of washed-up detritus after heavy storms. When the sands are clean, Tafelney offers one of the coastline's longest undisturbed beaches for anyone willing to get away from the tiny tarmac access point on its northern end.

Map on page 265

To Agadir

The road from Essaouira to Agadir is long, winding and remote. It is frequently doused in sea mists, even in mid-summer. The region is thinly populated, although roadside vendors selling local honey and argan oil *(see page 311)*, a strongly-flavoured cooking oil derived from the thorny argan tree, are fairly common. There are very few petrol stations along this stretch, so fill up before you start. Most of the coast, remote and parched, is the preserve of camel drivers and shepherds. It is accessible at Immessouane, once a tiny, picturesque fishing harbour, although most of the coast's secret beaches can only be discovered on foot.

Imessouane, once a pleasant little fishing hamlet with good beaches, on an otherwise remote stretch of coast, has been completely destroyed as a holiday getaway thanks to a new fish processing plant that has turned the little bay into an industrial site. One can only hope that the local population have at least benefited from opportunities for employment.

Tamri ❹, set in banana plantations, and Cap Ghir, the most westerly point of the High Atlas, are quiet, undeveloped places. As the road descends to Agadir, it meets sand-heaped shorelines, blasted by crashing waves, their profiles broken by natural sculptures of sea-battered rocks. These are some of Morocco's best beaches, tempting escapes from Agadir's commercialised attractions. ❏

BELOW:
Cap Tafelney.

THE HIGH ATLAS

Climb the highest mountain in North Africa, swim under waterfalls in the Ourika Valley, visit the seat of the Almohad Dynasty – the Atlas Mountains are packed with attractive possibilities

Map on pages 272–3

A ny mountain range 700km (450 miles) long and with summits over 4,000 metres (13,000ft) must be counted as a major topographical incident on planet earth. Since the first attempts by Europeans in the early 19th century to follow Arab trade routes across this great barrier, the number of foreign travellers penetrating the Atlas for pleasurable exploratory purposes until World War II probably never exceeded 1,000. The slogan "Death to the infidel!" applied to all unaccompanied strangers in this China of the West.

The Atlas mystique lasted even after a prominent pass, Tagharat, and a distinct summit, Gourza (3,280 metres/10,700ft,) had been reached by outsiders in 1871. The Hooker-Ball-Maw expedition observed, "The climate is admirable, the natural obstacles of no account, but the traditional policy of the ruling race has passed into the very fibre of the inhabitants, and affords an obstacle but impassable to ordinary travellers."

These days the Atlas is more accessible, and its inhabitants, having developed keen entrepreneurial instincts, are more hospitable towards visitors. Three main roads penetrate the High Atlas from **Marrakesh ❶** *(see page 243)*: the spectacular Tizi N'Test pass *(see page 289)*, the less interesting S511 through the western Atlas to Agadir (in winter); and the well-maintained Tichka Pass to Ouarzazate *(see page 289)* West of the Tizi N'Tichka, the High Atlas rises up to the jagged peaks of the Toubkal Massif, before descending to the Tizi N'Test pass. From the Tizi N'Test, the Atlas Occidental continues westwards, north of the city of Taroudannt, running down to meet the Atlantic Ocean between Agadir and Tamri. South of Toubkal the Jebel Siroua is a remote outlying plateau of extinct volcanic plugs filling the gap between the High Atlas proper and the Ouarzazate–Taroudannt road.

A taste of the Atlas

If you are staying in Marrakesh but not planning to travel very far afield, it would be a shame not to venture into the Atlas for at least a day or two. The easiest excursion – still recommended despite being a tourist draw – is to the **Ourika Valley**, about an hour's drive south along the S513, or a 1½-hour bus journey from Bab er Rob in Marrakesh.

The road, following the river, leads to the village of **Setti Fatma ❷**, high in the cleft of the valley. A busy mule track cuts deeper south, but the main attraction is the series of seven waterfalls on the far side of the river, the first of which is reached after an easy climb through the rocks and trees. In the summer this is a popular spot for young tourists and *Marrakshis*. There is a small café and swimming in a deep, icy rock pool. Above, wild monkeys stalk the craggy heights and

PRECEDING PAGES: the Dades Valley with the High Atlas behind.
LEFT: a mountain livestock market in full swing.
BELOW: dressed for the part.

shower walnuts. In the village there are a couple of hotels and a number of cafés. Newly established is the beautiful and inspiring Pinatel organic herb garden at the mouth of the valley, set up by two brothers for the production of organic essential oils.

One of the pleasures of walking in the Atlas is to order a tajine (a slow-cooked stew) in a local café before setting off for the day and finding it ready and waiting on your return.

THE TOUBKAL MASSIF

Shimmering in haze beyond the pink walls of Marrakesh, long flecks of snow barely 60km (38 miles) away brush the rugged profile of the southern horizon. This is the Toubkal Massif, the craggy mass of rocky peaks and deep valleys that contains the highest summits of the Atlas chain. Roads teeming with peasants and domestic animals, scooters and lorries belching diesel fumes, cross the hot Haouz plain to **Asni ❸** where there is an important Saturday market. A turning to the right before the market leads up to Moulay Brahim and the Kik Plateau. To the south of Asni, somewhere in the distance at the head of the Mizane Valley, towers **Toubkal ❹**, at 4,167 metres (13,670ft) the highest mountain in North Africa. Asni marks the end of French cuisine and comfortable quarters.

As nothing is done by the clock in country districts, pick-up trucks come and go according to demand along the 17km (11 miles) between Asni and the Mizane roadhead at **Imlil ❺**, a good base from which to explore the Toubkal area. A few thousand people come to Imlil in spring and early summer to climb Toubkal. For a mountain of this height and accessibility to have had its first recorded ascent (by a French party under the Marquis de Segonzac) as late as 1923 testifies to the tribal fortress mentality maintained by the natives well into the 20th century. Visitors also go hiking round the district – there are five- to 10-day circular tours, staying overnight in remote huts, Berber outposts and sometimes open-air bivouacs.

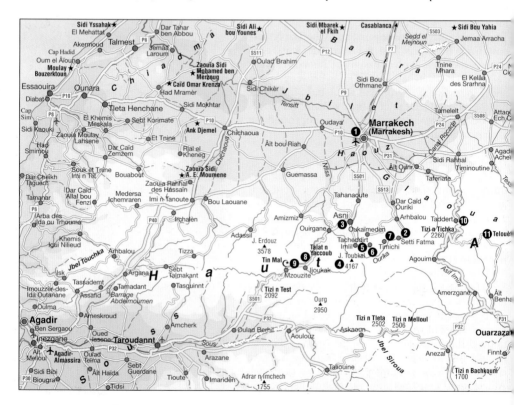

Map
on pages
272–3

Trekking companies predominate in these activities and deal with all the logistical problems of organising porters, provisions and accommodation. The more self reliant can always backpack and dispense with the local services on offer, although it would be wise to seek advice on routes and weather conditions beforehand, especially during winter.

There is now a Bureau des Guides in Imlil and anyone travelling independently for the first time in the area is recommended to pay it a visit, even if they have no intention of hiring a guide. Nationally qualified guides are called *accompagnateurs,* and are registered with the Ministry of Tourism. Several are resident in the Imlil district, although it must be said that their skills can vary; some are highly competent, others very much less so (try to get a recommendation if you can). They all speak French, with a few counting English, Spanish or German among their language skills. The guides will not only lead you on the right path, but will also take charge of the hiring of mules and the provision of supplies on longer expeditions. As a rule, one mule can carry the baggage of three trekkers equipped for three to four days. But mules cannot cross snow and on the Toubkal path they will stop at the snow line, from where their loads are carried by porters.

Prices for guides and mules/muleteers are regulated, although the rules are not always respected. If you expect extra duties, such as the guide also doing your cooking, or if you choose to take a muleteer and no guide, don't be surprised if you have to pay more than the usual rates. All prices are exclusive of their food, which you are expected to provide.

From Imlil, for those shod in boots, there are a number of easy day hikes up to the Tamatert pass in the east, *(see page 275)* or the **Mzic pass** in the west, both

A stork in the ruins of Telouet. These birds are believed to bring good luck.

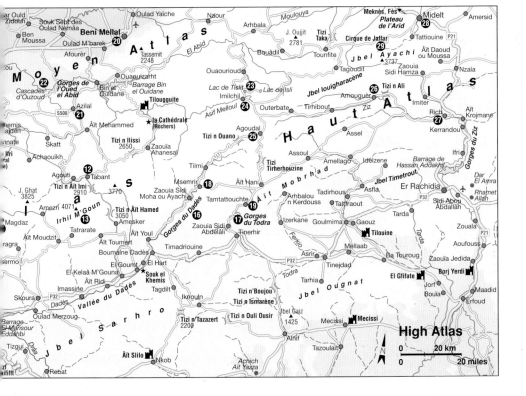

TIP

To find out about
trekking facilities in
advance of your stay
in Morocco, *see Travel
Tips*. In Marrakesh, the
hotels Ali and
Foucauld are the
places to meet up with
guides from the
mountains and check
out the possibilities of
treks, mountain
biking, whitewater
rafting and other
activities.

BELOW: tattooed girl
near Setti Fatma.

giving superb views back and beyond to the continuing chain of ridges and peaks overlooking the villages and green terraced fields of the Berbers.

Aremdi is the last village in the Mizane Valley before the long hike up to the high mountains. It is an important trekking centre with a range of *gîtes*, a small hotel and a campsite. The valley here is more open than in Imlil and is a beautiful place to spend a day or two acclimatising before the rigours of an arduous trek, or even recuperating before descending to the manic bustle of the souk in Marrakesh.

Sidi Chamharouch, which is a pastoral shrine with associated shops catering for pilgrims, lies two hours along the mule trail in the upper Mizane. Like a beacon, its white roof draws many on a day's outing; walk or ride a mule. Among this huddle of little houses squeezed into a niche at the foot of a rock slope all Berber life is exposed to public view.

Allow four to five hours to hike up the valley to the CAF Toubkal Refuge (formerly called the Neltner Refuge). The recently enlarged refuge has much improved dormitory facilities and a large communal area for cooking and eating. A spring supplies the hut, via a buried pipe, although it is still recommended that you boil drinking water. Gully water in the stream below flushes the toilets. Refreshments and simple meals can be ordered from the warden. During the summer months it is sensible to book a place in the refuge via a message carried by the in-season shuttle of mules and porters from Imlil (do this a day before going up to the hut). Camping below the hut is becoming increasingly popular; there is a plan to clear a proper site for tents, with improved sanitary and rubbish clearing facilities.

If you climb Toubkal outside the summer trekking season (mid-May until

mid-October; remember that you have to leave the refuge by 6.30am) you may need crampons and an ice-axe for complete comfort as well as stout boots and proper clothing. Knowing the prevailing conditions, a guide will advise exactly.

The ascent is perfectly straightforward, merely a gradual walk up a stony slope, until one reaches the notorious upper scree, where care must be taken as one false move might be dangerous. Moreover, the path has been ruined by the careless footwork of by thousands of tired limbs.

The route is graded by Atlas mountaineer Peyron as "*type boulevard*" and, indeed, after about four hours, the summit appears like a big open corral. You'll find people – usually the T-shirt and flip flop brigade – stamping their feet and trotting round to keep warm.

Treks and traditions

A popular trek, which can been lengthened or shortened according to taste, takes the path from Imlil over the **Tamatert pass** to the crossroads village of **Tacheddirt ❻**, in a relaxing 3½ hours. It is an appealing Berber settlement epitomising traditional ways of life. There is accommodation in a mountain hut or in a couple of *gîtes* in nearby villages.

The major climb to the **N'Addi pass** (2,900 metres/9,600ft) that looms behind the village is rewarded by views of ravines and peaks zebra-striped with long streaks of snow. Riding a mule will be allowed only on the easy down slope to the broad pastures of Oukaimeden below. A ski resort during the winter, in spring this site is quiet and almost deserted and its CAF hut (tel: 31 90 36) is like a hotel, with all mod cons, and admirably run by Jean and Michelle. Other accommodation possibilities are the small but comfortable Hotel Angour (Chez

Map on pages 272–3

At first sight the Atlas appear to be remote. In fact, one-quarter of Morocco's population lives on ground over 1,000 metres (3,300ft) above sea level.

BELOW: snow in the High Atlas.

Juju, tel: 31 90 06), and the reopened Kenzi Hotel, a huge alpine-style pyramidal hotel currently struggling to get enough guests to keep it going.

A local viewpoint with an orientation table behind the Moroccan-style chalets commands a wide vista towards Marrakesh; there are prehistoric rock engravings along the north side of the pasture plateau. Huge flocks of sheep and goats graze here in early summer, brought up by villagers from the lower valleys. The massive hulk of Angour dominates the scene. While an asphalt road goes back to the city, a mule path winds westwards, over the Tizi N'oukaimeden, down paths through stunted walnut forests and evergreen oak, back to the terraced fields of the Mizane and Asni, a good five-hour hike.

At the head of the Tacchedirt Valley lies the Tacchedirt pass, leading to the large village of **Timichi** ❼, from where paths lead over the **Tizi N'Ouattar**, again to Oukaimeden, or continue to Setti Fatma at the head of the Ourika Valley *(see page 271)*. For the really adventurous, the towering **Likemt pass** offers routes over to the southern side of the Atlas, descending eventually to Ammzouzerte, in the Tifnout Valley, at the head of which lies the remote Lac d'Ifni *(see page 276)*. Seen from the height of the moraine that blocks its southern end, the lake is like a blue-green jewel set in a bowl made by towering naked peaks. From its northern shore a path sets off across rocky ground to a tortuous gully that leads up to the mountain's highest and most spectacular pass, the **Tizi Ouanouns**, to regain the head of the Mizane Valley, which descends first to the Toubkal Refuge and finally back to Imlil. The entire round trip is a one-week trek, without rest days or excursions to explore or climb nearby peaks.

All this merely scratches the surface of an area rich in opportunities for trekking, with many more routes heading off west of Imlil for almost as many days as you have the energy to walk.

The restored Tin Mal Mosque, seat of the Almohad Dynasty.

BELOW:
a switchback ride.

To Ouirgane and Tin Mal

Back on the **Tizi N'Test** road, continuing south of Asni *(see page 272)*, the route continues to **Ouirgane**, a country resort sporting two hotels which make good lunch stops: the more upmarket is the Roserie (run by a one-time manager of Marrakesh's La Mamounia), which is an excellent place for a drink, but never quite lives up to expectations as a place to stay. More satisfying is the Sanglier Qui Fume, under new ownership since 1997, a characterful country retreat, perfect for an overnight stay in the country.

A little further on is **Ijoukak** (where a piste leads into the less visited **Agoundis Valley**). Close by stands the ancient kasbah of **Talat N'Yaccoub** ❽, surrounded by olive groves, with the foaming Oued Nfiss lapping at the foot of its ramparts. Dominating an adjacent knoll, with the snows of the western Igdet as a backdrop, is the **Agadir N'Gouj**, a former stronghold of the Goundafi tribe that was notorious in the 19th century for its dungeons. The entire location is now regarded as one of the outstanding beauty spots of the Great Atlas chain.

Higher up on the other side of the stream is the 12th-century **mosque of Tin Mal** ❾, birthplace of the Almohad movement that eventually gave rise to the famous Berber dynasty of the Middle Ages. This

Map on pages 272–3

mosque, which is roughly contemporary with the Koutoubia in Marrakesh, has now been renovated and is one of the few in Morocco that non-Muslims can visit (outside prayer times).

The mountain behind the mosque is **Gourza**, first climbed by the Hooker botanical expedition in 1871. The Test road narrows near the top of the pass but it then has a good surface all the way to Taroudannt. Animals winding along in Indian file and sentinels watching over groups of dromedaries are some of the images that will be etched on travellers' minds, but the area is actually an environmental disaster, as vast forests have been chopped down for building materials and firewood. Here, and similarly along the eastern boundary of the Toubkal Massif plainly marked by the Tichka pass commercial road, the watershed divides the lush from the barren. A quilt of green fields stitched round a few oases occasionally brightens the monotony.

THE WESTERN HIGH ATLAS

The Toubkal area is bordered on the west by the S501 Tizi N'Test road. Beyond rises the Occidental or Western High Atlas, remote to most tourists but surprisingly densely populated and supporting a thriving agricultural economy. The **Seksawa Valley**, its boxy dwellings planted on mountain sides prickling with television aerials, is the principal road by transit lorry from Marrakesh. Adventurous tourists bent on exploration away from the crowds will find many diverting sights in this region.

One rewarding way of visiting the area is by mountain bike (they can be hired in Agadir). The mountains are not as rugged as the Toubkal, and the area is more densely covered by piste. As a base for such expeditions, one could do

The mountain range was named the Atlas by Europeans inspired by the Greek myth. According to the story, after the Titan Atlas was turned to stone by Perseus his burden became a mountain, supporting the heavens. Bowed by the weight, Atlas genuflected towards the setting sun in northwest Africa.

BELOW:
souk in Msemrir.

much worse than Imouzzer-des-Ida-Outanane *(see page 308)*, with its excellent hotel and nearby waterfalls.

EAST OF THE TOUBKAL MASSIF

On the eastern side of the Toubkal Massif the Yagour plateau (rife with pre-historic rock engravings) and the Zat Gorge lead down to the **Tizi N'Tichka**, meeting the main P31 road from Marrakesh just above **Taddert**  ❿. This is a one-street town, lined with grill shops and the last truck stop before a dizzy series of heart stopping hairpin bends takes you up to the 2,260-metre (7,412-ft) pass. The Auberge des Noyers, a survivor of the Protectorate period, has rooms and a walnut shaded terrace at the back where you can drink cold beers.

View of Telouet from the kasbah, the one-time power base of the Glaoui.

The Tizi N'Tichka is a superb drive, but it is mainly a transport artery and is little used as a start point for trekking. About 20km (12 miles) east of the Tichka and deliberately side-tracked by the main road built in 1936, lies **Telouet** ⓫, the old Glaoui seat of power situated on the old caravan route. It is famous for its kasbah, deserted after the fall from grace of the self-styled Sultans of the South *(see page 39)*. First visited by a European in 1889 and once host to Wilfred Thesiger on his treks through the Atlas, the crumbling ruin is sufficiently intact to give an impression of past splendour. Local children will fetch a custodian who can unlock its gate and give a small tour, pointing out the once magnificent reception rooms and the bower from which the privileged guests of the Glaoui could watch *fantasias* staged in the arena below.

BELOW:
an ammonite.

Further up the Animter Valley the path leads through a fertile valley up to the isolated Tamda Lake, full of trout and surrounded by stones, tightly packed with tiny fossils. The surrounding mountains are bare and lonely and largely

GEMS AND FOSSILS

In the Atlas and Middle Atlas, makeshift stalls selling rocks packed with crystals and semi-precious stones, such as amethysts and quartz, can prove irresistible. The usual advice is, be cautious, as some of the items being hawked are not genuine. That said, many are, and you will sometimes see European gem traders examining stones under a magnifying glass. At one such stall, in 1996, a British geologist discovered an intensely blue pyramid-shaped rock, which the stallholder told her was lapis lazuli. Realising that it wasn't but still intrigued by the rock, she bought it for a few dirhams and on her return home took it to London's Natural History Museum. Tests revealed it to be an entirely new mineral containing silicon, aluminium, calcium, magnesium, iron and oxygen.

Fossils, too, are found on these stalls, including some impressive examples of ammonites *(see left)*, Morocco being one of the world's best sources of this fossil. And it was again in Morocco, in 1996, that the bones of a meat-eating African dinosaur as large as *Tyrannosaurus rex* were found. Though scientists had known of *Carcharodontosaurus saharicus* prior to the find, only one other skeleton of the dinosaur had been found previously, and that had been lost.

uninhabited. Eastwards the path meanders across the Tizi N'Fedhrat to the picturesque village of Magdaz *(see page 280)* and the start of the mountains of the M'Goun Massif (the Central High Atlas) with its fertile valleys and canyons.

Map on pages 272–3

THE CENTRAL HIGH ATLAS

The trekking base centre on the north side of this sector is the **Bouguemez (Wgmmaz) Valley**, a broad expanse of greensward sprinkled with small villages, with an administrative post at Tabant. Once a Shangri La, it now has good vehicle access via a mostly tarmac road from the market town of **Ait Mhammed** (near Azilal, the provincial capital, *see page 282*). Trekking is normally problem-free after early May but can be difficult in winter and spring, when heavy snows can block the road. The new road (turn right just before Ait Mhammed when coming from Azilal) has shortened and eased the journey, and Landrover taxis regularly ply the route between the market town and Ait Bouguemez.

An outdoor centre and guides school has been opened at **Tabant ⑫** by the CFAMM (Centre de Formation aux Métiers de la Montagne). The town also provides contact with the local mountain rescue group and has telephone facilities. Accommodation is provided in *gîtes*, some of which offer facilities such as *hammams*, hot showers and electricity powered by generators or solar panels.

The tremendous barrier ridge of **Irhil M'Goun ⑬**, 20km (12 miles) long, dominates the area; it remains a formidable test of endurance until sleeping quarters are established. Comparatively easy to reach are the mammoth whalebacks of **Azurki** (3,677 metres/12,100ft) and **Ouaoulzat** (Wawgoulzat) (3,736 metres/12,340ft), which take about four or five hours each.

...I became lost in the castle, and found my torch shining upon white but manacled bones in a dungeon. With the turbulent history of Telouet they could have been either a hundred or less than five years old.

– GAVIN MAXWELL
Lords of the Atlas, 1966

BELOW:
among the aspen trees in winter.

Mules and porter assistance are essential in the Central High Atlas; it is virtually impossible to cover the terrain or the distances without them. Thus supported, there are fine expeditions to be made to big limestone synclines such as **Tignousti** and **Rat**, and cross-country and river bed journeys of several days to attractive villages such as **Magdaz** , where the famous poetess Mririda n Ayt Attik was born under the tutelary pyramid of Lalla Tazerzamt. The spectacular sheer sided gorges of Tessaout and Arous, draining southwest and northwest respectively from M'Goun, invite wet-suited wanderers and rock climbers.

Climbing in a gorge in the Central High Atlas.

Canyons and gorges

The most frequented canyon trek in the region is the **M'Goun (Achabou) Gorge**. It winds south from the Central Massif to the Dades valley at El Kelaa M'gouna) on the P32 road. In one place it forces a passage between overhanging rocks for 8km (5 miles), while the total river distance from El Mrabtin to the Issoumar/ Bou Taghrar dirt road is 50km (30 miles) and takes two days. Supported by mules and porters, supervised parties go from Tabant Bou Guemez over the Ait Imi pass to El Mrabtin, an arduous leg even without the burden of a rucksack. The best time to tackle it is June to late July when assorted plunges and wading shallows are appropriate for bathing suits and gym shoes. There are no technical difficulties, but pack animals unable to follow through the narrower sections are obliged to detour along a dizzy man-made staircase on the canyon wall.

Berbers use the river bottom as a conventional thoroughfare, and you will stumble upon family groups crouching among the boulders, brewing mint tea. The trek is subject to the water level and to weather conditions (it can be dangerous in thunderstorms). A guided tour lasting three or four days can be taken from El Kelaa. To quote Peyron: "Not all of it is hard work; there are moments then the magic of the canyon plays on the mind inducing serenity and reverie."

Another way into this region is from **Demnate**  (100km/60 miles from Marrakesh) along the lorry pistes of Tifni, the Outfi pass and Ait Tamlil. Tour operators work most of these valleys but rarely ascend their great mountains except for the Mgoun summit.

Coming from the south, the valleys off the P32 Dades road from Ouarzazate to Skoura, El Kelaa and Boumalne (the so-called Route des Kasbahs) are harder still, and the preserve of seasoned climbers and walkers accustomed to treeless and waterless wastes. Guiding services can be found at El Kelaa M'gouna. Getting a lift to Boutaghrar on the Oued M'Goun cuts out the worst of the walk there.

The Dades and Todra Gorges

The Sahara side of the Central High Atlas is cut by several gorges of some repute. Two have become well known as scenic routes following improvement to their piste tracks. The **Gorges du Dadés**, emerging at Boumalne, and the **Gorges du Todra** at Tinerhir, both on the P32, can be traversed along their lengths.

The two gorge circuit takes five or six hours by four-wheel-drive. Proceeding up the Dades the verdant narrow valley meanders from village to village. The road, looping west to avoid obstacles, rejoins the river at Ait

Arbi, with its characteristic watch towers set among gardens shaded by venerable walnut trees. Dazzlingly bright, the white limestone spurs jut into the valley. The vertiginous incision of the gorge commences outside Ait Oudinar.

After a ford to the east bank the piste has been blasted from sheer cliffs. Fields with industrious Berbers hoeing and ploughing appear as the gorge widens out. Near the last ford a glimpse west into the broad Oussikis hollow reveals the density of villages crammed round a jigsaw of green patches. The Berbers spend their lives trying to recover and develop arable land.

So we come to **Msemrir** ⑱ (65km/40 miles) with its colourful Saturday market and the historic meeting place between two of the major nomadic tribes, the Haddidou and Merghad, enemies to a man until they came together under the Yafelmane federation. The dirt road ahead begins a long crawl to the Ouerz pass. In just over a kilometre (½ mile) a prominent right-hand fork is reached at point 1996, where there is a survey pillar, signpost and drinking fountain. The piste curves east between stark escarpments to reach the Ouguerd Zegzaoune pass in an empty area of the "badlands". Even at this height the heat is intense, and a mirage lurks round every hairpin bend.

A longer descent and another fork south deposits you in **Tamtattouchte** ⑲ on the seasonal Temda stream, the chief feeder to the gorge lower down and the site of several *marabouts*. The road winds south and in 5km (3 miles) enters the upper Todra Gorge. Floods sometimes close the canyon to vehicles. Parts of the new piste have been raised above the river bed, first on the west side and latterly in the main gorge on the east side, which begins just after the tight bend at point 1599. One extraordinary sight is palm trees sprouting from the stony bed. When the river vanishes in the dry season, the bed is used as a highway by

Map
on pages
272–3

Many of the names of the villages are preceded by the Berber word Ait, *meaning "of the people".*

BELOW:
kasbah living.

pedestrians and animals. Though less forbidding than the Dades, its rock walls soar 400 metres (1,300ft) and the defile at its narrowest point is impressive. The Hotel Yasmina is the first of a number of hotels and restaurants in the gorge, preceding a series of pretty Todra villages along the west bank. Gardens, small fields, date palms and fig trees presage the magnificent oasis of **Tinerhir**, noted for its gold and jewellery workshops, castellated buildings and decayed palace (20km/19 miles from Tamtattouchte).

THE EASTERN HIGH ATLAS

Beni Mellal ⓴, on the P24 to Marrakesh, is a large market town, offering several places to stay. The town also marks the frontier proper between the High and Middle Atlas mountains. Going north towards Khenifra, the Middle Atlas branch out on their own, an ever-increasing distance separating the two ranges as the Middle Atlas reaches north. Beni Mellal is a good stop-over for motorists wishing to visit the Cascades d'Ouzoud, impressive waterfalls off the S501, a detour off the main P24. The good road twists up to the vast **Bin el Ouidine** reservoir *(also see page 230)* and then on to **Azilal ㉑**, a market town with a basic hotel, bank and modest restaurants.

The **Cascades d'Ouzoud ㉒** are signposted off to the right about 10km (6 miles) beyond Azilal. From the road's end, an easy path snakes through trees to the base of the falls, passing low-key cafés on the way. There are no restrictions on swimming; people simply strip off to their bathing costumes and plunge in. Rock climbing is also popular. There will always be a few visitors around, but the falls only get busy on weekends and holidays, when locals head here from Beni Mellal and Marrakesh.

TIP

Beni Mellal offers the most comfortable accommodation for visiting the Cascades d'Ouzoud. The other options, the Auberge du Lac at Bin el Ouidine, the Hotel Tanout at Azilal, and Dar Essalam at the falls themselves, are all basic, with no heating and sometimes no hot water.

BELOW: in the hunting season, Beni Mellal.

To Imilchil

Northeast of Beni Mellal is the departure point for the arduous off-road journey to Imilchil and beyond. Along the secondary 1901 road (there's a hotel at El Ksiba) towards Arhbala, a fork south at Azarar Fal proceeds to the Abid bridge over the Ouirine River, where the tarmac runs out. In dry weather the continuing piste can be managed by ordinary cars with good ground clearance; tour firms use a variety of four-wheel-drive vehicles. Drive through sundry villages among oak forests, over several rivers, up to **Tassent** and along its ravine with tricky zig-zags and broken edges, past the old French army memorial to a moderate descent to **Lac de Tislit ㉓**, with its twin, **Lac de Isli**, out of sight further to the east. The complete journey takes five hours. The lakes establish a natural boundary between the Central and Eastern massifs. This magnificent high grazing area translates as the Celestial Fields of Berber legend. According to the tale, the lakes of Isli (the man) and Tislit (the woman) were formed by the tears of two young people whose love was thwarted by their feuding families.

Today the September *moussem* at **Imilchil ㉔** is dominated by the Brides' Festival, held to celebrate the legend *(see page 65)*. Young men and women dressed in their traditional finery go courting from tent to tent while families negotiate the chattels a marriage might produce. It is a rare aspect to a gathering that is otherwise a religious-cum-rural fête noted for its enormous market. The *moussem* has become known world-wide and has consequently transformed the event into an important stopover for four-wheel-drive mountain safari tours.

Accommodation in Imilchil itself (the festival is held a few kilometres south of the town) is available in two small unclassified hotels, as well as some Berber inns and cafés. The village also runs to a weekly market, stores and a local

It was in the region of Azilal in the late 1970s that scientists found the bones of the so-called "Atlas Giant" (Atlasaurus Imelakel), a 165-million-year-old dinosaur that proved to be one of the oldest and largest saurians ever unearthed.

BELOW: Lake Tislit, which is noted for its rich birdlife.

authority headquarters. There are gentle river walks beside turreted buildings or longer strolls on piste tracks across kilometres of pasture between the lakes.

Vantage points near Imilchil are **Amalou N'Tiffirt** (2,470 metres/8,100ft), which takes one hour; and **Bab N'Ouayyad** (2,804 metres/9,200ft), which takes three hours. Summits here tend to be merely long hikes. **Msedrid** (3,077 metres/10,100ft) is probably the most frequented and takes two days without four-wheel-drive assisted approach.

Those touring on wheels can leave Imilchil by the pulverising trail south to **Agoudal** ㉕, one of the highest inhabited villages in Morocco. After some spectacular scenery over the Tizi Tirherouzine pass, the track eventually arrives in **Ait Hani** where a piste continues to Todra. Alternatively, there is an equally thrilling piste from Agoudal to Msemrir and the Dades Gorge, crossing the Tizi N'Ouano. For the less adventurous there is now a good piste from the site of Imilchil's *moussem* that quickly turns into tarmac after **Amouguer** ㉖ and emerges at **Rich** ㉗, close to the road to **Midelt** ㉘. The latter, spectacularly perched on the edge of a high plain, has hotels and restaurants and is a good stop-off en route to the Tafilalt Valley in the south. It is also an important market for carpets, fossils and minerals (azurite, malachite and aragonite).

Secret canyons

Northwest of Agoudal, towards **Anergui**, over the vast undulating tableland called Kousser, the terrain is cracked by several precipitous watercourses. The spectacular Tiflout is the master canyon, fed by snaking tributaries of some complexity. This system of ravines introduces another dimension to Atlas exploration. Potholing, caving, and rock climbing techniques, sometimes calling for

In addition to the many carpet shops in Midelt, take a look inside Kasbah Myrien, a carpet workshop run by Franciscan nuns, that produces good quality kilims and Berber blankets.

BELOW: pomegranates for sale at the Brides' Festival, Imilchil.

Map
on pages
272–3

bold swims in squeezes (tunnelled rocks), require equipment and experience. These gorges and their mysterious branches have been used for centuries by the Haddidou Berbers as shortcuts during their migrations. Jungle tracks among creepers, waterfalls bulging over sheer drops into pools, and raging torrents can all be experienced. Wood and rock bridges (passerelles) must be treated with caution. One of the main arteries is the Melloul, a stretch of 20km (12 miles) between Anergui and Imilchil populated by cliff dwellers. The others are the Tiflout (35km/22 miles), Wensa (15km/9 miles) and Sloul (15km/9 miles). Approaches and exits add to these distances and represent the serious work.

The Jaffar Cirque

The extremities of the Eastern High Atlas culminate in the Jebel Ayyachi (3,750 metres/12,300ft), whose backbone is double the length of Irhil M'Goun. The **Jaffar Cirque** ㉙, named after a local saint, is an inlet with parking places that marks the best departure point for an ascent of the mighty **Ayachi** (3,737 metres/12,300ft). A crumbling 24-km (15-mile) piste known as the axle breaker also extends from Midelt, and there is a similar but longer unmade track from Tounfite. Picturesque rock cataracts, the ravines of the Ijimi Valley and clumps of dwarf conifers combine to make the area a popular picnic spot.

Snow cover on the mountain is normal until at least June. Most attempts to reach the summit start at dawn from a bivouac at 2,200 metres (7,200ft), about 30 minutes above the road, and a fit party can attain the summit in 5½ hours. Seen from the north in full winter robe, 40 km (25 miles) long and with a dozen named summits, the mountain is one of the most arresting spectacles in Morocco. ❑

BELOW:
a bride of Imilchil.

THE SOUTH

*South of the High Atlas spread the spectacular landscapes
of the south – sandcastle architecture, vast palm oases
and the great river valleys of the Draa and the Ziz*

Map
on pages
290–291

othing north of the Atlas prepares one for "Le Grand Sud", a vast expanse of desert and semi-arid mountains stretching to the Algerian border. There is hardly a road in the region that cannot be described as spectacular. It is a film-maker's dream: wide valleys studded with palm-packed oases, mud-built castles rearing out of the ground, jagged blue mountains stretching across almost every vista. Martin Scorsese filmed *Kundun* in southern Morocco, glorying in the wide desert landscapes hung with backdrops of the snow covered Atlas mountains. The people are equally striking: leather-skinned nomads herding flocks; veiled, sombre-clad women evoking Sara and Salome; shy girls flitting among vegetable gardens and disappearing into shadowy back alleys.

Southern Morocco runs westwards from Figuig, on the Algerian border, to Goulimine in the southwest (the gateway to the Western Sahara, *see The Deep South, pages 305–19*), a distance of almost 1,000km (600 miles). It is bounded by the Atlas Mountains to the north and by the Algerian border to the south, where it is lapped by the sands of the Sahara.

Of particular interest are the central valleys, the Draa, the Dades, Ziz and Tafilalt. The geography of the region is formed by the Anti-Atlas, a range of outlying semi-arid mountains that break up the south. In the east, the Sarhro wedges the Draa up against the Jebel Aklim Massif; in the north the Dades drains between the Sarhro and the Atlas proper; eastwards the Tafilalt peters out on the edges of the Grand Erg Occidental.

The Draa is Morocco's longest river, a huge wadi that finds its source in rivers flowing south from the Atlas and is augmented by streams from the Anti-Atlas. It survives the increasing aridity of its southward journey, turns west to form the border with Algeria, and eventually emerges exhausted at Tan Tan on the Atlantic coast.

PRECEDING PAGES:
in the Todra Gorge.
LEFT:
the Jewish Kasbah
in Amazraou.
BELOW:
woman of Rissani
in the Ziz Valley.

Routes to the south

From Marrakesh, three passes cross the Atlas Mountains to the south. The most spectacular is the Tizi N'Test (2,100 metres/6,890ft), which leads to Taroudannt via 306 km (140 miles) of hair-raising bends *(see page 272)*. The second route south from Marrakesh is over the Tizi N'Tichka (2,260 metres/7,415ft) to Ouarzazate (190km/118 miles), along a wider, better maintained road *(see page 278)*. Buses and grand taxis serve both routes, but they stop at many small villages along the way and progress is slow: buses via the Tizi N'Test take 7–8 hours, and via the Tizi N'Tichka around 6 hours (four in a *grand-taxi*). In winter both passes are often closed, in which case the only passage south will be via the less interesting route via Imi N'Tanoute to Agadir.

Kasbahs of the stars

If your main aim of travelling south is to see the Draa Valley, the Tizi-N'Tichka to Ouarzazate, the gateway to the Draa, is the best route to take. Most of the Atlas villages along the route are covered in the chapter on the Atlas Mountains, but 18km (12 miles) before Ouarzazate, there is a short side road to the **Kasbah Ait Benhaddou ❶**, probably the most celebrated kasbah in Morocco. Featured in numerous films (including the 1999 blockbuster *Gladiator*), it is a fortified warren of narrow streets across the valley on a small hill. Today, this UNESCO World Heritage Site is still inhabited and many of its residents are happy to show you around their homes and recount stories of their filming experiences.

Access to the kasbah from the road is through the small modern town of shops, restaurants and *auberges* that have sprung up to service the stream of visitors. Beyond here it is necessary to wade, or take a mule, across the Mellah River. The kasbah is really a town of many smaller kasbahs, all built from the same deep red earth and often with intricate details carved into their walls. The huge gate is not part of the original design, but a film fantasy built for *Romancing the Stone* so that Michael Douglas could drive a plane through it.

A few kilometres north of the kasbah, across a broken-down bridge, is the much smaller, but once beautifully decorated **Kasbah Tamdaght**, now abandoned to a family of storks. From here the piste continues north along the old trade route to Telouet *(see page 278)*.

Springboard for the Draa

Ouarzazate ❷, the capital of the south, sits astride the Draa, at the end of the Tichka road, dominated by the Atlas range that fills its northern horizon. It is a

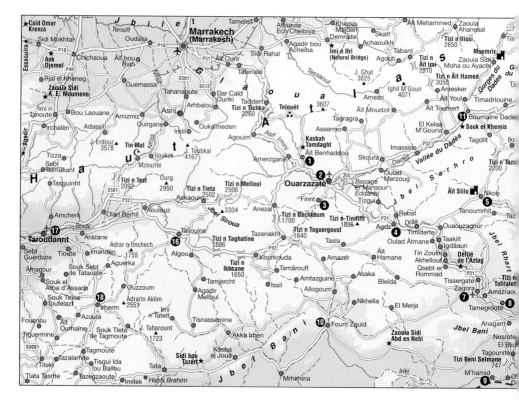

Map below

crossroads through which everyone must pass, and was originally a base of the French Foreign Legion. It is now increasingly important to Morocco's film location industry, and is served by a plethora of hotels and an international airport. It is a modern town of little character or interest, but hidden away are a number of features that bring to life its short history.

The Legionnaires have left their mark in the church, which is still maintained by Catholic nuns, and **Chez Dimitri** restaurant. Once a wild drinking hole, Dimitri's is now famous as one of the best restaurants south of the Atlas, thanks to its colourful founder. Dimitri was an energetic Greek, who jumped ship in Casablanca as a 14-year-old in 1928 on his way to the United States. He eventually made his way to the Legionnaire post of Ouarzazate, where he set up his soon to be celebrated restaurant. His son, who now runs the place, grew up rubbing shoulders with the likes of Orson Welles, and had his own moment of film fame playing the son of Anthony Quinn in *Lawrence of Arabia*. Despite the rapid development of numerous hotels and restaurants, Dimitri's is still the most memorable eating place in town. There are hotels of all standards here *(see Travel Tips)*, but the modest La Gazelle has the most character. Dating from 1962, it offers comfortable, modest rooms arranged around a pleasant garden courtyard behind its popular restaurant.

Scattered around the church and hotel are the bizarre sculptures of the Legion's last remaining representative in the town, an eccentric Austrian who rose to the rank of corporal and then chose to stay behind in Ouarzazate as the Legion pulled out, only to blow his own arm off with a grenade.

Overlooked by the Club Med is the **Kasbah Taourirt**, whose Glaoui palace, empty and partially open to the public, has some fine painted wooden ceilings.

Early morning traffic of mules, donkeys and people is a sign that there is a souk close by: watch out for a large encampment of tents.

BELOW: typical pisé architecture.

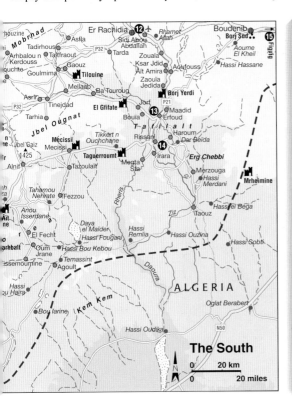

The South

0   20 km

0   20 miles

Much of the rest of the kasbah village is still occupied and worth a visit. Just to the west of town is the **Kasbah Tiffoultoute**, now a restaurant with a few rooms offering basic accommodation. Yet another Glaoui abode, the kasbah is frequently the setting for fashion shoots and film and video fantasies. The singer Paula Abdu shot a music video here.

Further along the road from Tiffoultoute, a piste heads off west, passing a small lake, to the peaceful oasis of **Finnt ❸**. A short excursion from Ouarzazate, this green oasis is hidden deep in a small river valley surrounded by barren hills. It is the perfect place to sip tea and explore a microcosm of rural life in the Moroccan south.

Along the Draa Valley

South of Ouarzazate, the road winds through arid hills, cut by an impressive gorge with a black patina, eventually descending into the oasis of Agdz. Before the descent, a dirt track signposted **Cascades du Draa** offers a delightful excursion. Although reached via a terrifyingly steep piste, the destination is an Arcadian gorge, with waterfalls and pools suitable for swimming plus a modest café.

A small market town with a carpet-clad square, **Agdz ❹** is surrounded by a sea of palm trees. Left from the square a small road leads to a camp site with a pleasant café. Nearby is a huge rambling kasbah, still occupied and under restoration. The resident family is very friendly and willing to give visitors a tour of their home. If you do nothing else here, climb up to the government fort (once a Legionnaire garrison) to admire the view.

South of Agdz, the valley widens considerably. Here the banks are clothed in tall reeds and often brightly decked in freshly washed clothes. Across the

BELOW:
Ait Benhaddou.

Map on pages 290–291

valley stands the **Kasbah Timiderte**; isolated like a medieval fortress, it is one of the classic images of the southern Draa. As the towering metropolises of mud multiply, the Sahara begins to make its presence felt, costumes change, and the colourfully-clad women of the mountains are replaced by black-swathed and much darker skinned people. As the road approaches Zagora the changes are increasingly acute, the enclosed villages more densely packed, and reed-built palisades check the increasing quantities of drifting sand. White-domed *marabouts* stand stark against the brown and ochre of the earth.

A turn-off at **Tansikht** marks the start of the road to **Tazzarine** and **Alnif**, which now has a tarmac surface and links up with the road between Erfoud and Rissani in the Tafilalt. Once an arduous two-day drive across a bone-crunching piste, it is now much improved and hire cars can make the crossing from Zagora to Rissani without the need for too much back-tracking. This is also a rewarding drive along the southern slopes of the Jebel Sarhro, containing some of Morocco's most dramatic desert mountain scenery.

As you drive east from **Tansikht**, the road runs first through the large village of **Nkob** ❺. It is the southern focus of the Ait Atta Berbers of the Jebel Sarhro and has a lively souk on Sunday. It is also the southern starting point for the spectacular piste crossing the Tizi N'Tazazert and an important base for winter treks and camel expeditions across the mountains to destinations as far away as Merzouga. A few *gîtes* have developed and the semi-nomadic Ait Atta make marvellous guides, combining great dignity and hospitality. The region of the Sarhro is a rugged wilderness with an extraordinary geology that has given it a reputation as the "Monument Valley" of Morocco.

Further along the road is **Tazzarine** ❻, famous for its henna. Although the

BELOW: Agdz.

town is less attractive than Nkob, it is situated in a spectacular valley and has a pleasant campsite and a few simple hotels.

Zagora ➐ is the main market of the south. The nomadic Ait Atta, Saharan Berbers who found their way into Morocco in the 17th century, mix with old Arab families who emigrated from the Arabian peninsula in the 12th century. Clinging to the side of Jebel Zagora, on the south bank of the river, are the remains of an 11th-century fortress built by the Almoravides, testament to the antiquity of the town despite its dusty modern streets. A signpost declares Timbuktu a mere 51 days camel journey away. Zagora was once a confluence of trade routes. Camel caravans from the south broke their journey here before making their onward journeys east and north.

Holy centre

About 12km (7 miles) south of Zagora is **Tamegroute** ➑, a dusty little town which has a tiny weekly souk. Tamegroute is dominated by a *zaouia* of the Sufi Naciri brotherhood that has been a centre of religious learning since the Almoravides spearheaded a wave of religious re-awakening in the 11th century. It was also the cradle of the Saadian dynasty *(see page 30)*. The *zaouia* incorporates a *madrassa* which, although now a modern school, has its origins in the 17th century. Alongside the school is a celebrated library (another modern building) which counts among its treasures Islamic commentaries written on gazelle skin dating from before the 13th century. It is open to visitors.

The *zaouia* also attracts some of the most underprivileged members of Moroccan society, people suffering from mental or physical illness, or simply lost souls who find their way to its peace and charity from as far away as Casablanca.

Tamegroute also supports a pottery whose products are famous for a distinctive green glaze derived from a cocktail of ingredients including locally mined magnesium.

BELOW: evening near Erg Chebbi, Merzouga.

Desert dunes

South of Tamegroute the first sand dune appears around Tinfou, marked by the Auberge Repos de Sable (tel: 04-84 85 66). Owned by an artist couple living in Rabat, and run by their son, the auberge is a ramshackle gallery of Moroccan contemporary and folk art.

M'hamid ❾ marks the end of the road south. Once a Beau Geste outpost, garrisoned by the Legion's camel corps, it was later a target of the Polisario guerrillas *(see page 48)*. Sand and date palms crowd the last few kilometres of road before the town, which is rapidly becoming a centre for camel trekking and a pit stop for four-wheel-drive excursions into the desert. However, the town itself has little to recommend it other than a few rather predatory small hotels and a weekly souk held on Monday. Perhaps more comfortable is the campsite just before the town, which also organises camel excursions into the Erg El Yehudi.

West of M'hamid is a track to **Foum Zguid ❿** (four-wheel drive only). The area between, which still has a strong military presence (the Algerian border is never more the a few kilometres away), offers a taste of the true Sahara. The Iriki Basin has Morocco's most extensive area of dunes, a wide mirage-haunted region, occasionally inundated by freak rains in the surrounding hills. The area is inhabited by ancient Arabic speaking nomads, descendants of the Bedouin of Arabia, who live amicably alongside Berber Ait Atta tribesmen. A permanent winter campsite has been set up in the picture-book oasis of **Oum Laalag** in the middle of the Iriki Basin. Surrounded by scattered palms, with a spring and three wells, the oasis is sited between the dunes and the Jebel Bani (the northern limit of the depression) and is a perfect place from which to explore the desert, though you will need the help of a local guide.

Map
on pages
290–291

By camel, Zagora is 51 days from Timbuktu – or so the notice claims.

BELOW: in the grain market, Taroudannt.

A hotel with a pool, like this one at Boumalne, is recommended from late spring through autumn when average southern temperatures range from 30–40°C (86–104°F).

Canyons and roses

Return to the head of the Draa Valley to explore the **Valée du Dades**, popularly known as the Valley of Kasbahs, east of Ouarzazate. The Dades finds its water high in the Central High Atlas and this bursts out of the mountains in one of Morocco's most spectacular canyons, the **Gorges du Dades**. At its mouth is the town of **Boumalne ⓫**, a centre for roses and their associated perfume industry (a festival is held each spring to celebrate the opening of the rose buds). Like its sister, the **Gorges du Todra**, this 1,000-metre (3,280-ft) canyon, sheer in places, becomes a raging torrent in spring when the snow thaws on the Atlas. These gorges comprise one of the best bird-watching areas in Morocco, with Black Wheatear, Red-rumped Wheatear, Moussier's Redstart, Tristam's Warblers, Crimson-winged finch common, along with many types of lark, sand grouse, buzzards and falcons.

The parallel Todra Gorge was once populated by Jews, who still remember Todra in a popular Hebrew folksong. Of the two gorges, the Dades, which is longer and in places wider, is probably the more beautiful. Extraordinary rock formations like elephant hide look as if they have only recently lost their molten ability to move. *(For more information about the Todra and Dades gorges, see The High Atlas, pages 271–85.)*

The Ziz and the Tafilalt valleys

Beyond **Tinerhir**, the road traverses arid hills to arrive at the crossroads town of **Er Rachidia ⓬**, a modern town and the regional seat of government. A few kilometres south of here is the **Source Bleu de Meski**, head of the other great valley of the south, the Ziz. Once an idyllic oasis, the clear pools have been cemented and a characterless café has done its best to destroy what atmosphere remains. Walk a little way downstream, however, and the landscape opens out into a vista of picturesque villages and hills, and you will meet young girls swathed in black, who come to collect water in copper pots.

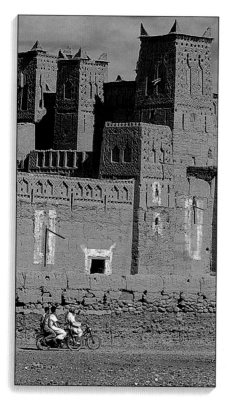

After Meski, the Ziz River and the Tafilalt appear, a great scar of a valley that cuts through barren hills. The drive to Erfoud is spectacular as the road first descends from the plateau to the sheer-sided valley floor and then winds its way through a string of villages. The people of the Tafilalt are very different from the communities inhabiting the Dades and the Draa to the west. The home territory of the ruling Alaouite dynasty, the Tafilalt is an isolated Arab community, whose roots in the valley are far older than those of the Berber tribes surrounding them today. Their villages are impenetrable fortresses of covered and winding alleys; they themselves are inward-looking.

Erfoud ⓭, another recently developed town, has no medina and its streets are laid out in a grid, but it is pleasant nonetheless and well prepared to meet the needs of tourists. A base for exploring the Tafilalt, it has several hotels, restaurants, petrol stations and mechanical repair shops.

Rissani ⓮, at the end of the Tafilalt, is another great trading crossroads, and home to Morocco's most African market, a continuous mêlée of haggling and jostling, where enormous trucks compete with laden donkeys. Rissani is said to be one of the world's largest date palmeries, with some 4 million trees and more than 100 varieties of dates (a festival is held each autumn to herald the harvest). Like Tamegroute, the city is also an important religious centre, based on the tomb of Moulay Ali Sherif, the founder of the ruling Alaouite dynasty. Behind are the ruined remains of the Alaouite Ksar Akbar. Surrounding Rissani are deep rutted tracks, which turn to mud in rain, linking yet more isolated adobe villages and *zaouias* dating as far back as the 13th century.

Close to Rissani lies **Sijilmassa**, founded by an Arab general at the beginning of the 8th century. At its peak in the Middle Ages it had developed into a fabulously wealthy city that dominated the south of Morocco, gaining its wealth through the all important trans-Sahara trade. Today it is nothing more than a pile of barely distinguishable rubble, not really meriting a visit.

East of Erfoud and Rissani are the dunes of **Erg Chebbi**, often referred to as Merzouga after the small village and military outpost towards their southern limit. The dunes here are the highest in Morocco and regularly host film crews shooting on location. On a clear winter day, it is possible to see the snow-capped M'Goun Massif, more than 150km (93 miles) away, from the summits of the dunes. Before dawn Land Rovers set off in droves from Erfoud's smarter hotels taking tourists to experience a true desert sunrise. If you want to experience the dunes in relative peace, it is advisable to avoid the well-worn track leading to the cluster of small cafés at the dropping-off point for the tourist convoys. Camping among the dunes is possible, and it's recommended if you really want to experience the powerful appeal of the desert, but you may be visited by a policeman wanting to check on your passport details.

Map on pages 290–291

TIP

The Kasbah Derkoua (tel: 055-57 71 40), a few kilometres before the dunes of Erg Chebbi, is a pleasant auberge. Its owner has spent most of his life deep in the desert; the kasbah is a haven of good food, natural charm and peace.

LEFT: testing marrows. **BELOW:** drawing water in Taroudannt.

Eastern outposts

Between Er Rachidia and the Algerian border crossing at Figuig is 400km (250 miles) of gravel plain, with little to relieve the eye, save the occasional palm plantation in the Oued Guir, a scattering of *ksour* and the mountains in the distance. Humanity here is mostly represented by military outposts.

At the end, rarely visited, is **Figuig** , which is even more remote from the north, for the road from Oujda is longer and emptier than the one from Er Rachidia. Like an island in the ocean, Figuig is an oasis of date palms and gardens. Springs, some hot, feed a maze of irrigation channels. Separate and jealous communities, barricaded within now crumbling *ksour*, fought each other for lack of other enemies until the French provided them with a common foe.

Figuig was once a major staging post on the overland route to Mecca. It supported a significant Jewish population up until the 1950s. Today, traffic to Algeria is much reduced and most of the town's inhabitants are soldiers. Despite all this, Figuig has an undeniable attraction; it is a haven of calm, a fertile destination after a long journey through a seeming void.

The Jebel Siroua

BELOW:
the Dades Valley.

West of the crossroads at Ouarzazate, the P32 climbs between the Anti-Atlas and the volcanic peaks of the **Jebel Siroua**, a high, sparsely populated plateau, roasting in summer, heavy with snow in winter. It is a harsh and remote range, dominated by old volcanic plugs, of which Mount Siroua at 3,304 metres (10,837ft) is the highest. Few people come here to trek and those who do usually come in late spring or autumn to avoid the extremes of weather. The most popular access routes to the high peaks are from the south, where the road passes

fields of saffron and runs through the carpet-weaving villages of the Siroua Berbers. Along the way the road passes through **Tazenakht**, a market for carpets. Further west is **Taliouine** ⑯ a snug but essentially one-horse town. There are few guides who specialise in this area, although some of those who are well known nationally lead the odd trek here each year. The only really competent guide based in the area is Jadid Ahmed at the Auberge Souktana in Taliouine.

Just before Taliouine, a huge rambling ruin appears, another Glaoui kasbah. It is still inhabited by descendants of the Glaoui's servants; dozens of noisy children usually swarm round visitors in an over-enthusiastic welcome but they will happily guide you through the ruins. Alongside is a particularly unattractive hotel, which is all cement and charmless despite its fine view. Not far from the town is the much more attractive Auberge Souktana, which also offers hiking excursions into the Siroua hills.

For those with time to spare, but little inclination to hike, a tarmac road cuts into the Siroua from Taliouine to **Askaoun**, an uninspiring government centre in the middle of one of the most beautiful and unspoilt parts of the Atlas. From Askaoun a road turns west to Aoulouz, back on the P32, while a spectacular track north heads towards the peaks of the Atlas then swings east, away from the Tifnout Valley, joining the Tizi N'Tichka road at Agouim. A long and arduous trip, it should not be regarded as an easy excursion to make in a small hired vehicle. You will need a four-wheel drive vehicle and a local guide.

To Taroudannt

The journey on to Agadir from Taliouine enters the Sous Valley, a huge fertile river plain. The walled city of **Taroudannt** ⑰ sits, like a miniature Marrakesh,

Map on pages 290–291

A sand fish, usually seen in the dunes. Other reptiles include lizards and snakes, the most dangerous of which is the venomous horned viper

BELOW: crossing the Draa near Zagora.

Map
on pages
290–291

Spices heaped in Taroudannt's souk, which is one of the best in the south.

BELOW: welcome to the Palais Salem.

in the heart of the valley. Centuries ago Taroudannt served as a staging post for dynasties on the road to power, and was a temporary seat of government before the capture of Marrakesh itself. In 1912, it was also the stronghold of El Hiba, the "Blue Sultan", whose short-lived revolt against the French protectorate ended in his bloody expulsion at the hands of High Atlas Berbers allied to the colonial power.

Few monuments to the city's rich history now remain, apart from the walls, which still follow their Almoravide plan. The **Palais Salem Hotel** (tel: 85 21 30) is worth a visit, even if you are not staying there. Converted from the 19th-century palace of the then pasha, the hotel's public rooms maintain some of their original splendour and the ground-floor rooms enclose small, luxuriant gardens of which the towering banana trees form the crowning glory. About the only other historical site in the town is the impressive **Bab Kasbah** in the eastern side of the walls.

Taroudannt's chief attraction is its souk, and as a result this once quiet, largely tourist-free city has become firmly established as a popular coach excursion from Agadir. Prices and hassle have both increased accordingly, but the small scale of the souk and the individualistic crafts on offer make it an enjoyable and easy place through which to wander. There are a couple of notable antiques shops whose owners have a fine eye for the unusual and sometimes outright bizarre. But do not expect ancient winding alleys and beautiful old *riads*, however, as much of the medina is made up of dilapidated concrete houses with barely a pavement in sight.

Outside Taroudannt, on the road to **Amezgou**, is the **Gazelle D'Or** (tel: 85 20 39), which is one of the most exclusive hotels in Morocco, if not the world. It

is famous for its huge gardens and tasteful interior decor, and was once the home of a French baron. Patronised mostly by wealthy Europeans, it cultivates an exclusive country club atmosphere, and regularly attracts international celebrities, including, infamously, Sarah Ferguson, the Duchess of York, who spent a holiday here with John Bryan before she separated from the Duke.

South of Taroudannt

From Taroudannt, route 7025 climbs the Anti-Atlas massif of Jebel Aklim to the town of **Irherm** ⓮, a small market and administrative centre at one time noted for its silversmiths. The road beyond descends spectacularly, through striated hills and huge valleys (dwarfing what villages there are) to **Tata**, an oasis on the edge of the Algerian Sahara. From Tata, the road to Tissint, Foum Zguid and back north, is tarmaced. This eastwards route is rewarded with views of enormous wadis, sometimes filled with the distinctive black camel and goat hair tents belonging to nomadic herdsmen.

West of Tata, the road arrives at Goulimine, gateway to the deep south and the Western Sahara *(see page 313)*, which is famous for its Saturday morning camel market. Alternatively, a turn-off north, onto the P30 a few kilometres before the town, leads to the resort of Agadir via Tiznit. ❏

On Location

The most famous film to conjure up an image of Morocco is *Casablanca*. However, the film, like many others at the time, was entirely filmed on a back lot in Los Angeles. Yet Morocco has been a real destination for film makers since the very beginning of cinema. Way back in 1897, the Lumière brothers shot *Le Cavalier Marocain* on location. Marlene Dietrich also made her US debut in 1930 with a film called *Morocco* directed by Von Sternberg, who shocked many with Dietrich's lingering screen kiss to another woman before striding off into the desert dressed in full tuxedo and high heels. The Marx brothers also came to Morocco to make *A Night in Casablanca* in 1946, and Hitchcock made good use of Marrakesh's mystery in the opening sequence of *The Man Who Knew Too Much*.

Other classics that have taken advantage of Morocco's rich landscapes are Orson Welles' *Othello* (1952), shot in Essaouira, El Jadida and Ouarzazate, David Lean's *Lawrence of Arabia* (1962), John Huston's *The Man Who Would Be King* (1975) and *Sheltering Sky*, directed by Bertolucci (1990).

More recently, the Hollywood blockbuster *The Mummy*, the award-winning film *Kundun*, and *Terms of Engagement* were all at least partly filmed in Morocco, on location budgets running to many millions of dollars. The country now rivals South Africa as the continent's premier filming location.

Much of this success is attributed to the energy of the Centre Cinematographique Morocain, the country's film commission. Set up during the Protectorate period, the CCM licenses the industry, approves scripts and issues filming permits. In a country known for its over large bureaucracy, it is an enthusiastic and efficient organisation run by people who are film-makers themselves.

The surprise hit *Hideous Kinky* retold the story of the 1960s in Morocco from a child's perspective and made great use of Marrakesh's medina. All in all, the publicity created for Morocco from hosting such films does more to promote the country than even its own Ministry of Tourism.

However, it is not just Morocco's stunning scenery and improving infrastructure that attracts producers. There is a growing wealth of skilled technicians and talented craftsmen, who can turn their hands to producing costumes, props and scenery of all types. In *Kundun*, Moroccan craftsmen not only built replicas of Tibetan temples but also made most of the costumes and props – to such authenticity that Tibetan monks, who came to act in the film, wept on seeing the sets.

Moroccan film production companies have sprung up in Marrakesh, Casablanca and Rabat, and film lighting hire is available. Literally thousands of Moroccans are now employed not just as extras, but as technicians, assistant producers, directors, designers and actors. The industry is creating real employment opportunities and making a significant contribution to the economy. Allied to it is a constant stream of TV commercials, music videos and fashion shoots all helping to turn Morocco into a new California. ❑

RIGHT: David Lean's classic *Lawrence of Arabia* was partly filmed in Morocco.

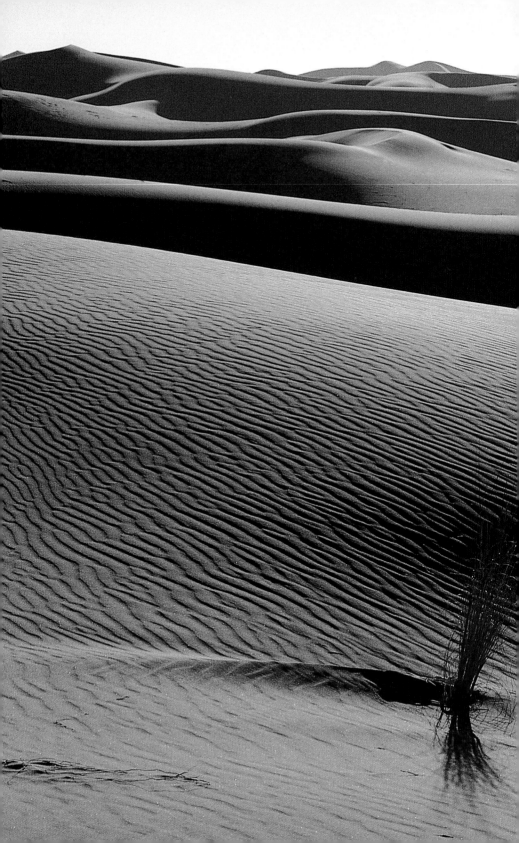

AGADIR AND THE DEEP SOUTH

Agadir, where Morocco strives hardest to create a "playground resort", is a springboard for expeditions into the Anti-Atlas and along the coast to Goulimine, the gateway to the Western Sahara

T he city of **Agadir** ❶ has changed greatly in recent years. It has expanded enormously and its tourist infrastructure has become more sophisticated, with new and better quality hotels, restaurants and nightclubs opening all the time. The city is Morocco's premier beach resort and attracts as many tourists as the rest of the country put together. It is not, however, typically Moroccan and it would not look out of place on the Costa del Sol; there is no ancient medina and no historic monuments or souks to visit; the frantic concentration of life that is so characteristic of Moroccan towns is lacking here. But that is not to say that it cannot be a pleasant city to visit. With its international airport, it is easy to get to, and it is an ideal base from which to venture into some of Morocco's most spectacular scenery. The centre of town is clean and has numerous well-tended green spaces.

The predominantly Berber city is home to an impressive university that has been instrumental in a revival of Amaziah (Berber) culture *(see page 64)*. There is also a French Institute that holds exhibitions and cultural events.

Rising from the ashes

During the night of 29 February 1960, an earthquake destroyed Agadir. The quake wasn't a strong one, but its epicentre hit the old town kasbah with devastating effect. The town had for centuries been a fishing port and a market centre for the valley of the Oued Sous, which runs out to sea to the south. But on the morning of 1 March, most of the town was rubble: some 15,000 people died and 20,000 were made homeless, as 3,650 buildings were destroyed. Agadir had effectively to be rebuilt from scratch.

Modern Agadir was conceived as a showcase for the new country. A modern port, administration centre and new tourist complex were built almost in segments, a process that has taken many years and is still continuing today. New residential quarters have spread out from the city centre and new access roads have been constructed, planted with palms that one day will line wide straight dual carriageways linking the city to the main Marrakesh road.

Fishing is a major industry of the city, which claims to be the largest sardine fishing port in the world, and there is a continuous stream of Spanish refrigerated trucks carrying fresh fish northwards to the markets in the Iberian peninsula. Within the port itself there is a yacht mooring and a good restaurant, while in the nearby square from late morning until late evening in summer (early evening in winter) tightly packed stalls

Maps:
Area 308
City 306

PRECEDING PAGES: a sea of dunes. **LEFT:** a view of Agadir. **BELOW:** Agadir's sandy and protected bay is great for children.

serve freshly grilled seafood at inexpensive prices in a lively bustling atmosphere. Invisible around the headland is the heavier industrial docks.

Sunshine coast

TIP

To help while away the time while sunbathing on the beach, visit the Crown English Bookshop (8 Avenue Moulay Abdellah), which also exchanges second-hand books.

For tourists, however, the city's prime attraction is its 10km (6 miles) of broad sandy beach and an average of 300 days of sunshine a year. In summer Agadir, which is cooler than the interior of the country, is prone to morning sea fogs, while the winter climate is often sunny and clear with temperatures in the mid-20s Centigrade (upper 70s Fahrenheit). The beach is huge and impeccably clean. Lining its promenade are hotels, beach clubs, bars, cafés and restaurants. At the centre of the bay is a ridge of rocks, exposed at low tide, that shelters much of the beach from Atlantic breakers and makes for safe swimming most of the time (flags provide warnings of dangerous conditions). Beach activities on offer include paragliding around the bay, towed behind a speedboat.

Inland, between Boulevard 20 Août and Boulevard Mohammed V is a wedge of tourist shops, restaurants, hotels and residences. Similar tourist complexes have sprung up along the beachfront, especially to the south around the Tikida Beach Club. They are not particularly Moroccan, conforming more to the international idea of beach resort facilities. Tavernas and pubs abound, as do German, Italian and hamburger-style restaurants. More unusual are the Korean establishments including the stark Coreen Jazz-bar (open until 2am) on the northern end of the beachfront (catering for the large numbers of Asian seamen who dock in Agadir) and the entertaining Samurai Japanese restaurant (tel: 84 03 35, part of the TRYP Hotel) where the samurai-carrying chef prepares dishes at the tables.

The best view of the city is from the **kasbah** Ⓐ on the hill which dominates

BELOW: hiding in a tree at the Medina d'Agadir.

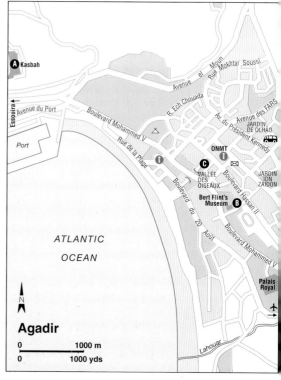

ATLANTIC
OCEAN

Agadir

| 0 | 1000 m |
| 0 | 1000 yds |

the northern end of the bay. It's a bit far to walk, but the road winds around the hill giving superb views down onto both the fishing and industrial ports before turning back on itself to overlook the beach and the city. The kasbah is the one historic monument left in the town; an inscription over the entrance in both Dutch and Arabic dates back to the middle of the 18th century.

Map on page 306

Other places of interest in the town are **Bert Flint's Museum** ❽ in the basement of the municipal theatre (9.30am–1pm and 2.30–6pm; admission charge), which houses a fine collection of jewellery; and the **Vallée des Oiseaux** ❻ (Wed–Sun 9.30–noon, 2.30–6pm, Tue 9.30–noon; admission charge), a park-cum-zoo between Hassan II and Avenue 20 Août, with various aviaries and animals in pens, including a group of Moroccan moufflon, a cross between a goat and a sheep. Outside town, on the Inezgane road, is the **Medina d'Agadir**, a new but traditionally constructed kasbah, built by an Italian architect called Coco Polizzi, and housing not only a collection of handicraft shops but also busy traditional craft workshops making everything from doors to mosaic tables and floors for architectural projects around the country.

Sporting Agadir

Apart from the beach there are good sports facilities. These include some excellent golf courses, the Royal (tel: 63 12 68) and the larger Dunes (tel: 83 46 90), the latter run by Club Med, but open to non-residents. The Royal Tennis Club (tel: 84 01 45) is on Hassan II in the centre of town. There are also a number of possibilities for horse riding, but the Royal Equestrian Club (tel: 22 79 76), accepts individuals for lessons and excursions on an hourly basis or longer.

Numerous agencies in Agadir, including Massira Travel (tel: 84 00 75) offer

Paragliding, just one of many sports that Agadir has to offer.

BELOW: in the Vallée des Oiseaux.

sea fishing expeditions and excursions into the hinterland. Safari Quads (tel: 01 38 37 00) specialises in daily excursions on all-terrain vehicles. If you want more independence, car and motorcycle hire is available from a plethora of offices on Mohammed V or Hassan II.

Around Agadir

Twelve kilometres (7 miles) north of Agadir is a signposted turning to **Imouzzer des Ida Outanane ❷**, a spectacular drive through the so-called Paradise Valley, a palm lined gorge with cascading springs, ending in the prettily sited village, some waterfalls and the delightful Hotel des Cascades (tel: 82 60 23). A little beyond the turning for Imouzzer is the smaller resort of **Tarhazout**, a popular surfers's beach, with its own campsite and, it is rumoured, the imminent construction of a huge new beach development.

If all the tourist frivolity of Agadir leaves you wanting more real contact with the local life of the city, visit the Foyer Rose du Sud School (tel: 22 74 99) by the local Association of Parents and Friends of Mentally Handicapped Children in the Sous. Their school, entirely funded by private donations, is an inspiring project and the children are delightful. The director, Mr Essamadi, would be delighted to organise a visit for anyone sufficiently interested and, of course, would gratefully accept any donation towards the running of the school.

South of Agadir

As you leave Agadir, heading south, the real Morocco crowds back around the roadside. For the first few kilometres, you're still in the estuary plains of the Oued Sous: flat fertile land where trees line the road and villages are rows of

The nature reserve of the Oued Massa, 51km (32 miles) south of Agadir offers opportunities for bird- and wildlife-watching. The reserve is home to the rare Bald Ibis and runs an Arabian oryx-breeding project.

BELOW: Tafraoute.

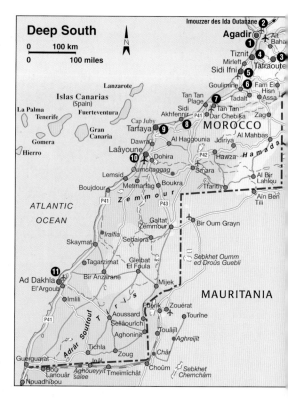

small, cell-like shops in arcades where metalworkers labour next door to butchers. The road skirts the town of **Inezgane**, southern Morocco's most important fruit and vegetable market, and splits into three in the centre of **Ait Melloul**. One road leads up the Sous River, westwards to Taroudannt and the High Atlas, a second road runs south to Tiznit, and a third crosses the mountains to Tafraoute. A triangle of roads connects Ait Melloul and Tiznit to Tafraoute, and the fastest way to reach the valleys around Tafraoute is to keep to the wider, straighter road via Tiznit. This is what the coach excursions have to do. But if you have a car and a certain amount of nerve, it's worth travelling on the narrower road. Both routes pass through mountains, but you will get to them more quickly by a northern route. The way is full of surprises, such as the curious sight of the town of **Ait Bahia**, a jumbled cluster of low, white, mostly modern buildings, invisible until you top a mountain ridge.

Older villages cling to hillsides, crowding together on top of cols and hillocks; most have walls the colour of the mountainside. The slopes are corrugated with terraces ploughed by donkeys driven by black-clad women. Craggy red ochre outcrops at the peaks look like a continuation of the terraces' reinforcing walls, such is the harmony between the unchanging habits of the mountain people and the sombre majesty of the mountains.

The rocks of Tafraoute

The landscape around **Tafraoute ❸** is startling. From crumbly sandstone looms a jutting ridge of pink granite, purple in shadow, the Jebel Lekst. Below it, a lush series of palmiers: thousands of date palms spread in the Vallée des Ameln, and above them villages in earth colours: umber, pink, red and yellow ochre. The

Map on page 308

Nothing ever came from the Sous but oil and lies and locusts

— MOROCCAN BALLAD

BELOW:
Oumesnat, a village near Tafraoute.

granite behind them looks like a series of cascades, geysers solidifying as they fall. This remote area is prosperous, partly due to its fertility but mostly because the majority of the men travel to the cities to seek their fortunes. Tafraoute businessmen are among the most successful in Morocco. Sending money home, they build large town-style houses in their home villages, ready for the day when they retire.

Dozens of villages cluster about Tafraoute; they're more fun to explore than the town, whose main square has several souvenir shops, all overlooked by the imitation kasbah which is the Hotel les Amandiers ("Almonds" – an allusion to the almond blossom that decks the Tafraoute area in early spring). The first villages to see are **Oumesnat**, to the northeast of Tafraoute, **Agard Oudad** to the south, and **Adai** to the southwest.

Along the road to Tiznit, on the outskirts of town, are huge weathered boulders of granite, weird contorted shapes in striking contrast to the rigid outlines of the date palms. To the left is a signpost to "Les Roches Bleus", huge fauvist boulders painted by Belgian artist Jean Veran. Whether or not you like the style, this is a superb location to explore or to camp out for the night. The grandeur of the mountains and the 1,000-year-old lifestyle are as impressive here as along the northern route. In early spring the hillsides are covered with almond blossom, but once you are out of the mountains, there's a long stretch of pre-Sahara to cover before reaching Tiznit.

Walled city

The 6km (4 miles) of four-square ramparts around **Tiznit** ❹ look more solid than most: and so they ought since they are only just over 100 years old. The one

Woman in Tiznit, well concealed against the elements as well as prying eyes.

BELOW: silver for sale in Tiznit.

just inside the walls: the souk des bijoutiers (jewellers' market). A short walk from the *mechouar* (main square), grouped around a courtyard, the jewellers work delicate silver filigree into swords and daggers as well as heavy Berber bracelets and necklaces. Also worth seeing is the minaret of the Grand Mosque, with its curious wooden perches, also found in the southern Saharan town on Agdz in Niger.

Tiznit's walls are pisé, built of impacted earth the colour of ginger biscuits, as are most of the walls in the pre-Sahara and the mountains of the Anti-Atlas, which rear abruptly from the plain. Tiznit's other claim to fame is its municipal campsite, just outside the walls, which is one of the best run in the country.

Deserted terrain

Sharp contoured valleys divide mountainsides covered with green stubble that looks smooth from a distance, but turns out, on closer inspection, to be a mass of nobbly boulders and ground-hugging cactus. Barbary figs (prickly pears) and low, bushy argan trees grow in deeper soil. The argan, *argania spinosa*, is unique to Morocco and grows only along its southwestern seaboard. It produce a fruit like an olive, which is pressed for oil *(see below)*. The goats like these trees too; it is not unusual to see them in the branches, nibbling the leaves.

Below the tortuous mountain road, which descends as abruptly, the landscape is more deserted. This is where the pre-Sahara really begins . In vast open spaces stand swirled mountains like frozen sand dunes; others, with dark patterns, look as if a dry brush laden with dark green paint has been drawn over a light brown background. The sheer extent of these landscapes can be unnerving; there is no human reference point. The abrupt appearance of a marching line of

Map on page 308

Today the argan tree, which is a prehistoric relic from an earlier geological period, is under threat and is the focus of a protection campaign funded by a German government aid agency.

BELOW: a goat nibbles the leaves of an argan tree.

ARGAN OIL

The stones of the argan berries form the basis of a traditional oil, made by what must be one of the most labour-intensive extraction processes in existence. It requires 30kg (66lbs) of berries and eight hours of intensive manual labour to produce 1 litre (2.2 pints) of oil. The work is done entirely by women.

The fruit is collected during the summer months when it is sun dried and stored. Then the dried flesh of the fruit is removed, to be used as animal fodder, and the stones cracked open to remove the almond-like nut inside. The nut is then roasted and ground in a small stone hand mill. The milled nut residue is also used as high-quality animal feed. The decanted oil is not only used for cooking but is also a valuable local medicine, used to treat everything from stomach ailments to heart failure, poor blood circulation and even fertility problems. In the West it is gaining popularity as a cosmetic product.

The oil is sold throughout the region, on its own or mixed with ground almonds (in a kind of Moroccan peanut butter called *amalou*), and you will probably see it being sold on road sides. However, because of its high value, it is difficult to guarantee that the oil you buy is really pure and not mixed with olive, or even ordinary, cooking oil.

pylons can turn the landscape into what seems like a post-industrial wasteland. But it isn't, it is just a desert.

As an alternative to travelling straight on to Goulimine, a secondary road heads west back towards the coast, coming first to **Mirleft**. This is a tiny hamlet set back from numerous beaches, the most impressive of which is **Sidi Mohammed**, a small sandy bay dominated by rocky outcrops eroded into caves and arches. Alongside the beach is the super Italian-run Hotel de la Plage (tel: 08 71 90 56), which offers more pleasing accommodation than anything found in Tiznit or Goulimine. Alessandra and Michele also run their trekking and adventure agency, Cobratours (tel: 08 71 91 05) from the hotel, offering treks along the coast and into the Atlas as well as trips into the desert to the south.

Man in blue, but not necessarily a "blue man" – see Meet the Blue Men, page 319.

Sidi Ifni

The road continues southwards, never going far from the coast and running across the tops of cliffs until it arrives in **Sidi Ifni ❺**, a Spanish enclave until 1969. Ifni is an extraordinary place, full of colonial architecture and with a kind of run-down charm, as if time has stood still. The focus of the town is the old Plaza España dominated by the ruined governor's mansion. Off on the seaward side, next to the old church, is the Hotel Belle Vue, with spectacular views over the Atlantic. From the square an operatic sweep of steps runs down to the Hotel Ait Bamrane and the surf-battered beach. Far off in the sea spray are the remains of a téléferique tower that the Spanish used for hauling goods up to the town from a safe deep-water anchorage, in the days when the town was blockaded by the Moroccans. Across the river is the *marabout* complex where the local *moussem* is held in summer.

BELOW: gathering of the clan.

From Sidi Ifni the road winds through the hills of argan trees to Goulimine. A few kilometres before the town a 20-km (12-mile) piste leads to the impressive **Fort Bou Jerif**, once a Foreign Legion outpost, now a comfortable auberge and campsite that has become a major staging post for four-wheel-drives on the road south. Run with military efficiency by a French couple, it is well signposted and there is little chance of getting lost among the winding dusty tracks that lead to it. Nearby lives an intriguing German who has become an expert snake charmer and keeps a collection of venomous snakes for the curious.

Further along the Oued Noun are the ruins of a 14th-century Portuguese fort and a track that comes out on the coast at Foum Assaka, the start of the impressive **Plage Blanche**, a huge series of white beaches and dunes that run down to the mouth of the Oued Draa. Another, more difficult access to the dune area is possible at **Aoreora** via a piste 72km (45 miles) south of Goulimine.

The town of **Goulimine** ❻ (some signposts say Guelmim), despite its romantic desert reputation, has very little to write home about. It is primarily an administrative centre and its chief claim to fame is as the venue of a camel and livestock market every Saturday morning. Though this is touted as the place to see blue men *(see page 319)*, it is really a venue for local farmers who rub shoulders with less rustic salesmen dressed in their blue men costumes.

The town is also close to a group of oases, and you'll have no trouble finding somebody to take you out to one or all of them. Your guide will probably offer to introduce you to a blue man, or to a nomad, and if you're really lucky, he might just have some carpets and jewellery with him. Of course, what you believe, who you meet and what you buy is up to you. Even if you feel pressured, there is a friendly feeling in Goulimine, particularly if you stay there. The

Map on page 308

Goulimine is the venue for a camel and livestock market on Saturday mornings.

BELOW: the date harvest.

only classified hotel is the Salam, which is basic but has showers in some rooms. The dining-room is a little fly-blown; bedrooms open off an upstairs courtyard with lurid murals, but because there's so little else to do, you can find yourself making friends and spending hours just talking there.

Tan Tan and Tarfaya

Laayoune was the scene of brutally repressed demonstrations in 1999 that hastened the departure from government of Driss Basri, Morocco's hard-line minister of the interior. Basri was fired by King Mohammed VI after more than 20 years in the position under Hassan II.

On the road south, the occasional convoy of monstrous trucks heading to the burgeoning city of Laayoune and garrisons in Ad-Dakhla, forces on-coming vehicles half off the road. Table-top mountains surrounding Tan Tan look no more substantial than sandcastles. **Tan Tan ❼** is made up of custard yellow buildings (the sort of colour that paint manufacturers might call "Sahara"). The turquoise dome of a mosque stands out, visible from the edges of the basin in which the town sits. There is a military feel to the place: lots of flags, men in uniforms and garrison compounds. There are some hotels, but none of any special note. The sea is 25km (16 miles) away at **Tan Tan Plage**, a dusty half-way house, divided into a sardine port (a guarded private complex) and a genteel resort. Small, elaborate seaside bungalows in a nouvelle-Moorish style would be better placed next to the Mediterranean. The wind whips creamy spray from Atlantic breakers before they hit a crescent beach of sand, layered rock and the odd boulder. During the week at least, nothing much stirs apart from boys mussel-hunting in rock pools.

This is an exhilarating route, where the desert meets the sea and where the tarmac road wanders in and out from the coast, occasionally dusted over with blown sand. Between Tan Tan and Tarfaya, the crumbling tableland comes to an abrupt end, and then gives way to unstable cliffs. Butterflies play along the

BELOW: flag raising on 6 November, Laayoune.

THE GREEN MARCH

The reason for the military lorries and surfeit of troops from Tan Tan southwards is political. It was from Tan Tan that troops, followed by King Hassan II and 350,000 unarmed Moroccans, waving flags and copies of the Koran, marched to claim Moroccan sovereignty of the then-Spanish Sahara in 1975 *(see page 47).*

The anniversary of the Green March (Marche Verte) is celebrated as a national holiday every 6 November; posters, postcards and even the crockery of Laayoune's Hotel Massira commemorate the event in bold green and red. Morocco is today obliged by the United Nations-brokered ceasefire to limit its standing army in the south to a mere 140,000 men.

Consequences for travellers are nowadays few and not really irksome. You are likely to be stopped by the Gendarmerie Royale on either side of Tan Tan, where the white roadside checkpoint buildings are as bare as cells, and the Moroccan flag flapping on its pole is the only sound as a gendarme writes down your name, address, car registration, marital status, and the first names of both parents. This rigmarole is much more likely if you are heading south; going north, you are unlikely to be given more than a cursory once-over.

edge of the red earth, while pounding Atlantic surf blackens the rocks below.

Flocks of seagulls congregate on certain stretches of road; beside it are Land-Rovers, swathed in nets and wearing fishing rods like huge antennae, and fishermen casting from the cliffs. At times, the road swoops down into a valley of brackish water – a sea inlet, a river outlet, or a salt lake (it's never quite clear which). Here and there are desert cafés painted green or white or yellow, one-storey concrete cabins whose cheery colours seem to underline their isolation.

A whole village of cafés has grown up in **Sidi Akhfennir** ❽, 100km (63 miles) north of Tarfaya, at the base of a headland pitted with gaping caves. This is a useful petrol stop: you can rely on getting petrol around every 100km from Tan Tan to Laayoune. But you cannot rely on French or English being spoken, and you may need to know the Arabic for water as well as please and thank you *(see Travel Tips)*. At the Caidat of Sidi Akhfennir get permission to visit the most notable of the estuaries that bisect the route south. Khan N'fiss is a wildlife reserve and wonderful wild campsite. The estuary is huge, bounded by emerald-green marshes, silken white dunes and populated by a few fishermen, outnumbered by flocks of flamingos, cormorants and even the odd osprey. Beyond the dunes on the north bank is a vast beach, wild, remote and scattered with the flotsam of the Atlantic. There are gulls here and the occasional heron. Harsh, semi-arid plains alternate with shifting sand dunes, looking (deceptively) as cosy as any seaside version.

The journey south is eerily quiet. Other vehicles become quite an event; the occasional well-hidden pothole in an otherwise reliable surface is less welcome. North of the little, Spanish-influenced port of Tarfaya, the spooky mood is enhanced (or aggravated) by the hulks of abandoned ships and large fishing

Map on page 308

The sea off the Western Sahara is among the richest fishing grounds in the world.

BELOW:
Sahawris.

TIP

Swarms of locusts are a potential hazard along this stretch of road. Like pink smoke clouds when they're in motion, they are like a rose-coloured carpet as they bask on the road. If you hit some, drive slowly through, and clear them from the engine and the grille with a stick as soon as the swarm has gone.

BELOW:
houses in Tarfaya.

boats leaning half grounded just offshore. They're too recent to look like wrecks, and some seem as if they're only resting, but they're definitely dead. The local authorities have helpfully installed a plaque identifying each of the wrecks and the dates when they ran aground.

Tarfaya 9 has lost much of its passing trade since the road south now bypasses the port. However it is worth a visit as it has had an intriguing history and still exudes a certain sleepy charm. It was established initially as a trading post by a determined although undoubtedly eccentric Scotsman called Mackenzie in the mid-19th century. Mackenzie built a fort-like outpost on a tiny rocky island which he inevitably called Port Victoria. He eventually sold out to the then-Sultan Moulay Hassan for a fantastically large sum of money, although not before trying to raise a consortium to build a trans-Saharan canal.

The port next hit the headlines during World War I, when the Spanish caught a German submarine unloading arms to supply the Blue Sultan's resistance to the colonists. That galvanised the Spanish to settle the site as Villa Bens. Their garrison buildings have since been taken over by the Moroccan military, but an abandoned theatre still stands next to a small overgrown square. Tarfaya today is mostly a small fishing and administrative port, which also exports sand for the otherwise rocky beaches of the Canary Islands.

If you are planning to stay the night in Tarfaya, don't expect to find anything but the most basic accommodation.

City of the desert

The animation, size and modernity of **Laayoune** 10 are a jolt to the senses after the denuded bleakness of the desert. Passing through two police checkpoints and

a huge ornate gateway, and crossing the Green March bridge, you realise that Laayoune has been designed as a city of the desert. Since the Green March and King Hassan's return visit 10 years later, a lot of money and energy have gone into making the city an emblem of the benefits that Morocco can give to the people of the Sahara. A new hospital and airport have been built, and public housing and civic buildings are in vernacular style: dome-topped houses and a courthouse like a desert fort.

There is no medina, and the huge modern square, the **Place de l'Allegeance**, is not the focus it sets out to be. The real animation of Laayoune is in street after street of shops and markets selling daily produce and livestock. For visitors, Laayoune puts on its best face in the Hotel Parador: a mock castle enclosing a series of lush courtyards and shallow pools and one swimming pool; there's Arab decor and green trellises throughout. The alternative is the Hotel Massira, mostly booked out by groups or by the UN on their mission to organise the seemingly-never-to-happen referendum. These two hotels both serve alcohol, but otherwise the entire town is dry, apart from the rather grim Hotel Nagir and the UN MINURSO base. However, the two best restaurants in town, the Poissonière and the Restaurant Phillippe, are happy for clients to bring their own wine (provided of course you have remembered to stock up before leaving Agadir, the nearest source).

Big plans are afoot for the development of tourism in the Sahara, but they still have a long way to go. Trips to the sand sea, an area of shifting dunes, are easy to organise, and are occasionally laid on (together with folklore displays, camel rides and dromedary kebabs). Regular visitors to the region are from the expatriate community in the nearby Canary Islands, who use regular flights to

Map on page 308

Mining for phosphates, one of the main industries of the south, is now in decline due to the slump in world phosphate prices.

BELOW: run aground north of Tarfaya.

Map on page 308

Laayoune as an easy way of complying with Spanish immigration laws. **Laayoune Plage**, 20km (13 miles) west, is attractive chiefly because it is so empty. The city also has a large fishing port, much visited by foreign fishing fleets. A trip to Laayoune can be fascinating, but come for the pleasure of the trip rather than the town.

Phosphate mines

Inland from Laayoune the road runs alongside the deep wadi, **Saguia el Hamra**, before cutting through inhospitable desert, past old earthern defences built by the Moroccan army against the Polisario, towards **Smara** and **Boukra**, once the largest phosphate mine in the world. Halfway along, the road comes up alongside the forlorn looking Boucraa conveyer belt, trundling the now-uneconomic phosphate for more than 100km (63 miles) across the stony ground from the mine to loading piers on the coast near Laayoune port. This has now been surpassed as the longest conveyer belt in the world by one in Australia.

The mine itself can be found down a turning before Smara. If you make it to the mine, you will find a surprisingly green oasis and a comfortable club set up by the engineers, which serves very good food using fresh vegetables grown in their own gardens. The mine itself is a huge open pit, surrounded by spoil heaps, excavated by the mother of all Tonka toy diggers that amazingly moves on compressed air-powered skids.

Smara is mostly a military garrison today, but was once the centre of the desert empire of Sheik Ma el Ainin, who was a hero of the Moroccan resistance against France, and was the father of El Hiba, the Blue Sultan. Today little is left of Ma el Ainin's town except the mosque and a few roofless black stone walls, but once it was an impressive stronghold built with the help of craftsmen from the north of Morocco. The site was sacked by French forces in 1913 and occupied by the Spanish in 1934, as the still-used beehive barracks testify. If you've had enough of the desert at this point, the P44 from Smara to Tan Tan offers an alternative to the coast road. Be sure to fill up with fuel though, as the one petrol station on the way is often empty.

BELOW: reading the Koran in a mosque in Smara.

Remote outpost

Past Laayoune, Ad-Dakhla is a serious 500-km (300-mile) drive across barely inhabited desert. The road passes **Boujdour**, on the coast, 89km (55 miles) south of Laayoune. It is then a very long drive to **Ad-Dakhla ⓫** and after hardly seeing any other human habitation, it seems metropolis-like, although its few cafés and hotels have little to offer anyone in search of comfort or nightlife.

The old Spanish cathedral and square, like that in Laayoune, offers a brief cultural respite from the garrison nature of everything else. The big attraction of the place is its setting of lagoons and beautiful beaches, great places for diving and, at the right time of year, for whale- and sea lion-watching. Ad-Dakhla is also the last staging post for the twice weekly police-organised convoy crossing the border into Mauritania – when it isn't closed. ❑

Meet the Blue Men

Any trip south of Agadir is likely to involve an encounter with *un homme bleu*, a blue man of the Sahara – one of those romantic desert nomads depicted in Hollywood epics as blue-turbaned aristocrats mounted on pure white camels. It was a blue man that swept Kit (played by actress Debra Winger) to safety and desert madness in Bertolucci's 1990 film *The Sheltering Sky*.

At least, you might *think* that you're meeting a blue man. In truth, he is probably fake. Southern Morocco only brushes the Sahara, a desert that spans the width of Africa, but Moroccans make the most of it – especially when there are tourists to satisfy. In the town of Goulimine, one of the places where the blue men traditionally came to sell camels, the promise of nomads draws Saturday coach-tours from Agadir, the day when the weekly camel market is held. Most of the traders are, therefore, not real blue men at all but townspeople intent on making a profit.

Desert nomads still operating as such are found further south and east. Real blue men, though fallen upon hard times, are not particularly interested in entertaining tourists, and their pride is legendary. Wyndham Lewis, who visited the region and recorded his adventures in his book *Filibusters in Barbary*, published in 1932, said: "At their feet you may look. A downcast eye, fixed upon the exceedingly filthy blue feet belonging to these lords, will not attract a bullet."

Real blue men belong to the Taureg tribes, which spread through Mauritania, the Western Sahara, southern Algeria and southwest Libya. Physically, they are unusually tall, with a regal demeanour emphasised by flowing robes, Their headdress wraps over the nose and chin to keep out the sand-laden wind.

Traditionally it was the dye in their robes that imbued the skin with an indigo hue. In the 15th century an enterprising Scottish cloth merchant is supposed to have travelled to Agadir and introduced a dark-blue coloured calico which was greatly admired. The fact that its dye permeated the skin was the cloth's main attraction. Before buying, a customer would test the cloth between wet thumb and forefinger to ensure the dye came off well.

The Taureg are associated with a rich intellectual heritage, and literature and poetry are valued. The women are known for *guedra*, an erotic dance which they perform on their knees. The shows performed for Westerners' benefit are likely to be fairly sedate affairs, but at one time the *guedra* was the speciality of prostitutes.

Such vestiges of their culture apart, the nomads' traditional way of life has eroded fast, due to improved methods of transport in the Sahara, the breakdown of the traditional status quo, and severe droughts which have destroyed many of the traditional areas of grazing for their goats. Many nomads have congregated in the towns, picking up odd jobs here and there, abandoning their culture and leading a sedentary life. The Maghrebi governments have more pressing problems than the protection of endangered minorities. The blue men of the Sahara have had to be pragmatic to survive. ❑

RIGHT: a blue man

INSIGHT GUIDES
Travel Tips

Insight FlexiMaps

Maps in Insight Guides are tailored to complement the text. But when you're on the road you sometimes need the big picture that only a large-scale map can provide. This new range of durable Insight Fleximaps has been designed to meet just that need.

Detailed, clear cartography
makes the comprehensive route and city maps easy to follow, highlights all the major tourist sites and provides valuable motoring information plus a full index.

Informative and easy to use
with additional text and photographs covering a destination's top 10 essential sites, plus useful addresses, facts about the destination and handy tips on getting around.

Laminated finish
allows you to mark your route on the map using a non-permanent marker pen, and wipe it off. It makes the maps more durable and easier to fold than traditional maps.

The world's most popular destinations
are covered by the 125 titles in the series – and new destinations are being added all the time. They include Alaska, Amsterdam, Bangkok, Barbados, Beijing, Brussels, Dallas/Fort Worth, Florence, Hong Kong, Ireland, Madrid, New York, Orlando, Peru, Prague, Rio, Rome, San Francisco, Sydney, Thailand, Turkey, Venice, and Vienna.

INSIGHT GUIDES

The world's largest collection of visual travel guides

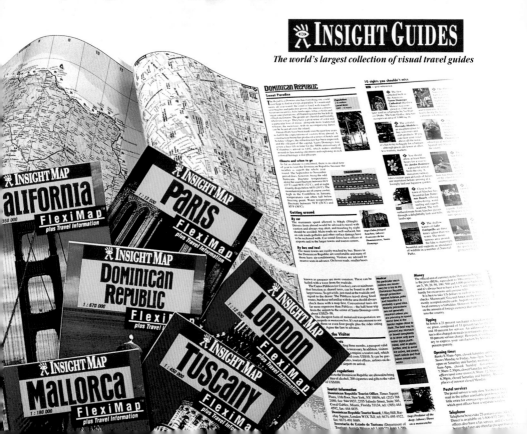

CONTENTS

Getting Acquainted

The Place 322
Climate Table 322
Geography 322
The People 323
Time Zones 323
The Economy 323
Government 324
Islam 324

Planning the Trip

What to Bring 324
What to Wear 324
Entry Regulations 325
Health 325
Money Matters 325
Public Holidays............326
Festivals......................326
Getting There 326
Tour Operators 327
Special Facilities..........327

Practical Tips

Emergencies 328
Weights & Measures....328
Business Hours 329
Media..........................329
Post & Telecoms..........329
Telephoning Home 330
Tourist Offices 330
Distances....................330
Embassies
    & Consulates 331
Extensions of Stay 331

Getting Around

On Arrival 331
Orientation 331
Airport/City Links 332
On Departure 332

Internal Flights 332
Car Hire 332
City Transport 333
Local Transport............333

Where to Stay

Hotel Standards 334
Agadir 334
Al Hoceima..................335
Asilah..........................335
Asni 335
Azrou 335
Beni Mellal 335
Casablanca 335
Chaouen......................336
El Jadida 336
Erfoud 336
Er Rachidia..................336
Essaouira 336
Fez..............................337
Ifrane 337
Imlil 337
Immouzer des Ida
    Outanane 337
Immouzer du Kandar ..337
Larache 338
Laayoune 338
Marrakesh 338
Meknes 339
Oualidia 339
Ouarzazate..................339
Ouirgane 339
Oujda 339
Oukaimeden................339
Ourika 339
Rabat 339
Sidi Harazem 340
Tafraoute 340
Tangier........................340
Tan Tan........................340
Taroudannt..................340
Tetouan 340
Zagora 340

Where to Eat

Menu Decoder 341
Restaurant Listings......341

Attractions

Excursions 344

Nightlife

Bars............................345
Nightclubs & Discos 345
Gambling 345
Folklore & Fantasias 345

Shopping

Where to Shop 345
What to Buy 346
Export Procedures 346
Complaints..................346

Sport

Golf 347
Hunting & Fishing 347
Hiking 347
White-Water Rafting 348
Skiing..........................348
Bird-watching 348
Mountain Tourism........348

Language

Moroccan Arabic 349
Pronunciation 349
Glossary......................350
French 351

Further Reading

Listings 352
Other Insight Guides 353

Getting Acquainted

Area 710,850 sq.km (274,461 sq. miles), including the Western Sahara.
Population: 29 million.
Language Arabic, Berber and French.
Religion Muslim, with a tiny percentage of Jews and Christians.

Time Zone: Greenwich Mean Time
Currency: Dirhams.
Weights & Measures Metric
Direct Dialling 00 212

Geography

Northern Morocco is a natural amphitheatre, with the Rif mountains (to the north) and the Atlas mountains (to the south and east) enclosing the basin of the river Sebou and the meseta or table land, which reaches south to Essaouira. The Sebou basin and the meseta are the country's richest and most fertile areas; the Atlantic plains and the lower valley of the Sebou support cereals and vines; higher plateaux around the edge of the meseta are covered by forest and pasture. The river basins and low coastal plains have been the natural settings for Morocco's northern cities: the ports of Casablanca and Rabat; Marrakesh between the meseta and the Atlas mountains; Fez and Meknes on the rich soils south of the Sebou.

The Rif mountains, falling abruptly to the Mediterranean on their northern side, slope more gently towards the Sebou to the west and south. Fields and olive groves surround tiny stone villages: the only towns of any size are industrial and touristic centres on the Mediterranean coast (Tangier, Tetouan, Al Hoceima), or in the foothills (such as the market town of Chaouen). Along the spine of the Rif, hashish is grown: the (illegal) hashish trade centres on Ketama, inland of Al Hoceima.

Climate Table

MONTH		J	F	M	A	M	J	J	A	S	O	N	D
Agadir	Temp	20	21	23	23	24	25	27	27	27	26	24	21
	Rain	55	33	22	17	7	<1	<1	1	8	14	35	47
	Sun	7.7	8.2	9.3	9.9	10.0	9.6	9.4	8.7	8.6	7.9	7.6	7.2
Casablanca	Temp	17	18	20	21	22	24	26	26	26	24	21	18
	Rain	78	61	54	37	20	3	<1	1	6	28	58	94
	Sun	5.2	6.3	7.3	9.0	9.4	9.7	10.2	9.7	9.1	7.4	5.7	5.3
Fez	Temp	15	18	20	22	26	31	36	36	32	26	20	16
	Rain	80	72	71	64	37	12	1	3	15	36	61	85
	Sun	5.0	6.6	7.1	8.1	8.5	10.0	11.3	10.5	8.6	7.4	5.6	4.3
Marrakesh	Temp	18	20	23	25	29	33	38	37	33	28	23	19
	Rain	29	31	31	33	20	8	2	3	10	17	27	34
	Sun	7.0	7.3	8.2	9.1	9.3	10.7	11.5	10.6	9.7	8.0	7.1	6.7
Melilla	Temp	17	18	19	21	23	26	29	29	27	24	20	18
	Rain	52	30	28	28	38	8	1	1	11	27	33	66
	Sun	5.1	5.5	6.0	6.8	7.9	8.7	9.1	9.4	6.2	5.9	5.0	4.9
Ouarzazate	Temp	17	19	23	26	30	35	39	40	35	27	21	17
	Rain	8	5	15	7	6	5	2	10	21	20	17	19
	Sun	7.4	8.6	9.5	10.2	10.9	11.6	10.0	8.9	8.9	8.4	7.7	7.1
Tarfaya	Temp	20	20	21	21	22	22	23	23	24	23	23	21
	Rain	9	5	3	1	<1	<1	<1	<1	6	1	15	10
	Sun	6.6	6.9	7.7	8.5	7.9	7.8	6.5	7.0	7.2	7.1	5.9	6.6

Key:
Temperature: Average daily maximum (°C)   *Rain:*   Average monthly rainfall (mm)
Bright sunshine: Average daily hours   *Source:*   Meteorological Office Statistics

The People

The original people of Morocco are the Berbers: originally nomadic tribes and historically fierce. But the name Berber itself is thought to be derived from an Arab word for non-Arabs; and from the late 7th century AD, Arabs and Berbers have shared the country and alternately held power – until colonial domination by Europeans. In troubled times, the Berbers retreated to strongholds in the Rif and Atlas – where they have always been their own masters, and which still remain predominantly Berber today. The Arab population is today concentrated in the north and in the cities: in mountain and country areas three Berber languages are still spoken, and national news is broadcast in Berber at certain times of the day. But centuries of intermarriage have blurred the Arab/Berber divide.

The population of Morocco is officially estimated at a little over 29 million people, 90 percent of whom live north of a line drawn between Tiznit and Oujda.

Growth in recent decades has been remarkable: from 6.5 million in 1935, to 12.5 million in 1964, to well over double that today. And it is a young population; four out of 10 Moroccans are under 15.

The Atlas mountains run in parallel ridges across Morocco from southwest to northeast. The Middle Atlas (up to 3,000 metres/10,000 ft) is part flat-topped, part corrugated, damp and green with forests of oak and huge cedars. The western plateaux are interrupted by volcanic scenery. Some of the predominantly Berber population of the Atlas are still nomadic.

The grand chain of the High Atlas (4,167 metres/13,670 ft at its highest point, the Toubkal) runs for 761 km (473 miles), across virtually the width of Morocco. Sandstone and granite peaks, snow-covered until June, contrast with the pisé villages, narrow field-terraces, and bright green valleys to the west of the Tizi n-Tichka pass. Further east, the mountainsides are devoted to goats.

A fault line runs from Agadir to Figuig, splitting the Anti Atlas and High Atlas ranges. At first it follows the valley of the river Sous, whose basin is desolate scrub except in the lower valley between Taroudannt and Agadir, where early fruits are grown. To the south is the pre-Cambrian bulge of the Anti Atlas. Argan trees and small holdings flourish on the slopes facing west towards the sea. South and east again, the country is no more than desert, scored by oases-dotted river valleys. The pre-Sahara, made up of vast bare rocky plateaux, is swept by dusty winds and occasionally punctuated by flat-topped hillocks or shifting dunes. The Sahara proper is less hospitable still, except at the chains of oases. What were once watercourses are dry for most of the year, except after the occasional desert storm. Trickles of water are more common towards the hazy coast of sands and crumbling cliffs.

The northeastern extreme of the country comprises chiefly plateaux of 1,000 metres (3,000ft) or more. In the main they are too dry to cultivate: even the valley of the river Moulouya, running out of the Atlas and east of the Rif, provides only a narrow corridor of cultivated soil. The wealth of the region, dominated by the town of Oujda, comes from the Mediterranean coast, irrigated and dammed, where the climate allows pockets of agriculture and market gardening.

Time Zones

Moroccan time is the same as Greenwich Mean Time and there is no daylight saving; when it is noon in Morocco, it is noon in London (11am during the UK's daylight saving), 7am in New York and 8pm in Perth.

Climate

Three types of climate hold sway in three distinct regions: coastal regions have warm dry summers, are wet for the rest of the year and mild in winter: the coast is drier south of Agadir, where it is free of Atlantic depressions in winter. Agadir has a well-protected climate, with a narrow range of temperatures; but in common with the rest of the Atlantic coast, cold offshore water can cause cloud and fog. The mountains get hot, dry summers and very harsh winters; parts of the High Atlas are under snow well into the summer. The remainder of the country has a continental climate, getting hotter and drier in summer to the south, but moderated by the sea to the west. In the inland Sahara very dry, hot summers give way to warm sunny days and cold (sometimes frosty) nights in winter. (*See chart on page 322.*)

The Economy

Agriculture: Exports include cereals, dates, figs, olives and almonds, sugar-cane, and most notably early fruits: oranges and tomatoes are the best known, but the Sous area has been experimenting with banana growing and the cultivation of roses.

Minerals are dominated by rich reserves of phosphates; some three-quarters of the world's stock. The export of phosphates and its derivatives has historically accounted for over 40 percent of export earnings.

Energy has to be bought: there are some reserves of anthracite, and oil shales are beginning to be exploited, but most oil is imported. Hydro-electric power has contributed less to national needs as northern Africa has become gradually drier. A large lump of the country's foreign exchange comes from wages sent back home by Moroccans living abroad, notably in France and Belgium.

Government

Morocco is a Muslim kingdom governed since 1961 by Mohammed V, Hassan II and now Mohammed VI. It was Mohammed V who changed his own title from sultan to king, and reigned when Morocco secured independence from France and Spain in 1956. In 1962, King Hassan put forward a new constitution which described Morocco as a Muslim sovereign state and a social democratic and constitutional monarchy, and which led to parliamentary elections. There have been periods of emergency rule, attempted coups and government by decree. The political structure remains parliamentary, with the King firmly established in power.

Islam

There is not much evidence of hard-line Islam in Morocco. Alcohol is not restricted by law and many European habits of government and administration are followed. For example, New Year's Day is a holiday and Sunday is the closing day for offices and larger shops. It is generally only in souks that *jemaa* – the word means mosque – is observed on Fridays after noon.

Nonetheless Morocco is a Muslim country, for all its compromises with Western calendars and customs, and never more obviously than during the holy month of Ramadan, when all Moroccans observe the daily fast.

Islam in the country is a peculiarly Moroccan hybrid – the faith of the Arabs adapted by the tribes of Berbers. There is more emphasis on individuals and saints than rigid Islamic codes would sanction.

In the city, the minarets of the mosques are a constant visible reminder of faith, and the call to prayer is heard five times a day. The mosque – and the wisdom and learning traditionally associated with it – are (often literally) central to town and city life. Koranic schools and conclaves of Islamic scholars reinforce orthodoxy, the most important tenet being that there is no God but God and Mohammed is his Prophet. There are no priests, no intermediaries: in praying five times a day, the Muslim is talking directly to God. At the same time, even without priests, centres of religious devotion have immense influence – and power.

The first and most visible element of country Islam is the popularity of the *marabout* or local saint – visible, because the countryside is dotted with small white buildings with domed roofs. Each is the tomb of a local holy man; the tomb itself sometimes known as a *marabout* (otherwise called a *koubba*). Around these local saints, cults of devotion have grown up over centuries.

Rich cults have *zaouia* – educational colleges that were set up next to the *marabout* in the same way as a mosque set up a *madrassa* – but as an alternative to the city-based orthodoxy taught at the mosque. Every cult has its *moussem* – an annual festival in honour of the saint.

Ramadan

The ninth month of the Muslim calendar was the one in which God revealed to Mohammed the truths which were written as the Koran. In remembrance of this and in obedience to one of Islam's "five pillars", Muslims must observe a fast during the hours of daylight (*see page 63*).

For travellers: The unique atmosphere of Ramadan – the festive spirit in the evenings – can be weighed against slight material inconveniences (most cafés and restaurants close during the day). Non-Muslims are not required to observe the fast, but abstinence from smoking, eating or display of physical affection in public is tactful.

Planning the Trip

What To Bring

Although cash tips are common, certain goods go down well too, with children who have posed for photographs or anyone who has helped you. European or American cigarettes (light tobacco) are worth carrying; so (for children) are coloured ball-point pens, small notebooks or wrapped sweets. Clothes (e.g. picture T-shirts and Levi's) can occasionally be useful currency when bartering for larger items (such as rugs or killims) in the souks, though now that such things are easily available in Morocco this is much less true than it used to be.

ELECTRICITY

Most of the country's supply is rated 220 volts, but some places have a 110 volt supply; sockets and plugs are of the continental European type, with two round pins.

What To Wear

Dress for comfort. Light-coloured, lightweight cottons are advisable, and in the south, a sun hat in summer. Hotels are rarely dressy, although some four and many five-star hotels have formal restaurants where men will feel more comfortable in a jacket and tie, and women in a dress. When touring or sightseeing, let tact be a guide: keep skimpy clothes for the beach and remember that jewellery and fine clothes mark the wealthy tourist in a poor country; expensive bags or cameras may also attract more attention than you'd like.

Entry Regulations

VISAS & PASSPORTS

Holders of full British passports (but not a British Visitor's Passport), and holders of valid US, Canadian, Irish, Australian, New Zealand or Scandinavian passports need no visa for a stay of up to three months. Children under 16 without their own passports must have their photograph stamped in the passport of one of their parents (be aware that since 1998 all UK children travelling abroad require their own passports by British law).

CUSTOMS

Clothes, jewellery and personal effects including cameras and up to 10 rolls of film can be taken into the country temporarily, without formality. Foodstuffs and medicines in reasonable quantities for personal use may also be imported. Duty-free allowances for alcohol, tobacco and perfumes are 250 grammes of tobacco or 200 cigarettes or 50 cigars; one litre of wine; one litre of spirits; a quarter-litre of *eau de cologne*. To import firearms, a licence is needed from the Direction de la Sûreté Nationale in Rabat.

Customs procedure on entry will vary according to point of arrival; baggage is often searched, and will need to be cleared by a customs official before entering the country.

Health

Vaccinations and Protection against Malaria

No vaccinations are required by the Moroccan government for entry into the country, unless you have come from a recognised infected area (e.g. a yellow fever, cholera or smallpox zone). For your own safety, however, inoculations against typhoid, polio, cholera, and tetanus are advised by some doctors. A course of malaria tablets may also be advisable if you intend travelling in the south: these are normally taken for a week before, during, and

Common Ailments

Stomach upsets are the most common ailment: diarrhoea remedies or relief will come in handy. To cut down on the chances of getting an upset stomach, avoid food that has been left standing or has been re-heated; use bottled water in remote areas. The next most common cause of illness is usually **sunstroke**, especially when combined with alcohol; light cotton clothing, moderate exposure and protective lotions all reduce the risk of sunstroke.

for four to six weeks after travel. The risk of malaria is highest in the summer: insect repellent gels or creams are sensible precautions.

Some protection against hepatitis may be useful if travelling in remote country areas. Injections of immuno-globulin give protection for about four weeks: they are of no use for long trips, therefore, and should be discussed with a medical advisor. Contact with standing fresh water (swimming or paddling in oases, river valleys and lagoons) may carry the risk of bilharziasis, so take local advice. Rabies is present: take medical advice immediately if you are bitten.

Aids

Being Muslim and conservative, Morocco is not a high-risk area for aids. Nonetheless, it is a developing country and its medical facilities do not compare with those in the West. The disease can be transmitted either through sexual contact, or through medical treatment using infected needles, blood or blood transfusion equipment. Most Moroccan pharmacies now stock disposable needles, and clinics and hospitals are usually reliable: check with a consulate or embassy if you are in doubt over treatment. It is possible to buy medical "kits" containing sterile hypodermic needles and plasma which can be carried in case of an emergency.

Money Matters

The Moroccan Dirham (Dh) is divided into 100 centimes (often called Francs). In rural areas people often count in Rials (which no longer exist). There are 20 Rials to 1Dh. Recent official rates have hovered around £1 = 16 Dh and US$1 = 11Dh. Check the Bank of Morocco official rate card which is available at all money exchange desks in hotels and banks.

There is one simple rule: Moroccan currency may not be imported or exported. Visitors can import as much foreign currency (in cash or travellers' cheques) as they wish. Changing unwanted Dirhams back into hard currency at the end of your trip must be done at the airport, and you must have exchange receipts totalling twice the amount you wish to change back and have your flight boarding card. You will have to accept an unfavourable rate and whatever currency the cashier has available.

ATMs:

Most Moroccan airports now have an ATM, which have also become common in most large towns. However, do not rely solely on cash machines for funds as they are frequently out of order or crash while you are using them, and are still rare outside major centres. The Wafabank machines tend to be the most reliable.

Travellers' Cheques

Travellers' cheques in either Sterling, French francs or US dollars, are the safest way of carrying money in Morocco, although not all bank branches will exchange them and those that do, increasingly charge a per cheque commission. It is useful, especially if entering Morocco outside banking hours to have some cash as well as cheques, as not all exchange facilities accept travellers' cheques and credit cards.

Credit Cards

Credit cards are accepted in many 3-star and above hotels, the more expensive restaurants and most car hire companies.

Money Transfer

Western Union money transfer is by far the quickest way of telexing money from aboard. Western Union has offices in all major cities but also operates through Wafabank and the post offices. The process should take four hours maximum.

Public Holidays

There are two sets of holidays, religious and secular: the former based on the Muslim (lunar) year, and the other on the Western (Gregorian) calendar.

Religious holidays are as follows. For exact dates according to the Western calendar – they get earlier each year by 11 days (12 in a leap year) – consult the Tourist Office.

Festivals

Every religious holiday is marked by festivity in Morocco. The other staple of festival life is the *moussem*: a local festival (or pilgrimage) in honour of a saint or holy man. In the country you may stumble across one of these, a flash of colour and excitement in the daily round of subsistence.

But there are several *moussems* which are on a larger scale and worth going out of your way for. Ceremonial dancing and *fantasias* (displays of horsemanship) may accompany them. There are also folklore and harvest festivals. Most of these are moveable feasts and exact dates should be checked before you travel or when you arrive.

February
Tafraoute: an almond blossom festival.
May
El Kelâa des Mgouna (Ouarzazate region): festival of roses.
June/July
Marrakesh: national folklore festival in early to mid-June.
Goulimine: *moussem*.

Muslim holidays

These religious holidays are observed by most businesses.
Aid es Seghir (marking the end of Ramadan)
Aid el Kebir (feast of Abraham's sacrifice of a sheep instead of his son).
Muslim New Year
Mouloud (the Prophet's birthday). Celebrated with candlelit processions in Salé near Rabat.

State holidays

New Year's Day – 1 January
Manifesto Independence – 11 January
Labour Day – 1 May
Allegiance of Oued Edtahab – 14 August
Anniversary of the King's and People's Revolution – 20 August
Youth Day – 21 August
Green March – 6 November
Independence Day – 18 November.

Sefrou (Fez region): cherry harvest. Asilah: an international music festival, including classical, folk and popular: from the last week in July, for one month.
August
Setti Fatma (Marrakesh region) *moussem*
September
Imilchil (High Atlas): marriage *moussem* of the Aït Haddidou tribe, a sort of costumed mass pledge.
Moulay Idriss (Meknes region): this is the country's biggest *moussem* commemorating the founder of Morocco's first Arab dynasty, Idriss I
Fez: *moussem* of Moulay Idriss II, the founder of Fez.
October/November
Agadir: art and folklore festival. Erfoud: a date festival.
Mouloud (moveable)
In the fortnight before and after Mouloud, the Prophet's birthday, there are processions and *moussems* in Meknes, Salé (near Rabat) and Asni (Marrakesh region).

Getting There

BY AIR

The national airline, Royal Air Maroc RAM), has Casablanca airport as its hub. There are direct flights from London Heathrow and from New York JFK to Tangier, Casablanca and Marrakesh. From Casablanca connecting flights go onto most large cities and even to Essaouira, although many destinations are infrequently served.

Websiste: www.royalairmaroc.com
In the UK, GB Airways (tel: 01293 664 239) in conjunction with British Airways flies six days a week to Casablanca and Marrakesh, a couple of times a week to Tangier and once to Agadir.

There are very few cheap charter flights to Morocco, and so schedule flights become heavily booked and are expensive, especially during peak periods (July/August, Easter, Christmas). If you are travelling to Tangier and having problems finding an affordable flight, it may be worth investigating flights to Gibraltar or even Malaga (from where you must take a bus to the ferry in Algeciras). Ferries leave throughout the day and cost about DH450 return for foot passengers. *See Getting There By Sea.*

Royal Air Maroc Offices

Belgium: 46–48 Place de Broukerie 1000 Brussels. Tel: 219 24 50; fax:219 98 38
E-mail: info@royalairmaroc.be
Canada: 1001 de Maisonneuve Ouest, Suite 440, Montreal QC. Tel: 285 1937
France: 38 Avenue de l'Opera, 75002, Paris. Tel: 44 94 13 00.
Germany: Kaiserstrasse 12, 60311 Frankfurt. Tel: 92 00 14 20.
Great Britain: 205 Regent Street, London W1. Tel: 020-7439 4361; fax: 020 7734 6183.
E-mail: Ramlondon@btinternet.com
Italy: Via Bissolati 76-00187, Rome. Tel: (06) 47 82 33 36.
E-mail: ram98@mail.nexus.it.
The Netherlands: Stadhouderskade 2 1054 ES Amsterdam.
Tel: 515 85 92/93.
E-mail: ramams@euronet.nl

Spain: Calle Princesa 7, 28008. Madrid. Tel: 91 54 87 800. email: ram-mad@maptel.es
United States: 666 Fifth Avenue AT 53rd Street, New York, NY 10103, USA. Tel: 974 3850. email: ram@kingdomofmorocco.com
For Royal Air Maroc offices in Morocco, *see page 332.*

BY SEA

The most logical point of entry by sea is from **Algeciras** in southern Spain across the Strait of Gibraltar to **Tangier** (around 2½ hours by ferry) or the Spanish territory of **Ceuta** (around 90 minutes). Tangier is better connected to public transport in Morocco. These short hops are the best bet for those in cars, since there are sailings through the day. Where possible, avoid all routes in July and August, when migrant workers clog ports. Passport control takes place on board the boat. You must have your passport stamped before disembarking.

There are also hydrofoil services to Tangier from **Algeciras, Gibraltar,** and **Tarifa,** Spain's southernmost town and the nearest to Morocco (the crossing takes just 35 minutes, (but note that non-EU passport holders cannot leave from Tarifa). Hydrofoils don't run if the sea's too rough and are less frequent than the ferries. Spanish car ferries also run from Almeria and Málaga to the Spanish enclave of Melilla (6½ and 7 hours respectively). Finally, there are car ferries run by the

Ferries and Hydrofoils

A number of ferry and hydrofoil companies ply the route between Spain and Morocco. They include Euroferrys and Trasmediterrania. www.euroferrys.com www.trasmediterrania.com
In London, ferry bookings can be made through Southern Ferries, 179 Piccadilly, W1V 9DB, tel: 020 7491 4968; fax: 020 7481 3502.

Compagnie Marocaine de Navigation from Sète, in southern France, to Tangier (35 hours) or via the Balearic islands to Nador.

BY RAIL

Trains leave London Victoria and connect via the Algeciras ferry with Tangier, Rabat and Casablanca, by way of Paris (change to Gare d'Austerlitz in Paris). The journey time, London to Tangier, is around 48 hours. Travellers aged 26 and under can save by buying youth or student fares.

BY ROAD

Two options: drive through France to catch the ferry at Sète, or through France and Spain to take one of the Algeciras ferries *(see By Sea).* Generally, travelling to Morocco by car is expensive (allow for toll fees in France and Spain as well as ferries, petrol and overnight accommodation).

For travel through France you will need Green Card insurance, and for Spain a bail bond, both issued by your regular insurer. Few British insurers are prepared to cover cars in Morocco. Your best bet is to purchase insurance when you arrive: see Assurances aux Frontieres in Tangier's harbour. You will also need to take your Vehicle Registration Document.

Tour Operators

The Moroccan National Tourist Office provides a comprehensive list of tour operators. Here is a selection of UK firms:

GENERAL
General
Abercrombie & Kent: up-market hotels in Essaouira, Tangier, Mohammedia, Marrakesh, Fez, Zagora, Erfoud, Taroudannt and Ouirgane. Tel: 0845 0700617.
Cadogan Travel: good hotels in Agadir, Tangier, Marrakesh; Imperial Cities tour. Tel: 02380 828304.
Club Mediterranée: Club holidays in

Agadir, Marrakesh and Ouarzazate. Tel: 020-7348 3333.
Hayes & Jarvis: Imperial Cities Tour; Agadir and Marrakesh. Tel: 0870 898 9890.
Travelscene: Tel: 020-8427 4445.

Specialist
The Best of Morocco. Offers package holidays and tailor-made tours. Tel: 01380 828533.
Exclusive Golf Tours Specialists in golfing holidays in Morocco and elsewhere. Tel: 020 8679 6571.
Morocco: Made to Measure Every destination and every type of holiday catered for. Tel: 020-7235 0123/2110.
Naturetrek Bird-watching and botanical tours. Tel: 01963 733051.
Ramblers Holidays Ltd Walking in the Atlas. Springboard Marrakesh. Also walking in Southern Morocco. Tel: 01707-331133.
Walks Worldwide Tailor-made walking tours. Tel: 01542 62255.

Adventure Tours
Exodus Travels Provides the most complete adventure programme in Morocco of any British agency. Tel: 020-8675 5550.
Explore Worldwide Tel: 01252 760000
Sherpa Expeditions Walking and adventure holidays in the High Atlas. Tel: 020 8577 2717.

Special Facilities
GAY TRAVELLERS
Morocco no longer offers visitors the free and easy attitude it once did towards homosexuality. Tangier

Students

There are few official discounts available to students in Morocco. The chief benefit of student status is the use of an Inter Rail pass on the railways. There are also discount fares for students from Royal Air Maroc. Domestic discount fares can be booked in advance from RAM offices (but not on spec at the airport) on proof of student status. .

in particular has been officially cleaned up. What the Moroccan law describes as an "unnatural act" between two persons of the same sex is punishable by imprisonment (six months to three years) and fines. Despite this, male gay sex is still available. Marrakesh and Tangier are most popular with gay travellers.

DISABLED TRAVELLERS

No official register exists of facilities within Morocco for people with disabilities. Relatively few hotels are overtly suitable for wheelchair access, particularly those converted from older buildings such as palaces. Getting around towns can also be difficult.

TRAVELLING WITH CHILDREN

Moroccans adore children, and they are welcome everywhere. However, few cities have attractions specifically aimed at children: Agadir and Rabat have zoos, and there are a few privately-run children's playgrounds.

The big hotels in Agadir have most to offer in the way of child-oriented entertainment, but somewhere such as Marrakesh, with its nightly circus-cum-fair on the Jemaa el Fna, horse-drawn carriages, colourful souks and great hotel pools offer plenty to stop children from getting bored.

Eating out can be problematic, particularly if your child has typically narrow tastes. However, a daily diet of omelette/chicken and chips can be reasonably nutritious when supplemented by fresh fruit, yoghurts and fresh fruit milkshakes. You will find prepared baby foods, but not toddler standbys such as baked beans or tinned spaghetti.

If you buy milk to give to babies, you should boil it first (hotels will gladly do this for you).

Nappies (diapers) and baby wipes are sold in many of the larger grocer's and in some pharmacies (but not all). "Pull-ups" (trainer pants) are much more difficult to obtain, so bring these with you.

Practical Tips

Emergencies

SECURITY & CRIME

Crime against tourists is not common, but neither is it unknown. In a survey published by the British consumer magazine Holiday *Which?*, it was found that 4.3 percent of visitors to Morocco had been victims of theft: smaller than 1 in 24. But any guide in the packed souks of Fez and Marrakesh will advise you to hold tightly to your bag. What tends to be most intimidating, especially in the imperial cities, is harassment from *faux-guides* (literally, false guides) who try to force their services on you. The government has recently clamped down on them, but with unemployment so high the problem is bound to resurface. The best way to deal with them if you don't want their help is to decline firmly but with good humour. Above all, don't become agitated – it only prompts abuse. *(Also see "Guides" under Orientation, page 331.)*

Emergency telephone numbers:

Police: 19.
Fire services/ambulance: 15.

Elementary precautions:

Avoid wearing jewellery, or carrying too much money in the streets: use hotel safe deposit boxes. If you're on the move, use a secure pocket or money belt to a shoulder bag for valuables; if you wear a bag, sling the strap over the head, not just the shoulder.

If you are attacked, don't put up a fight: better to lose money than risk being hurt. If driving, don't leave bags visible in the car, always lock your vehicle and leave it empty

Weights & Measures

Metric measures are used throughout Morocco: distances are in kilometres, quantities in litres and weights in grammes or kilogrammes.

To convert
multipy by
Kilometres to miles	0.621
Metres to feet	3.28
Kilograms to pounds	2.204
Grams to ounces	0.035

overnight. Better still, do as the locals do and have a *gardien* can watch over it (3 or 5DH for short stays; up to 50DH for the night).

Left luggage:

For a small charge, luggage may be left at railway stations or offices of the Compagnie Transport Marocain (CTM): it should be safe.

Loss Of Belongings

If belongings have been stolen, a police report must be made. Do not be put off by hotel staff; insurance companies invariably require a local police report before they will entertain a claim for theft. If tour company representatives are on hand, they may be able to help, and should certainly be informed. If your belongings do not arrive at the airport, it is the responsibility of the airline: ask for a Property Irregularity Form to fill in. Many travel insurance policies will then allow reasonable expenses on clothes and other essentials.

MEDICAL SERVICES

There are private clinics in all main towns, along with government hospitals in many. Consulates will give advice about English-speaking doctors, as will tour companies' representatives (and noticeboards) at hotels. Be sure to come to Morocco with full medical insurance, including cover for repatriation. All services will be charged for immediately, except in cases of extreme need or emergency. Ask for and keep receipts.

Pharmacies in towns sell many kinds of medicines and contraceptives (but not tampons or sanitary towels – these may be available from general stores in town). Medicines are expensive: aspirin, insect bite cream and stomach settlers are best bought at home. There is a late night pharmacy in each major town: it is often located in the town hall (Municipalité).

Business Hours

Business hours in Morocco are very variable, but typical times are:

Banks: Monday–Friday
Winter: 8.30–11.30am and 2.30–4pm.
Summer: 8.30–11.30am and 3–5pm.
Ramadan: 9.30am–3pm.
Many major branches of banks now incorporate money exchange kiosks (with separate entrances) that have longer opening hours and are open over the weekend.
Offices: Monday–Friday
Winter: 8.30am–noon 2.30–6pm.
Summer: 8.30am–4.30pm.
Ramadan: 9.30am–4pm.
Government offices close early on Friday and many private businesses open their offices on Saturday mornings.
Post offices: Monday–Friday winter and summer: 8.30–11.45am and (except Saturday) 2.30–6.30pm.
Ramadan: 9.30am–3pm.
Many post offices have a desk selling stamps which is open through lunch time and into the early evening. Larger post offices have a telephone section that keeps longer hours (there are also many late-night *teleboutiques*).
Shops: Monday–Saturday
Winter 8.30am–noon and 2.30–6.30pm.
Summer 8.30am–4pm or 8.30am–noon and 4–7pm, depending on the type of shop.
Ramadan: 9.30am (or as late as 11am)–4pm, with some opening 7–11pm.

Some shops close on Fridays (the Muslim holy day) or even Saturday if the owner is Jewish. In the new parts of cities shops often close on Sunday. Other shops remain open throughout the week.

Media

NEWSPAPERS & MAGAZINES

The Moroccan media is undergoing something of a revolution since censorship has become more relaxed. A selection of the French language newspapers are *L'Opinion*, the strongly royalist *Le Matin du Sahara* and *Maroc Soir*. Weekly newspapers such as *Le Journal* and *Gazette du Maroc* tend to be more outspoken and produce more critical articles. The two main French language financial papers are *La Vie Economique* and *L'Economiste*. *Femmes Du Maroc* and *Citadine* are the two French-language women's glossies, which as well as being fashion magazines carry a great deal of information on social issues and national events.

International newspapers and magazines are found in the larger hotels and magazine kiosks in the cities. English language newspapers are usually a day old at best.

RADIO & TELEVISION

Moroccan TV consists of two channels, of which the stupefying TVM (the original government-run channel) is under pressure to make itself more interesting. 2M, originally a private channel that went bankrupt and was taken over by the government, has kept its editorial independence and is considered much better. Satellite television (and increasingly TPS) is common in homes across the country and is available in hotels.

RTM runs a radio station which broadcasts daily programmes in English, Spanish and Berber as well as the more usual Arabic and French. It is complemented by Median (Radio Mediterranée Internationale) that broadcasts from Tangier to the whole of the Maghreb.

Telephone Codes

022: Zone of Casablanca
023: Zone of Settat (includes Azzemour, Azilal, Beni Mellal, El Jadida, Ksiba, Mohammedia).
044: Zone of Marrakesh (includes Demnate, El Kelaa Mgouna, Essaouira, Ouarzazate, Oukaimeden,Safi, Tinerhir, Zagora).
055: Zone of Fez (includes Erfound, Er Rachidia, Guercif, Ifrane, Khenifra, Meknes, Moulay Idriss, Rissani, Sefrou).
056: Zone of Oujda (includes Figuig, Nador and Saidia).
037: Zone of Rabat (includes Khenitra, Moulay Bousselham. Ouezzane, Skhirate, Souk el Arba, Temara).
048: Zone of Laayoune (includes Agadir, Guelmime, Sidi Ifni, Tafraoute, Tan-Tan, Taroudant and Tiznit).
039: Zone of Tangier (includes Al Hoceima, Asilah, Chaouen, Larache, Tetouan).

Post & Telecoms

In the past, visiting a post office in Morocco could take hours and involved fighting through huge rugby scrums only to find that you had been queueing at the wrong window all along. Today both Isstallit al Maghrib (the telephone company) and the post office have become a great deal more efficient.

The post office now has computerised tills and a separate Post Rapide service for national and international express parcel services. Stamps are widely available from tobacconists (*tabac*) and stationery shops.

The sale of a second mobile phone licence to Medi Telecom, an international consortium, and the privatisation of 40 percent of the national telephone company have reduced the cost of telephone calls and prompted a new climate of efficiency at Maroc Telecom. There are many more public telephones accepting prepaid cards, and phone and fax shops are common. Most

Telephoning Home

Most exchanges are now automatic and direct dialling abroad is now the rule. Dial 00 for an international call, wait for a second dial tone, then dial the country code. The codes are as follows:
Australia: (61)
Belgium: (32)
Canada: 1)
Denmark: (45)
France: (33)
Germany: (49)
Great Britain: (44)
Ireland: (353)
New Zealand: (64)
Portugal: (351)
Spain: (34)
United States: (1)

exchanges are now automatic and direct dialling abroad is now the rule.

The Internet

Using e-mail in Morocco is very cheap, thanks to an abundance of Internet cafés that have sprung up across the country. Internet access costs from around 10Dh an hour.

Tourist Offices

OUTSIDE MOROCCO

Australia: 2/11 West Street, North Sydney, NSW 2060. Tel: 957 6717/922 4999. Fax: 9923 1053. E-mail: maroc@magna.comau
Belgium: Avenue Louise 402, 1050 Brussels. Tel: 646 6320
Fax: 646 7376.
Canada: Place Montreal Trust,Suite 2450, 1800 Avenue McGill College, Montreal QC H3A 3JS.
Tel: 842 8111/8112.
Fax: 842 5316.
France: 161 Rue Saint Honoré, 75001 Paris. Tel: 42 60 63 50.
Fax: 40 15 97 34.
Germany: Graf Adolf Strasse 59, 40210 Dusseldorf.
Tel: 370551/552.
Fax: 374048.
Great Britain: 205 Regent Street, London W1R 7DE.
Tel: 020-7437 0073.
Fax: 020 7734 8172.
Italy: Via Larga 23, 201202 Milan.
Tel: 5830 3633.
Fax: 5830 3970.
Spain: Ventura Rodríguez, No 24–1 1ZQ-28008 Madrid. Tel: 5427431.
Fax: 559 4594
United States: 20 East 46th Street,

Websites

For information on Morocco, visit the following websites:
www.tourism-in-morocco.com
www.maroc.net
www.mincom.gov.ma

Suite 1201, New York 10017.
Tel: 5572520. Fax: 9498148.

IN MOROCCO

National Tourist Offices (Office Nationale Marocain du Tourisme, ONMT: headquarters in Rabat) are often complemented by a municipal Syndicat d'Initiatif. Both can give plans, maps, advice and provide guides, but the onmt are usually better staffed, with more guides on hand. Most offices are open Monday to Saturday mornings from 8am.
Agadir: Place Prince Heritier Sidi Mohammed (off street: on first floor level of paved square opposite post office). Tel: (048) 84 63 77.
Casablanca: 55 Rue Omar Slaoui. Tel: (022) 27 11 77.
Fez: Place de la Résistance. Tel: (055) 62 34 60/65 43 70.

Distance in kilometres From City to City

	AGADIR	BENI MELLAL	CASABLANCA	CHAOUEN	EL JADIDA	ER RACHIDIA	ESSAOUIRA	FEZ	LAAYOUNE	MARRAKESH	MEKNES	OUARZAZATE	OUJDA	RABAT	TANGIER	TAZA	TETOUAN	TIZNIT
AGADIR																		
BENI MELLAL	467																	
CASABLANCA	511	210																
CHAOUEN	841	480	330															
ELJADIDA	417	271	99	429														
ER RACHIDIA	681	375	545	548	606													
ESSAOUIRA	173	370	351	681	252	745												
FEZ	756	289	289	225	388	364	640											
LAAYOUNE	849	1116	1160	1490	1066	1330	822	1396										
MARRAKESH	273	194	238	568	197	510	176	483	922									
MEKNES	740	278	229	202	328	346	580	60	1389	467								
OUARZAZATE	375	398	442	772	399	306	380	687	1024	204	652							
OUJDA	1099	632	632	499	731	514	983	343	1748	826	403	820						
RABAT	602	260	91	239	190	482	442	198	1251	321	138	528	541					
TANGIER	880	538	369	118	468	608	720	303	1529	598	267	811	609	278				
TAZA	876	409	409	345	508	484	760	120	1525	603	180	790	223	318	423			
TETOUAN	892	536	358	61	484	604	736	281	1541	615	258	820	555	294	57	370		
TIZNIT	93	560	604	934	510	774	266	849	556	366	833	468	1192	699	973	969	985	

Marrakesh: Place Abd el Moumen Ben Ali, Boulevard Mohammed V. Tel: (044) 43 62 39. Fax: (044) 43 60 57.

Meknes: Place Administrative. Tel: (055) 52 44 26. Fax: (055) 51 60 46.

Ouarzazate: Avenue Mohammed V. Tel: (044) 88 24 85. Fax: (044) 88 52 90.

Oujda: Place du 16 Août. Tel: (056) 68 56 31. Fax: (056) 68 90 89

Rabat: 22 Avenue al Jazair (Ave d'Alger). Tel: (037) 73 05 62. Fax: (037) 72 79 17.

Tangier: 29 Boulevard Pasteur. Tel: (039) 94 80 50. Fax: (039) 94 86 61.

Tetouan: 30 Avenue Mohammed V. Tel: (039) 96 19 15. Fax: (039) 69 19 14.

Embassies & Consulates

Algeria: 46 Rue ibn Ziad, Rabat. Tel: (037) 76 54 74.

Canada: 13 Bis Rue Jaffar Assadik, Agdal, Rabat. Tel: (037) 67 28 80.

France: 3 Rue Sahnoun (Agdal). Tel: (037) 68 97 00.

Germany: 7 Rue Madnine, Rabat. Tel: (037) 70 96 62.

Great Britain: 17 Boulevard de la Tour Hassan, Rabat. Tel: (037) 72 96 96; email: britemb@mtds.com There is also a consul in Tangier at 41 Avenue Mohammed V, tel: (039) 94 15 57; email:uktangier@mtds.com

Italy: 2 Rue Idriss el Azhar, Rabat. Tel: (07) 70 65 98.

The Netherlands: 40 Rue de Tunis, Rabat. Tel: (07) 73 35 12/3.

Spain: 13 Rue Madnine, Rabat. Tel: (07) 70 94 81.

USA: 2 Avenue de Marrakech, Rabat. Tel: (07) 76 22 65.

Extensions Of Stay

Contact the local police department well in advance if your stay is likely to exceed 90 days. Proof of funds will be required, along with reasons for staying. It is easier, at least in the north, to leave Morocco inside the 90 day period, and re-enter.

Getting Around

On Arrival

When you arrive you will be given an official form to fill in stating profession, addresses in Morocco and length of stay. Each time you register at a hotel you are required to fill in a similar form which is submitted to the police.

An international health and inoculation certificate (no more than 10 days old) and an anti-rabies certificate (not less than 6 months old) is needed to take pets into Morocco.

Orientation

Reaching a Moroccan town or city is often a bewildering experience. The largest are divided into the old and new towns. The old town – or medina – is the traditional quarter. Often surrounded by ramparts and entered through grand gateways, it will contain a disorientating maze of narrow streets and souks running between squares. It may also contain the fortified kasbah – ramparts within ramparts. At the other extreme is the *nouvelle ville* – usually planned and laid out by the French, with grand, straight avenues connecting roundabouts. The grandest avenue is often named after Mohammed V, and it's usually here or in the main square of the new town that you'll find the tourist office *(addresses, page 330)*. This is the place to find an official guide. On the roads, signposts are clear, and the long roads have few turnings. It's worth taking local advice about the state of mountain or desert roads at any time of year, but particularly in the mountains during winter.

Guides

The experience of arriving in an unfamiliar town or city is inevitably accompanied by the offer of a guide's services. The guide may be a small boy, a student or a professional hustler; and he will be persistent, rarely taking your first no for an answer. The government has clamped down on these so-called *faux-guides* in recent years, and if they are caught by the police they are liable to be thrown in prison. However, economic necessity forces many young men to still try their luck.

If you've decided you need a guide, such meetings can be fruitful, but it is essential to agree on a fee in advance (15 DH an hour is fairly standard). The rate for official guides (hired at the tourist office or your hotel) is around 150 DH for half a day .

At some point your guide will doubtless try to steer you into the souks, where he or she will earn commission on what you spend. If you are not interested in shopping, point this out before setting out.

MAPS

The reliable maps produced by European companies are: Hallwag (1:1,000,000); Lascelles (1:800,000); Michelin No. 969, Maroc Nord et Centre (1:1,000,000). Also good is the companion fold-out map to *Insight Pocket Guide: Morocco*, which contains town plans of major towns as well as a clear country map, and *Insight Fleximap: Morocco*, which is laminated and hard-wearing.

Serviceable town and city plans are available free of charge from the National Tourist Office. Large scale topographical maps of the Atlas are difficult to obtain. In Morocco try the shop at 31 Avenue Hassan I, Rabat. Main agent in the UK is West Col Productions, Goring, Reading Berks. RG89AA (tel: 01491 681284).

In the US: Michael Chessler

Books, PO Box 2436, Evergreen, CO80 439-2436. Maps of Toubkal National Park are available at Imlil and Asni.

Airport/City Links

There are taxi services between international airports and their respective towns. With the exception of **Casablanca** (which, with Rabat, now has a rail link between the airport and the city), distances are small, so in theory taxi fares should be low. There are official fare tables published, but you're unlikely to see them around the airport: most of the *grands taxis* on the airport run are unmetered, and drivers may want to haggle over fares. Use the guide prices below as a rough estimate. Casablanca airport is 30 km (19 miles) south of the city: the taxi fare will be about 140 dirhams. **Agadir** airport is 22 km (13 miles) south of town, and the taxi fare is around 80 dirhams; **Fez** airport is 10 km (6 miles) south of the town (taxi around 100

dirhams); **Marrakesh** airport is 6km (4 miles) southwest of the city (taxi around 80 dirhams); **Tangier** airport is 15 km (9 miles) southwest of the city (taxi around 100 dirhams).

There is also a **rail service** between Casablanca Airport and Casablanca and Rabat (departures are in line with flight arrivals) and there is a **bus service** between the airports of Agadir and Marrakesh and their respective cities.

On Departure

Moroccan money is not supposed to be exported. If, on departure, you want to reconvert your dirhams into hard currency, you must show your receipt/s for the original exchange.

Be sure to reconfirm your return air ticket 72 hours before departure. There is no departure tax.

Internal Flights

There are internal flights between most cities, even as far south as

Laayoune and Dakhla. The advantages of flying are clear cut: speed and reliability. The chief drawbacks are also obvious: cost and the infrequency of internal flights. The best reason to use an internal flight would be to complete the lion's share of a long circuit., such as from Laayoune to Casablanca or Tangier, but the journey would cost around four times as much as the bus or train.

ROYAL AIR MAROC OFFICES

In Morocco

Agadir: Avenue General Kettani. Tel: (048) 84 07 93.
Casablanca: 44 Avenue de L'Armée Royale. Tel: (022) 31 11 22.
Fez: 54 Avenue Hassan II. Tel: (055) 62 04 56.
Laayoune: Place Dcheira Immeuble Nagjjir. Tel: (048) 89 40 71.
Marrakesh: 197 Avenue Mohamed V. Tel: (044) 43 62 05.
Ouarzazate: 1 Boulevard Mohammed V. Tel: (044) 88 50 80.

Hiring a Car

The major international hire companies are all represented in Morocco and it is possible to make arrangements to pick up a vehicle at any of the airports. In cities there are always local companies who will undercut the rates of the major companies. This will be useful for short rentals (which are proportionately more expensive): but for a rental lasting the whole trip, it may be cheaper to organise a car in advance on a special **holiday tariff** – either through a travel agent or direct with one of the major companies.

Car hire prices are usually quoted exclusive of a 19 percent government tax: be sure this has been added to the price which is agreed. A week's inclusive hire of a basic car (Renault 4) can be had for about 3,000 Dh (£200/$300) from local companies. Booked from London, prices from specialist brokers start at roughly

the same level, but prices from the majors start at around £250/$375. Remember that the international companies have a better network of offices if anything goes wrong. For gruelling itineraries with a lot of mountain driving, consider hiring cars from group B (Fiat Uno) or C (Renault 19): they feel a bit more secure on tight corners. Land-Rovers for more adventurous routes can be hired locally, often with a chauffeur.

Agadir
Europcar: 5 bis, Avenue Mohammed V. Tel: (048) 84 02 03.
Hertz: Bungalow Marhaba, Avenue Mohammed V. Tel: (048) 84 09 39.
Casablanca
Avis: 19 Avenue des FAR. Tel: (022) 11 35
Hertz: 25 Rue Aloraibi Jilali. Tel: (022) 29 44 03.
Fez
Avis: 50 Boulevard Chefchaouni.

Tel: (055) 62 67 46.
Budget: Avenue Hassan II. Tel: (055) 62 09 19.
Europcar: 45 Avenue Hassan II. Tel: (055) 62 65 45.
Hertz: 1 Boulevard Lalla Meryem. Tel: (055) 62 28 12.
Marrakesh
Avis: 137 Avenue Mohammed V. Tel: (044) 43 37 27.
Europcar: 63 Boulevard Zerktouni. Tel: (044) 43 12 28.
Hertz: 154 Boulevard Mohammed V. Tel: (044) 43 99 84.
Tangier
Adil: 84 Boulevard Mohammed V. Tel: (039) 94 22 67.
Avis: 54 Boulevard Pasteur. Tel: (039) 93 30 31.
Budget: 7 Avenue du Prince Moulay Abdellah. Tel: (039) 93 79 94.
Europcar: 87 Boulevard Mohammed V. Tel: (039) 94 19 38.
Hertz: 36 Avenue Mohammed V. Tel: (039) 93 33 22.

RAM on the Web

For information on departure times, tariffs and reservations: callcenter@royalairmaroc.co.ma

Oujda: Hôtel Oujda, Boulevard Mohammed V. Tel: (056) 68 39 09.
Rabat: Avenue Mohammed V. Tel: (037) 70 97 66.
Tangier: 1 Place de France. Tel: (039) 93 55 01.
Tetouan: 5 Avenue Mohamed V. Tel: (039) 96 16 10.

City Transport

In cities take *petits taxis*: small saloon cars, theoretically metered, and with a different livery in each town. They'll take up to three people. They are cheap and usually have a meter, but it's wise to ask the approximate fare before you get in: and there's no harm in politely but firmly disputing an exorbitant fare at the end of a journey.

In **Marrakesh** (and also in Taroudannt), an alternative means of urban transport are the glossy horse-drawn *calèches,* with large wheels, loud horns and folding leather canopies. These can be as cheap as taxis for three or four people, though increasingly exorbitant prices prevail when tourists are many. Official rates are posted inside the vehicle, but congratulate yourself if you manage to pay no more than what they recommend. City buses are occasionally useful and very cheap.

Local Transport

The choice in local transport is between trains, buses and taxis.

TRAINS

The rail network extends south to Marrakesh, and links up with Safi, El Jadida, Casablanca, Rabat, Tangier, Fez, Meknes and Oujda. First-class and second-class in autorail trains are air-conditioning. Travellers under the age of 26 can use Eurotrain or Inter-Rail passes

on Moroccan trains. In any case, prices are cheap (for example: Tangier to Marrakesh costs around 290Dh first class; 190 DH second class). Plan your journey in advance (timetables are available from stations and tourist offices and published in daily newspapers). It can be worth travelling first-class at busy times and over popular routes, especially if you are not joining the train at the start of a journey. Train stations are usually found near the centre of the *ville nouvelle.* Be sure to get out at the right station: for example, in Rabat you will probably want Rabat Ville, not Rabat Agdal (a pleasant suburb); likewise you will need Meknes, not Meknes amir Abdelkader.

RAIL INFO ON THE Web

For information on, routes, departure times and tariffs, contact www.oncf.org.ma

BUS TRAVEL

This is the cheapest way to get around, and there's no better way to get to know Morocco in detail. There is a national network, CTM, which runs comfortable air-conditioned buses; a network between Casablanca, Agadir and the south, SATAS; and a lot of small local companies who may or may not run according to a timetable. Allow plenty of time to travel by bus: most of them stop frequently.

Fares are 20 percent cheaper than trains. Comfortable Supratours express coaches run by ONCF (the railway company) ply the southwest and northern coasts (where the railway doesn't run): these cost 50 percent more than standard bus fares.

Most large cities have acquired a new, centralised bus station in the last few years. These are equipped with efficient information centres that can advise on routes, etc.

In **Fez**, all buses now leave from the station below Borj Nord.

In **Meknes**, most buses leave and depart from the station outside Bab Khemis, but limited delivery

and pick-up continues at Bab Mansour.

In **Marrakesh**, the main bus station is next to the Bab Doukala, on the edge of the medina. However, the Supratours buses go from next to the railway station and the CTM has a second station in the Gueliz on Boulevard Zerktouni, not far from the Collisee cinema.

In **Casablanca** the CTM bus station is off Avenue des Far, behind the Hotel Safir. In **Rabat** the main bus station is inconveniently 2km (1 mile) away from the centre of town in Place Zerktouni.

GRANDS TAXIS

These are large cars, usually Mercedes, which rattle along with up to six passengers on routes from town to town, charging a fixed price. They will leave when they are full: it's possible to charter an entire taxi, but make sure you know the going rate. The fare is liable to be a third as much again as a bus, but the journey is likely to take half the time, or less. In remote or desert areas, Land Rovers often replace taxis, and open trucks act as local buses.

Private Transport

BY CAR

Drivers must be over 21, and be fully insured against claims by third parties. The insurance is automatic on renting a car. If taking your own vehicle, the European insurance Green Card is required and you will also need the registration document. If your own particular company doesn't issue Green Card insurance for Morocco (few do) you will need to purchase it when you arrive in Morocco (see *Getting There*). Your own national licence is valid, but it does no harm to carry an International Driving Permit as well (it has French and Arabic translations), available from motoring organisations. An international customs carnet is required for caravans.

The old system of giving priority to the right (*priorité à droite*) is still generally in force. This means that traffic going on to a roundabout has priority over the traffic already engaged. However, junctions increasingly sport give-way signs indicating priority. Major roads are well surfaced, minor ones good with lapses (some treacherous potholes) and mountain roads often not as bad as you'll have been led to expect. A toll-funded motorway is gradually being built between Casablanca and Tangier. So far it has reached just north of Larache, but with a tedious 40kph (25 mph) section in Rabat. There is also a new motorway between Rabat and Fez and new stretches under construction to Tetouan and Marrakesh. Tolls are low, at least by European standards.

Beware of other drivers: the driving test in Morocco is notoriously open to corruption.

Fuel (*essence* or, more likely, super for petrol/gas; gas-oil for diesel) is available in towns and along the highway, but fill up before striking out on a long journey away from main roads. An increasing number of petrol stations sell lead-free (*sans plomb*), especially Afriquia. Petrol gets cheaper to the south, but costs around 8 Dh a litre on average. Parking in towns of any size is likely to cost a few dirhams, collected by an official attendant, who may offer car cleaning services – at a price.

Where to Stay

Hotels

Most Moroccan hotels are classified, and their rates roughly correspond to their star rating. Tariffs are always posted at reception, so check the rate when you arrive. Generally, the standard of facilities for each star rating are as as outlined in the box on the right.

It is sensible to book ahead during busy periods (for example, Easter, Christmas and high summer, and at all times in Marrakesh).

AGADIR

There are probably more large hotels and holiday clubs in Agadir than in any other Moroccan resort, but in summer they tend to be booked up by package tour groups. Most are on Boulevard Mohammed V, which runs parallel to (though not alongside) the beach; smaller establishments occupy side-streets.

Hotel Sahara: ☆☆☆☆
Avenue Mohammed V
Tel: (048) 84 06 60
Fax: (048) 84 06 48
The largest and most resplendent of the package hotels, with every amenity, including air-conditioning in all rooms, swimming-pool, sauna, cinema and tennis courts, night-club with resident band. But a fair way from the sea.

Iberotel Tikida Beach ☆☆☆☆
Chemins des Dunes
Tel: (048) 84 54 00
Fax: (048) 84 22 21
A huge hotel, with private beach, numerous activities and health spa. Popular nightclub.

Club La Kasbah Agadir
Boulevard du 20 Aout
Tel: (048) 84 01 36
Fax: (048) 84 03 75

Hotel Standards

Prices here a rough guide and refer to the price of a double with bath per night.

Five-star hotels (over 1,500 Dh for a double) are truly luxurious and in some cases their tariffs are on a par with those in luxury hotels in Europe. Morocco's top 5-star hotels, renowned for their character and style, are La Mamounia in Marrakesh, Palais Jamai in Fez, El Minzah in Tangier and, the most exclusive of all, La Gazelle d'Or in Taroudannt.

Four-star establishments are usually very good but less refined than 5-star (from 750 DH for a double). You can expect decent plumbing, a good pool (sometimes heated in winter), often a night-club, but not always tennis courts. In warmer regions nearly all 4-star hotels have air-conditioning. Their disadvantage is that they can lack character.

In a **3-star hotel** (around 300–700 DH for a double) guests can expect a reasonable restaurant and bar, private facilities in all rooms and often a pool. Sometimes they are not as modern as 4-star hotels, but tend to be efficiently run.

Two-star hotels (about 250–300 DHfor a double) have private facilities in most rooms, sometimes a modest bar and restaurant, but rarely a pool.

One-star hotels vary tremendously. Most have at least some rooms with showers. Occasionally one will also find a restaurant or a bar, but not a-pool. Expect to pay around 200 DH for a double.

Unclassified hotels, auberges and maison d'hôtes vary more widely than any other category and can charge what they like. Depending on their standard and the aspirations of their owners, they can charge from as little as 50 DH, but usually charge between 80–200 DH. That said, there are some very upmarket masion d'hôtes, with prices to match.

Holiday villas beyond indulgence.

BALEARICS ~ CARIBBEAN ~ FRANCE ~ GREECE ~ ITALY ~ MAURITIUS
MOROCCO ~ PORTUGAL ~ SCOTLAND ~ SPAIN

If you enjoy the really good things in life, we offer the highest quality holiday villas with the utmost privacy, style and true luxury. You'll find each with maid service and most have swimming pools.

For 18 years, we've gone to great lengths to select the very best villas at all of our locations around the world.

Contact us for a brochure on the destination of your choice and experience what most only dream of.

INTERNATIONAL
CHAPTERS

☒ INSIGHT GUIDES

The world's largest collection of visual travel guides

Insight Guides – the Classic Series
that puts you in the picture

Alaska	China	Hungary	Munich	South Africa
Alsace	Cologne			South America
Amazon Wildlife	Continental Europe	Iceland	Namibia	South Tyrol
American Southwest	Corsica	India	Native America	Southeast Asia
Amsterdam	Costa Rica	India's Western	Nepal	Wildlife
Argentina	Crete	Himalaya	Netherlands	Spain
Asia, East	Cuba	India, South	New England	Spain, Northern
Asia, South	Cyprus	Indian Wildlife	New Orleans	Spain, Southern
Asia, Southeast	Czech & Slovak	Indonesia	New York City	Sri Lanka
Athens	Republics	Ireland	New York State	Sweden
Atlanta		Israel	New Zealand	Switzerland
Australia	Delhi, Jaipur & Agra	Istanbul	Nile	Sydney
Austria	Denmark	Italy	Normandy	Syria & Lebanon
	Dominican Republic	Italy, Northern	Norway	
Bahamas	Dresden	Italy, Southern		Taiwan
Bali	Dublin		Old South	Tenerife
Baltic States	Düsseldorf	Jamaica	Oman & The UAE	Texas
Bangkok		Japan	Oxford	Thailand
Barbados	East African Wildlife	Java		Tokyo
Barcelona	Eastern Europe	Jerusalem	Pacific Northwest	Trinidad & Tobago
Bay of Naples	Ecuador	Jordan	Pakistan	Tunisia
Beijing	Edinburgh		Paris	Turkey
Belgium	Egypt	Kathmandu	Peru	Turkish Coast
Belize	England	Kenya	Philadelphia	Tuscany
Berlin		Korea	Philippines	
Bermuda	Finland		Poland	Umbria
Boston	Florence	Laos & Cambodia	Portugal	USA: On The Road
Brazil	Florida	Lisbon	Prague	USA: Western States
Brittany	France	Loire Valley	Provence	US National Parks: East
Brussels	France, Southwest	London	Puerto Rico	US National Parks: West
Budapest	Frankfurt	Los Angeles		
Buenos Aires	French Riviera		Rajasthan	Vancouver
Burgundy		Madeira	Rhine	Venezuela
Burma (Myanmar)	Gambia & Senegal	Madrid	Rio de Janeiro	Venice
	Germany	Malaysia	Rockies	Vienna
Cairo	Glasgow	Mallorca & Ibiza	Rome	Vietnam
Calcutta	Gran Canaria	Malta	Russia	
California	Great Britain	Mauritius, Réunion		Wales
California, Northern	Greece	& Seychelles	St Petersburg	Washington DC
California, Southern	Greek Islands	Melbourne	San Francisco	Waterways of Europe
Canada	Guatemala, Belize &	Mexico City	Sardinia	Wild West
Caribbean	Yucatán	Mexico	Scandinavia	
Catalonia		Miami	Scotland	Yemen
Channel Islands	Hamburg	Montreal	Seattle	
Chicago	Hawaii	Morocco	Sicily	
Chile	Hong Kong	Moscow	Singapore	

Complementing the above titles are 120 easy-to-carry Insight Compact Guides, 120 Insight Pocket
Guides with full-size pull-out maps and more than 100 laminated easy-fold Insight Maps

Huge ACCOR-chain complex with just about every facility you could wish for, including a children's club.

Hotel Club Salam ☆☆☆
Boulevard Mohammed V
Tel: (048) 84 08 40
Fax: (048) 84 08 21
Club-style hotel with tennis courts, swimming-pool and night-club. Efficiently-run. Entertainment.

Hotel Miramar ☆☆
Boulevard Mohammed V
Tel/Fax: (048) 84 07 70
Comfortable small hotel (just 12 rooms) with bar and restaurant. Situated above the harbour.

Hotel Petit Suede ☆
Avenue Hassan II
Tel: (048) 84 07 79
Fax: 84 00 57
Comfortable and adequate, but only a third of the rooms have showers.

Hotel Diaf ☆
Rue Allal ben Abdellah
Tel: (048) 82 58 52
Modest, clean, friendly. A few rooms have showers.

Hotel Karam ☆☆
10 Place de la Foire
Tel: (048) 84 42 49
Fax: (048) 84 12 34
With restaurant and pool. Shower or bathroom in most rooms.

Hotel Sindibad: ☆☆
Place Ibrahim Tamri
Tel: (048) 82 34 77
Fax: (048) 84 24 74
Well-run small hotel with a pool.

Residence Farah: ☆☆
Rue de la Foire
Tel: (048) 84 39 33
Fax: (048) 84 33 64
Self-catering option.

AL HOCEIMA
Mohammed V ☆☆☆☆
Place de la March Verte
Tel: (039) 98 22 33
Fax: (039) 98 33 14
Formerly government-run, this is the oldest of the hotel complexes. Rooms and apartments have been attractively refurbished.

Hotel Quemado ☆☆☆
Beachfront
Tel (039) 98 33 15
Fax: (039) 98 48 87
Beachfront complex offering villas,

rooms, pool, tennis and watersports.

Hotel Karim ☆
27 Avenue Hassan II
Tel: (039) 98 21 84
Modest, but with good restaurant and bar.

Hotel Nacional ☆☆
23 Rue de Tetouan
Tel: (039) 98 21 41
Small but adequate. Most rooms have bathrooms.

ASILAH
Hotel Al Khaima ☆☆☆
2k Route de Tanger
Tel: (039) 41 74 28
Fax: (039) 41 75 66
Slightly out of town, on the Tangier road. Has pool, bar and disco, and is close to the beach but separated from it by the busy road (rooms to the rear will be quieter).

Hotel Oued el Makhazine ☆
Avenue du Melilla
Tel: (039) 41 70 90
Comfortable and pleasant, with sea views and bar.

ASNI
Grand Hotel du Toubkal ☆☆☆
Tel: (044) 48 45 84
Has been closed for a couple of years, but due to reopen in 2002. Comfortable base for exploring the Toubkal National Park. Restaurant, bar and, in summer, a central heating (valuable out of season).

AZROU
Auberge Amros ☆☆☆☆
Just outside town on Meknes road.
Tel: (055) 56 36 63
Comfortable modern hotel with pool in rural setting. French restaurant.

Hotel Panorama ☆☆☆
Centre of town
Tel: (055) 56 20 10
Fax: (055) 56 18 04
Well run, with restaurant, bar and central heating in winter.

Azrou Hotel: ☆
Route de Khenifra.
Tel: (055) 56 21 16.
Small, pleasant and lively. Features restaurant, bar and central heating.

Hotel des Cèdres ☆
Place Mohammed V
Tel: (055) 56 23 26.
A congenial small hotel, with restaurant and central heating.

BENI MELLAL
Hotel Chems ☆☆☆☆
Route de Marrakech
Tel: (023) 48 34 60
Pool and pleasant gardens but undeserving of its four stars. Lack of maintenance.

Hotel Ouzoud ☆☆☆
Route de Marrakech.
Tel: (023) 48 37 52
Fax: (023) 48 85 20
Large modern hotel which, along with Hotel Chems, serves as a stop-over for groups visiting Marrakesh. Swimming pool.

Hotel Gharnata ☆☆
Boulevard Mohammed V.
Small, quite comfortable hotel with central location.
Tel: (023) 48 34 82

Hotel du Vieux Moulin ☆ A;
Boulevard Mohammed V
Tel/Fax: (023) 48 27 88
Welcoming auberge, with decent restaurant.

CASABLANCA
Hotel Royal Mansour ☆☆☆☆☆
27 Avenue des F.A.R
Tel: (022) 31 30 11
Fax: (022) 31 48 18
The original of a growing chain of Meridien hotels in Morocco, it has more character than is usual in international chains. Its atrium courtyard is a pleasant place for a drink or coffee.

Hotel Hyatt Regency ☆☆☆☆☆
Place des Nations Unies
Tel: (022) 26 12 34
Fax: (022) 20 44 46
Even if you are not staying here, it is fun to come and have a drink in the 'Casablanca' bar, inspired by the film.

Holiday Inn Crown Plaza ☆☆☆☆☆
Avenue Hassan II
Tel: (022) 29 49 49
Fax: (022) 29 34 34
Sheraton ☆☆☆☆☆
100 Avenue des F.A.R

Tel: (022) 31 78 78
Fax: (022) 31 51 37
Hotel Safir ✩✩✩✩
160 Avenue des F.A.R
Tel: (022) 31 12 12
Fax: (022) 31 65 14
Renowned for its excellent value
and special deals.
Hotel Riad Salam
Boulevard de la Corniche
Tel: (022) 39 13 13
Fax: (022) 39 13 45
The only luxury hotel overlooking
the beach and situated near the
Royal Anfa Golf Club. Includes a
centre for sea-water therapy.
Idou Anfa ✩✩✩✩
85 Boulevard d'Anfa
Tel: 022) 20 02 35
Fax: (022) 20 00 29
City location, near the Twin Centre.
Fair value. Luxury amenities and
nice pool.
Ibis Moussafir ✩✩✩
Avenue Bahmad
Tel: (022) 40 19 84
Fax: (022) 40 07 99
Like other members in the
Moussafir chain, it is within spitting
distance of the railway station.
Simply furnished, but very clean
with good bathrooms and excellent
service. Good value. Best to book.
Hotel Plaza ✩✩
18 Boulevard Haphouet Boigny
Tel: (022) 29 76 98
Small, well-run hotel with restaurant
and bar.

CHAOUEN

Parador ✩✩✩✩
Outa el Hamam
Tel: (039) 98 63 24
Fax: (039) 98 61 36
Old-style Spanish parador with pool
(summer only), restaurant, bar and
good views.
Hotel Asma ✩✩✩
Place Sidi Abelhamid
Tel: (039) 98 60 02
Rather dated-looking 1970s-style
hotel, but with most amenities and
a great view.
Hotel Magou ✩✩
23 Rue Moulay Idriss
Tel: (039) 98 62 57
Comfortable small hotel with
restaurant and bar.

Price Guide

Prices here a rough guide and
refer to the price of a double with
bath (if available) per night.
Five-star: over 1,500 Dh, though
it can be quite a lot more.
Four-star: from 750 Dh
Three-star: 300–700 Dh
Two-star: about 250 Dh.
One-star Up to 200 Dh

Hotel Madrid ✩✩
Avenue Hassan II
Tel: (039) 98 74 96
Friendly, individualistic hotel, with
Moroccan decor.
Hostal Gernika
49 Rue Onssar
Tel: (039) 98 74 34
Run by artistically-inclined Spanish
woman. Spotlessly clean with a
pretty terrace. An excellent budget
option.

EL JADIDA

Royal Golf ✩✩✩✩
KM 7 Route de Casablanca
Tel: (023) 35 41 41
Fax: (023) 35 34 73
Luxury hotel with all amenities
(tennis courts, pool, hammam,
nightclub, exercise room, several
restaurants, etc) just north of El
Jadida with views of the
neighbouring golf course and the
Atlantic Ocean.
Doukkala Abou Jadail ✩✩✩
Avenue de la Ligue Arabe
Tel: (023) 34 37 37
Fax: (023) 35 05 01
Sporty beach club hotel.
Hotel le Palais Andalous ✩✩✩
Boulevard Docteur de Lanouy
Tel: (023) 34 37 45
Fax: (023) 35 16 90
A converted palace built around a
courtyard. Plenty of charm and
reasonable rates.
Hotel de Provence ✩✩
42 Avenue Fkih Er Rafi
Tel: (023) 34 23 47
This is a pleasant hotel that was
formerly run by an Englishman. A
few of the rooms have bathrooms.
A licensed bar and a good
restaurant.

ERFOUD

Hotel Salam ✩✩✩✩
Route de Rissani
Tel: (055) 57 64 25
A luxurious older-style hotel with
much dignity, overlooking the
palmerie. Pool.
Auberge-Kasbah Derkaouah ✩✩✩
Tel: (055) 57 71 40
About 24km (14 miles) souheast of
town, on the piste to the Merzouga
Dunes, this complex of bungalows,
rooms and tents is a haven of good
food, unforced charm and peace.
The owner, who has spent most of
his life in the desert, helps make it
a memorable place to stay.
Telephone to make a reservation,
and also to ask for directions on
finding it.

ER RACHIDIA

Hotel Rissani: ✩✩✩✩
Route d'Erfoud
Tel: (055) 57 21 86
Fax: (055) 57 25 85
As the most luxurious hotel in town
and the only one with a decent
pool, it serves as a stop-over for
coach tours. Views over Oued Ziz.
Hotel Meski ✩✩
Avenue Moulay Ali Cherif.
Tel: (055) 57 20 65.
Unpromising exterior leading to a
warren of large, clean, but austere,
rooms. Restaurant, but no bar. Pool
of sorts, but very murky.

ESSAOUIRA

Riad Mogador ✩✩✩✩
BP 368
Tel: (044) 78 35 56
Newish and well-run hotel which is a
rival to the well-established,
similarly conventional-style Hotel
des Iles. Slightly out of the centre.
Hotel des Iles ✩✩✩✩
Boulevard Mohammed V
Tel: (044) 47 53 29
Fax: (044) 47 54 72
Well-run, if fairly dull hotel
overlooking the beach.
Hotel Tafoukt ✩✩✩
58 Boulevard Mohammed V
Tel: (044) 47 25 05
Situated south of town on the road

running parallel with the coast. Congenial, with licensed restaurant.

Villa Maroc ☆☆☆
10 Rue Abdellah Ben Yassine
Tel: (044) 47 61 47
Fax: (044) 47 58 06
Stylish and comfortable. Moroccan meals cooked to order. Open fires out of season. Be sure to make reservations. Prices above average for the category.

Hotel Riad Al Medina ☆☆☆
9 rue Attarine
Tel/Fax: (044) 47 57 27
Individualistic and attractive *maison d'hôte* in 18th century property. Not as stylish as Villa Maroc, and prices here have risen steeply.

Hotel Sahara ☆☆
Avenue Okba Ibn Nafaa
Tel: (044) 47 22 92
Fairly large and very efficient.

Auberge Tangaro
4 km south of Essaouira, on the way to Diabet
Tel: (044) 47 84 78
Split-level room, romantic location, but no electricity (candles suffice). Half-board terms.

FEZ

Hotel Palais Jamai: ☆☆☆☆☆
Bab Guissa
Tel: (055) 63 43 31
Fax: (055) 63 50 96
19th-century palace with beautiful gardens and views of Fez. It reopened after extensive refurbishment in 1999, Stay here if you possibly can. It is well worth spending extra for a room with a medina view.

Hotel Merinides: ☆☆☆☆☆
Avenue Borj du Nord
Tel: (05) 64 52 26
Fax: (05) 64 52 25
Modern hotel near Borj Nord, high above the medina, with fabulous views. Less expensive than other hotels in the luxury category.

Jnan Palace ☆☆☆☆☆
Avenue Ahmed Chaouki
Tel (055) 65 22 30
Flashy hotel set in extensive grounds in the new town. All facilities, including well-equipped business centre. A better choice for a conference than for a holiday.

Sheraton ☆☆☆☆☆
Avenue des F.A.R
Tel: (055) 93 09 09
Fax: (055) 62 04 86
As regards atmosphere, this new town hotel is not a patch on Palais Jamai, but better service. Tennis courts.

Maison Bleue *(maison d'hote)*
2 Place de L'Istiqal Batha
Tel: (055) 63 60 52
Fax: (055) 74 06 86
Very beautiful and charming family owned hotel with three suites above arguably Fez's best restaurant.

Hotel Menzeh Zalagh ☆☆☆
Rue Mohammed Diouri
Tel: (055) 62 55 31
Fax: (055) 65 19 95
Medium-sized hotel with a good reputation and views towards Fez Jdid. When booking (advisable), specify the original Menzel Zalagh and not the more functional Zalagh 2 down the road. Pool.

Hotel de la Paix ☆☆☆
44 Avenue Hassan II
Tel: (055) 62 50 72
Fax: (055) 62 68 80
Popular hotel off the main drag in the new town. A few rooms have air-conditioning.

Ibis Moussafir ☆☆☆
Avenue des Almohades
Tel: (055) 65 18 52
Fax: (055) 65 19 09
Plaza de la Estacíon.
In the nouvelle ville, this is one in a chain of good-value railway hotels. Attractive decor, garden and pool. Very popular, so be sure to book.

Splendid Hotel ☆☆☆
9 Rue Abdelkrim el Khattabi.
Tel: (055) 62 21 48
Fax: (055) 65 48 92
Good value hotel with air-conditioning (welcome in Fez in summer), pool and a bar. Okay rooms, though nothing special.

Hotel Batha ☆☆☆
Place Batha
Tel: (055) 63 64 37
Fax: (055) 63 82 67
Excellent position near Bab Boujeloud, gateway to Fez el Bali. Slightly run down for a modern hotel, though fairly comfortable rooms. Pool which is in shadow most of the day .

Hotel Amor ☆☆
31 Rue Arabie Saoudite
Tel: (055) 62 27 24
Out of the clutch of hotels close to the railway station Amor is one of the most comfortable. Good value.

IFRANE

Hotel Michlifen ☆☆☆☆☆
Tel: (055) 56 66 07
Fax: (055) 56 66 23
Recently renovated and by far the best hotel in the area, with pool and all amenities.

Hotel Perce Neige ☆☆
Rue des Asphodelles
Tel: (055) 56 63 50
Reasonable rooms, but the dining room has little to recommend it.

IMLIL

La Kasbah du Toubkal
Tel: 00 44 (0) 1883 744392
www.kasbahdutokal.com
An environmentally friendly study centre and auberge which has been renovated by an English–Moroccan partnership (book through UK office; telephone number above). Rooms with en suite bathrooms, all with a fabulous view over the valley. No star-rating, but expensive.

IMMOUZER DES IDA OUTANANE

(Agadir region)
Hotel des Cascades ☆☆☆
Tel: (048) 82 60 16
Excellent hotel in the country north of Agadir, with nice rooms and views.

IMMOUZER DU KANDAR

(Fez region)
Hotel des Truites ☆
Tel: (055) 66 30 02
Old family-run hotel with cosy bar and restaurant. Rooms are a bit basic but full of character.

Chalet du Lac
Tel: (055) 66 31 97
French-owned hunting and fishing auberge located next to Dayet Aoua. Ancient plumbing. The auberge was reputedly a favourite with King Hassan II.

LARACHE

Hotel Riad ☆☆
Rue Mohammed ben Abdellah
Tel: (039) 91 26 29
Charming and comfortable old hotel with bar.

Hotel España ☆☆
2 Avenue Hassan II
Tel: (039) 91 31 95
Larger licensed hotel which is very good value with beautiful rooms.

LAAYOUNE

Hotel Parador ☆☆☆☆☆
Rue Okba ibn Nafaa
Tel: (048) 89 45 00
Fax: (048) 89 23 46
A mock castle enclosing a series of lush courtyards and shallow pools (one swimming pool). Arab decor and green trellises throughout.

Hotel Massira
Tel: (048) 89 42 25
Acceptable alternative to Hotel Parador, though tends to get booked up by tour groups.

Hotel Nagjir
Tel: (048) 89 41 68
More basic option, but all rooms have bathrooms or showers plus a refrigerator.

MARRAKESH

If you arrive in Marrakesh without a hotel booking (inadvisable) and have difficulty finding a room, your best bet is to try the streets off Avenue Mohammed V in Gueliz (the New Town), where there are many two- and three-star hotels.

Amanjena ☆☆☆☆☆
Route de Ouarzazate
Tel (044) 40 35 53
Fax: (044) 40 34 77
The first Amanresort in Africa. The ultimate in luxury, comprising palatial pavilions set among palm and olive trees.

Hotel La Mamounia ☆☆☆☆☆
Avenue Bab Jdid
Tel: (044) 44 89 81
Fax: (044) 44 49 40
Winston Churchill liked staying here. Former palace close to the medina: expensive but truly luxurious; renowned for its superb gardens.

Palmeraie Golf Palace ☆☆☆☆☆
Tel: (044) 30 10 10
Fax (044) 30 50 50
New luxury hotel (eight restaurants, five pools, horse riding, fitness centre, etc) attached to superb 18-hole golf course designed by Robert Trent Jones.

Hotel Es Sadi: ☆☆☆☆☆
Avenue Quadissia (in the upmarket Hivernage area west of the Koutoubia)
Tel: (044) 44 88 11
Fax: (044) 44 76 44
Not half as flashy as the Mamounia, but more affordable and very popular nonetheless. All amenities, including tennis courts.

Maison Arabe (5-star prices)
Near Bab Doukala
Tel: (04) 39 12 33
This beautiful hotel, once a famous restaurant, is owned by Fabrizio Ruspoli, an Italian, who has poured his soul into making it an unusual place to stay. No pool and no restaurant but attracts many discerning guests.

Hotel Tafilalet ☆☆☆☆
Route de Casablanca
Tel: (044) 80 70 71
Polished, personal service, quite a way out of town; 84 rooms.

Hotel Grand Imilchil ☆☆☆
Avenue Echouhada
Tel: (044) 44 76 53
Fax: (044) 44 61 65
Good-value hotel with a pool, quite close to the medina. No bar.

Hotel Le Marrakech ☆☆☆
Place de la Liberté
Tel: (044) 43 43 51
Fax: (044) 43 49 80
Large hotel on the edge of the medina. Reasonable rates with most amenities.

Hotel Moussafir ☆☆☆
Avenue Hassan II
Tel: (044) 43 59 29
Fax: (044) 43 59 36
Efficient service, blue and white decor in rooms and good plumbing.

Hotel Nassim ☆☆☆☆
115 Avenue Mohammed V
Tel: (044) 44 64 01
Fax: (044) 43 67 10
Well-run city centre hotel in heart of Gueliz with cosy bar and a tiny pool.

Hotel Sheherzade ☆☆
Derb Riad Zitoun Kedim
Tel/Fax: (044) 42 93 05
The medina's most popular small hotel, based around two traditional *riads* with good rooftop terraces. Run by a Moroccan/German couple.

Hotel Islane ☆☆
279 Avenue Mohammed V
Tel: (044) 44 00 83
Fax: (044) 44 00 85
Clean, friendly and pleasant. Good position close to the Koutoubia. Check your room first to ensure it isn't too noisy.

Hotel Le Gallia ☆☆
30 Rue de la Recette
Tel: (04) 44 59 13
Delightful rooms attractively tiled; a leafy central courtyard.

Hotel de Foucald ☆
Avenue El Mouahidine
Tel: (044) 44 54 99
The hotel has lost a star and is no longer licensed, but allows customers to BYO and the bathrooms are much improved. It remains a firm favourite among hikers and adventure travellers mostly because of Thami, the best hotel receptionist in Morocco.

Hotel Ali unclassified
Rue Moulay Ismail
Tel: (044) 44 49 79
Most popular amongst backpackers and adventure travellers going on to the mountains. Cheap and cheerful, with a decent restaurant and buffet on its terrace in summer.

Hotel Essaouira unclassified
3 Sidi Bouloukate (medina)
Tel (044) 44 38 05
Attractive, simple accommodation. Friendly and spotlessly clean.

Riad Mia Remmal Metzger
Kaat Benahid Derb Bounouar, 12.
Tel: (044) 42 78 51

Delightful *riad* run as informal bed & breakfast by artist. This is a good option for those willing to trade hotel services for medina life.

MDIQ
Hotel Golden Beach ✩✩✩
Route de Ceuta
Tel: (039) 97 50 77
Fax: (039) 97 50 96
One of several club-style hotels that are spreading along the white sands between Ceuta and Tetouan.
Holiday Club Mdiq
Route de Ceuta
Tel: (039) 66 31 39
Rooms are basic but adequate. Sport facilities, including windsurfing, riding and tennis.

MEKNES
Hotel Transatlantique ✩✩✩✩
 Rue El Merinyine
Tel: (055) 52 50 50
Fax: (055) 52 00 57
This is a long established luxury-class hotel, with character.
Hotel Rif: ✩✩✩✩
Rue Zankat Accra
Tel: (055) 52 25 91
Fax: (055) 52 44 28
Much less refined than Transatlantique, but congenial and popular, with most amenities.
Hotel Volubilis ✩✩✩
45 Avenues des F.A.R
Tel: (055) 52 50 82
Medium-sized hotel with a bar and nightclub.
Hotel Akouas ✩✩✩
Rue Emir Abdelkader
Tel: (055) 51 59 67
Fax: (055) 51 59 94
Reasonable rooms and pleasant staff. Popular nightclub.

MIRLEFT
Hotel de la Plage
Tel: (048) 71 90 56
Small Italian-run hotel on the beach. Reasonable and friendly.

OUALIDIA
L'Hippocampe ✩✩✩
Tel: (023) 36 64 99

Fax: (023) 35 64 61
Bungalow-style rooms with views of the lagoon. Terraced garden, very good restaurant (oysters a speciality).
Auberge de la Lagoune
Tel: (023) 34 64 77
Pleasant auberge.

OUARZAZATE
Hotel Berber Palace ✩✩✩✩✩
Quartier Mansour Eddahbi
Tel (044) 88 31 05
Fax: (044) 88 30 71
Large Meridien hotel with five-star facilities and comfort. Popular with film production crews, and fashion shoot teams.
Hotel Riad Salem: ✩✩✩
Avenue Mohammed V
Tel: (044) 88 20 06
Fax: (044) 88 27 66
Medium-sized with tennis courts and large pool. Pleasant setting.
Hotel La Gazelle ✩✩
Avenue Mohammed V
Tel: (044) 88 21 51
Well-established with restaurant and bar. Modest rooms are arranged around a courtyard. Swimming-pool. A short walk from the centre. No air-conditioning.

OUIRGANE
Residence de la Roseraie ✩✩✩✩
Tel: (044) 43 91 28
Fax: 43 91 30
A great escape. Folded into the mountains, with rose garden, swimming-pool, stunning views, bungalows and apartments; 9 rooms, 16 suites.Horse-riding and tennis available.
Hotel Le Sanglier Qui Fume ✩✩
Tel: (044) 48 57 07
Fax: (044) 48 57 09
Under new ownership since 1997, this characterful auberge has a characterful restaurant and bar and a pool.
Chez Momo
Tel: (044) 48 57 04
Fax: (044) 48 57 27
Small, fairly new hotel set amongst trees by the river. Has a small swimming pool and an easy-going atmosphere.

OUJDA
Ibis Moussafir
Place de la Gare
Tel: (056) 68 82 01
Fax: (056) 68 82 08
Comfortable rooms. Pool, restaurant and Bar. Next to the station.
Hotel Lutetia ✩
44 Boulevard Hassan Loukili
Tel: (056) 68 33 65.
Well-run and quite comfortable, though no restaurant.
Hotel Royal ✩
13 Boulevard Mohammed Zerktouni
Tel: (056) 68 22 84
Most rooms have bath or shower. Clean and adequate.

OUKAIMEDEN
CAF Refuge
Tel: (044) 31 90 36
Run by Jean and Michelle, this offers very reasonable dormitory accommodation, with discounts for affiliated associations. Justly popular restaurant and very cheap bar. Crowded during the skiing season, it is a recommended base for Atlas hiking at other times .
Hotel Angour (aka Chez Juju)
Tel: (044) 31 90 05
Small, comfortable alternative, again with bar and restaurant.

OURIKA
Ourika Hotel ✩✩✩✩
BP 870
Tel: (044) 31 91 55
The one luxury hotel in this popular Atlas valley just south of Marrakesh. Restaurant, bar and swimming-pool.

RABAT
La Tour Hassan Meridien ✩✩✩✩✩
26 Rue Chellah
Tel: (037) 72 14 01
Fax: (037) 72 54 08
Since being taken over by Meridien and a complete renovation, the hotel has regained its place as the best accommodation in the centre of town.

Hotel Safir ☆☆☆☆
Place Sidi Makhlouf
Tel: (037) 73 47 47
Fax: (037) 73 39 94
Large, luxury hotel between the medina and Hassan Tower, overlooking the river. Most amenities.

Hotel Chellah ☆☆☆☆
2 Rue d'Ifni
Tel: (037) 70 10 51
Fax: (037) 70 63 54
Near the archaeological museum. Pleasant and comfortable.

Hotel Balima ☆☆☆
283 Avenue Mohammed V
Tel: (037) 70 77 55
Fax: (037) 70 74 50
Old-style hotel near the railway station and opposite the parliament building. Well-maintained, with bar, restaurant (of sorts) and good-size rooms. Its outside café is a lively meeting place.

SIDI HARAZEM

Hotel Sidi Harazem ☆☆☆☆
Tel: (055) 69 00 57
Fax: (055) 69 00 72
Ugly hotel dominating the springs; reasonable comfort, but wiser to choose a good hotel in Fez.

TAFRAOUTE

Hotel aux Amandiers ☆☆☆☆
Tel: (048) 80 00 08
Fax: (048) 80 03 43
Kasbah style hotel above the town square. Has en suite bathrooms and pool, but due for a renovation.

TANGIER

Hotel el Minzah ☆☆☆☆☆
85 Rue de la Liberté
Tel: (039) 93 58 85
Fax: (039) 93 45 46
Elegant but relaxed hotel with Moorish decor. Garden or sea views. Great bar and restaurant.

Hotel Solazur ☆☆☆☆
Avenue des F.A.R
Tel: (039) 94 01 64
Fax: (039) 94 25 86
A functional package-tour establishment, but offers most amenities and overlooks the beach.

Price Guide

Prices here a rough guide and refer to the price of a double with bath (if available) per night.
Five-star: over 1,500 Dh, though it can be quite a lot more.
Four-star: from 750 Dh
Three-star: 300–700 Dh
Two-star hotels: about 250 Dh.
One-star Up to 200 Dh

Tanjah Flandria ☆☆☆☆
6 Boulevard Mohammed V
Tel: (039) 93 30 00
Fax: (039) 93 43 47
Popular town centre hotel with pool.

Hotel Rembrandt ☆☆☆
Avenue Mohammed V
Tel: (039) 93 78 70
Fax: (039) 93 04 43
Classy old-style hotel that has recently been renovated.

Hotel Chellah ☆☆☆
Rue Alal ben Abdellah
Tel: (039) 94 33 88
Large, popular hotel with pool.

Hotel Djenina ☆☆
8 Rue el Antaki
Tel: (039) 942244.
Small and comfortable, with bar and restaurant. Recently renovated.

Hotel Continental ☆☆
36 Rue Dar el Baroud
Tel: (039) 93 10 24
Older colonial-style hotel behind the port, on the edge of the medina. What it lacks in modern comforts it makes up in atmosphere.

Hotel Miramar
168 Avenue des F.A.R
Tel: (039) 94 17 15
Well-run, with restaurant and bar.

Hotel el Muniria unclassified
Rue Magellan
Tel: (039) 93 53 37
Pleasant hotel with literary associations. Groovy bar which is sometimes packed and sometimes empty. Some rooms have showers.

TAN TAN

Hotel Etoile du Sahara ☆
17 Rue el Fida
Tel: (048) 87 70 85
Decent enough, with restaurant. Some rooms have showers.

TAROUDANNT

Gazelle d'Or ☆☆☆☆☆
3 kilometres from town
Tel: (048) 852039
Fax: (048) 85 27 37
Luxury bungalows under the High Atlas. Very exclusive. Attracts the rich and famous.

Hotel Palais Salam ☆☆☆☆
Tel: (048) 85 23 12
Fax: (048) 85 26 54
A palace built in to the city wall. Good service, mediocre food.

Hotel Saadiens ☆☆
Borj Annassim
Tel: (048) 85 25 89
Newish hotel unlicensed but with attached pastry shop and pool. Good value and very clean.

TETOUAN

Hotel Safir ☆☆☆☆
Avenue Kennedy
Tel: (039) 97 01 44
Fax: (039) 97 66 92
Large modern hotel on the Ceuta (Sebta) road. Tennis courts, pool and night-club..

Paris Hotel ☆☆
Rue Chakib Arsalane
Tel: (039) 96 67 50.
Central, modest hotel. Some rooms are very small.

VOLUBILIS

The Volubilis Inn ☆☆☆☆
Tel: (055) 69 40 70
Fax: (055) 69 40 12
Comfortable modern hotel in rural setting near Moulay Idriss. Pool and terrace overlooking the ruins.

ZAGORA

La Fibule du Draa ☆☆☆☆
Route de M'hamid
(044) 84 73 18
Fax: (044) 84 72 71
A favourite hotel built from pisé. Garden, pool and bar. Rooms are quite small.

Hotel Kasbah Asmaa
Route de M'hamid
Tel/Fax: (044) 84 75 27
Popular hotel with enthusiastic staff and good food.

Where to Eat

Where To Eat

Moroccan-style meals are available in most four and five-star hotels, in traditionally furnished restaurants. In cities such as Fez and Marrakesh, there are several restaurants in the medina which specialise in Moroccan meals combined with a floor show. These are mainly the preserve of the tourist trade, since Moroccans tend not to eat out or, if they do, they prefer French or Italian restaurants for the change.

The design of a Moroccan dining-room is similar everywhere. Low banquette seats against the wall, and even lower tables, are the norm in both restaurants and private homes. The classic Moroccan meal is eaten with two fingers and thumb of the right hand – but hotels and restaurants may not insist! When tea or coffee is served, it is a sign that the meal is at an end: prepare to leave after three cups or so.

You will probably need to book such meals in advance (even in your hotel): occasionally you may need to be part of a group to order a certain dish. If you're looking for a good restaurant, rely on word of mouth from other visitors rather than the recommendations of guides: the restaurants themselves pay a commission to the guides.

Price Guide

Prices here a rough guide and refer to the price of a meal per person.
$$$$: over 400 Dh.
$$$: 250–400 Dh
$$: 100–250 Dh
$: under 100 Dh

European style meals are served in three, four and five-star hotels, and in many city restaurants. Especially in Agadir, but also elsewhere, pizza and spaghetti restaurants are multiplying But there will always be cheap medina cafés – pick the cleanest and busiest.

AGADIR

Agadir likes to think of itself as a cosmopolitan resort, and this is reflected in the restaurants – sadly rather too many pizza, burger and pasta establishments, most of which are on Boulevard du 20 Août. The restaurant in Al Madina Palace and the Marrakesh Restaurant in the Agadir Beach Club Hotel are at the top end of the quality scale, with Moroccan and international cuisine accompanied by a floor show. Agadir is a great place for fish. For inexpensive, informal dining, take a seat at one of the makeshift stalls inside the harbour. A plate of fried squid, prawns and sardines costs about 35 dirhams. They serve from late morning through to the evening. On weekends, another possibility is to drive to Aouir, north of Agadir, where the rooftop restaurants specialise in tasty *tajines*.

Hotel Miramar
Tel: (048) 07 70
The restaurant in this hotel, overlooking the harbour end of the beach, is well regarded. Good quality French cuisine specialising in flambés, Licensed. $$

Restaurant du Port
Port d'Agadir
Tel: (048) 84 37 08
Great fish. Licensed. $$

Joharat
The best Moroccan restaurant in town. A very good lute player provides musical entertainment. $$

Samouri Japanese restaurant
TRYP Hotel
Tel: (048) 84 03 35
Samurai carrying chef prepared dishes at the table. $$

Chahoua
One of a number of Korean establishments catering to the many Korean fishermen in town. Simple but authentic. $

Menu Decoder

The following are the staples of Moroccan menus.
Brochettes: cubes of meat on kebabs, most often made from lamb or liver.
Cous-cous: a huge bowl of steamed semolina grains with vegetables and meat – usually mutton or chicken. It's supposed to be eaten by hand, but spoons are usually provided for Westerners, which is just as well. More of a domestic meal than a meal eaten out – at least as far as the Moroccans are concerned.
Djej: Chicken. A favourite chicken dish is *djej mqualli*, chicken with preserved lemons and olives.
Hout: Fish. This often goes under its French names – *loup de mer* (perch), *rouget* (red mullet), merlan (whiting), *thon* (tuna).
Harira: thick, spicy, sometimes creamy soup, based on lamb and pulses. It's often offered as a starter, but beware: it is enough to be a meal in itself.
Kefta: meatballs flavoured with coriander and cumin. Sometimes served with fried eggs.
Khobz: bread for mopping up harira or tajines, the traditional flat round loaves are ideal. Fairly dry, with a grainy texture. Left-over bread is used to make sweets.
M'choui: whole lamb, spit or oven roasted. M'choui is are usually found only on special occasions – at festivals, say – or in the more "traditional" restaurants.
Merguez: spicy beef or lamb sausages, often served with harissa, a fiery pepper condiment.
Pastilla: spiced pigeon meat encased in flaky, warkha pastry, often dusted with sugar or cinnamon – a traditional delicacy. Sweet versions are also found.
Tajine: stew – meat or fish, often with fruit and nuts, slowly cooked on a bed of oil over charcoal, vegetables, fruits and spices in an earthenware pot. One of Morocco's most visible dishes (because of the conical topped dish in which it is served).

ASILAH

Pepe's
Just outside the main gate to the medina.
One of the best of several fish restaurants. Simply cooked sardines, squid, swordfish, prawns, sole, is served with bread and salads. Pavement tables provide a good view of the evening promenade. Licensed. $$

Garcia's
Rue Moulay Hassan Ben el Mehdi
Tel: (039) 41 74 65
Well-established fish restaurant on the corniche. Similar fare to Pepe's, though slightly more upmarket.
Licensed. $$

CASABLANCA

The city may not have much to recommend it from the point of sight-seeing but it has good restaurants.

A Ma Bretagne
Ain Diab (corniche south of town, ot far from the koubba of Sidi Abderrahman)
Tel: (022) 36 21 12
Reputed to be one of the best restaurants in Morocco. Emphasis on fish in both sophisticated and simple guises. Ocean views. $$$$

Al Mounia
95 Rue du Prince Moulay Abdallah, off the Boulevard de Paris.
Tel: (022) 22 26 69
Excellent Moroccan cuisine. Floor shows add to the experience. $$$

Sijilmassa
Rue de Biarritz
The Moroccan character extends to providing floor shows. $$–$$$

Le Cabestan
Boulevard de la Corniche
Tel: (022) 39 11 90
Excellent French cuisine featuring plenty of fish. Near the lighthouse. $$$$

Restaurant du Port de Pêche
(through the port entrance)
Tel: (022) 84 37 08
Good fish option. $$

Ostrea (also in the port)
Tel: (02) 44 13 90
Good fish restaurant, with moderately expensive prices. $$

Price Guide

Prices here a rough guide and refer to the price of a meal per person.
$$$$: over 400 Dh.
$$$: 250–400 Dh
$$: 100–250 Dh
$: under 100 Dh

Le Chalutier
Centre 2000
Tel: (022) 20 34 55
Good French and international cuisine. $$

ESSAOUIRA

Dar Loubon
Rue de Rif
Tel (044) 47 62 96
Imaginative menu combining international and Moroccan influences. Delightfully bohemian ambience. $$$–$$$$

Taros
Place Moulay Hassan
Tel: (044) 47 64 07
Run by a Breton, this is a popular bar and restaurant with a club-like atmosphere. Has a fabulous terrace with views over the sea and the square. $$–$$$

Chez Sam's
Inside harbour perimeter, i.e. through the gate. Good seafood and lively atmosphere. $$

Châlet de la Plage
Tel: (044) 47 21 58
Large portions of good French and international food (emphasis very much on fish) at reasonable prices. It is possible just to drink at the bar and eat tapas – particularly useful when the few other bars in the town have closed. $$

FEZ

L'Ambra
47 Route d'Immouzer
Tel: (055) 64 16 87
Has an excellent reputation and is famous for its Moroccan specialities, particularly *pastilla*. Essential to book in advance.It is located on the outskirts of town so you will need to take a taxi. $$$

La Maison Bleue
2 Place de L'Istiqal Batha
Tel: (055) 74 18 43
Upmarket restaurant in intimate private house with an elegant subdued atmosphere. Excellent food and superb understated gnaou duo and lute player provide entertainment. Reservations essential. $$$

Fassia, Hotel Palais Jamai
Tel: (055) 634331
Fez's most beautiful hotel, occupying a former palace, has an excellent Moroccan restaurant.
$$$–$$$$

Dar Saada
21 Souk Attarine (near the Attarine Madrassa)
Tel: (055) 63 33 43
Traditional *dar*-type restaurant. Tends to get busy with tour groups, especially at lunch time. Quite good food. $$$

Palais de Fez (opposite the Kairouyine Mosque)
16 Rue Boutouil-Kairouyine
Tel: (055) 63 47 07
Another *dar*-style restaurant, offering similar Moroccan fare to Dar Saada. $$$

Firdaous
Bab el Guissa (near Palais Jamai)
Tel: (055) 63 43 43
Offers floor show and quite good food at moderate prices.$$$

Yang Tse
23 Rue Eriytheria
Tel: (055) 62 14 85
Popular Chinese restaurant.

Vittorio's
31 Rue Jabir
Excellent, well-established pizzeria/Italian, just off Mohammed V in the New Town.

MARRAKESH

Marrakesh's offers the best choice of restaurants in Morocco, reflecting the presence of a wealthy expatriate community and its large numbers of high-spending visitors.

Yacout
79 Sidi Ahmed Soussi,
Tel: (044) 44 19 03
At the top end of the price spectrum. One of the top restaurants in town (it attracts

Eat like the Locals

In contrast to Marrakesh's many expensive restaurants there is a street of small local restaurants, doing excellent inexpensive food of all types, behind Hotel Ali, in the Medina. Another such street lies to the right of the Casablanca road junction at the end of Mohammed V in the Gueliz. Standards of hygiene may make foreign tourists nervous but trade is reassuringly brisk.

international names). Classic Moroccan dishes, superbly cooked and presented; a terrific ambience; and exquisite decor. It is necessary to book.

Tobsil
22 Derb Abdellah Ben Hessaien
Bab Ksour
Tel: (044) 44 45 35
Excellent food served with grace, in beautiful *riad* lovingly restored by its French owner. Reservations recommended. $$$–$$$$

La Palais Gharnatta
56 Derb el Arfa, Riad Zitoun Jdid
Tel: (044) 44 5218
Superb Moroccan food in traditional *riad*. Family-run. Offers the most value of the up-market restaurants. Book in advance. $$$

Kasbah la Rotunda
19 Derb Lamnabha
Tel: (044) 44 00 98
Theatrical Italian-owned restaurant occupying old *riad*. Go for the decor as much as the food, both of which are extravagant. $$$$

Rotisserie de la Paix
68 rue de la Yougoslavie, Gueliz
Tel: (044) 43 31 18
Old-fashioned French restaurant with pleasant garden, and small back room with open fire for winter dining. Excellent grills. $$

Le Jacaranda
32 Boulevard Mohammed Zerktouni
Tel: (044) 44 72 15
Good French option, plus a few Moroccan choices. Stylish setting. $$$

Bagatelle
101 Rue Yougoslavie
Tel: (044) 43 02 74

Very civilised French restaurant with attractive vine-covered garden for summer dining.

Le Pavilion
Bab Doukala
47 Derb Zaouia
Tel: (044) 39 12 40
Beautifully decorated restaurant offering up-market French food in an orientalist setting. Book in advance. Closed Tuesday. $$$

Kim Son
Rue Ibn Toumert
Tel: (044) 43 01 59
Good Vietnamese option. $$

Le Cantanzaro
Rue Tarik ibn Ziad
Tel: (044) 43 37 31
Good and very popular pizzeria/Italian. $$

Puerto Banus
Rue Ibn Hanbal
Tel: (044) 44 65 34
Marrakesh's only Spanish restaurant. Intimate and attractive with good food. $$

MEKNES

Le Dauphin
5 Avenue Mohammed V
Tel: (055) 52 34 23
Refined French and Moroccan food. $$$$

Hotel Transatlantique
Rue El Merinyine
Tel: (055) 52 00 02
This long-established luxury-class hotel; it serves old-fashioned Moroccan food at its best. $$$–$$$$

Riad
79 Ksar Chaacha-Dar Kakbira
Tel: (055) 53 05 42
Lovely garden restaurant serving excellent Moroccan cuisine. $$$

Hacienda, about 2 miles (3 km) outside Meknes on the Fez road.
Tel: (055) 52 10 91
A good French/Moroccan restaurant, with bar, dancing and al fresco dining. $$

OUARZAZATE

Chez Dimitri
22 Boulevard Mohammed V
Tel: (044) 88 26 53
Dimitri's has a French Foreign

Legion feel: large old-fashioned bar, wooden tables and chairs, old military memorabilia on the walls. Its namesake, Dimitri, died in 1991 but his son has now taken over. At dinner there is usually a table d'hôte menu as well as à la carte. Choices include hearty casseroles, comprising rabbit or lamb. Extremely reasonable prices and obliging staff. $–$$

Hotel La Gazelle
Avenue Mohammed V
Tel: (044) 88 21 51
At the western end of town. A good alternative to Chez Dimitri. $

OUIRGANE

La Roseraie
Tel : (044) 43 91 30
Beautiful luxury hotel enfolded by by the mountains. Good restaurant serving international and Moroccan cuisine. Open to non-residents. $$$

Au Sanglier qui Fume
Tel: (044) 48 57 07
A roadside auberge, which serves homely French cooking. Lunch is served in the garden in summer $$.

OURIKA

L'Auberge de Ramuntcho,
Aghbalou
Tel: (044) 48 45 21
Slightly more sophisticated alternative to the simple cafés and grill bars. $

RABAT

Dinarjat
6 Rue Belgnaoui (Medina)
Tel: (037) 70 42 39
Excellent Moroccan food in a beautiful old house. Andalusian music adds to the refined atmosphere. $$$

L'Oasis
Rue el Osqofiah
Off the Place Pietry (site of the flower market)
Tel: (037) 72 05 57
Good Moroccan option. $$

Le Mont Doré
l'Ocean (next to the medina)
Another inexpensive Moroccan restaurant serving good food.

La Pagode
Behind the railway station
11 Rue Baghdad
Tel: (037) 76 33 83
Good Vietnamese and Chinese
cuisine in attractive surroundings.

La Mamma
6 rue Tanta
Behind Hotel Balima (off Boulevard
Mohammed V)
Tel: (037) 70 73 29
Extremely popular with *Rabatis*, as
well as visitors. Great pizzas and
Italian/international fare. Always
busy, but they can usually squeeze
you in without a reservation.

TANGIER

El Korsan
85 Rue de la Liberté
Tel: (039) 93 58 85
Good Moroccan cuisine in
sumptuous surroundings. Also good
seafood. $$$

Restaurant Hammadi
(end of Rue Italie)
Reasonable Moroccan cooking in
kitsch surroundings. $$

Rubis Grill
3 lbn rochd
Tel: (09) 93 14 43
Popular expat hangout serving grills
and international cuisine. $$

Guitta's
110 Rue Sidi-Bouabid
Tel: (039) 93 73 33
Good international option which has
been going since Tangier's days as
an international zone. Renowned for
its Sunday lunch. $$

Pagode
Rue El Boussouri
Tel (039) 93 8086
Excellent and popular Chinese in
the centre of town. Attractive
ambience. $$

San Remo-Chez Toni
15 Rue Ahmed Chaouki
Tel: (039) 93 84 51
Long-established and popular
Italian. $$

Attractions

Excursions

There is, of course, an infinite
number of touring routes and
excursions throughout Morocco that
could be contrived: and the main
text of this book should help in the
planning of a suitable itinerary.
Below, however, are lists of the
must-see excursions and routes
radiating from the most popular
holiday centres.

From Agadir

The mountain villages and scenery
around **Tafraoute** (150 km/95
miles) southeast; the old
Portuguese fishing port of
Essaouira (180 km/112 miles)
north.

From Marrakesh

The pass roads through the High
Atlas of **Tizi n-Test** (to the south)
and **Tizi n-Tichka** (to the
southeast); the highest peak of
Morocco, **Jebel Toubkal**, due south,
visible for miles around, and
climbable from Imlil; the **southern
valleys** of oases and kasbahs, east
and south of Marrakesh and
reached via Ouarzazate, 204
km/126 miles from Marrakesh –
specifically the **Draa** valley, the
Dadès valley and the **Todra Gorge**;
the really dedicated will press
further east into the Sahara to the
Tafilalt to watch sunrise over the
dunes. Via Beni-Mellal 200 km/125
miles northeast), you can reach the
reservoir at **Bin el Ouidane** and the
waterfalls (cascades) at **Ouzoud**.

From Meknes or Fez

The cedar forests around **Azrou** and
Ifrane (80 km/50 miles and 60

km/37 miles south of Fez); the
Kandar massif (30 km/19 miles
south of Fez); the holy city of
Moulay Idriss and the nearby
Roman ruins of **Volubilis** (30 km/19
miles north of Meknes); the end of
the Middle Atlas mountains to **Taza**,
and further east, the end of the Rif
at the **Beni-Snassen** mountains.

From Rabat

Head inland! There are only coastal
towns to visit closer than Meknes:
Salé, Rabat's other half;
Casablanca (90 km/56 miles/) and
El Jadida (187 km/117 miles/).

From Tangier

The large market town of **Tetouan**
and the pretty white houses at
Chaouen and **Ouezzane** are in the
foothills of the Rif. **Asilah** is a good
place to head on the west coast.
You might also contemplate a day
trip to **Gibraltar.**

Further Afield

Hiking into the mountains and riding
into the desert can both be
arranged with relative ease. English
speaking travel agencies arrange
Land Rover "safaris" deep into the
desert, along prearranged routes,
and these obviously have
considerable attractions over
random forays, especially since
reliable maps are hard to come by.
Hiking in the High Atlas is well
catered for, with mules, guides and
mountain huts – the latter
maintained by the French Alpine
Club (caf). First base is at Imlil, two
hours from Marrakesh (you can
take a bus as far as Asni then buy a
place in a truck or taxi for the
remaining 17 km (11 miles). Again,
specialised tour operators can
provide guaranteed expertise, as
well as a bit of security for your
adventure. But there's no reason to
ignore independent possibilities, at
least if it's summer and you're
reasonably fit. The Toubkal National
Park is well charted (IGN maps
available from either Imlil or Rabat),
the terrain not difficult (except for
coping with the loose scree
underfoot). All in all, very little
specialist equipment is necessary.

Nightlife

Nightlife

Resort nightlife is restricted to Tangier, Casablanca and its outskirts (Ain Diab and Mohammedia) and Agadir (where it is, in fact, fairly subdued). But the most exciting city at night, and with the most Moroccan feel, must be Marrakesh, where activity on the Jemaa el Fna (musicians, magicians, entertainers) can keep going until dawn.

Tangier still lays claim to being the city that keeps the latest hours. As well as late bars and hotel discotheques, the enjoyable Morocco Palace (11 Avenue Prince Moulay Abdellah) offers belly dancing and disco dancing well into the early hours. Some of the beach bars also offer nightlife.

BARS

Bars are a late 20th century addition to Moroccan nightlife, and not always a happy one. It's as though they are symbols of the clash between Moroccan Islam, with its traditional rule of total abstinence from alcohol, and Moroccan modernity, with its liberal, urban, Westernised way of thinking. They can be loud and intimidating or furtive and uneasy. **Hotel bars** are a different matter, and can be insular. The best bar-life is found in Tangier and Marrakesh.

NIGHTCLUBS & DISCOS

Nightclubs (often with belly dancing) and **discos** in tourist centres and cities are aimed at the tourists and the Westernised urban population and visiting Gulf Arabs intent on letting their hair down. Most are in hotels.

GAMBLING

There are **casinos** in Marrakesh (in the Hivernage district of the new town) and in the resort area of Mohammedia, just north of Casablanca.

FOLKLORE & FANTASIAS

In medina restaurants or on main roads out of town, the most common evening entertainment is a combination of a typically Moroccan meal with a display of folklore: folk music and dancing, or (in the open countryside) an equestrian fantasia. Although these evenings often have a rather "packaged" feel, they can be genuinely spectacular – especially the fantasias. There may, of course, be the chance of coming across real festivals (while touring, for example), where the excitement is more spontaneous. The early evening in any town or city is vibrant as everyone comes out after an afternoon siesta. Evening street life is notably exciting in Marrakesh, where the celebrated Jemaa el Fna whirls with people; dancers, snake charmers, traders, beggars and musicians and tourists. Have plenty of change in your pocket while you watch the performers: a contribution is expected from everyone, visitors above all – and especially from all photographers.

Shopping

In Morocco touting is an everyday occupation; selling is a polished and sinuous art form, the rigmaroles of buying can be prolonged, even wearisome. One thing is worse: attempting not to buy goods is more exhausting.

Dealing with it: The only rule about bargaining for something you really want is to know the price you are prepared to pay, and start well under it (at, say, a third). Tactics and strategies on both sides (incredulous laughter, walking towards the door), and bids, which come gradually closer, will probably end with the buyer paying a little more than his original maximum; part of the seller's art is to determine approximately how much more.

Fixed prices: The first priority, then, is to ascertain a fair market price for goods on offer. This is often possible in the state-run Handicraft Centres (Centre or Maison de l'Artisanat) in major towns. The quality of goods here is underwritten by the government, and there is always a shop with fixed prices on display. These will be higher than the prices that should be possible through bargaining, but the lack of hustle and pressure mean that some people are bound to prefer shopping here.

Where To Shop

The following list contains the more upmarket places to shop, especially for quality Moroccan crafts, furniture and antiques.

CASABLANCA
Art de fez, 6 Rue General Laperine.

FEZ

Au Petit Bazaar de Bon Accueil, 35 Talaa Seghira, Fez el Bali.
Boutique Majid, Abdelmajid Rais el Fenni, 66 Rue des Chrétiens.

MARRAKESH

Bazaar du Sud, 117 Souk des Tapis.
Chez Alaoui, Souk Shouari.
Chez le Brodeuses Arab, 12 Rue Rahba Lakdima.
Coopartim, Ensemble Artisinal, Ave Mohammed V.
Fondouk el Fatmi, Bab Ftouh
Fondouk el Quarzazi, Bab Ftouh.
La Lampe d'Aladdin, 99 and 70 bis Rue Semmarine.
Mamounia Arts, 47 Rue Dar el Bacha, Bab Doukkala.
Maison d'été, 17 Rue de Yougoslavie. .

Moroccan Arts, 67 Sabeb Moulay Hadj, El Ksour.
L'Oiseau Bleu, 3 Rue Tarik Ibn Ziad.
L'Orientaliste, 15 Rue de la Liberté.

RABAT

Gallerie Cheremetieff, 16 bis Rue Annaba.

TANGIER

Adolfo de Velasco, 28 Boulevard Mohammed V. Antiques and crafts.
Boutique Majid, 66 Rue des Chrétiens.
Bazaar Tindouf, opposite El Minzah hotel.

Export Procedures

Beware of buying anything that can't be carried away. Many traders will offer export facilities (e.g. for large carpets) and, although there are no customs formalities to be met, the shipping of goods could take months. There is little comeback against a souk trader who has been paid in cash and fails to deliver. However, paying by credit card is getting easier, and the card companies may provide a back-up.

Complaints

Complaints can be taken to the local police. A complaints book is kept by every classified hotel (for complaints of all kinds, not just relating to accommodation). Copies of complaints are then forwarded to the headquarters of the tourist office in Rabat. The Syndicat d'initiatif or ONMT offices can also help in passing on complaints.

What to Buy

The traditional crafts of Morocco still make the best bargains. First and most prominent of the handicraft traditions are **carpets**, hand knotted and in some cases, still coloured with vegetable dyes. Designs (apart from the Turkish inspired patterns of Rabat carpets) are predominantly traditional to Berber tribes. Their use of colours and schemes of stylised illustration are supposed to enable experts to pin down not only the area but sometimes the individual tribe or even family that made them. Top quality carpets sell for thousands of dirhams; more affordable and more easily portable are Berber rugs, kilims or blankets. For Berber patterns, try the small country souks around Marrakesh.

Leather goods are widespread: from unpolished leather bags and belts, through the distinctive pointed slippers (babouches), to ornate pouffes, studded and dyed. Some leather goods are finished in a style closer to Italian designer luggage – in all cases, price should go hand in hand with quality, so check the hide and workmanship

before buying. Printed boxes and bookbindings are often found, but, with their shiny tooling, have become the victims of their imitators and too often look tacky.

Jewellery is available everywhere, although one of the best places to buy it is Tiznit, with its famous silversmiths' souk. Dull silver is the basic material: heavy but beautifully decorated bracelets, delicate filigree rings, chunky necklaces of semi-precious stones (or occasionally of plastic, for the unwary) are most common. Slightly more unusual, and sometimes antique, are decorated daggers, scabbards, or Koran boxes, covered with silver-wire decoration. Whatever the piece, the fastenings are often a weak point. Beware, too, of silver-plating masking what the Moroccans call b'shi-b'shi – meaning rubbish.

Marquetry is another traditional craft: wooden furniture, ornaments, chess-sets, and small wooden boxes made in cedar, thuya, and oak. Many wooden goods are inlaid with veneers or mother of pearl. Often the quality of finish is less than ideal: hinges

or joints are points to watch. The woodworkers' ateliers at Essaouira are an ideal place to buy (and to watch the manufacture).

Pottery ranges from the rough earthenware of household pots and crocks to gaudy (and predominantly tourist-orientated) designs in the main towns.

Edibles As well as spices, nuts, olives and Moroccan sweets, possible buys include argan oil, produced in the southwest. It is sold, either on its own or mixed with ground almonds (a nut butter called amalou). However, because of its high value, it is difficult to guarantee that the oil is not mixed with olive oil.

One way of being sure that the oil you buy is 100 percent pure is to buy it from one of the women's cooperatives that produce it. The best of these are organised by the Projet Conservation et Development de Arganeraie, which markets its oil to supermarkets under the brand name Cooperative Tissaliwine, in Europe and Morocco, and has the EU approved certificate of producing an organic product.

Sport

GOLF

The main golf tournament is the Hassan II trophy, held in November at the Royal Dar es-Salam in Rabat. The Moroccan Open is held in January. Lessons and caddies are available at all courses. Some courses require a handicap card.

Agadir: Royal Golf d'Agadir, 9 holes. Built in 1955. Tel: (048) 83 46 90. Golf les Dunes, 27 holes. Built in 1992. Course comprises: Tamarisk (9), par 36; Eucalyptus (9), par 36; Oued (9), par 36.
Tel: (08) 83 46 90.
Ben Slimane (near Casablanca): Royal Golfe de Bani Slimane, 9 holes. Built in 1992.
Tel: (033) 32 87 93.
Casablanca: Royal Golf d'Anfa, 9 holes. Built in 1945.
Tel: (022) 36 53 55.
Royal Golf Mohammedia.
Tel: (03) 32 46 56.
El Jadida: Royal Golf d'El Jadida, 18 holes. Built in 1993.
Tel: (033) 35 41 41.
Meknes: Royal Golf de Meknes, 9 holes. Built in 1943.
Tel: (055) 53 07 53.
Marrakesh: Royal Golf de Marrakech, 18 holes, par 72. Built in 1923. Tel: (044) 44 43 41. Palmerie Golf, 18 holes. Built in 1993. Tel (044) 30 10 10. Amelkis: 18 holes. Built in 1995.
Mohammedia: Royal Golf de Mohammedia, 18 holes, par 72. Built in 1925. Tel: (033) 32 46 56.
Ouarzazate: Royal Golf de Ouarzazate, 18 holes. Built in 1993. Tel: (044) 88 26 53.
Rabat: Royal Dar-es-Salam, 45 holes. Built in 1971. Course comprises: Red (18), par 73; Blue

Golfing Information

For more information on courses and facilities, contact:
The Royal Moroccan Golf Federation
Royal Dar-Es-Salaam Golf Club
Rabat
Tel: (037) 75 59 60
Fax: (037)75 10 26.

(18), par 72; Green (9), par 32.
Tel: (037) 75 59 60.
Tangier: Royal Golf de Tanger, 18 holes, par 70. Built in 1914.
Tel: (039) 94 44 84.
Tetouan: Royal Golf Cabo Negro, 18 holes. Refurbished.
Tel: (039) 97 83 03.

HUNTING

From the first Sunday in October, on Sundays and public holidays until January or early spring, it's open season on game birds and wild boars. Game includes quail (season closes late January); snipe woodcocks, pigeons and turtle doves; and partridges, ducks, rabbits and hares (season closes early January). The season for wild boar runs until mid-February, on Thursdays as well as Sundays and holidays; but hunting is only allowed with beaters.

Licensing is strictly controlled, and hunting without a licence is an offence. It is theoretically possible to organise the temporary import of one's own guns, but it is more convenient to leave to an expert the formalities and the procurement of a local shooting licence.

For further information contact the Moroccan National Tourist office or the Moroccan Hunting Federation, 2 Rue Alkhil, Rabat. Tel: (037) 70 78 35; Fax: (037) 20 18 59.

FISHING

Trout fishing is popular in Morocco: to the extent that the rivers and lakes that are easily reached have been overfished. The fly fisher's choice is extreme: fishing in

isolated streams and pools of the Middle and High Atlas, or casting into custom-stocked lakes (most of them in the Middle Atlas) where the permits are expensive and the catch weighed before leaving.

Coarse fishing: Lakes and reservoirs of the Middle Atlas are the most popular setting for coarse fishing; around Azrou, Ifrane and Immouzer du Khandar in particular, and in the reservoir of Ben el Ouidane. Species include some of the world's largest pike, as well as black bass and perch.

Permits are required for trout and coarse fishing; these are usually available locally (through hotels or tourist offices.

Sea fishing is rich, too, and does not require a permit. From massive sea bass off Dakhla and Laayoune in the south, to the summer visits of tuna north of Casablanca, and swordfish off Tangier or lobster and langouste in Rabat and Agadir, fish are populous and varied. Bream, mackerel and sardines are common also. The Mediterranean and the South Atlantic coasts are the most fruitful: deep sea fishing from boats is relatively easy to arrange, and spearfishing with aqualung is possible with a permit.

HIKING

Several adventure tour operators run hiking holidays in the Atlas and Anti-Atlas mountains. These come with experienced guides and porters. However, it is possible to devise your own hikes in situ, especially in the Toubkal National Park south of Marrakesh. Unless you are a very experienced (and properly equipped) mountain hiker, hire a local guide and pack mules and follow the standard routes. The price of such services, including accommodation and sometimes food, are set and published, though they may be negotiable when business is quiet. Good springboards, where hiking has been turned into an important local industry, are Imlil (a few kilometres from Asni), Oukaimedan, and

Tabant. Basic accommodation on hikes is found in mountain refuges or in the homes of locals.

Also see the box on Mountain Tourism, *below*.

WHITE-WATER RAFTING

In spring, when the snows melt, and in late autumn, when rains fall, the rivers of the High and Middle Atlas quickly swell. Good rafting is to be had on the Dades and Ourika rivers in the High Atlas, and (more demanding) the Oum er Rbia River in the Middle Atlas. Several adventure tour operators now including rafting in their programmes, along with mountain biking. If you want to join an organised rafting programme contact:

Dynamic Tours, 34 Boulevard Zerktouni, 11th Floor, Casablanca. Tel: (022) 20 26 82.

Sport Travel, 154 Avenue Mohammed V, Marrakesh. Tel: (044) 43 99 68.

Ribat Tours, 3 Avenue Moulay Youssef, Rabat. Tel: (037) 76 03 05.

Tizi Randonnee, 42 Avenue de l'Istiqlal, Kenitra. Tel: (037) 37 53 54,

For general information, contact the Federation Royale Marocaine de Canoe-kayak, Centre National des Sports, BP 332, Avenue Ibnou Sina, Rabat. Tel: (037) 77 02 81.

SKIING

The peculiarity of the High Atlas climate enables the tourist board to boast of Marrakesh being a base from which you can go skiing in the morning and sunbathe in the afternoon. The ski resort of Oukaimeden (2,650 metres/8,700 ft;), an hour's drive south of Marrakesh, expects snow from December to April – but the snow is not to be relied on. The skiing is stiff; skis and boots can be hired. The other resort, Mischliffen, is reached through cedar forests from Azrou or Ifrane: the setting rather than the skiing is the attraction.

Specatator

BIRD-WATCHING

Some of the migratory birds lucky enough to have avoided death by shotguns are rare and beautiful: Morocco lies under one of the two major migratory routes for European birds wintering in Africa. Storks, ibis, and flamingoes are seen in the wetlands of river estuaries and coastal lagoons. Eagles and falcons sometimes wheel high in a semi-desert sky. Several tour companies offer bird-watching holidays; their expertise will help determine the place and time to go. Mid-October is one of the best times.

Particularly good areas include: **Oualidia**, where the lagoons and

Info in Marrakesh

In the absence of a national mountain guides' office in Marrakesh, the hotels Ali and Foucauld act as the place to meet up with guides from the mountains and check out the possibility of joining a trek or outdoor pursuit.

salt pans attract flamingo, black-winged stilt, avocet, Audoin's and Slender-billed gulls; the islands off **Essaouira**, where a colony of Eleonora's falcon breed; **Oued Massa** for crested coot, Pale Crag Martin, osprey and the rare bald Ibis; the **Sous valley** for Moussier's redstart, bush and great grey shrike, Lanner falcon and chanting goshawk; the **Anti-Atlas** for long-legged buzzards, cream-coloured courser and black wheatear; **Jebel Sarho** for desert sparrow, trumpeter bullfinch, brown-necked raven and rat-rumped wheatear and larks.

Other Sports

Tennis, and (along the coast) watersports are easy to find in most tourist areas, through hotels. One of the most popular activities, though, is riding – mule-trekking in the rugged terrain of the mountains, or galloping on horseback along the sandy beaches of the coast.

Mountain Tourism

For those intent on hiking in the Atlas Mountains, the Moroccan National Tourist Office publishes free each year a guide covering most of the mountain areas. It lists prices of guides, mules, accommodation as well as naming recognised mountain lodgings called *gîtes*, licensed guides, and for good measure, recommends prices of pick-up trucks to access points in the hills. This essential little booklet is available by writing to GTAM, Departement du Tourisme, 64 Avenue Fal Ould Oumeir, Agdal, Rabat, and is printed in an English as well as a French edition. Topographical maps can be harder to come by. The Departement cartographic in Rabat is the source, but offers only limited possibilities to buy from them, while specialist map shops outside Morocco are only able to get hold of occasional stocks. For stockists in the UK, try West Col Production, tel: 01491 681284.

There are also a number of Moroccan agencies specialising in organising group trips to the mountains or desert. They work mostly with foreign agencies but will also take on private groups approaching them directly. Individual mountain guides have also been quick to appreciate the value of the internet and many now even have their own websites. The range of activities has greatly expanded in recent years and it is now possible to go rafting, mountain biking and cross-country motorcycling as well as the more usual hiking, camel trekking or horse riding. These agencies are also listed in the Moroccan Government's booklet on mountain tourism.

Language

Moroccan Arabic

Arabic is the official first language of the kingdom, although many people speak dialects of the Berber language, especially in and south of the High Atlas. Moroccan Arabic is unlike other forms of Arabic, so Arabic phrase books are not a good investment (although classical Arabic speakers will be understood). The easiest way to communicate for most Westerners is to use French, the second language, commonly used alongside Arabic on signposts, menus and in shops. The average Moroccan puts the average visitor to shame in his command of second, third and fourth languages. English, German or Spanish will be understood in many hotels or markets – or wherever tourists are found.

It's very useful to have a few words of Arabic as a matter of courtesy, and to establish friendly relations. A few useful words are listed below; an accent shows the stressed syllable.

WORDS & PHRASES
In Conversation

Hello/*Márhaba, ahlan*
(reply)/*Marhba, ahlan*
Greetings/*As-salám aláykum* (peace be with you)
(reply)/*Waláykum as-salám* (and to you peace)
Welcome/*Áhlan wasáhlan*
(reply)/*Áhlan wasáhlan*
Good morning/*Sabáh al-kháyr*
(reply)/*Sabáh al-kháyr*
Good evening/*Masá al-kháyr*
(reply)/*Masá al-kháyr*
Good night/*Tisbáh al-kháyr* (wake up well)

(reply)/*Tisbáh al-kháyr*
Good bye/*Máa Saláma*
How are you?/*Káyf hálak?* **(to a man)**/*Káyf hálik? (to a woman)*
Well, fine/*Al-hámdu li-llá*
Please/*min fádlak* (to a man)/*min fádlik* (to a woman)
After you *Tafáddal* (to a man)/*Tafáddali* (to a woman)/*Afáddalu (to more than One)*
Excuse me/*Samáhli*
Sorry/*Áfwan or mutaásif* (for a man)/*Áfwan or mutaásifa* (for a woman)
Thank you *(very much)*/*Shúkran (jazilan)*
Thank you, I am grateful/*M'tshakkrine*
Thanks be to God/*Al-hámdu li-llá*
God willing *(hopefully)*/*Inshá allá*
Yes/*Náam or áiwa*
No/*La*
Congratulations!/*Mabrúck!*
(reply)/*Alláh yubárak fik*
What is your name?/*Sh'nnu ismak?* (to a man)/*Sh'nnu ismik?* (to a woman)
My name is.../*Ismi...*
Where are you from?/*Min wáyn inta?* (for a man)/*Min wáyn inti?* (for a woman)
I am from... England/*Ána min Ingíltra*
Germany/*Ána min Almánia*
the United States/*Ána min Amérika*
Australia/*Ána min Ustrália*
Do you speak English?/*Tkellem Inglisia?*
I speak...English/*Kan tkellem Inglesa*
German/*Almámi*
French/*Fransáwi*
I do notspeak Arabic/*Ma kan tkellemichi Arbia*
I do not understand/*Ma báfham*
What does this mean?/*Shka te ani?*
Repeat, once more/*Sh'hal*
Do you have...?/*Ándkum...?*
Is there any...?/*kayn...?*
There isn't any.../*Ma kaynsh*
Never mind/*Ma'alésh*
It is forbidden.../*Mamnú'a*
Is it allowed...?/*Masmúh...?*
What is this?/*Sh'nnu hádha?*
I want/*Baghi*
I do not want/*Ma Baghish*
Wait/*Istánna* (to a man)/*Istánni* (to a woman)
Hurry up/*Yalla/bi súra'a*
Slow down/*Shwáyya*
Finished/*Baraka*
Go away!/*Imshi!*
What time is it?/*Adáysh as-sáa?/kam as-sáa?*
How long, how many hours?/*Sha'al?*

General

embassy/*sifára*
post office/*máktab al-baríd*
stamps/*tawábi'a*
bank/*bank*
hotel/*otél/fúnduq*
museum/*máthaf*
ticket/*tadakir*
ruins/*athár*
passport/*jiwáz as-sáfar*
good/*m'zyan*
not good, bad/*mashi m'zyan*
open/*maftúh*
closed/*múghlk*
today/*al-yáum*
tonight/*Al barah ghadda*
tomorrow/*búkra*

Eating/Drinking out

restaurant/*máta'am*
fish/*sámak/hout*
meat/*láhma*
milk/*halíb*
bread/*khúbz*
salad/*saláta*
delicious/*záki*
coffee/*káhwa*
tea/*shái*
cup/*kass*

Pronunciation

Pronunciation

í	as in	see
ya	as in	Soraya
ai	as in	eye
ay	as in	may
aw	as in	away
kh	as in	the Scottish loch
gh	as in	the Parisian
dh	as in	the

Double consonants

Try to pronounce them twice as long.
An apostrophe ' indicates a glottal stop.

Days of the Week

Often used to identify towns and villages, which are named after the day of their weekly souk: thus Souk-Tnine is the town which has a market on Monday. On many road signs, the day is mentioned where the map or guidebook omits to mention it. The days are numbered from Sunday, with the exception of Friday, the day of Muslim worship, which has no number.

El had	the first day: Sunday
Et tnine	the second day: Monday
Et tleta	the third day: Tuesday
El arba	the fourth day: Wednesday
El khemis	the fifth day: Thursday
Ej djeema	day of mosque or assembly: Friday
Es sebt	the sixth day: Saturday

with sugar/*bi súkkar*
without sugar/*bla sukkar*
wine/*sh'rab*
beer/*bíra*
mineral water/*mái ma'adaniya*
glass/*kass*
bottle/*karaa*
I am a vegetarian/*Ána nabbáti* (for a man)/*nabbátiya* (for a woman)
the bill/*al-hisáb*

Getting around

Where...?/*Wáyn...?*
downtown/*wást al bálad*
street/*shária*
Amir Mohammed Street/*Shária al-amir Mohammed*
car/*sayára*
taxi/*táxi*
shared taxi/*servís*
bus/*tobis*
airplane/*tayára*
airport/*matár*
station/*mahátta*
to/*íla*
from/*min*
right/*yamín*
left/*shimál*
straight/*dúghri*
behind/*wára*
near/*karíb*
far away/*ba'id*
petrol, super/*benzín, benzín khas*

Numbers

zero	*sifir*
one	*wáhad*
two	*itnín*
three	*taláta*
four	*árba'a*
five	*khámsa*
six	*sítta*
seven	*sába'a*
eight	*tamánia*
nine	*tísa'a*
ten	*áshara*
eleven	*hidáshar*
twelve	*itnáshar*

Shopping

market/*súq*
shop/*dukkán*
money/*fulús*
cheap/*rakhís*
expensive (very)/* gháli (jídan)*
receipt, invoice/*fatúra, wásl*
How much does it cost?/*Adáysh?/bi-kam?*
What would you like?/*Sh'nou khsek?*
I like this/*Baghi hádha*
I do not like this/*Ma baghish hádha*
Can I see this?/*Mumkin ashúf hádha?*
Give me/*A'atíni*
How many?/*Kam?*

Looking for a room

a free room/*ghúrfa fádia*
single room/*ghúrfa munfárida*
double room/*ghúrfa muzdáwija*
hot water/*mái skhoon*
bathroom, toilet/*hammám, tuwalét*
shower/*dúsh*
towel/*foota*
How much does the room cost per night?/*Sha'al al bit allayla?*

Emergencies

I need help/*Bídi musáada*
doctor/*doct/Bídi musáada*
hospital/*mustáshfa*
pharmacy/*saidalíya*
I am ill, sick/*Ána marídh* (for a man)/*Ána marídha* (for a woman)
diarrhoea/*ishál*
operation/*amalíya*
police/*shúrta*
lawyer/*muhámmi*
I want to see/*Ba'ghi anshoof*

GLOSSARY

agadir/**fortified granary**
agdal/**garden**
Aid el Kebir/**feast day celebrating Abraham's Sacrifice of the Lamb**
Aid es Seghir/**feast day held after the first sighting of the moon after Ramadan**
El Andalus/**Muslim Spain**
aït/**community**
bab/**gate**
baraka/**blessing, often thought magical**
bled el makhzen/**land of government**
bled es siba/**land of dissidence**
caid/**district judge**
djemma/**assembly, but also mosque**
djinn/**spirit**
Fassi/**person from Fez**
fondouk/**lodging house with stables**
Gnouai/**a black African tribe in the south**
Hadith/**the written traditions of Islam**
Hadj/**the pilgrimage to Mecca**
hammam/**steam bath**
horm/**sanctuary**
imam/**prayer leader**
jebel/**mountain**
koubba/**white, domed building containing the tomb of a saint**
ksar (ksour)/**fortified** *pisé* **building or community** (plural)
l'tam/**veil**
Maghreb/**collective name for Morocco, Algeria and Tunisia**
makhzen/**government**
marabout/**saint**
Marrakshi/**person from Marrakesh**
mechouar/**square, assembly area**
medrass (medersa)/**Islamic college and living quarters for students** (plural)
medina/**old town**
mellah/**Jewish quarter**
mihrab/**niche indicating direction of Mecca in mosque**
minaret/**tower of mosque**
Moriscos/**Muslim refugees from spain in 15th century**
moujehaddin/**Islamic soldiers engaged in Holy war**
Moulay/**indicates descendancy from the Prophet**
Mouloud/**Prophet's Birthday**

moussem/**religious festival**
msalla/**prayer area**
muezzin/**caller to prayer**
oued/**river**
pisé/**mud and rubble**
quibla/**direction of Mecca in a mosque**
Shia/**branch of Islam which recognises Ali as the successor to Mohammed**
shouaf/**fortune teller**
shereef/**ruler who is descendant of Prophet**
stucco/**elaborate plaster work**
Sufi/**religious mystic**
Sunni/**orthodox Muslim**
tizi/**mountain pass**
tabia/**mud used in pisé architecture**
zaouia/**religious fraternity**
zellige/**elaborate tile mosaics**

French

WORDS & PHRASES

How much is it?/C'est combien?
What is your name?/Comment vous appelez-vous?
My name is.../Je m'appelle...
Do you speak English?/Parlez-vous anglais?
I am English/American/Je suis anglais/américain
I don't understand/Je ne comprends pas
Please speak more slowly/Parlez plus lentement, s'il vous plaît
Can you help me?/Pouvez-vous m'aider?
I'm looking for.../Je cherche
Where is...?/Où est...?
I'm sorry/Excusez-moi/Pardon
I don't know/Je ne sais pas
No problem/Pas de problème
Have a good day!/Bonne journée!
That's it/C'est ça
Here it is/Voici
There it is/Voilà
Let's go/On y va. Allons-y
See you tomorrow/A demain
See you soon/A bientôt
Show me the word in the book/Montrez-moi le mot dans le livre
yes/oui
no/non
please/s'il vous plaît
thank you/merci

(very much)/(beaucoup)
you're welcome/de rien
excuse me/excusez-moi
hello/bonjour
OK/d'accord
goodbye/au revoir
good evening/bonsoir
here/ici
there/là
today/aujourd'hui
yesterday/hier
tomorrow/demain
now/maintenant
later/plus tard
this morning/ce matin
this afternoon/cet après-midi
this evening/ce soir

ON ARRIVAL

I want to get off at...
Je voudrais descendre à...
What street is this? A quelle rue sommes-nous?
Which line do I take for...? Quelle ligne dois-je prendre pour...?
How far is...?
A quelle distance se trouve...?
Validate your ticket
Compostez votre billet
airport/l'aéroport
train station/la gare
bus station/la gare routière
Métro stop/la station de Métro
bus/l'autobus, le car
bus stop/l'arrêt
platform/le quai
ticket/le billet
return ticket/aller-retour
hitchhiking/l'autostop
toilets/les toilettes
This is the hotel address
C'est l'adresse de l'hôtel
I'd like a (single/double) room...
Je voudrais une chambre (pour une/deux personnes) ...
....with shower avec douche
....with a bath avec salle de bain
....with a view avec vue
Does that include breakfast? Le prix comprend-il le petit déjeuner?
May I see the room? Je peux voir la chambre?
washbasin/le lavabo
bed/le lit
key/la cléf
elevator/l'ascenseur
air-conditioned/climatisé

ON THE ROAD

Where is the spare wheel?/Où est la roue de secours?
Where is the nearest garage?/Où est le garage le plus proche?
Our car has broken down/Notre voiture est en panne
I want to have my car repaired/Je veux faire réparer ma voiture
the road to.../la route pour...
left/gauche
right/droite
straight on/tout droit
far/loin
near/près d'ici
opposite/en face
beside/à côté de
car park/parking
over there/là-bas
at the end/au bout
on foot/à pied
by car/en voiture
town map/le plan
road map/la carte
street/la rue
square/la place
give way/céder le passage
dead end/impasse
no parking/stationnement interdit
motorway/l'autoroute
toll/le péage
speed limit/la limitation de vitesse
petrol/l'essence
unleaded/sans plomb
diesel/le gasoil
water/oil/l'eau/l'huile
puncture/un pneu de crevé
bulb/l'ampoule

SHOPPING

Where is the nearest bank (post office)?/Où est la banque/Poste?
I'd like to buy/Je voudrais acheter
How much is it?/C'est combien?
Do you take credit cards?/Est-ce que vous acceptez les cartes de crédit?
I'm just looking/Je regarde seulement
Have you got...?/Avez-vous...?/
I'll take it/Je le prends
I'll take this one/that one/Je prends celui-ci/celui-là
What size is it?/C'est de quelle taille?
Anything else?/Avec ça?
size (clothes)/la taille

size (shoes)/*la pointure*
cheap/*bon marché*
expensive/*cher*
enough/*assez*
too much/*trop*
a piece/*un morceau de*
each/*la pièce (eg ananas, 15F la pièce)*
bill/*la note*
chemist/*la pharmacie*
bakery/*la boulangerie*
bookshop/*la librairie*
grocery/*l'alimentation/l'épicerie*
tobacconist/*tabac*
markets/*le marché*
supermarket/*le supermarché*

SIGHTSEEING

town/*la ville*
old town/*la vieille ville*
mansion/*l'hôtel*
hospital/*l'hôpital*
staircase/*l'escalier*
tower/*la tour (La Tour Hassan)*
walk/*le tour*
museum/*la musée*
exhibition/*l'exposition*
tourist/*l'office de*
information/*tourisme/le*
office/*syndicat d'initiative*
free/*gratuit*
open/*ouvert*
closed/*fermé*
every day/*tous les jours*
all year/*toute l'année*
all day/*toute la journée*
swimming pool/*la piscine*

DINING OUT

breakfast/*le petit déjeuner*
lunch/*le déjeuner*
dinner/*le dîner*
meal/*le repas*
first course/*l'entrée/les hors d'oeuvre*
main course/*le plat principal*
made to order/*sur commande*
drink included/*boisson compris*
wine list/*la carte des vins*
the bill/*l'addition*
fork/*la fourchette*
knife/*le couteau*
spoon/*la cuillère*
plate/*l'assiette*
glass/*le verre*
napkin/*la serviette*
ashtray/*le cendrier*

Further Reading

Books

HISTORY

Morocco by Neville Barbour. London: Thames & Hudson, 1965. The standard historical work from the Phoenicians to the 1960s.
Lords of the Atlas, by Gavin Maxwell. London: Century, 1983. Compelling story of the Glaoui dynasty in the last two centuries.
The Conquest of Morocco, by Douglas Porch. London: Jonathan Cape, 1986. French adventurism and Moroccan history at the end of the 19th century.

FICTION

The Spider's House, by Paul Bowles. London: Arena Publishing. Spy story set against daily life in Fez in the period leading up to independence.
The Sheltering Sky, by Paul Bowles. Familiar to many in the film adaptation by Bernardo Bertolucci, this is Bowles's most famous existentialist work.
   Other books by Bowles set in Morocco include **Without Stopping** and **Let it All Come Down**.
For Bread Alone by Mohamed Choukri. Grafton, 1987. Autobiography of a man who grew up poor and illiterate. Translated into English by Paul Bowles.
Hideous Kinky by Esther Freud. London: Hamish Hamilton, 1993. Comic novel about a young girl's adventures with her hippie mother in Morocco in the 1960s.
The Lemon and **Love with a few Hairs** Mohammed Mrabet. Al Saqi Books. Fiction by one of the leading Moroccan novelists.
The Sand Child by Tahar Ben Jellouan. Quartet. Novel by foremost Moroccan novelist, which won the French Prix Groncourt.

FOOD AND COOKING

Taste of Morocco, by Robert Carrier. Century, 1988. Excellent introduction to food and recipes. Sumptuous photographs.
Good Food from Morocco, by Paula Wolfert. John Murray, 1989. Comprehensive introduction to Moroccon cuisine; a diverting read.

TRAVEL LITERATURE

Morocco: The Traveller's Companion by Margaret and Robin Bidwell. I.B. Tauris, 1992. An anthology of extracts by writers on Morocco.
The Voices of Marrakesh by E. Canetti. London: Marion Boyars. Impressions by Nobel Prize winner.
Tangier: City of the Dream by Iain Finlayson. Harper Collins, 1992. A gripping account of Tangier in its louche heyday.
The Dream at the End of the World by Michelle Green. Bloomsbury, 1992. Gossipy account of expatriate life in Tangier.
Morocco That Was, by Walter Harris. London: Eland Books, 1983 (first published 1921). Accounts of the end of feudal Morocco and the beginning of French rule from the correspondent of the London *Times*.
Travels with a Tangerine, by Tim Mackintosh-Smith. John Murray, 2001. Engrossing account of author's travels in the footsteps of the 14th-century Arab geographer Ibn Battouta.
A Year in Marrakesh, by Peter Mayne. Eland Books, 1984. Engrossing, personal account.
By Bus to the Sahara, by Gordon West. London: Black Swan. A journey through Morocco during the 1930s, calling at the palaces of various Moroccan caids.
Days: Tangier Journal, 1987–1989, by Paul Bowles. Reflections on Bowles's life in Tangier.

GENERAL

Morocco, by Rom and Swaan Landau, London: Elek Books, 1967. Worth tracking down for its photographs of mosque interiors.

The World of Islam: Faith, People, Culture, edited by Bernard Lewis. Thames and Hudson. Excellent general introduction to the Islamic world, lavishly illustrated.

The Moors: a comprehensive description by Budgett Meakin. London: Sonnenschein, 1902. A good claim to be the first guide book to Morocco.

WOMEN

Beyond the Veil, by Fatima Mernissi. London: Al Saqi Books. Polemic on women's position in Islam by Moroccan feminist educated in Morocco and America.

PHOTOGRAPHIC/ART BOOKS

Matisse in Morocco, by Jack Cowart; Pierre Schneider; John Elderfield; Albert Kostenevich; Laura Coyle. Thames and Hudson, 1990. Stunning record of Matisse's two fruitful trips to Tangier in 1912. Lavishly illustrated.

Living in Morocco: Design from Casablanca to Marrakesh by Lisl (photographs) and Landt Dennis. Thames and Hudson, 1992. Sumptuous exploration of Moroccan arts and crafts.

Berbers of the Atlas by Alan Keohane. London: Hamish Hamilton. Impressive photographic study of the time Alan Keohane, one of the main contributors to *Insight Guide: Morocco*, spent living and travelling with the Berbers.

Other Insight Guides

Other Insight Guides highlighting destinations in this region:

The expanded and updated *Insight Guide: Tunisia* explores the country's heady mix of African, Arab and European influences. Includes background essays on the culture, as well as a comprehensive places section and detailed listings. The latest edition contains many new maps and images.

Insight's second series, Insight Pocket Guides, includes the titles *Insight Pocket Guide: Morocco* and *Insight Pocket Guide Tunisia*, featuring tailor-made itineraries extracting the best of these North African countries. Each title comes with its own pull-out map.

Insight Products

To find out more about Insight Guides' range of products, visit the company's website: Insightguides.com

A third series, Insight Compact Guides, also includes Morocco among its destinations. A handy on-the-spot reference book.

To complete its range of travel guides, Insight produces a range of laminated, all-weather Flexi Maps. Its title on Morocco includes town plans of Tangier, Fez, Rabat, Casablanca and Marrakesh.

Feedback

We do our best to ensure the information in our books is as accurate and up-to-date as possible. The books are updated on a regular basis, using local contacts, who painstakingly add, amend and correct as required. However, some mistakes and omissions are inevitable and we are ultimately reliant on our readers to put us in the picture.

We would welcome your feedback on any details related to your experiences using the book "on the road". Maybe we recommended a hotel that you liked (or another that you didn't), as well as interesting new attractions, or facts and figures you have found out about the country itself. The more details you can give

us (particularly with regard to addresses, e-mails and telephone numbers), the better.

We will acknowledge all contributions, and we'll offer an Insight Guide to the best letters received. Please write to us at:

Insight Guides
APA Publications
58 Borough High Street
London SE1 1XF
Or send e-mail to:
insight@apaguide.demon.co.uk

ART & PHOTO CREDITS

AFP/Corbis 49
AKG London 18, 26
Mary Andrews/Ffotograff 69
Apa Publications 276
Archivo Iconographico/S.A.Corbis 29
Associated Press 39, 40L, 47
David Beatty 6/7, 8/9, 10/11, 12/13, 14, 56, 58, 59, 60, 67, 83, 98/99, 100/101, 142/143, 147, 198, 200, 231, 247, 279, 288, 289, 293, 294, 295, 302/303, 309, 313
Bettmann/Corbis 73
Columbia Pictures 301
J.D. Dallet 259
Ethel Davies 2B, 88, 89, 95, 166/167, 168, 275, 312
Jose Navarro/Ffotograff 277
Wolfgang Fritz 45, 113, 124/125, 128, 131T, 150/151, 156, 162, 165, 197, 208, 210, 211, 233T, 256, 262, 263, 268/269, 271, 297L, 310, 311, 319
Veronica Garbutt 2/3, 80
Tony Halliday back flap bottom, back cover bottom,78, 247T, 248, 253L/R, 256T, 273T, 278T, 280T, 291, 292, 295T, 299T
Robert Harding 5B, 93, 106
Blaine Harrington 1, 4BL, 57, 61, 62, 81, 172, 184, 185, 187, 188, 189L/R, 189T, 199, 200T, 202, 238/239, 242, 243, 244T, 250, 258
Steinar Haugberg 92, 182/183, 201, 203
Holiday Which? 286/287, 320
Hulton Getty 31, 41, 42
Hulton Deutsch/Corbis 116
Alan Keohane 63, 66, 68, 87, 94, 96, 108/109, 110, 111, 114, 115,

115T, 117, 119, 120T, 121, 131, 132, 133, 137, 138, 139, 152, 157, 159, 160, 164T, 176, 180, 194T, 226/227, 229, 232, 233, 234, 235, 236, 237, 246, 249, 251T, 252, 264, 267, 280, 304, 305, 306, 307, 307T, 314, 315, 316, 317, 317T, 318
Alain Le Garsmeur 21, 25, 30, 32/R, 33, 36L/R, 38, 40R, 71, 72, 74, 119T
Louvre Museum 16/17
Magnum 70
Mary Evans Picture Library 23, 35
Middle East Pictures 20, 22, 54/55, 76/77, 102/103, 130, 136, 216, 299
Kim Naylor 82, 120, 134R, 190, 191, 196
Christine Osborne/MEP 4/5, 79, 84, 118, 144, 148, 173, 190T, 192, 194, 209, 265, 266, 282
Polly Phillimore 212, 215
Jorg Reuther 127, 135
Rex Features 43, 50, 51
Jens Schuman 164, 174/175, 219, 245, 251, 281, 284, 297R
Spectrum Colour Library 97
Topham Picturepoint 19, 34, 37, 44, 46, 48, 75
Bill Wassman 126,134L, 149, 158, 161, 206/207, 221, 222, 228, 260/261, 270, 274, 283, 285
Phil Wood/Apa back flap top, back cover left, back cover top, spine top & centre, front flap top & bottom, 85, 86, 113T, 122, 122T, 123, 133T, 134T, 136T, 137T, 138T, 139T, 140, 140T, 141, 145, 146,

146T, 147T, 153, 155, 155T, 156T, 157T, 161T, 163, 169, 170T, 171, 171T, 172T, 173T, 177, 178, 178T, 179, 180T, 181, 193, 195, 197T, 199T, 201T, 213, 213T, 214, 217, 217T, 218T, 219T, 220, 220T, 223, 231T, 234T, 244, 253T, 254, 255, 255T, 264T, 272T, 276T, 278, 291T, 296, 296T, 298, 300, 300T, 308, 310T, 312T, 313T, 315T

Picture Spreads

Pages 64/65: *Top row, left to right:* Middle East Pictures, Alan Keohane, Mary Andrews. *Centre row:* Alan Keohane, Ethel Davies. *Bottom row:* Ingrid Morato, Alan Keohane, Alan Keohane, Alan Keohane.
Pages 90/91: *All photography:* Alan Keohane.
Pages 204/205: *Top row, left to right:* Blaine Harrington, Jose Navarro/Ffotograff, Patricia Aithie/Ffotograff, Patricia Aithie/Ffotograff. *Centre row:* Alan Keohane, Blaine Harrington. *Bottom row:* Blaine Harrington, Phil Wood, Christine Osborne, Alan Keohane.
Pages 224/225: *Top row, left to right:* Middle East Pictures, Alan Keohane, Alan Keohane, Alan Keohane. *Centre row:* Christine Osborne, Blaine Harrington. *Bottom row:* Phil Wood, Christine Osborne, Alan Keohane.

Map Production Stephen Ramsay
© 2000 Apa Publications GmbH & Co.
Verlag KG (Singapore branch)

INSIGHT GUIDE
MOROCCO

Cartographic Editor **Zoë Goodwin**
Production **Linton Donaldson**
Design Consultants
Carlotta Junger, Graham Mitchener
Picture Research **Hilary Genin, Monica Allende**

Index

Numbers in italics refer to
photographs

a

Abd el Aziz 35, *36*
Abd el Krim 36
Abd el Krim Khatib 43–4
Abd el Malik 30, 31
Abd el Moumin 28
Abou el Hassan 29, 163
Abou Yahya 29
Abou Youssef 29
accommodation
    Continental Hotel (Tangier) *120*
    El Minzah Hotel (Tangier) 115
    Gazelle D'Or 300
    Grand Hôtel Villa de France
        (Tangier) 116, *117*
    Hostal Gernika (Chaouen) 134
    Hotel du Lac (Bin el Ouidane) 230
    Hotel les Merenides (Fez) 188
    Hotel Muniria (Tangier) 121
    Hyatt Regency Hotel
        (Casablanca) *170*
    La Mamounia hotel (Marrakesh)
        244
    maisons d'hôte (Marrakesh) 249
    Palais Jamai Hotel (Fez) 201, *202*
    Palais Salem Hotel (Taroudannt)
        300
    Volubilis Inn 209, 212
Adai 310
Ad-Dakhla 318
Afourer 230
Agadir 30, *304*, 305–8
    beach 306
    Bert Flint's Museum 307
    earthquake of 1960 305
    Foyer Rose du Sud School 308
    kasbah 306–7
    Medina d'Agadir *306*, 307
    Vallée des Oiseaux *307*
Agadir N'Gouj 276
Agard Oudad 310
Agdz 292, *293*
Agoudal 284
Agoundis Valley 276
agriculture 149
    argan oil 263, *311*
    dates 297, *313*
    fruit and nut orchards 140, 235
    olives 234
    Operation Ploughing 141
Ahmed el Mansour el Dehbi 30,
    31–2, 88, 148
Ahmed el Raisuli 146

Ahmed Tijani 201
Ain Leuh 233
Ait Bahia 309
Ait Benhaddou *292*
Ait Hani 284
Ait Melloul 309
Ait Mhammed 279
Ajdir 138
alcohol *see* **food and drink**
Al Hoceima 136, *137*
Alnif 293
Amezgou 300
Amouguer 284
Amzrou
    Jewish Kasbah *288*
Anergui 284
Aoreora 313
Arbaoua 148
architecture 83–8, 132, 171
    defensive structures 85–6
    Islamic influence 83–5
    kasbah 86
    ksour 85–6
    medinas 84
    modern 88
    palaces 86–7
    pisé 86, *291*
    Portuguese 178
    riads of Marrakesh *249*, 250
Aremd 274
Arhbala 231
art and crafts
    see also **museums and galleries**
    babouches 197, 253
    braid weaving 196
    carpets 158, 299
    Fez pottery 202
    leatherwork 201
    Salé pottery 164
    Tamgroute pottery 294
    textiles (El Jadida) 179
    wood crafts 198
arts and entertainment
    American Legation (Tangier) 118–9
    Dar el Bellarg arts centre
        (Marrakesh) 250
    Dawliz (Tangier) 117
    French Cultural Centre (Tangier)
        115
    French Institute (Casablanca) 171
    French Institute (Marrakesh) 258
    Salle Bastianelli (Tangier) 115
    Theatre Sidi Bellyout
        (Casablanca) 171
Asilah 30, 145, *147*
    Bab el Kasaba 146
    medina *144*
    music festival 145–6
    Palace 146

Askaoun 299
Asni 272
Auer, Jane 72–3
    Two Serious Ladies 72
Azemmour 30, 177
Azigza lake 232
Azilal 282
Azrou 95, *232*, 233

b

Bacon, Francis 73–4
Balch, Antony 74
    William Buys A Parrot 74
baraka 46, 59–60, 220
Barbary Coast 145
beaches
    Agadir 306
    Al Hoceima 137
    Casablanca 173
    El Jadida 177
    Essaouira 266
    Larache 147
    Layoune Plage 318
    Oualidia 179–80
    Plage Blanc 313
    Plage des Amiraux 123
    Plage des Nations 164
    Plage Rose-Marie 165
    The Rif 128
    Saidia 140
    Sidi Kaouki 266
    Sidi Mohammed beach (Mirleft)
        312
    Temara Plage 165
    Tangier 122–3
    Tarazhout 308
Ben Arafa *40*
Beni Mellal 282
Bin el Ouidane 230, 282
    Hotel du Lac 230
Black Sultan *see* **Abou el Hassan**
Blue Source of Meski 296
Bou Bou Ider 236
Boucraa 318
Bouguemez Valley 97, 279
Bou Iblane 95
Bou Inan 194–5
Boujdour 318
Boumalne 295
    Rose Festival 296
Bowles, Paul 58, *70*, 71–3, 111
    The Sheltering Sky 71, 72, 301,
        319
    The Spider's House 223
Burroughs, William 71, *72*, 74,
    111, *119*, 121–2
    The Naked Lunch 74, 119, 121

c

Cala Iris 137, *138*
Cap Beddouza 180
Capote, Truman 71
Cap Malabata 123
Cap Sim 266
Cap Spartel 122–3, 145
    lighthouse *122*
Cap Tafelney 266–7
car hire 114
Casablanca 60, 169–73
    Ain Diab 173
    A Ma Bretagne restaurant 173
    beach 173
    Borj Sidi Mohammed ben
        Abdullah 169
    Boulevards Zerktouni and Anfa
        170
    Caftan Show 171
    Derb Omar 169
    Deux Tours 170
    French Institute 171
    Hassan II Mosque *57*, 88, *168*,
        172, 173
    Home d'Enfants Murdoch-Bengio
        171
    Hyatt Regency Hotel *170*
    Marabout of Sidi Abderahmen 173
    nightlife 173
    Pâtisserie Bennis 172
    Place des Nations Unies 169
    Place Mohammed V *169*
    Quartier Habbous 172
    shopping 169–70, 171
    Theatre Sidi Bellyout 171
    Villa Des Arts 171
Cascades d'Ouzoud 282
Caves of Hercules 21, 22, 122, 123
Ceuta 30, 35, 129, 130
    Church of Our Lady of Africa *130*
Chaba Zahouania 93
Chaouen 132, *133–4*
    Grand Mosque 134
    Hostal Gernika 134
    Kasbah 134
    Plaza Uta el Hamman 133
Cheb Kader 93
climate 95
    chergui 113, 122, 177
    in Marrakesh 243
    in Tangier 113
Cooke, Robin see Raymond, Derek
Cotta Roman ruins 123
culture and etiquette
    hammam etiquette 58
    marriage 62, 67, *69*
    traditional dress 67, 129, 131,
        133, 139

d

Dades Gorge 280–81, 296
Dades Valley 296, *298*
Dalia 123
Dayet Aoua 234–5
Delacroix, Eugène 71, 115
    Fantasia in Front of Meknes
    Jewish Wedding in Morocco 29
    Religious Fanatics in Tangier 26
Demnate 280
desert 289, 294, 297, 316–8
Diabat 266
Draa Valley 289, 290, 292–4
    Cascades du Draa 292
Driss Basri 50
drugs 71, 119, 123, 136
    kif (hashish) production 129, *136*

e

eating out
    A Ma/a ma ?? Bretagne
        restaurant (Casablanca) 173
    Café Palm d'Or (Marrakesh) 257
    Chez Dimitri restaurant
        (Ouarzazate) 291
    Hafa café (Tangier) 121
    Lachari restaurant (Ksar es
        Seghir) 123
    Le Détroit café (Tangier) 120
    Marrakesh 252
economy 47, 62, 129
    in Fez 192
    in Marrakesh 243
    privatisation 50
    tax-free ports 129, 130
El Jadida *176*, 177
El Kebab 231
El Ksiba 230
Erfoud 296
Erg Chebbi 297
Er Rachidia 296
Essaouira 263–6
    Avenue de l'Istiqual 264
    Gnoua Festival 265
    Museum of Sidi Mohammed Ben
        Abdellah 265
    Place Moulay Hassan 264
    ramparts *262, 264*
    Rue Mohammed Zerktouni 264
    Villa Maroc 266

f

festivals and events 62
    Brides' Festival (Imilchil) 283,
        284, 285
    Caftan Show (Casablanca) 171
    cherry harvest festival (Sefrou)
        235
    Date Festival (Rissani) 297
    fantasia 179
    Folk Festival (Marrakesh) 249,
        257
    Gnaou Festival (Essaouira) 265
    Moussem of Moulay Abdellah 179
    music festival (Asilah) 145–6
    Ramadan 63
    Rose Festival (Boumalne) 296
Fez 27, 185–202
    Andalous Mosque 187, 202
    Andalous Quarter 202
    Madrassa Attarine *194*, 199
    Bab Boujeloud *193*
    Bab Ftouh 202
    Bab Guissa 201
    Borj Nord 188
    Borj Sud 188
    Madrassa Bou Inania 29, *82*, 85,
        194–5
    Chouras Tanneries 201
    Dar el Makhzen Palace 86
    Madrassa Es Sahrij 202
    Fez el Bali 191, 193–5
    Fez Jdid 188, 189
    Grand Rue de Fez Jdid 190
    Hebrew cemetery 190
    Hotel les Merenides 188
    Kairouyine Library 200
    Kairouyine Mosque 60, 187,
        198, 199–200
    Kissaria 198
    medina 192
    mellah 189
    Merinid Tombs 187, *188*
    Musée du Batha 190–91
    Nejjarine Fondouk museum 199
    Nejjarine fountain 195, 198, *199*
    New Town 185, 187, 202
    Palace *189*
    Palais Jamai Hotel 201, *202*
    Place des Alaouites *189*
    Place Nejjarine (carpenters'
        souk) 198
    Place Seffarine 200
    Madrassa Seffarine 200
    Shrine of Moulay Idriss II *185*,
        199
    Souk el Attarine 197–8
    Souk el Henna 198
    Talaa Kebira 193–4, 196–8
    Talaa Sghira 193–4
    tomb of Idriss II 27
    Tour de Fes 187
    Zaouia of Moulay Idriss II 187
    Zaouia of Sidi Ahmed Tijani 201
film industry and locations 243,

291, 297, 301
Centre Cinematiographique
    Morocain 301
Hideous Kinky 243, 301
Kundun 289, 301
Lawrence of Arabia 107, 291, *301*
Othello 178, 263, *264*, 301
Romancing the Stone 290
The Mummy 243, 301
The Sheltering Sky 301, 319
The Third Man 258
Firouato cave 236
FInnt 292
Flint, Bert 250, 307
food and drink 79–81, 145, 171,
    180, 219, 272
    alcohol 67, 81
    celebratory food 63, 80–81
    mineral water 229
    Moroccan wine 216
Forbes, Malcolm 120–21
Forbes, Rosita 146
Fort Bou Jerif 313
Fougerolles, André 95
Foum Zguid 295
French Foreign Legion 41, 291,
    295, 313
Fuiguig 298

g

gays 62, 71–4, 111, 133
    gay bars in Tangier 122
gems and fossils *278*
Goulimine (Guelmim) 313
Guillaume, Augustin 39–40
Gysin, Brion *74*, 92, 111, 120
    The Process 74
Gzanaia 145
    Diplomatic Forest 145

h

hammam 58
Harris, Walter 115, 117, 119–20,
    146
    Morocco That Was 117, 146
Harun er Rashid 26
Hassan II 44–50, 61, 127, 136–7
Herbert, the Hon. David 71, 75,
    111, 117
Hermes, Patrick 250
High Atlas 271–85
    see also individual place names
history 21–50, 111, 133, 153
    Act/Treaty of Algeciras 35, 112
    Almohads 28, 87
    Almoravides 27–8, 87
    Battle of the Three Kings 3, 148

Berber dynasties 27–9
border war with Algeria 44
European presence 30, 33,
    35–41, 43, 112, 128–9, 133,
    145
Green March *47*, 83–4
Gulf Crisis (1990–91) 61
Idrissid dynasty 26–7
Independence (1956) 41, 111
Merinids 28–9, 88
Muslim occupation of Spain
    25–6, 27, 28, 29
nationalist movement 37–41
piracy 29–30, 131–2, 145, 157
Roman occupation 21–2
Saadian dynasty 30, 88, 247–8
Treaty of Fez 112, 145
Vandal invasion 22
Wattasid dynasty 30
Western Sahara problem 47–9
Hopkins, John 74
    Tangier Buzzless Flies 74
horses 221, 223
Hutton, Barbara *75*, 111, 119

i

Ibn Battouta 118
    El Rihla 118
Ibn Khaldoun 195
Ibn Toumert 28
Idriss ibn Abdullah (Idriss I) 26
Idriss II 26
Idriss Ier reservoir 236
Ifrane 95, 234
Ighrem 300
Ijoukak 276
Imilchil 283
    Brides Festival 283, *284*, *285*
Imlil 272, 273
Immessouane 267
Immouzzer des-Ida-Outanane 278,
    308
    Paradise Valley 308
Immouzzer du Kander 234
industry
    fishing 305
    fish processing 267
    perfume 296
    potteries 164, 180
    mining 180, *317*, 318
Inezgane 309

j – k

Jaffar Cirque 285
Jebel Tazzeka National Park 236
Jilala 61
Juba II 22, 160

Kasbah Ait Benhaddou 290
Kasbah de Boulaouane 181
Kasbah de Mehdiya 149
Kasbah Derkoua 298
Kasbah Tamdaght 290
Kasbah Timiderte 293
Kassita 141
Keen, Emily, Sherifa of Ouezzane
    117, 135
Kenitra 149
Ketama 136
Khenifra 231–2
Ksar el Kebir 148
Ksar es Seghir 123
    Lachari restaurant 123

l

Lac d'Ifni 276
Lake Isli 283
Lake Tislit *283*
Lalla Haya 229
language 60, 145
Larache 147
    beach 147
    Oued Loukos 147
    Place de la Libération 147
    Stork's Castle 147
Laayoune *314*, *315*, 316–7
    Place de l'Allegeance 317
Layounne Plage 318
Likemt pass 276
Lixus 22, *147*, 148
Loti, Pierre 259
Loveless, Jane 266
Lyautey, Hubert Gonzalve *36*, 37,
    158, 185, 187

m

Maaziz 229
Magdaz 280
Mahjoubi Aherdan 43–4
Majorelle, Louis/Jacques ?? 257
Mamora Forest 149
Marrakesh 28, 243–59
    Agdal Gardens 257
    Bab Aghmat/Rhemat 256
    Bab Agnaou 85, 256
    Bab Doukkala gallery 254
    Bab Debbarh 256
    Bab er Rob 256
    Madrassa Ben Youssef 85, *253*,
        254
    Ben Youssef Mosque 254
    Café Palm d'Or 257
    city walls 256
    Dar el Bellarj arts centre 250
    Dar El Glaoui 256

Dar Si Said Museum 251
Dar Tizkiwin 250
eating out 252
El Badi Palace 86, *248*, 249, *257*
El Bahia Palace 249, 259
French Institute 258
Gueliz *242*, 243, 244, *258*
Jemaa el Fna 243, *244*, *250*,
   251–2
Kasbah Mosque 247
Koubba el Baroudiyn 254
Koutoubia Mosque 28, 87, *245*,
   246–7
La Mamounia Hotel 244
maisons d'hôte 249
Majorelle Gardens *256*, 257, *259*
Mamounia Gardens 256
Marrakesh Folklore Festival 249,
   257
medina 243–4
Menara Gardens *256*, 257
Mouassine Mosque and Fountain
   255
Musée de Marrakech 254–5
Palmerie 257
Riad Tamsna 250
Saadian Tombs 32, *247*
Souk des Babouches 253
Souk des Teinturiers 255–6
souks 252–3, *254*, 255
Souk Smarine 253
Squallet el Mrabit 256
Matisse, Henri 116, 259
   Café Marocain 116
Mayne, Peter 74
   The Alleys of Marrakesh 74
   The Narrow Smile 74
media
controls on press and
   broadcasting 61–2
Mehdi ben Barka 44, 45
Meknes 32–3, 88, 209, 215–23
Aguedal Basin 221
Bab el Berdain (Gate of the
   Saddlers) 222
Bab Mansour 85, *217*, 219
carpenters' souk 222
city walls *222*
Dar el Kebira 220
Dar el Makhzen 220
Haras Regional 221
Heri as Souani 220–21
Koubbet el Khiyatin 219
medina 221
Bou Inania Madrassa 221–2
Museum of Moroccan Arts 221
New Town 223
Place el Hedim/Hadim 219, *223*
Place Lalla Aouda 219

royal golf course 219
Royal stables 221
Shrine of Sidi Ben Aissa 222
Tomb of Moulay Ismail 219, *220*
Meknes Region 209–23
   see also individual place names
Melilla 30, 35, 129, 130
Meski 296
Mgoun (Achabou) Gorge 280
M'hamid 295
Midelt 284
Middle Atlas 299–36
   see also individual place names
   lakes region 234–5
Mirleft 312
   Sidi Mohammed beach 312
Mischliffen-Jebel Hebri 95
Mohammed V *41*, *42*, *43*, 60
Mohammed VI *49*, *50*, 61, 68, 127
Mohammed ben Youssef 38, 39
Mohammed el Mutawakkil 30–31
Mohammed ibn Abdullah 33
Mohammedia 165
Mohammed Oufkir 45
monarchy 43–50
mosques and madrassas 84–5
   Andalous Mosque (Fez) 187, 202
   Attarine Madrasa (Fez) *194*, 199
   Madrassa Ben Youssef
      (Marrakesh) 85, *253*, 254
   Ben Youssef Mosque
      (Marrakesh) 254
   Madrassa Bou Inania (Fez) 29,
      82, 85, 194–5
   Madrassa Es Sahrij (Fez) 202
   Grand Mosque (Chaouen) 134
   Grand Mosque (Rabat) 158
   Great Mosque (Rabat) 159
   Hassan Mosque (Rabat) 87
   Hassan II Mosque (Casablanca)
      57, 88, *168*, *172*, 173
   Kairouyine Mosque (Fez) *60*,
      187, *198*, 199–200
   Kasbah Mosque (Marrakesh) 247
   Koutoubia Mosque (Marrakesh)
      28, 87, *245*, 246–7
   Medrassa Bou Inania (Meknes)
      221–2
   Medrassa/Madrassa ?? el
      Hassan (Salé) *164*
   Madrassa Moulay Idriss 210
   Mouassine Mosque and Fountain
      (Marrakesh) 255
   Oudaya Mosque (Rabat) 157
   Seffarine Madrasa (Fez) 200
   Sidi Bouabid mosque (Tangier)
      114
   Tin Mal mosque 276–7
Moulay Bousselham 148

Moulay el Hassan 33
Moulay Idriss el Akhbar 27, 209–10
Moulay Idriss 209–10
   moussem 211
   Shrine of Moulay Idriss el Akhbar
      27, *209*, 210–11
Moulay Ismail 32–3, 157, 216–20
Moulay Yazid 33
mountains
   Amalou N'Tiffirt 284
   Anti-Atlas 289
   Atlas 229–36, 271–85
   Ayyachi 97, 285
   Azurki 97, 279
   Bab N'Ouayyad 284
   Beni Snassen 140
   Bou Hello 135
   Gourza 277
   Irhil Mgoun 279
   Jebel Aklim 300
   Jebel Irhoud 231
   Jebel Masker 97
   Jebel Mouchchene 229
   Jebel Sarhro 293
   Jebel Siroua 271, 298–9
   Jebel Tazzeka 236
   Msedrid 284
   Ouagoulzat (Wawgoulzat) 279
   Rif 127–41
   Sirwa 298
   Tazzaka 236
   Tidiguin 127–8
   Toubkal Massif 96, 271, 272–7
Msemrir *277*, 281
Musa ibn Noseir 25
museums and galleries
   Archaeological Museum (Rabat)
      159–60
   archaeological museum
      (Tetouan) *22*, 132
   Bab er Rouah (Rabat) 161
   Bert Flint's Museum (Agadir) 307
   Cybergallery (Casablanca) 171
   Dar Si Said Museum (Marrakesh)
      251
   Galerie Delacroix (Tangier) 115
   Musée d'Art Contemporain de
      Tanger (Tangier) 115
   Musée de Marrakesh
      (Marrakesh) 254–5
   Musée du Batha (Fez) 190–91
   Museum of Moroccan Arts
      (Meknes) 221
   Museum of Moroccan Arts
      (Rabat) 157
   Museum of Moroccan Arts
      (Tetouan) 132
   Museum of Sidi Mohammed Ben
      Abdellah (Essaouira) 265

National Ceramic Museum (Safi) 180
Nejjarine Fondouk museum (Fez) 199
Oudayas Museum (Rabat) 158
Palace Museum (Tangier) *120*
Villa Des Arts (Casablanca) 171
music 92–3, 139
Andalusian 93, 139
Berber music 93
Chabbi 92
El Malhoune 61
gnaoua 59–60, 93
Master Musicians of Jajouka 92
rai 92–3, 139
The Rolling Stones 92
Mzic pass 273–4

n – o

N'Addi Pass 275
Nass el Ghiwane 61
nightlife
Casablanca 173
Tangier 118, 121–2
Nkob 293
Northwest Coast 145–9
see also individual place names
Oualidia 179–80
Ouarzazate 290–92
Chez Dimitri restaurant 291
Kasbah Taourirt 291–2
Kasbah Tiffoultoute 292
Ouezzane 134–6
Ouirgane 276
Oujda 139
Oukaimeden 95, 96
Oulmes 229
Oumesnat *309*, 310
Oum Laalag oasis 295
Ourika Valley 257, 271

p

people 57–69
Abids 33
Arabs 57
Berbers 21, 25–6, 38, 57, 67, 107, 229, 280, 281, 293
Blue Men 312, 313, *319*
Jewish community 22, 59, 189–90
Jiballi 117, 129, 132, 133, 146, 217
Riffians 127, 128–9
Tafilalt Arabs 296
women *44*, 50, 57, 67–9, 159
Pillars of Hercules 21
Plage Blanc 313

Plage des Amiraux 123
Plage des Nations 164
Plage Rose-Marie 165
politics 43–50
first constitution 44
Istiqlal Party 43–4
Moroccan Liberation Army (MLA) 43–4
Organisation of African Unity (OAU) 43, 44
People's Movement 44
second constitution 45
Union Socialiste des Forces Populaires (USFP) 44, 46, 50
Port de Jorf 179

r

Rabat 60, 153–63
see also **Salé**
Archaeological Museum 159–60
Avenue Mohammed V 159
Bab er Rouah 161
Chellah Necropolis *160, 161, 162*–3
Dar El Makhzen (House of Government) 161
flea market 159
Grand Mosque 158
Great Mosque 159
Hassan Mosque 87
Kasbah of the Oudayas *156–8*
Marché Central 158
Mausoleums of Mohammed V and Hassan II *155,* 156
medina 158–9
Museum of Moroccan Arts 157
Old Wool Market 157
Oudaya Gate 85, 157
Oudaya Mosque 157
Oudayas Museum 158
Oued Bou Regreg (Father of Reflection) 163
Parliament building 159
railway station 153
riverside 156
Royal Palace 161
Rue Souika 158
Sala Colonia 21–2, 162
shopping 158–9
Tour Hassan (Hassan Tower) 28, *155*, 156
Ras el Ma 236
Raymond, Derek 73
religion
Aissawa Brotherhood 223
Christianity 22
Islam 22, 25–33, 57, 58, 60, 63, 67

Islamic Conference Organisation 45
Judaism 22
Shereef of Ouezzane 134–5
Sufir Naciri brotherhood 294
Rich 284
Richardson, James 263, 264
Travels in Morocco 263, 264
Rif, The 127–41
see also individual place names
beaches 128
Rissani 296–7
Date Festival 297
rivers
Aggai 235
Dades 289
Draa 289, 290, *299*
Fertassa 213
Gigou 236
Moulouya 138
Neckor 138
Nfis 276
Oued Boufekrane 223
Oued Bou Regreg (Father of Reflection) 163
Oued Sebou 149
Oum Er Rbia (Mother of Spring) 177, 181, 232
Tafilalt 289, 296
Ziz 289, 296
Rommani 229

s

Safi 30, *180*
National Ceramic Museum 180
Saidia 139–40
St Laurent, Yves 250, 259
Salé 22, 163–4
see also **Rabat**
Bab Mrisa 163–4
Jardins Exotiques 164
medina 164
Madrassa el Hassan *164*
potteries 164
Shrine of Sidi Abdallah ben Hassan 164
Sefrou 235, *236*
cherry harvest festival 235
Seguia Al Hamra 318
Seksawa Valley 277
Setti Fatma 271–2
Pinatel organic herb garden 272
shopping
Casablanca 169–70, 171
Rabat 158–9
Tangier 114, 117
Tetouan 132
Sidi Abdallah ben Hassan 164

Sidi Akhfennir 315
Sidi Ben Aissa 222, 223
Sidi Bouzid 180
Sidi Chamarouch 274
Sidi Harazem 202
Sidi Ifni 312
Sidi Kacem 149
Sidi Kaouki beach 266
Sidi Mohammed ben Arafa 38
Sidi Mohammed ben Youssef see
    Mohammed V
Sidi Okba ibn Nafi 25
Sidi Yahya 140
Sidi Yahya Ousaad 231
Sijilmassa 297
Sillitoe, Alan 74
    The Loneliness of the Long
        Distance Runner 74
Sitwell, Osbert 259
Skhirate 165
Smara 318
Souk el Arba du Rharb 149
Spanish Enclaves 130
    see also Ceuta, Melilla
sport and recreation
    camel trekking 263, 293, 295
    diving 318
    golf 307
    hiking and mountain climbing
        233, 272–6, 280
    horse riding 223, 307
    mountain-biking 277–8
    paragliding 307
    sea fishing 307–8
    skiing 95–7, 233
    surfing and windsurfing 266, 308
    tennis 307
superstition 58–9

t

Tabant 279
Tacheddirt 275
Taddert 278
Tafoughalt (Taforalt) 140–41
    Grotte de Chameau 141
Tafradous 236
Tafraoute 308, 309
Talat N'Yaccoub 276
Taliouine 299
Tamatert pass 275
Tamda Lake 278
Tamegroute 294
Tamri 267
Tamtattouchte 281
Tangier 22, 30, 36, 71, 111–23
    American Legation 118–9
    beaches 122–3
    Boulevard Pasteur 114

British telegraph office 118
Carmen Macien foundation 119
Continental Hotel 120
Dar El Makhzen 120
Dawliz 117
El Minzah Hotel 115
French Cultural Centre 115
Galerie Delacroix 115
Grand Hôtel Villa de France 116,
    117
Grand Socco 117–8
Hafa café 121
Hotel Muniria 121
Kasbah 118, 119
Le Détroit café 120
Librairie des Colonnes 114
Madani perfumier 114
medina 117, 118–21
Musée d'Art Contemporain de
    Tanger 115
nightlife 118, 121–2
Palace Museum 120
Petit Socco 119
Place de France 114
Rue Assad ibn Farrat 120
Rue Ben Raisouli 119
Rue de la Liberté 115, 117–8
Rue des Cheratins 119
Rue d'Italie 118
Rue es Siaghin 118
Rue Mohammed Tazi 120
Rue Riad Sultan 120
St Andrew's church 115
Salle Bastianelli 115
shopping 114, 117
Sidi Bouabid mosque 114
Sidi Hosni 119–20
Spanish mission 118
Tomb of Ibn Battouta 118
tourist office 114
York House 120
Tansikht 293
Tan Tan 314
Tan Tan Plage 314
Tarhazhout 308
Tarfaya 316
Targuist 136
Tarik ibn Ziad 25
Tarmilate 229
Taroudannt 295, 299–300
    Bab Kasbah Gate ?? 300
Tassent 283
Tata oasis 300
Taza 236, 237
Tazaghärt 96
Tazenakht 299
Tazzarine 293–4
Telouet 278
Temara Plage 165

Temara Ville 165
    zoo 165
Tessaout Gorge 280
Tetouan 30, 131–2
    archaeological museum 22, 132
    Museum of Moroccan Arts 132
    Place Hassan II 131
Timichi 276
Tinerhir 282, 296
Tin Mal 276
Tizi N'Ouattar 276
Tizi N'Test pass 271, 289
Tizi N'Tichka Pass 271, 278, 289,
    290
Tizi Ouanouns pass 276
Tiznit 310–11
Todra Gorge 280, 281–2, 296
tourism 107, 113, 127, 128, 305,
    317

v – w

Volubilis 22, 211, 212–15
    see also Archaeological
        Museum, Rabat
wildlife
    Barbary apes 233
    Barbary deer 236
    bird-watching 147, 148, 296,
        308, 315
    desert reptiles 299
    Khan N'fiss wildlife reserve 315
    locusts 316
    monkeys 271
    Oued Massa nature reserve 308
    storks 273
    whale-watching 318
Williams, Tennessee 73
Windus, John 216
    A Journey to Mequinez 216
writers and artists 71–4, 116, 145
    see also individual writers' and
        artists' names
    Psychedelic Summer 74, 121

y – z

Yacoub el Mansour see Youssef
    Yacoub
Yacoub Youssef 28
Youssef ibn Tashfin 27
Youssef Yacoub 28, 153, 155
Zagora 294
Zegzel Gorge 140
Zireg Gorge 236